The Future of Asian Finance

EDITORS
Ratna Sahay, Jerald Schiff, Cheng Hoon Lim,
Chikahisa Sumi, and James P. Walsh

INTERNATIONAL MONETARY FUND

Cataloging-in-Publication Data
Joint Bank-Fund Library

The future of Asian finance / edited by Ratna Sahay, Jerald Schiff, Cheng Hoon Lim, Chikahisa Sumi, and James P. Walsh. – Washington, D.C. : International Monetary Fund, 2015.

      pages ; cm
  Includes bibliographical references and index.
  ISBN: 978-1-49831-719-1

1. Finance – Asia. 2. Economic development – Asia. 3. Asia – Economic conditions. I. Sahay, Ratna. II. Schiff, Jerald Alan. III. Lim, C. H. (Cheng Hoon). IV. Sumi, Chikahisa. V. Walsh, James P. (James Patrick), 1972- VI. International Monetary Fund.

HC412.F88 2015

Second Printing (August 2016)

Disclaimer: The views expressed in this book are those of the authors and do not necessarily represent the views of the International Monetary Fund, its Executive Board, or management.

Please send orders to:
International Monetary Fund, Publication Services
P.O. Box 92780, Washington, DC 20090, U.S.A.
Tel.: (202) 623-7430   Fax: (202) 623-7201
E-mail: publications@imf.org
Internet: www.elibrary.imf.org
www.imfbookstore.org

Contents

Foreword

Recognizing the increasingly important role finance will play in Asia, the International Monetary Fund (IMF) embarked on the "Future of Asia's Finance" project in early 2013. Our aim was to take stock of Asia's financial systems and chart possible paths that it might take to meet the rising economic expectations of its vast population and finance its increasingly consumption-based growth models.

The IMF is committed to playing a supportive role in helping its Asian member countries achieve the twin goals of inclusive growth and financial stability. These goals need to be considered in the context of major ongoing changes in the global financial system following the global financial crisis in 2008, as well as demographic shifts, rapid urbanization, large infrastructure needs, and the evolving structure of economic activity in Asia itself.

Asia demonstrated remarkable resilience throughout the global financial crisis and its aftermath. Although some export-dependent economies were hit hard, the region as a whole recovered quickly and reestablished itself as the global growth leader. One key reason for Asia's resilience was that the region's financial sector was in much better shape than many countries in the West, a sharp contrast to the experience during the Asian financial crisis in the second half of the 1990s. Looking ahead, Asia's relatively conservative business model, a strength going into the global financial crisis, may become a constraint if it holds back further development of the financial sector, such as equity and bond markets and long-term investor bases, that are needed for continued strong growth.

Although Asia's financial sector has been successful in supporting growth, sustaining the region's impressive growth momentum will require the financial sector to innovate further. There is tremendous potential to better manage and mobilize Asia's large savings to finance the region's human capital and infrastructure investment needs. Capital markets need to deepen further to strengthen financial intermediation and risk sharing, diversify sources of funding, and mitigate capital flow volatility. By moving in this direction, the financial sector will help Asia meet the challenges of population aging, reduce gaps between the rich and the poor, and escape the so-called middle-income trap. Given the growing size and influence of the Asian economies, a sound and dynamic financial sector in Asia will also be beneficial to the rest of the world.

So far the IMF's work on the "Future of Asia's Finance" project has focused on taking stock of Asian financial systems and their resilience to global stresses, as well as how they can be retooled to address demographic shifts and infrastructure needs and adapt to the new global regulatory regime. In this context, we have held several public events in the past two years.

- "The Future of Asia's Finance" seminar during the April 2013 IMF-World Bank Spring Meetings outlined the challenges facing Asia's financial sectors and provided a starting point for many of the topics in this book.

- The Joint IMF-Hong Kong Monetary Authority (HKMA) Conference, "The Future of Asia's Finance," held in February 2014, brought together government, private sector, think tank, and other representatives from the region to discuss the role of finance in Asia, including managing capital flows and dealing with regulatory reforms.

- At the October 2014 IMF-World Bank Annual Meetings Flagship Seminar, "Financing Asia's New Growth Models," a high-level panel discussed how to ensure sustainable, high-quality growth in Asia and how financial systems should respond to these challenges.

Drawing on the lessons from our previous and ongoing work, including the key takeaways from the seminars noted above, this book attempts to provide a comprehensive assessment of the state of Asia's financial sector, the challenges going forward, and further changes that can be expected. It also proposes policy responses to address the region's present and future challenges. Lessons learned from cross-country experiences are valuable and yet they need to be applied to Asia with care, recognizing the region's many unique characteristics and the wide diversity of financial systems within the region.

Through the "Future of Asia's Finance" project, the IMF intends to continue serving as an international forum for its Asian members for discussing the challenges faced by its financial systems to meet Asia's twin goals of sustaining high growth and financial stability.

Min Zhu
Deputy Managing Director
International Monetary Fund

Contributors

EDITORS

Cheng Hoon Lim is Assistant Director in the Monetary and Capital Markets Department of the IMF. She is responsible for leading and implementing the department's strategic priorities on macro-financial surveillance and review for advanced and emerging market economies. She has led IMF teams to assess the stability of financial systems in recent years and has worked extensively on IMF programs during the Asian crisis in the late 1990s and early 2000s. Ms. Lim has produced seminal work on the effectiveness of macroprudential policy instruments in mitigating systemic risk. She has also published on other topics, including inflation targeting, sovereign debt crisis and restructuring, contingent claims analysis of banking and corporate sectors, and the future of finance in Asia. In addition to the IMF, Ms. Lim has worked at the UK Financial Services Authority and the World Bank. Ms. Lim received her PhD from Cambridge University.

Ratna Sahay is Deputy Director of the Monetary and Capital Markets Department at the IMF. She is responsible for setting strategic priorities for the department, leading key projects on policy, and coordinating the work and resource management of the department. She has previously worked in the Research, Finance, Asian, European, Middle East, and Western Hemisphere Departments at the IMF, leading key analytical and policy projects as well as several missions to emerging market countries. She has also led regional surveillance projects and missions in the Middle East and Western Hemisphere Departments. She has served as Advisor to Stanley Fischer (First Deputy Managing Director) and Michael Mussa and Kenneth Rogoff (both Economic Counselors of the IMF). She has published widely in leading journals on financial market spillovers and financial crises, inflation, economic growth, fiscal policy and debt sustainability, and transition economies. She has taught at Delhi University, Columbia University, and New York University and holds a PhD in Economics from New York University.

Jerald Schiff is Deputy Director of the Asia and Pacific Department (APD) and IMF Mission Chief for Japan. He has previously served as a Senior Advisor in the Office of the Managing Director, Assistant Director of APD, and Divison Chief in the European Department. Mr. Schiff received his AB at Cornell University and MS and PhD degrees at the University of Wisconsin. He has also taught at Tulane University and American University School of International Service and worked in the U.S. Department of Treasury.

Chikahisa Sumi is Assistant Director in the Asia and Pacific Department (APD) of the IMF. He is APD's lead on the "Future of Asia's Finance" project. He is also Mission Chief for the Philippines and New Zealand. Mr. Sumi has also held key positions in the Japanese government, including Deputy Vice Minister of Finance and Deputy Commissioner of the Financial Services Agency. He also headed Japan's Debt Management Office. Born in Osaka, Japan, Mr. Sumi holds an LLB from the University of Tokyo (1982) and an MBA from Harvard University (1986).

AUTHORS

Geert Almekinders is a Deputy Division Chief in the IMF's Asia and Pacific Department.

Rina Bhattacharya is a Senior Economist in the Monetary and Capital Markets Department at the IMF.

Ding Ding is a Senior Economist in the Asia and Pacific Department at the IMF.

Sergei Dodzin is a Senior Economist in the Asia and Pacific Department at the IMF.

Mangal Goswami is currently the Assistant to the Director at the IMF–Singapore Regional Training Institute.

Fei Han is an Economist in the Monetary and Capital Markets Department at the IMF.

Phakawa Jeasakul is an Economist in the Monetary and Capital Markets Department at the IMF.

Andreas Jobst is a Senior Economist in the IMF's European Department.

Heedon Kang is a Financial Sector Expert in the Monetary and Capital Markets Department at the IMF.

Minsuk Kim is an Economist in the Strategy, Policy, and Review Department at the IMF.

Yitae Kevin Kim is a Senior Financial Expert in the IMF's Monetary and Capital Markets Department.

Raphael W. Lam is the IMF's Deputy Resident Representative in China.

Vanessa le Leslé is Deputy Head of Global Regulatory Strategy and Policy for Asia Pacific, at JP Morgan Hong Kong and was Senior Financial Expert at the IMF until 2013.

Wei Liao is an Economist in the Asia and Pacific Department of the IMF.

Fabian Lipinsky is an Economist in the Western Hemisphere Department at the IMF.

Erik Lundback is a Senior Economist in the Monetary and Capital Markets Department at the IMF.

Wojciech S. Maliszewski is a Senior Economist working on China and Hong Kong in the IMF's Asia and Pacific Department.

Alex Mourmouras is a Division Chief in the IMF's Asia and Pacific Department.

Aditya Narain is Deputy Director of the IMF's Monetary and Capital Markets Department.

Franziska Ohnsorge is a Lead Economist in the Development Prospects Group (DECPG) at the International Bank for Reconstruction and Development, and was Senior Economist at the IMF until 2014.

Li Lian Ong is Senior Vice President at GIC Private Limited, Singapore. She was Deputy Division Chief in the Monetary and Capital Markets Department of the IMF until 2014.

Shanaka Jayanath Peiris is the IMF's Resident Representative to the Philippines.

Srikant Seshadri is the IMF's Senior Resident Representative in Turkey.

Dulani Seneviratne is a Research Officer in the Regional Studies Division of the IMF's Asia and Pacific Department.

Jongsoon Shin is an Economist in the IMF's Asia and Pacific Department.

Jade Vichyanond is an economist in the IMF's Asia and Pacific Department, Macroeconomic Research Division.

James P. Walsh is Deputy Division Chief in the Monetary and Capital Markets Department at the IMF.

Jianping Zhou is a Senior Economist in the Monetary and Capital Markets Department at the IMF.

Yong Sarah Zhou is a Senior Economist in the IMF's Asia and Pacific Department.

Edda Zoli is a Senior Economist in the IMF's Asia and Pacific Department.

PART I

The Structure of Finance in Asia

CHAPTER 1

Introduction

RATNA SAHAY, JERALD SCHIFF, CHENG HOON LIM, AND CHIKAHISA SUMI

Asian economies are rich in diversity. Yet a common thread runs through them: In recent decades they have grown faster than have the economies of other regions. In fact, they now account for about 30 percent of the world's GDP. Asian markets have expanded and they are more interconnected with each other and the rest of the world. A growing and vibrant middle class—the backbone of stable and sustainable growth—and continued prosperity will transform Asia's growth models in the future. This growth will be driven more by domestic demand and consumption than by exports. Estimates show that by 2030, two-thirds of the world's middle class will be in Asia.

The potential for expanding consumption is high, as it accounts for only 20 percent of the world's GDP. A growing middle class with higher household incomes will demand a greater range of goods and services, especially financial services. The latter includes home mortgages and auto financing, working capital for more start-ups, equity financing as companies expand, trade credit for corporations going global, bonds to finance infrastructure, and financial products to provide stable incomes for retirees. Technological innovation, including mobile and Internet banking, is extending the reach of finance to rural and previously unbanked areas, leading to greater financial inclusion of low-income households and small and medium-sized enterprises.

Even as Asia continues to evolve and grow, however, pockets of uncertainty remain. After two lost decades of growth, Japan is making a concerted effort to tackle deflation and revive its economy through a three-pronged strategy— aggressive monetary easing, fiscal stimulus, and structural reforms. With an aging population and a large public debt, this task is not easy. China's mighty economy is slowing, and given its prominence in global goods markets, its spillovers are already being felt in declining commodity prices. India and Indonesia are counting on their newly elected governments to improve governance, modernize their economies, and reduce the gap between rich and poor. Economic and financial integration of the Association of Southeast Asian Nations (ASEAN) economies, a region of more than 600 million people and a GDP of over $2.5 trillion, is promising. Low-income countries in Asia are also reforming to promote broad-based and sustainable growth, but they face a more unfavorable global environment than do Asian trail blazers that have now reached high-income status.

On a broader level, there are several reasons to be concerned: changing demographics in countries that were once major engines for growth, falling exports resulting from weak external demand, and infrastructure bottlenecks that are hindering total factor productivity growth. Despite a prolonged period of very low global interest rates, world events are stoking fears of "secular stagnation" and negative spillover to the rest of the world. These include sluggish growth and high unemployment in some major advanced economies, political turmoil in the Middle East, and the Russia-Ukraine impasse.

Set against these forces at play, what does the future hold for Asia? How will the region transform its long-standing growth model of a manufacturing hub to meet the evolving needs of the region and the world? There is no single answer or simple solution. Asia has many faces, with countries at different stages of development. This book considers one aspect—the role of the financial sector in facilitating Asia's transformation. We argue that the financial sector will take on a bigger role than it has in the past and will, itself, become an engine of growth.

The financial sector will face many challenges, including:

- *Better managing accumulated saving.* An aging population in the countries that have been the region's major engines of economic growth—China, Japan, Korea, and Singapore—will put increasing downward pressure on that growth. To help ensure adequate retirement saving and alleviate fiscal pressures, the large saving accumulated in these countries will need to be managed better.

- *Efficiently mobilizing saving.* As demographic changes occur and Asia becomes less of a net saver, a long-term global shortage of saving could develop. This could, in turn, cause long-term interest rates to rise. To counter this potential development, the financial sector will need to more efficiently mobilize saving and governments will need to adopt policy measures that encourage rebalancing from surplus to deficit countries.

- *Investing in human and physical capital.* Many Asian countries have a young population, and can expect a demographic dividend in the future. However, many are currently burdened with a high young-age dependency ratio and are in need of large-scale investment both in human (education, health, and training) and physical (transportation, electricity, and telecommunication) capital to reap the benefits of an expanding labor force and avoid development of a youth-unemployment problem.

- *Deepening capital markets to escape a "middle-income trap."* Asian bond markets are still shallow and equity and venture capital play a limited role in corporate financing. Deepening capital markets to provide long-term and risk-sharing capital, reducing the dominance of state banks in several countries, and developing a domestic institutional investor base will help increase productivity, diversify sources of funding, and mitigate capital flow volatility.

- *Supporting economic and financial integration of ASEAN.* Most ASEAN countries are still at an early stage of development and have large infrastructure gaps. Establishment of an ASEAN Economic Community will provide opportunities for further liberalizing inter- and intraregional flows of goods, services, and capital. The financial sector can play a critical role in supporting integration initiatives and help unlock growth-enhancing cross-border flows of capital.

Rapid growth of the financial sector can, in itself, pose risks. Although Asian financial markets showed remarkable resilience during the global financial crisis of 2008, they are becoming bigger, more complex, and interconnected. At the same time, global regulatory reforms are also creating domestic and cross-border challenges for markets and regulators alike. The implementation of this agenda is influencing market structures and liquidity, financial products and flows, the size of banks and shadow banks, financial safety nets, and resolution frameworks. Asia will need to adapt to and influence these changes and be ready to manage emerging risks.

Understanding how this process will work requires looking deeply into Asia's financial systems, at what they have in common and how they differ, at why they proved so resilient to global financial shocks, and at how successful they have been at deepening and diversifying their financial services. It also requires digging down into how these issues affect the financial sector, and how market participants, supervisors, and households in turn react. Many of these questions have been raised in some countries, but in this book we try to look at them for various countries across the region, drawing insights for the high-income countries and financial centers, along with emerging markets and, when possible, low-income countries as well.

In this book, we adopt a chronological approach by first taking stock of the current state of play in Asia's financial sectors. We then assess how they must adapt to support the transformation of Asia's growth models to become more service oriented and to meet the high expectations of its diverse populations. Finally, we consider the challenges that will need to be addressed in this process.

Three chapters in Part I describe the structure of finance in Asia. Chapter 2 presents an overview of Asia's financial system and the next two chapters investigate how capital markets in Asia can be developed further to provide adequate stable funding for long-term investment and risk capital for innovation and entrepreneurship.

In Chapter 2, "A Bird's-Eye View of Finance in Asia," Heedon Kang, Phakawa Jeasakul, and Cheng Hoon Lim describe Asia's financial systems. As home to about half the world's population and highly heterogeneous economies, Asia's financial systems are quite diverse, ranging from global hubs for securities and derivatives trading to low-income economies where financial services have yet to reach much of the population.

Yet across the region, there are some striking similarities. Asian banking sectors tend to be large, constituting about 60 percent of the aggregate assets of financial institutions across the region. The role of government in banking is significant. Asian banks tend to be quite conservatively run—they focus on commercial lending, their liabilities are dominated by deposits rather than wholesale funding, and they tend to be well capitalized. Financial inclusion, as measured by access to finance by small and medium-sized enterprises and households, tends to lag other regions.

The simple and risk-averse business model was a strength going into the global financial crisis as it limited the exposure of Asian banking systems to subprime loans and securitization that beset advanced economies. At the same time, bank dominance has come at the cost of underdeveloped equity and bond markets in most countries. Also, the short duration of banks' liabilities limits their capacity to finance long-term investments such as infrastructure projects.

In Chapter 3, "Are There Crouching Tigers and Hidden Dragons in Asia's Stock Markets?" Fabian Lipinsky and Li Lian Ong explore the pricing of Asia's equity markets, which have become a key source of financing for firms. They find that idiosyncratic factors, such as the implementation of securities regulation, tend to play a more important role in driving equity price movements compared to the G7 markets. This suggests that improvements in the regulation of securities markets in Asia could enhance the role of stock markets as stable and reliable sources of financing into the future.

In Chapter 4, "Bond Markets: Are Recent Reforms Working?" Mangal Goswami, Andreas Jobst, Shanaka J. Peiris, and Dulani Seneviratne find that bond markets have grown rapidly, albeit unevenly, across emerging Asia in the aftermath of the global financial markets. Foreign investors have come in and, at the same time, the availability of hedging instruments has risen. Emerging Asian financial systems are starting to fire up the "twin engines," with the corporate bond market developing into an alternative and viable nonbank source of private sector and infrastructure funding. Deeper corporate bond markets will help channel resources from aging savers in industrialized Asia to infrastructure investment in emerging Asia, as highlighted in Chapter 8. In addition, developing a local institutional investor base and encouraging offshore issuance will help deepen bond markets and reduce the volatility of asset prices to global shocks.

Having established where Asia's financial sectors currently stand, Part II of this book asks: Where are they going?

In Chapter 5, "Is Asia Still Resilient?" Phakawa Jeasakul, Cheng Hoon Lim, and Erik Lundback discuss the lessons Asia learned after the Asian financial crisis, and how it has applied those lessons in recent years. Following the Asian financial crisis, Asia reduced its macro-financial vulnerabilities, introduced more exchange rate flexibility, built foreign exchange reserves, cleaned up the balance sheets of banks and firms, and stepped up the regulation and supervision of its financial sectors. This helped ensure a rapid bounce-back from the global financial crisis in 2008. While most of Asia withstood the "taper tantrum" of asset prices in mid-2013 following the Federal Reserve's hint of monetary tightening, some Asian countries that had re-leveraged and built up higher domestic imbalances were hit hard.

A quantitative analysis comparing more recent macro-financial conditions with those before the Asian financial crisis suggests that parts of Asia have become less resilient because of growing domestic imbalances from rapid credit growth and elevated house prices, higher leverage in the household and corporate sectors, and deteriorating external positions. Maintaining Asia's standing in the world as an engine of growth will require proactive policies to reduce vulnerabilities and push ahead with structural reforms.

In Chapter 6, "The Future of Asia's Financial Sector," Rina Bhattacharya, Fei Han, and James P. Walsh look farther ahead at how evolving economic structures, higher growth, and demographic changes in Asian economies are likely to affect the region's financial sectors. Although the sustained economic growth in the medium term should boost the region's financial sectors, the pace of financial sector growth is likely to slow down as the Asian emerging markets converge to advanced economy income levels. The different pace of demographic change will also have an impact. Asia's aging economies, chiefly the advanced economies and China, will begin to see a decline in saving in favor of consumption, while the region's younger economies, especially India and Indonesia, can expect further financial deepening as saving begins to increase. Further, rising incomes tend to go hand in hand with increasing sophistication and integration of financial institutions, which should work to make Asia's financial systems both more complex and more globally connected. This, in turn, will present new challenges for the region's regulators and supervisors, who will have to oversee increasingly networked, complicated, and large financial sectors.

Vanessa le Leslé, Franziska Ohnsorge, Minsuk Kim, and Srikant Seshadri show in Chapter 7, "Hong Kong SAR and Singapore as Asian Financial Centers—Complementarity and Stability," how these two cities have evolved from modest beginnings as entrepôt trade hubs into international financial centers in terms of their depth, scope, financial sophistication, and interconnectedness. To the extent that greater levels of interconnectedness might result in greater propagation of financial shocks, this chapter highlights the positive role that complementary coexistence of these financial centers can play in enhancing financial stability in the region and beyond. Regulatory and supervisory considerations of cooperation and coordination to facilitate such positive outcomes are presented.

Part III looks at three specific challenges that face Asia in the coming years: the nexus of aging societies in need of infrastructure investment, increasing openness to capital flows, and the evolving agenda of global regulatory reform.

Several countries in the region are aging rapidly, while infrastructure needs across the board are large. In Chapter 8, "Asia's Demographic Changes and Infrastructure Needs," Ding Ding, W. Raphael Lam, and Shanaka J. Peiris examine how Asia's heterogeneity can work in its favor. They find that enhancing financial innovation and integration in the region could facilitate intraregional financial flows and mobilize resources from the aging savers in industrialized Asia to finance infrastructure investment in emerging Asia. Strengthening the financial ties within the region, as well as with the global financial markets, alongside appropriate prudential frameworks, could also help diversify the sources of financing and reduce the cost of funding in emerging Asia.

The scope for financial integration is particularly evident in southeast Asia, where the 10 member countries of ASEAN have become highly integrated with global trade flows, yet financial integration has lagged. In Chapter 9, "ASEAN

Financial Integration: Harnessing Benefits and Mitigating Risks," Geert Almekinders, Alex Mourmouras, Jade Vichyanond, Yong Sarah Zhou, and Jianping Zhou look at the pros and cons of ASEAN's ongoing financial integration. ASEAN member countries plan to integrate further through the ASEAN Economic Community, due to be established in 2015. The process has so far been prudent and gradual, dominated by their concern that premature financial liberalization can exacerbate domestic vulnerabilities and heighten risks. However, breaking down barriers to financial flows within the region could further support growth, jobs, and financial inclusion, and help ASEAN in transforming from an export powerhouse to a growth model that is increasingly dependent on domestic investment and consumption.

In Chapter 10, "Capital Flows: A Prospective View," Edda Zoli, Sergei Dodzin, Wei Liao, and Wojciech Maliszewski look at capital flows in Asia in the last two decades, and discuss prospects going forward. They find that traditionally, the size and composition of capital flows in Asia have been driven to a large extent by the region's stronger growth prospects, global interest rates, and investors' risk appetite. Capital flows are likely to react to Japan's monetary easing, capital account liberalization, especially in China, increasing financial integration and development, and changes in saving patterns driven by demographics. Overall, this will increase the volume of capital flows in the region, and most likely also lead to higher volatility. Many Asian countries already use macroprudential policies to minimize systemic financial risk; improving and fine tuning these tools will be key for managing these flows.

Finally, in Chapter 11, "Operating within the New Global Regulatory Environment," Rina Bhattacharya, James P. Walsh and Aditya Narain look at the broader agenda for global regulatory reform and its potential effect on Asia. Asia's fast-evolving financial systems have always presented challenges for supervisors and regulators, and the new efforts to reduce systemic risk across the world have added to the task. They find that the region's financial supervisory frameworks are generally robust. Crisis management tends to be strong but, as elsewhere, the presence of too-important-to-fail banks or government-owned banks remains a concern. Shadow banking, which is still small across the region, is growing rapidly in some countries. Looking toward the global regulatory agenda, new rules on bank capital and liquidity are unlikely to affect most of the region's banks, which already tend to be well capitalized and liquid. But like the rest of the world, potential unintended consequences from regulatory reform, such as continued growth in nonbank finance and structural changes in market liquidity, will continue to challenge the region's regulators and supervisors.

This book paints a potentially bright future for Asia's finance to support the new growth models. Moreover, the Asian authorities are well placed to safeguard financial stability as financial markets deepen and financial institutions grow, based on lessons learned from the Asian financial crisis of 1997, the global financial crisis of 2008, and the integration of the European Union. The region's financial systems have underwritten an impressive growth record over the past generation, and we are optimistic that the financial sector in Asia will successfully meet the challenges ahead.

CHAPTER 2

A Bird's-Eye View of Finance in Asia

Heedon Kang, Phakawa Jeasakul, and Cheng Hoon Lim

MAIN POINTS OF THIS CHAPTER

- Despite their diversity, Asia's financial sectors share some similarities. These include the dominant role played by banks, the rising importance of capital markets, and the significant degree of influence exerted by governments.
- Banking sectors tend to be well capitalized and largely reliant on deposit funding. However, access to funding by small and medium-sized enterprises lags behind such access in other regions.
- Despite recent rapid growth, equity and bond markets remain underdeveloped and illiquid in part due to a paucity of real money and long-term institutional investors.
- Asia's financial sectors remain less complex than those of Europe and North America, but the growth of shadow banking and structured financial products is beginning to change this relative complexity. Cross-border interconnectedness is also increasing.
- The region's evolving needs will continue to spur development of the financial sector. Policymakers must carefully manage risks while continuing to further develop capital markets. This is necessary to overcome inefficiencies and mobilize savings to support vibrant economic growth.

INTRODUCTION

Asia is home to a diverse set of financial systems that vary in depth and sophistication. The region includes a number of emerging market and low-income economies in which banks play a dominant role. However, in these economies, banks' functions remain basic; capital markets and financial services, such as asset management and insurance, stay largely embryonic; and sizable financial intermediation occurs through informal channels. With financial sector development still at the fledgling stage, growth opportunities are abundant as these economies expand.

Asia is home to a number of advanced economies in which banking sectors are large and sophisticated, and capital markets are deep and well developed. In some of these economies, banks face declining profit margins because domestic opportunities for growth have become more limited. However, they are poised to gain a growing share of the regional market following the significant pullback by European banks in the wake of the global financial crisis.

Asia also is home to thriving international financial hubs, such as Hong Kong SAR and Singapore, which are highly interconnected within the region and with other global financial centers.

This chapter aims to provide answers to the following questions:

- What is the role of finance in Asia? Who are the key players and what are their main functions? Is shadow banking important?

- How does private credit intermediation take place in Asia? How does financial inclusiveness compare to inclusiveness in other regions?

- What role do Asian governments play in the financial sector? Is the extent of government involvement in the financial sector greater than it is elsewhere?

- How does financial sector complexity and interconnectedness in Asian economies compare with that in other parts of the world?

- How does the structure of Asia's financial system affect financial stability in the region?

THE ROLE OF FINANCE, KEY PLAYERS, AND MAIN FUNCTIONS

Asia as a whole has a large financial sector.[1] At the end of 2012 the estimated sum of aggregate assets of financial institutions and outstanding values of bond and stock markets in Asia amounted to 580 percent of the region's GDP. This compares with an estimated sum of about 700 percent of GDP in the euro area and in the United States. Across Asia, financial sectors vary considerably in size, ranging from 340 percent of GDP in emerging Asia to 880 percent of GDP in advanced Asia. Financial sectors in emerging Asia are considerably larger than those in its peers outside Asia (Figure 2.1).

Bond and equity markets provide alternative channels of funding and investment for public and private sectors. At end-2012, outstanding debt securities were 110 percent of GDP; about 65 percent of these were issued by governments. Japanese government bonds form the largest segment of Asian bond markets, accounting for almost half of outstanding debt securities. Stock markets are also large, with market capitalization amounting to 75 percent of the region's GDP, but they vary significantly in their relative importance across Asia. Hong Kong SAR and Singapore dominate the scene as regional financial centers (Figure 2.2).[2]

---

[1] This chapter only covers Australia, Hong Kong SAR, Japan, Korea, New Zealand, and Singapore for advanced Asia; and China, India, Indonesia, Malaysia, the Philippines, and Thailand for emerging Asia.

[2] See Chapters 3 and 4 for the structure and growth of capital markets, and Chapter 7 for the role of the two financial hubs in Asia.

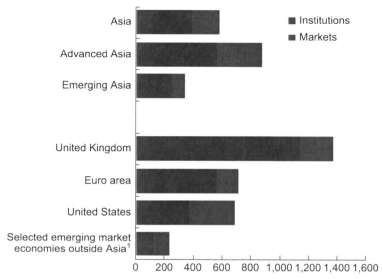

Figure 2.1   Selected Economies and Regions: Size of Financial Sectors (*Percent of GDP, end-2012*)

Sources: Bank for International Settlements, *Debt Securities Statistics*; Bankscope; Bloomberg, L.P.; country authorities' reports; Financial Stability Board, *Global Shadow Banking Monitoring Report 2013*; IMF, World Economic Outlook database; and IMF staff estimates.
[1]Brazil, Mexico, Russia, South Africa, Turkey.

Financial Institutions

Banks and nonbank depository institutions are the dominant financial institutions in Asia. Their assets amounted to 270 percent of GDP at end-2012, or 69 percent of the aggregate assets of financial institutions. Assets of banks accounted for 56 percent of the aggregate assets of financial institutions, while assets of nonbank depository institutions accounted for 13 percent. Mostly small in size, nonbank depository institutions are active in Japan and Korea, where credit cooperatives play an important role in providing access to finance for households and small businesses that are deemed less creditworthy. However, some nonbank depository institutions are exceptionally large, such as Japan's fully government-owned Post Bank, which is the largest financial institution in the world. Together, banks and nonbank depository institutions play a vital role in credit intermediation in Asia, with the following noteworthy aspects:

- Varied regulatory frameworks within the region result in different banking structures. In Japan, Korea, and Malaysia, banks are part of conglomerates owned by holding companies that are also active in insurance or investment banking. Australia, Hong Kong SAR, and Singapore subscribe to a universal banking model that provides both commercial and investment banking services. In Indonesia and Thailand most banks are stand-alone commercial institutions that conduct insurance or investment banking businesses through subsidiaries.

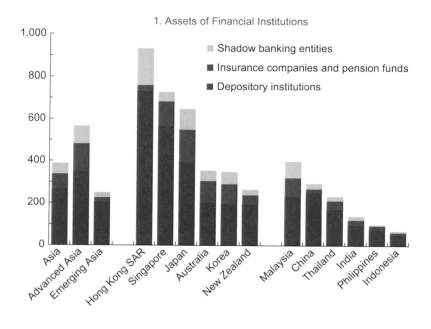

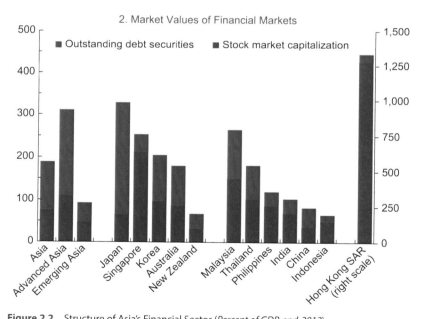

Figure 2.2 Structure of Asia's Financial Sector (*Percent of GDP, end-2012*)

Sources: Bankscope; Bank for International Settlements, *Debt Securities Statistics*; Bloomberg, L.P.; country authorities' reports; IMF, World Economic Outlook database; and IMF staff estimates.

- Asia has six global systemically important banks (G-SIBs). There are three in Japan: Mitsubishi UFJ Financial Group, Mizuho Financial Group, and Sumitomo Mitsui Financial Group; and three in China: Agricultural Bank of China, Bank of China, and Industrial and Commercial Bank of China. In other countries, highly profitable local opportunities have encouraged banks to retain a domestic focus. However, as European banks have retrenched in the wake of the global financial crisis, Australian and Japanese banks have gained overseas market share, expanding their international business by some 40 percent from the first quarter of 2007 to the third quarter of 2013. Japanese G-SIBs are among the top 10 global lenders in loan syndication and trade financing.

- Government ownership of banks is fairly common in Asia. Governments control about 23 percent of the aggregate assets of financial institutions, with 16 percent in commercial banks and 7 percent in policy banks.[3] Government ownership is markedly higher in emerging Asia, especially China, India, Indonesia, and Malaysia, but policy banks also have an important presence in Korea, the Philippines, and Thailand.

- By contrast, foreign ownership of locally incorporated banks is relatively limited, accounting for 3 percent of aggregate assets of financial institutions. The exceptions are Hong Kong SAR and New Zealand, where banking systems are dominated by U.K. and Australian banks, respectively. Many foreign banks operate as branches in Asia (Fiechter and others 2011). However, where their operations are large, foreign banks tend to establish subsidiaries, which are subject to the same regulatory and supervisory treatment as domestic banks. In a number of Asian countries, local authorities require foreign bank branches to hold capital as a ring-fencing measure. Among foreign banks, Citigroup, HSBC, and Standard Chartered have strong footprints in Asia.

The second-largest group of financial institutions includes pension funds and insurance companies. This group holds combined assets of 70 percent of the region's GDP, or 18 percent of the aggregate assets of financial institutions. Pension funds and insurance companies in Asia often exhibit significant home bias, with many investing more than 80 percent of their assets in domestic markets. This home bias is not evident in Hong Kong SAR and Singapore (Chan and Hull 2013). Important characteristics of pension funds and insurance companies are the following:

- Pension funds and insurance companies are more prominent in advanced Asia, where their assets accounted for 11 percent and 12 percent, respectively, of the aggregate assets of financial institutions at end-2012. In emerging Asia they accounted for 2 percent and 6 percent, respectively.

---

[3] Policy banks are financial institutions established by governments to achieve specific policy goals. Examples of policy banks include development banks, export-import banks, and postal banks.

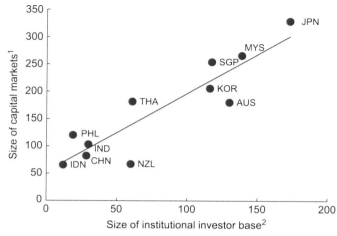

Figure 2.3   Asia: Institutional Investors and Capital Markets (*Percent of GDP*)

Sources: Bank for International Settlements, *Debt Securities Statistics*; Bloomberg, L.P.; country authorities' reports; IMF, World Economic Outlook database; and IMF staff estimates.
Note: AUS = Australia; CHN = China; IDN = Indonesia; IND = India; JPN = Japan; KOR = Korea; MYS = Malaysia; NZL = New Zealand; PHL = the Philippines; SGP = Singapore; THA = Thailand.
[1]Size of capital markets is based on the sum of stock market capitalization and oustanding debt securities.
[2]Size of institutional investor base is based on assets of investment funds, pension funds, and insurance companies.

- The paucity of "real-money investors," such as pension funds and insurance companies, appears to be linked to the underdevelopment of capital markets in a number of Asian economies. There is a high correlation between the size of the institutional investor base and the size of capital markets. This underscores the importance of developing a critical mass of long-term institutional investors to support financial deepening, including improved market efficiency and liquidity (Figure 2.3).

The third group comprises other nonbank financial institutions with assets amounting to 50 percent of GDP at end-2012, or 13 percent of the aggregate assets of financial institutions. These institutions are lightly or not regulated by authorities and are regarded as "shadow banks" according to the definition of the Financial Stability Board (FSB).[4] This group includes finance companies that mainly provide consumer finance, broker-dealers that act primarily as market makers facilitating transactions, and asset management companies that offer money market mutual funds and other collective investment vehicles. Both advanced and emerging Asia still have smaller shadow banking sectors (85 percent and 25 percent of GDP, respectively) than do their respective counterparts in

---

[4]The data on shadow banking is collected from the Financial Stability Board (FSB 2013, 2014) and national official websites. The FSB reports note that the shadow banking system can be broadly described as credit intermediation involving entities and activities outside the regular banking system. This chapter uses this broad definition of shadow banking.

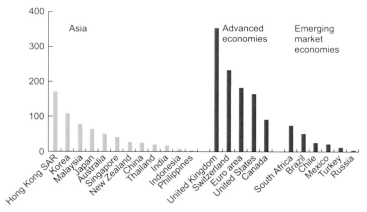

Figure 2.4 Selected Economies: Assets of Other Nonbank Financial Institutions (*Percent of GDP, end-2012*)

Sources: Financial Stability Board, *Global Shadow Banking Monitoring Report 2013*; country authorities' reports; and IMF staff estimates.

other regions. For example, both the euro area and the United States have shadow banking sectors of more than 150 percent of GDP, and both Brazil and South Africa have sectors of more than 50 percent of GDP (Figure 2.4). In emerging Asia, finance companies play a major role, accounting for more than 50 percent of the shadow banking system in India, Indonesia, and the Philippines. By contrast, shadow banks in advanced Asia mainly include asset management companies and broker-dealers that provide sophisticated investment and structured products. Two countries—China and Japan—accounted for more than two-thirds of the aggregate assets of Asia's shadow banking sector at end-2012, but they have experienced different trends since the global financial crisis, described below:

- Japan's shadow banking sector has shrunk, mirroring the experiences of other advanced economies. After reaching a peak of about 75 percent of GDP in 2007, the shadow banking sector dropped to 65 percent in 2012. Tighter lending conditions—driven by adoption of the 2006 Money Lending Business Act—contributed to this trend. The act imposed loan-to-income limits on loans from finance companies (also known as "money lenders"). Finance companies' assets declined from 22 percent to 15 percent of GDP during 2006–12 (Konno, Teramoto, and Mera 2012).

- In China, however, shadow banking activities have continued to grow in size and complexity. Nonbank financial intermediation amounted to 34 percent of China's GDP in 2013—growing strongly since 2010 (FSB 2014). Much of the nonbank credit provision in China, excluding bond financing, consists of commercial banks doing bank-like business away from their own balance sheets (IMF 2014). Two key factors have been driving this trend: a search for yield by retail investors who try to circumvent regulatory caps on bank deposit rates, and the desire of commercial banks to move certain types of loans off their books to avoid regulatory restrictions on lending activities. These restrictions include reserve requirements and caps on loan-to-deposit ratios.

Capital Markets

Asia's capital markets serve as a significant source of long-term financing for investment. In the past decade, Asia's bond and stock markets have grown more rapidly than those of their global peers, roughly doubling in size (Figure 2.5). This is particularly true in emerging Asia, where market capitalization has risen eightfold. Foreign exchange markets have become vibrant (Box 2.1), while stock and bond markets have become an important funding source for both private and public sectors. In Hong Kong SAR, India, Indonesia, Korea, Malaysia, the Philippines, and Thailand outstanding values of bond and stock markets have already surpassed banking sector assets.

Japan still has the region's largest bond market, and is home to the world's second-largest bond market. At end-2012, Japan accounted for 63 percent of total outstanding debt securities issued in Asia, compared with almost 85 percent a decade ago. The significant decline in Japan's relative prominence in the Asian bond market is largely due to the rapid growth of the Chinese bond market. Nonetheless, the Japanese government bond market is the largest market segment in Asia, accounting for 46 percent of outstanding debt securities and 76 percent of trading volume. Across Asia, about 60 percent of debt securities are issued by governments, another 30 percent by financial institutions, and the rest by nonfinancial corporations.

Concerted efforts to develop local bond markets in the aftermath of the Asian financial crisis have also borne fruit.[5] Asia's domestic issuances of bonds relative to international issuances are now larger than that in other parts of the world. Only 6 percent of Asia's debt securities are issued internationally, compared with 24 percent in non-Asian advanced economies and 14 percent in non-Asian emerging market economies.[6] This focus on local bond markets helps reduce excessive reliance on short-term funding provided by banks and mitigate currency

---

[5] Because long-term local-currency-denominated bonds can reduce the well-known problem of currency and maturity mismatches that some Asian economies suffered during the Asian financial crisis, policymakers have been putting considerable efforts into developing local bond markets. In 2002, the ASEAN+3 countries (includes China, Japan, and Korea) launched the Asian Bond Market Initiative, which was aimed at strengthening the regulatory frameworks and necessary market infrastructures, as well as promoting the issuance of local-currency bonds. In 2010, the Credit Guarantee and Investment Facility was established in collaboration with the Asian Development Bank to provide credit guarantees for investment-grade, local-currency bonds. See Chapter 4 for a more detailed account of various policy initiatives.

[6] A high figure for the share of debt securities issued internationally in the euro area (42.9 percent) is more likely to reflect a significant degree of financial integration within the currency union rather than an underdevelopment of local bond markets.

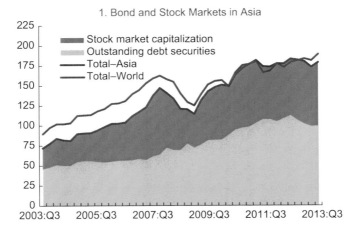

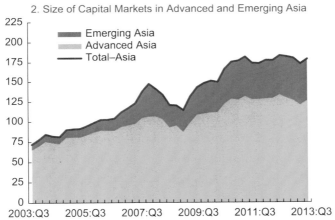

Figure 2.5 Asia: Capital Markets during 2004–12 (*Percent of 2012 GDP*)

Sources: Bank for International Settlements, *Debt Securities Statistics*; Bloomberg, L.P.; IMF, World Economic Outlook database; and IMF staff calculations.

and maturity mismatches. This, in turn, has increased the resilience of Asian economies over the past decade.

However, bond markets still have room to develop in many Asian economies, in which outstanding amounts of debt securities tend to be small relative to income levels (Figure 2.6). A primary reason is Asia's relatively low level of public indebtedness. With the exception of Japan, where government debt is high, most Asian countries have low public debt. Moreover, some governments, such as those in China and India, still rely significantly on nonmarket forms of funding, such as loans. The issuance of debt securities accounts for only about 40 percent of total government debt in China and India compared with a global average of 85 percent.

Box 2.1. Foreign Exchange Markets in Asia

Capital markets in Asia are supported by vibrant foreign exchange markets. Japan, Hong Kong SAR, and Singapore are among the five largest foreign exchange markets in the world; their combined turnover amounted to 21 percent of global turnover in 2013. Their prominence in the global foreign exchange market (behind only the United Kingdom and the United States, with 41 percent and 19 percent of global turnover, respectively) reflects the role of Hong Kong SAR and Singapore as regional financial centers and the Japanese yen as the third most commonly used currency globally.

Asian currencies are playing an increasingly important role in global foreign exchange markets. They accounted for 21.2 percent of global turnover in 2013, up from 16.7 percent in 2001. Asian currencies combined have surpassed the euro, which saw its share fall to 16.7 percent in 2013. The U.S. dollar has remained the prime global currency, with its share continually larger than 40 percent.

Interbank foreign exchange markets are relatively small in Asia, with transactions more oriented toward meeting nonfinancial customers' demand for currencies. In 2013, foreign exchange transactions directly for nonfinancial entities accounted for 23 percent of total turnover in emerging Asia (14 percent in emerging market economies outside Asia) and for 10 percent in advanced Asia (5 percent in advanced economies outside Asia). This suggests that foreign exchange transactions in Asia are more underpinned by real economic need than driven by financial transactions. In addition, foreign financial institutions generally have a smaller presence in Asia's foreign exchange trading markets. The exceptions are Australia, Hong Kong SAR, Japan, and Singapore, which are leading international hubs of currency trading, as well as New Zealand, where the banking system is dominated by Australian subsidiaries.

In addition, Asian bond markets have low levels of market liquidity, measured as the ratio of total turnover to the average outstanding amount of debt securities. Most Asian government bond markets have significantly less trading than does the highly liquid Japanese government bond market (Figure 2.7). Liquidity in corporate bond markets has generally been much lower than in government bond markets. Another challenge is the concentration in corporate bond markets, where the top 10 issuers accounted for 60–90 percent of an individual country's total corporate bond issuance in 2013 (Levinger and Li 2014). This suggests that access to bond market funding is primarily available to large and well-established corporations. China is an exception, with only 24 percent of corporate bond issuance attributed to the 10 largest issuers.

Five of the 10 largest stock markets by capitalization in the world are located in Asia, including three in advanced economies (Australia, Japan, and Hong Kong SAR) and two in emerging market economies (China and India). They are a key source of financing for local companies. Almost 20,000 companies were listed in Asia's stock markets as of end-2012, compared with more than 10,000 in the Americas and 13,300 in Europe, the Middle East, and Africa. New capital raised by stock issuance in Asia amounted to $198 billion in 2012, compared with $234 billion in the Americas and $102 billion in Europe, the Middle East, and Africa.

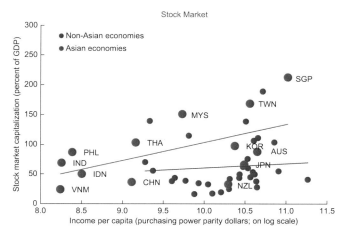

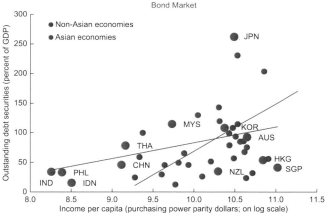

Figure 2.6 Selected Economies: Capital Markets and Economic Development (*Percent of GDP, end-2012*)

Sources: Bank for International Settlements, *Debt Securities Statistics*; Bloomberg, L.P.; IMF World Economic Outlook database; and IMF staff calculations.

Note: AUS = Australia; CHN = China; HKG = Hong Kong SAR; IDN = Indonesia; IND = India; JPN = Japan; KOR = Korea; MYS = Malaysia; NZL = New Zealand; PHL = the Philippines; SIN = Singapore; THA = Thailand; TWN = Taiwan Province of China; VNM = Vietnam.

Many equity markets in Asia face weaknesses, such as limited liquidity and inefficient pricing, raising concerns about market volatility and functionality. Only four Asian markets—China, Japan, Korea, and Thailand—are more liquid than the global average (Figure 2.8). "Noise trading" also remains a key feature of most stock markets in Asia excluding Japan (see Chapter 3). Given the relatively small number of free-float shares, Asian stock markets have not yet provided strong support for wealth management to a broader range of retail and institutional investors. Furthermore, Asian stock and bond markets outside Japan are

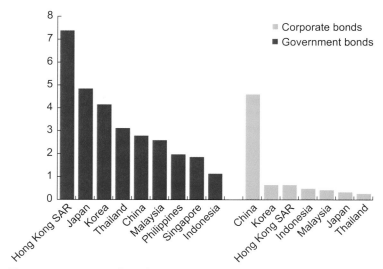

Figure 2.7 Asia: Bond Market Liquidity (*Total turnover, percent of average outstanding amounts, 2012*)

Sources: Asian Development Bank, AsiaBondsOnline; and IMF staff calculations.

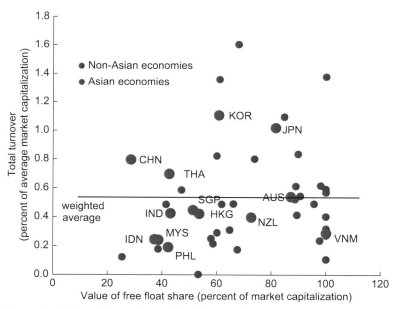

Figure 2.8 Selected Economies: Stock Market Liquidity

Sources: Bloomberg, L.P.; and IMF staff calculations.
Note: AUS = Australia; CHN = China; HKG = Hong Kong SAR; IDN = Indonesia; IND = India; JPN = Japan; KOR = Korea; MYS = Malaysia; NZL = New Zealand; PHL = the Philippines; SIN = Singapore; THA = Thailand; VNM = Vietnam.

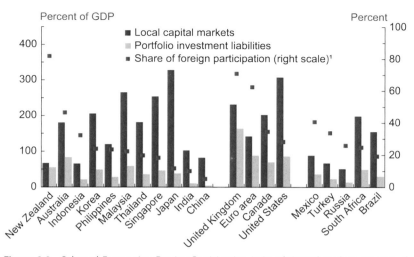

Figure 2.9 Selected Economies: Foreign Participation in Local Capital Markets (*Percent of GDP, end-2012*)

Sources: Bank for International Settlements, *Debt Securities Statistics*; Bloomberg, L.P.; IMF, *International Financial Statistics* and World Economic Outlook database; and IMF staff estimates.
[1]Based on amount of portfolio investment liabilities relative to combined value of outstanding debt securities and stock market capitalization.

more concentrated than they are in many advanced economies. For example, the 10 largest companies in Asia accounted for 45–75 percent of the region's total market capitalization at end-2012, compared with about 20 percent in Japan and the United States.

Foreign participation in Asia's capital markets tends to be lower than it is in other regions. At end-2012, it was less than 25 percent in most Asian markets, except Australia, Indonesia, and New Zealand (Figure 2.9). Foreign participation was much higher in advanced Europe and North America, as well as in emerging market economies outside Asia, such as Mexico and Turkey. Similarly, foreign ownership of government debt securities tends to be lower in Asia, with foreign holdings of Chinese and Indian government bonds at nearly zero because of restrictions on inflows. The low share of foreign investors can be seen as a double-edged sword. On the one hand, it helps contain instability caused by external funding shocks. On the other hand, it could inhibit risk sharing with a diverse investor base and limit market liquidity.[7] Furthermore, even with low foreign participation in Asian capital markets, market shallowness could reduce liquidity in a number of Asian economies. For instance, it takes almost 30 days for a foreign investor to liquidate an entire position in Malaysia and the Philippines

---

[7]A sudden, sizable pullback by foreign investors usually triggers market turmoil and a spike in risk premiums. The IMF's (2014) *Global Financial Stability Report* also notes that portfolio flows are likely to become more sensitive to global financial conditions.

TABLE 2.1

Asia: Shallowness of Local Government Bond Markets in 2012	
Number of Days Needed for Foreign Investors to Liquidate Their Entire Holding	
China	0.3
Indonesia	130.4
Japan	4.8
Korea	5.8
Malaysia	25.4
Philippines	27.7
Thailand	6.9

Sources: Asian Development Bank, AsiaBondsOnline; ArsIanalp and Tsuda (2012); and IMF staff estimates.

(Table 2.1). Based on this benchmark, Indonesia looks the most vulnerable given its relatively illiquid government bond market.

Intermediation of Private Sector Credit

Over the past decade, total credit to private sectors in Asia has gone through two distinct phases: a modest-increase phase prior to the global financial crisis and a more rapid-rise phase in recent years (Figure 2.10).[8] The first phase reflects the legacy of the Asian financial crisis, particularly in Asian emerging market economies hard hit by the crisis. The ratio of private credit to GDP increased, on average, by 7 percentage points in Asia during 2002–08, while it grew by about 40 percentage points in Europe. In the second phase, from 2008 to 2012, the ratio increased sharply in Asia, while the United States and many European advanced economies were facing a severe credit crunch. Within Asia, there has been a divergence in credit growth over the past decade. The ratio of private credit to GDP increased by 26 percentage points, on average, in advanced Asia, compared with only 18 percentage points in emerging Asia, where a longer period of deleveraging after the Asian financial crisis slowed financial deepening.

Banks, underpinned by a large pool of retail deposits, remain the dominant source of credit to the private sector, accounting for an average of 84 percent of total private credit in Asia at end-2012. Bond financing and cross-border bank credit accounted for an average of only 11 percent and 5 percent of total private

---

[8] Private credit intermediation is a process of transferring funds from an ultimate source to ultimate private users. It is estimated as the sum of (1) domestic bank claims to public nonfinancial corporations and the private sector (IMF, *International Financial Statistics*, line 22C and 22D), (2) cross-border bank credit to the private nonfinancial sector (Bank for International Settlements [BIS] locational and consolidated international banking statistics), and (3) debt securities issued by the nonfinancial private sector (BIS debt security statistics). See Dembiermont, Drehmann, and Muksakunratana (2013) for how to derive cross-border bank credit to the private nonfinancial sector.

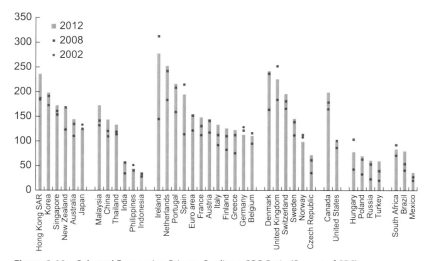

Figure 2.10 Selected Economies: Private-Credit-to-GDP Ratio (*Percent of GDP*)

Sources: Bank for International Settlements, *Consolidated Banking Statistics*, and *Debt Securities Statistics*; IMF, *International Financial Statistics*, and World Economic Outlook database; and IMF staff calculations.

credit in Asia, respectively. Characteristics of credit intermediation by banks include the following:

- Banks channel 60 percent of their total non-interbank assets to the private sector. Credit to the government and to nonresidents remains important in some countries (Table 2.2). For instance, Indian and Japanese banks have accumulated a large stock of government bonds, accounting for a quarter of total non-interbank claims. Banks in Hong Kong SAR and Singapore hold sizable foreign assets, accounting for 60 percent and 35 percent, respectively, of total non-interbank claims.

- Retail deposits expanded and bank lending grew as deposit insurance and guarantees made this channel more attractive to savers. In most Asian economies, deposit-to-credit ratios were over 100 percent at end-2012 (Figure 2.11). The exceptions were Korea and New Zealand, where the banking sectors saw a marked increase in net foreign liabilities during 2001–08. As a result, these countries introduced macroprudential measures, including the Macroprudential Stability Levy (Korea, August 2011) and the Core Funding Ratio (New Zealand, April 2010), to discourage excess reliance on international wholesale funding and thus contain systemic liquidity risk. The large pool of retail deposits helped Asian banks weather liquidity shortages during the global financial crisis.[9] It will also play an important role in putting Asian banks in a favorable position to meet the Basel III liquidity requirements, compared with peers in Europe and North America (Ötker-Robe and Pazarbasioglu 2010).

---

[9] See Chapter 5 for a detailed analysis.

TABLE 2.2

Asia: Composition of Banks' Non-Interbank Claims
(*Percent of total non-interbank claims, at end-2012*)

	Total Claims	Foreign Assets	Claims on Central Bank	Claims on Government	Claims on Other Financial Institutions	Claims on Private Agents
Australia	100	11	0	1	17	71
China	100	3	19	5	5	68
Hong Kong SAR	100	60	2	6	0	32
India	100	0	5	26	0	69
Indonesia	100	3	21	4	4	68
Japan	100	17	4	28	13	38
Korea	100	7	7	2	11	74
Malaysia	100	8	16	4	4	68
Philippines	100	8	21	14	6	51
Singapore	100	35	3	10	0	52
Thailand	100	4	17	3	5	72
Average	100	14	10	9	6	60

Sources: IMF, *International Financial Statistics*; and IMF staff calculation.

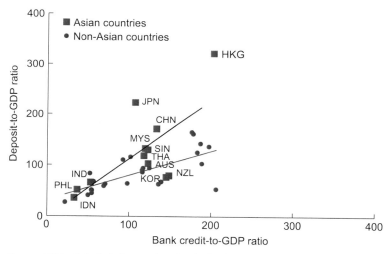

Figure 2.11 Selected Economies: Bank Credit and Deposits (*Percent of GDP, end-2012*)

Sources: FinStats; Haver Analytics; IMF, *International Financial Statistics*; and IMF staff calculations.
Note: AUS = Australia; CHN = China; HKG = Hong Kong SAR; IDN = Indonesia; IND = India; JPN = Japan; KOR = Korea; MYS = Malaysia; NZL = New Zealand; PHL = the Philippines; SIN = Singapore; THA = Thailand.

Corporate lending tends to outweigh household lending in Asia. Banks in China, India, and the Philippines allocated about 80 percent of private credit to nonfinancial firms at end-2012. After suffering large losses from the failure of big corporate borrowers during the Asian financial crisis, banks in some countries saw a temporary shift to household lending during 2000–05 (Mohanty and Turner 2013). As risks appeared to rise in housing markets, however, authorities actively implemented macroprudential and tax measures to contain them, which contributed to a rebound in the share of corporate lending after 2006.[10]

Although bank credit remains the dominant source of corporate financing, bond financing has become an increasingly important funding source for firms, accounting, on average, for 11 percent of total private credit in Asia. The outstanding balance of local-currency corporate bonds increased two-and-a-half fold from $1.4 trillion in 2003 to $3.3 trillion in 2012, representing 15 percent of GDP in Asia (Asian Development Bank 2013).[11] Various factors have contributed to the recent growth of corporate bond markets in Asia. These include policy initiatives, perceived earnings potential, a large interest rate differential, and rising foreign investor interest.[12] The size of corporate bond markets varies widely among Asian economies. In Korea and Malaysia, outstanding corporate debt securities amounted to 42 percent of GDP at end-2012, or a quarter of total private credit. However, the corporate bond market is still at an early stage of development in many Asian emerging market economies, such as China, India, Indonesia, and the Philippines, with share in private credit below 10 percent in these four countries.[13]

Direct cross-border bank lending plays a limited role. The growth of local bond markets after the Asian financial crisis provided an opportunity to move away from cross-border funding. In 2012 in most Asian economies, cross-border bank credit amounted to less than 10 percent of GDP, and, on average, about 5 percent of total credit. The exceptions were Hong Kong SAR and Singapore, where cross-border bank lending to private agents stood at about 20 percent of GDP at end-2012. Although Asia faced a larger decline in funding provided by international banks, many Asian economies—unlike many countries in emerging Europe—were able to weather an acute sudden stop of funding during the global financial crisis, given the limited role of cross-border bank credit (IMF 2011).

Targeted policies remain in place to address barriers to financial access faced by small and medium-sized enterprises. Capital market deepening has increased the options for firms but so far their use has been limited to relatively large issuers. Asian small and medium-sized enterprises often encounter poor access to finance

---

[10] Macroprudential instruments have been used more extensively in Asia than in other regions. This is particularly true of measures related to the housing market such as limits on loan-to-value ratios and caps on debt-service-to-income ratios (for example, China, Hong Kong SAR, India, Indonesia, Korea, Malaysia, Singapore, and Thailand). These instruments have helped dampen mortgage loans and slow the growth of housing price (Zhang and Zoli 2014).

[11] Corporate bond issuance increased from 2 percent of GDP in 2010 to over 3.5 percent in 2012, while newly originated long-term syndicated bank loans fell from 2.5 of GDP to below 2 percent over the same period (Levinger and Li 2014).

[12] See Chapter 4 for detailed information.

[13] From 2008 to 2012, the size of domestic corporate debt securities doubled in China to 10 percent of GDP, but their contribution to private credit is much smaller than is bank lending to private agents, which is 130 percent of GDP.

relative to their peers in other regions. Fewer than 45 percent of small and medium-sized enterprises in emerging Asia have access to credit lines, compared with 70 percent in Latin America and 60 percent in emerging Europe. This financial exclusion is especially stark in China, where fewer than 20 percent of small and medium-sized enterprises have access to bank credit lines. The financial access of small and medium-sized enterprises has gradually improved because of government measures such as credit guarantees (Japan, Korea), mandatory lending (Indonesia, the Philippines), and coinvestments for start-ups (for example, the Spring Seeds capital scheme in Singapore). A few emerging market economies in Asia have also recently developed financial infrastructure that could promote small and medium-sized business lending, including credit information systems (the Philippines, 2011) and movable collateral registers (China, 2007).

Financial inclusion for individuals lags in emerging Asia relative to other regions, but mobile technology has begun to turn this around. Two interesting aspects follow:

- Only 45 percent of adults in emerging Asia have bank accounts, compared with over 95 percent in advanced Asia. The disparities are even larger among rural or low-income households. Among the bottom 40 percent of income earners and those who live in rural areas, only about 30–35 percent hold a bank account in emerging Asia, compared with 90 percent in advanced Asia. Urban residents in emerging Asia generally have better access to banking services than do their rural counterparts. Gaps in access still persist, even in cities, in areas such as credit cards.

- However, the recent growth of mobile technology has rapidly improved financial inclusion. Not only has mobile banking emerged as a convenient way to manage payments and fund transfers, it has also offered new opportunities for banks to reach unbanked customers at low marginal costs. According to Bain & Company (2012), Asia is the leader in mobile banking penetration. In several economies, including China, Hong Kong SAR, India, and Korea, more than 35 percent of survey respondents said they have used mobile banking for financial transactions—well above levels seen in other countries outside Asia (Figure 2.12).[14] Given the rapid development and evolution of mobile banking, policymakers will need to ensure that secure settlement systems and proper oversight are put in place to balance technological innovation and customer protection while promoting financial inclusion.

Government Involvement

Government involvement in the financial sector is significant in many Asian economies. A number of IMF Financial Sector Assessment Programs for Asian

---

[14] In 2008, Jibun Bank was launched in Japan as the first virtual bank in the world. Founded by a joint partnership between Bank of Tokyo-Mitsubishi UFJ and the telecommunication company KDDI, Jibun Bank offers various banking products and services exclusively for its customers over mobile phones.

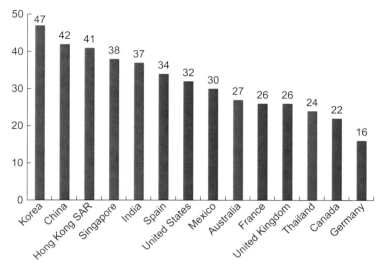

Figure 2.12 Selected Economies: Mobile Banking Penetration (*Percent of respondents reporting mobile banking transactions in the last three months, 2012*)

Source: Bain & Company (2012).

economies have highlighted the large role of the government, particularly through ownership of financial institutions, the use of financial sector policies to foster financial sector development and influence credit intermediation, and the provision of explicit and implicit government guarantees to backstop financial institutions and enhance financial access of small and medium-sized enterprises. Some of these aspects of government involvement reflect proactive efforts to preserve financial stability and support economic development. Other government actions—such as directed lending—can distort incentives and hinder financial sector development.

The degree of government ownership of financial institutions varies widely. In major Asian economies—with the exception of Australia, Hong Kong SAR, New Zealand, and Singapore—the share of government-controlled credit institutions was at least 20 percent of the aggregate assets of credit institutions in 2013 (Figure 2.13).[15] Furthermore, government ownership extends to insurance and securities companies in some countries. Factors contributing to significant government ownership vary:

- *Historical factors.* In China and India, governments continue to maintain ownership of commercial banks.

---

[15]The analysis is based on the controlling power of governments over credit institutions, which include banks and other financial institutions that provide credit. Hence, it does not present a picture of the exact amount of government shareholding in financial institutions. In particular, in Singapore, the government has a sizable stake in the DBS Bank, its largest bank, with no controlling power.

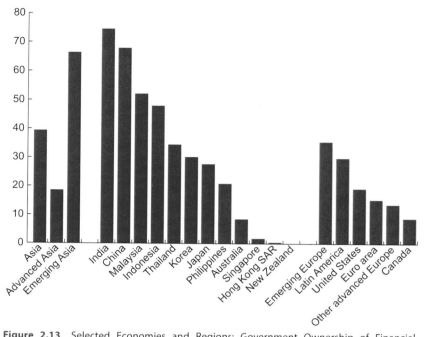

Figure 2.13 Selected Economies and Regions: Government Ownership of Financial Institutions in 2013 (*Assets of credit institutions owned by governments as a percentage of the aggregate assets of credit institutions*)

Sources: Bankscope; and IMF staff estimates.

Note: The analysis covers credit institutions with assets greater than US$5 billion available from the Bankscope database.

- *Legacy of financial crises.* In countries such as Indonesia, Korea, and Thailand, which were severely hit during the Asian financial crisis, state interventions led to significant government ownership of commercial banks.

- *Policy-driven government involvement.* In Malaysia, the government has large de facto interests in a number of major financial institutions through government-linked investment companies, some of which are related to the public pension system. In Japan, the government, in addition to fully owning the Post Bank, provides funding to various financing vehicles aimed at supporting the government's social goals. Policy banks, such as development banks and export-import banks with explicit mandates, play important roles in many countries, including Korea, the Philippines, and Thailand.

Governments have considerable influence on credit intermediation because they are using or incentivizing the financial sector to support broader policy goals. This may affect both aggregate amounts and sectoral allocation of credit. The policy goals follow:

- *Managing overall credit conditions.* In countries such as China and Vietnam, where monetary policy operations are not based on interest rates, administrative limits on lending remain a key policy instrument. Prudential regulation, such as penalizing banks with loan-to-deposit ratios below a specific target, has also been used in Indonesia to stimulate overall credit growth.

- *Affecting the sectoral allocation of credit.* Implicit guidance, such as supervisory pressure, and regulatory measures, such as lower risk weights, are commonly used to influence commercial banks' decisions. These directed lending practices are more prevalent in China, India, Indonesia, and Korea. Even in cases in which policy banks provide direct lending to priority sectors, excessive support is often observed (for example, housing finance in the Philippines). Moreover, some governments use policy banks to support government social programs without properly acknowledging the contingent fiscal cost (for example, subsidization of rice production in Thailand).

- *Promoting lending through guarantees.* In Japan and Korea, governments set up specialized agencies to provide guarantees for credit risks of lending to small and medium-sized enterprises. In Malaysia, a similar scheme, called Cagamas, was launched to promote the local corporate bond market.

Governments have also been active in maintaining financial stability by addressing systemic risks during normal times and providing support during crises:

- *Addressing systemic risks.* Following the Asian financial crisis, authorities in many Asian countries stepped up systemic risk monitoring and assessment, including the regular publication of financial stability reports. In addition, governments sometimes implement structural measures to strengthen financial systems. For instance, the Chinese government played an active role in bank restructuring in the early 2000s.

- *Providing support during stress periods.* According to Standard & Poor's "Banking Industry Country Risk Assessment Update: October 2013," governments are highly supportive of the banking industry in all major Asian economies, except New Zealand. Asian governments are more likely to intervene than are governments in major non-Asian economies, particularly with the goal of restoring financial stability during periods of distress.[16] During the global financial crisis, for example, the Japanese and Korean authorities engaged in very large scale liquidity injections and took measures to ensure continued access to finance by small and medium-sized enterprises. In Singapore, the authorities provided a temporary blanket deposit guarantee, while the Australian government offered a fee-based, unlimited guarantee for wholesale funding and large-amount deposits.

---

[16] Governments in major economies in other regions, both advanced and emerging market, are considered to be only supportive to the banking industry in their jurisdictions.

COMPLEXITY AND INTERCONNECTEDNESS

In the run-up to the global financial crisis, Asia's financial system was generally less complex than was those of its counterparts in the euro area and the United States. Many structural features associated with the crisis were absent (IMF 2012b). For example, the Asian financial sector did not shift toward a market-based model, but remained largely dominated by commercial banks. Asian banks also continued to rely on traditional activities such as accepting deposits and making loans rather than on sophisticated activities such as trading and underwriting. The sector was neither highly leveraged nor significantly exposed to opaque structured financial products (Jeasakul, Lim, and Lundback 2014).[17] Shadow banking played only a minor role, and domestic financial entities were weakly interlinked.

Even after the global financial crisis, some aspects of Asia's banking system have remained relatively unsophisticated. First, Asian banks continue to rely heavily on interest income, which accounted, on average, for more than two-thirds of total income at end-2012. At the same point, non-interest income—such as trading income, fees, and commissions—accounted for only 20 percent of total income, compared with more than 50 percent in Switzerland and the United Kingdom (Figure 2.14). Second, interbank linkages are lower in Asia (IMF 2013). The sum of two ratios, interbank assets to total assets and interbank liabilities to total liabilities, was about 20 percent in Asia at end-2012, less than 40 percent in the euro area, and 30 percent in Latin America.

However, Asia has been embracing financial innovation and diversification since the global financial crisis, with strong growth in shadow banking activities and structured products. Nonbank financial intermediation can enhance financial depth and broaden access to finance, and diversified financial products can make financial markets more efficient because they lead to more risk sharing. If the associated risks are allowed to grow unchecked, however, they could undermine financial stability and damage the real economy.

The rapid growth of domestic interlinkages in some Asian economies has intensified contagion risks. In China, for example, bank claims to nonbank financial institutions grew by about 50 percent during 2012–13, and commercial banks' interbank assets accounted for 20 percent of total assets in 2013.[18] The increasing bilateral exposures between shadow and traditional banks are also found in other Asian economies. Lee and Cheng (2012) show that such bilateral exposures have doubled since 2006 in Korea and the Financial Stability Board (2013) notes that funding and credit risks have increased markedly in

---

[17] For instance, Asian financial institutions' subprime-market-related losses and write-downs amounted to $27 billion, only 3 percent of total losses and write-downs by the top 100 banks and securities firms around the world.

[18] IMF (2011) shows that Chinese money markets are actively used by many small and medium-sized banks (and nonbank financial institutions) to fund their activities, and by large banks to place their surplus funds.

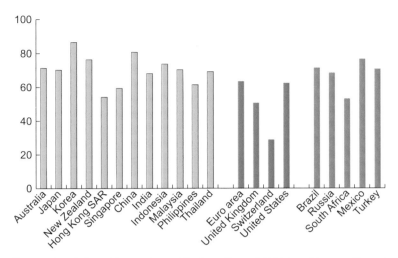

Figure 2.14 Selected Economies and Regions: Share of Net Interest Income (*Percent of total income, end-2012*)

Sources: Bankscope; and IMF staff calculations.

India and Indonesia due to the linkages between commercial banks and shadow banking entities.

The use of structured foreign exchange derivatives in Asian currencies has also recently grown. Foreign exchange derivatives provide a way to hedge currency risks, but some exotic contracts may actually raise currency risk exposures. A case in point is the so-called knock-in-knock-out (KIKO) foreign exchange options, which were sold in 2006–07 to many Korean small and medium-sized enterprises seeking to hedge against a prolonged appreciation of the Korean won. As the won depreciated sharply during the global financial crisis, these contracts resulted in sizable losses. This, in turn, amplified depreciation pressures on the won, hurting other entities with open foreign exchange positions. A similar phenomenon may now be emerging in Hong Kong SAR, where the offshore renminbi foreign exchange option market has a daily turnover of about $7 billion, up from about $10 million in 2010 (Deutsche Bank 2013). Unlike the onshore renminbi foreign exchange market, in which only simple and standardized options can be traded, the offshore renminbi foreign exchange market is dominated by targeted accrual redemption notes, which are similar to the KIKO options (J.P. Morgan 2014). As happened in Korea, a sharp movement of spot rates in the offshore market may lead corporations in Hong Kong SAR to suffer nonnegligible losses and create counterparty risks for dealer banks.

Exchange traded funds (ETFs) have become increasingly popular in Asia, with assets under management growing from $53 billion in 2008 to $167 billion in 2013 (Deutsche Bank 2014). Trading volumes in Asian ETFs increased by 100 percent to $654 billion in 2013. By comparison, trading volumes in the

United States, the world's largest ETF market, grew by less than 8 percent, though in 2013 they totaled $14 trillion. The vast majority of ETFs in Asia are the plain-vanilla type, providing investors with a low-cost and efficient way to access a wide variety of asset classes. As the demand for ETFs has grown, however, so have product complexity and investors' appetite for riskier ETFs. For example, ETFs based on synthetic replication methods have slowly become popular. The use of swaps and other derivative instruments to generate benchmark returns, instead of the passive holding of underlying assets, could complicate ETF risk assessment. In particular, opaque ETFs may create risks similar to those created by many structured financial instruments before the global financial crisis.

The level of Asia's cross-border interconnectedness through financial linkages remains relatively limited, compared with the level in advanced Europe and North America. Gross foreign assets and liabilities in Asian economies (excluding Hong Kong SAR and Singapore) increased, but were still modest (160 percent of GDP in 2012), compared with those in the euro area and North America (430 percent and 300 percent of GDP, respectively) (Figure 2.15).[19] Furthermore, emerging Asia lags significantly behind its peers. For example, the sum of gross foreign assets and liabilities was 135 percent of GDP in 2012 in Asia, compared with a sum of 420 percent in emerging Europe and 215 percent in Latin American. However, Hong Kong SAR and Singapore, two financial hubs, had correspondingly large foreign assets and liabilities (above 1,500 percent of GDP).

Intraregional financial linkages are limited. Asia has very strong regional trade linkages, as well as financial linkages with other regions, but financial linkages within the region are relatively small.[20] Asian economies held very small cross-border portfolio investments and banking claims on each other. The intraregional linkages within Asia accounted for only 5 percent of total global bilateral positions at end-2012, far below levels observed in Europe (42 percent).[21]

Emerging Asia is not particularly active in interregional financial activities.[22] For instance, Asian financial institutions, with the exception of Australia and

---

[19] In many Asian economies, foreign assets are largely in the form of official foreign reserves. For example, in China, India, Japan, Korea, Malaysia, and the Philippines, foreign reserves reached 20–50 percent of GDP at end-2012, representing over 16–70 percent of foreign assets.

[20] In terms of trade linkages, IMF (2012a) shows that Asian economies are tightly interconnected intra- and interregionally, with China as a core and a gatekeeper of the cluster. Over the past two decades, intraregional trade among the Asian cluster economies has grown strongly.

[21] Total global bilateral position is calculated as the sum of cross-border portfolio investments from the Coordinated Portfolio Investment Survey and cross-border banking claims from the BIS locational banking statistics. The position can be divided into two types according to location. One is the cross-border position between two countries within a region, or intraregional linkages, and the other is the cross-border position between two countries in different regions, or interregional linkages. The two positions accounted for 51 and 49 percent of total global bilateral positions, respectively, as of end-2012.

[22] Japan, however, acts as a global lender and investor, holding 12 percent of cross-border banking claims and 10 percent of portfolio investments vis-à-vis the rest of the world, Australia plays a role as a regional lender and investor, providing 14 percent of the banking claims vis-à-vis Asian economies at end-2012.

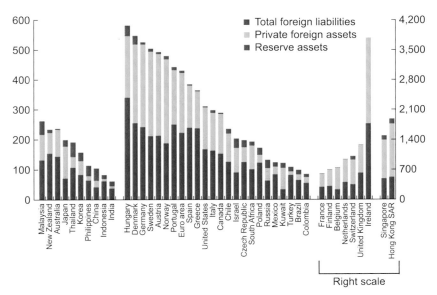

Figure 2.15 Selected Economies: Gross Foreign Assets and Liabilities (*Percent of GDP, end-2012*)
Sources: IMF, *International Financial Statistics*; and IMF staff calculations.

Japan, held very small cross-border portfolio investments and banking claims on countries outside Asia. Such investments and claims accounted for only 3 percent of the global bilateral positions, while those in North America accounted for 14 percent at end-2012.

Global interconnectedness has risen since the global financial crisis, however. Asian economies have seen a sharp increase in cross-border financial interconnectedness, pulling global capital inflows into the region. Australian and Japanese banks are also actively filling a gap created by European banks as they retreat from the region. Gross foreign assets and liabilities in Asian economies increased by 60 percent on average during 2007–12, while some European countries (Austria, Belgium, Italy, Portugal, and Spain) saw declining positions. Asia's portfolio investment assets grew by 40 percent during the same period, compared with a decline of 3 percent in the euro area (Figure 2.16).[23] Furthermore, while cross-border bank flows to the euro area and the United Kingdom fell by 30 percent, bank flows to Asian economies (excluding Japan and Australia) increased by 60 percent between 2007 and the third quarter of 2013. Even though the Federal Reserve's tapering announcement caused volatility in capital flows into and out of Asian emerging market economies in 2013, the overall capital inflow to Asia has remained resilient. These included inflows from Australian and Japanese banks driven by business opportunities emerging from the retreat of European banks (see Chapter 10).

---

[23] Asia's portfolio investment liabilities grew by 23 percent over the same period, compared with a decline of 4 percent in the euro area.

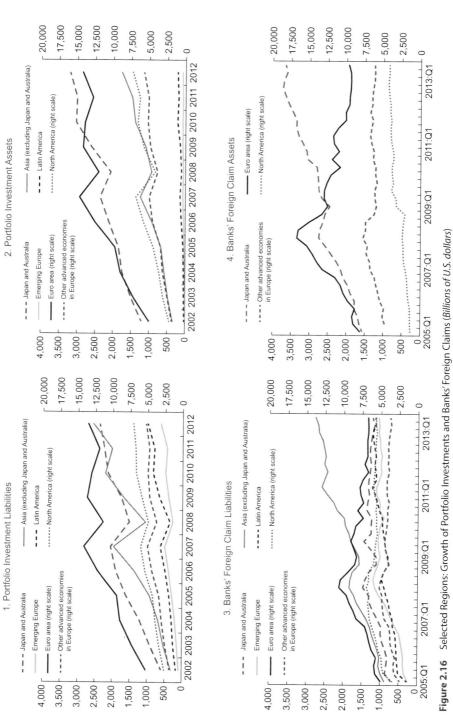

Figure 2.16 Selected Regions: Growth of Portfolio Investments and Banks' Foreign Claims (*Billions of U.S. dollars*)

Sources: Bank for International Settlements, *Consolidated Banking Statistics* on ultimate risk basis; IMF, Coordinated Portfolio Investment Survey; and IMF staff calculations.

CONCLUSION

Asia's distinctive financial sectors raise specific concerns for the region's governments. The region fared relatively well during the global financial crisis as a result of favorable macroeconomics, prudent supervision, and other factors. However, as in all countries, regulators and supervisors in Asia need to focus on potential instability and closely monitor and properly manage potential risks (see Chapters 5 and 11).

Because Asia's financial sector is banking focused, regulators and supervisors must continue to ensure that banks do not jeopardize financial stability. The lessons for Asia are similar to those for other regions: it is crucial to ensure that borrowing costs reflect not only banks' cost of capital, but also the costs of risky activities. Asia has some advantages—its banks are not as complex as those of emerging markets; it has fewer G-SIBs; and interbank linkages, both domestic and cross border, are relatively small. This may change in the future.[24] Rapid growth can also be expected to shift Asia's corporate-dominated bank balance sheets toward more household lending, necessitating the development of risk-management tools in this area.

Asia's rapidly developing capital markets also will raise supervisory challenges. Asia's large equity markets are already an important source of funding for large companies, but it could become more liquid and a better source for capital (see Chapter 3). The rapid development of bond markets in recent years also raises the hopes for a more diverse and disintermediated financial system that allows banks to focus on providing funding to small and medium-sized enterprises while large-company and longer-term financing move into bond markets (see Chapter 4).

To support the long-term sustainable development of Asia's financial system, policymakers and financial market participants need to take new steps to develop domestic institutional investors. The lack of a critical mass of long-term or real-money investors has slowed the development of Asia's capital markets. A greater presence of pension funds, insurance companies, and other institutional investors would provide an important source of funds for companies issuing securities and for infrastructure projects. It could add to secondary market liquidity, and thus price discovery as well (see Chapter 8).

The broad range of government involvement in Asia could lead to sizable public contingent liabilities. Guarantees for certain types of lending, deposits, or bonds could lead to substantial fiscal costs, especially when systemic risks materialize. Guarantees tend to be implicit and may naturally arise due to government ownership of financial institutions. A case in point is China, where there is as yet no formal deposit insurance scheme, but nevertheless recognition that deposits in the country's largely publicly owned banking system are safe. Even in countries that have explicit financial safety nets and specialized agencies for providing guarantees, governments are widely expected to backstop potential financing gaps. Such contingent liabilities could exacerbate the negative feedback loop between

---

[24] Chapters 6, 9, and 10 provide details on Asia's financial sector.

banks and sovereigns during crises, when additional government supports, such as guarantees on banks' liabilities and purchases of nonperforming assets, are extended to safeguard financial stability.

Other adverse effects of government involvement have also been identified. Government involvement can create moral hazard by reducing the perceived risk of individual activities. It might also lead to the misallocation of resources by providing distorted incentives. For example, many nonviable small and medium-sized enterprises in Korea continue to receive financing because of the government's credit guarantee scheme for lending to small and medium-sized enterprises. Moreover, restrictions on financial institutions' activities or on foreign participation in local capital markets appear to have hindered financial sector development in some countries. Unintended consequences also commonly arise as a result of other government policies. For instance, the regulation requiring banks to hold a substantial amount of government securities in India has led to limited liquidity in the country's secondary government bond market.

The rapid development and evolution of mobile banking gives rise to new types of risks that need to be properly addressed. While mobile banking has helped promote financial inclusion, policymakers need to ensure that secure settlement systems and proper oversight are put in place to balance technological innovation with customer protection against cyber crime.

REFERENCES

Arslanalp, Serkan, and Takahiro Tsuda. 2012. "Tracking Global Demand for Advanced Economy Sovereign Debt." IMF Working Paper 12/284, International Monetary Fund, Washington.

Asian Development Bank. 2013. *Asia Bond Monitor.* Manila: Asian Development Bank.

Bain & Company. 2012. "Customer Loyalty in Retail Banking: Global Edition." Boston, December 4.

Chan, Lydia, and Stephen Hull. 2013. "Asian Home Bias: Creating a Framework for Equity Portfolio Diversification." *Investment Insights,* Blackrock.

Dembiermont, Christian, Mathias Drehmann, and Siriporn Muksakunratana. 2013. "How Much Does the Private Sector Really Borrow? A New Database for Total Credit to the Private Nonfinancial Sector." *BIS Quarterly Review* March: 65–81.

Deutsche Bank. 2013. "The Burgeoning CNH FX Option Market." *CNH Market Monitor,* October 25, Deutsche Bank Markets Research.

———. 2014. *ETF Annual Review & Outlook.* Frankfurt: Deutsche Bank Securities Inc.

Fiechter, Jonathan, İnci Ötker-Robe, Anna Ilyina, Michael Hsu, Andre Santos, and Jay Surti. 2011. "Subsidiaries or Branches: Does One Size Fit All?" IMF Staff Discussion Note No. 11/4, International Monetary Fund, Washington.

Financial Stability Board (FSB). 2013. *Global Shadow Banking Monitoring Report 2013.* Basel: Financial Stability Board.

———. 2014. *Global Shadow Banking Monitoring Report 2014.* Basel: Financial Stability Board.

International Monetary Fund. 2011. "People's Republic of China: Financial System Stability Assessment." *IMF Country Report No. 11/321.* Washington: International Monetary Fund.

———. 2012a. "Enhancing Surveillance: Interconnectedness and Clusters." IMF Policy Paper, March, International Monetary Fund, Washington.

———. 2012b. "The Reform Agenda: An Interim Report on Progress toward a Safer Financial System." *Global Financial Stability Report.* October, Chapter 3. Washington: International Monetary Fund.

————. 2013. "Changes in Bank Funding Patterns and Financial Stability Issues." *Global Financial Stability Report*, October, Chapter 3. Washington: International Monetary Fund.

————. 2014. "Making the Transition from Liquidity- to Growth-Driven Markets." *Global Financial Stability Report*, April, Chapter 1. Washington: International Monetary Fund.

Jeasakul, Phakawa, Cheng Hoon Lim, and Erik Lundback. 2014. "Why Was Asia Resilient? Lessons from the Past and for the Future." IMF Working Paper 14/38, International Monetary Fund, Washington.

J.P. Morgan. 2014. "China and the Credit Nexus: Capital Demands, Rate Distortions, NPLs Move West." *Asia Pacific Equity Research*, April 4.

Konno, Sayako, Ai Teramoto, and Yuka Mera. 2012. "Compiling Statistics of Shadow Banking." In *Proceedings of the Sixth International Finance Corporation Conference on Statistical Issues and Activities in a Changing Environment*. Basel: Bank for International Settlements.

Lee, Bumho, and Wonkyung Cheng. 2012. "Shadow Banking in Korea and Potential Risk." Discussion Paper Series No. 2012–11 (in Korean), Bank of Korea, Seoul.

Levinger, Hannah, and Chen Li. 2014. "What's behind Recent Trends in Asian Corporate Bond Markets?" Current Issues, January, Deutsche Bank AG, Frankfurt.

Mohanty, Madhusudan, and Philip Turner. 2013. "Banks and Financial Intermediation in Emerging Asia: Reforms and New Risks." BIS Working Paper No. 313, Bank for International Settlements, Basel.

Ötker-Robe, Inci, and Ceyla Pazarbasioglu. 2010. "Impact of Regulatory Reforms on Large and Complex Financial Institutions." IMF Staff Position Note No. 10/16, International Monetary Fund, Washington.

Standard and Poor's. 2013. "Banking Industry Country Risk Assessment Update: October 2013." Standard and Poor's, New York.

Zhang, Longmei, and Edda Zoli. 2014. "Leaning against the Wind: Macroprudential Policy in Asia." IMF Working Paper No. 14/22, International Monetary Fund, Washington.

CHAPTER 3

Are There Crouching Tigers and Hidden Dragons in Asia's Stock Markets?

FABIAN LIPINSKY AND LI LIAN ONG

MAIN POINTS OF THIS CHAPTER

- Asia's stock markets tend to be more influenced by idiosyncratic factors than do the stock markets of the Group of Seven (G7)[1] countries, beyond the systematic factors and local fundamentals that are identified in the analysis.
- There is a significant relationship between the strength of implementation of securities regulations and the "noise" in stock pricing.
- Improvements in the regulation of securities markets in Asia could enhance the role of stock markets as stable and reliable sources of financing into the future.

INTRODUCTION

The Chinese proverb "crouching tiger hidden dragon" is an apt description of Asia's stock markets today. It refers to the mysteries or undiscovered potential that lie beneath the surface, appropriately capturing the stage of development of the region's stock markets. These stock markets continue to be a key source of financing for local firms, but their potential is yet to be fully realized. They are an important destination for foreign investment, yet some are seen as somewhat opaque and idiosyncratic.

The role of Asia's stock markets as important drivers of growth in the region is underappreciated. Though not widely known, the share of stock market capitalization as a percentage of GDP in most Asian countries is comparable to that of their total banking sector assets, with debt securities markets coming in a distant third (Figure 3.1). This contrasts with developments in many advanced economies, where banking sectors continue to dominate financial intermediation

---

This chapter is based on Lipinsky and Ong (2014); see this paper for more references to the related literature.

[1] The G7 comprise Canada, France, Germany, Italy, Japan, the United Kingdom, and the United States.

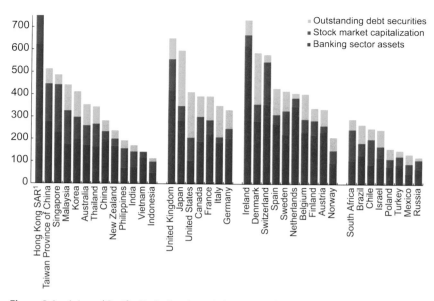

Figure 3.1 Asia and Pacific (Excluding Japan), the Group of Seven, and the Rest of the World: Structure of the Financial Sector at End-2012 (*Percent of GDP*)

Sources: Bank for International Settlements; Bloomberg, L.P.; Haver Analytics; and IMF staff calculations.
[1]The Hong Kong SAR column is truncated for presentation purposes, given the relatively large size of its financial system, with stock market capitalization amounting to almost 13 times GDP and outstanding debt securities issued domestically amounting to 54 percent of GDP at end-2012.

(see Chapter 1). Statistics published by the World Federation of Exchanges illustrate the breadth and depth of Asia's stock markets. For example, they show the following:

- Equity issuances have been an important source of financing in many Asian countries. New capital raised by stock issuance in Asia in 2012 amounted to $198 billion, compared with $234 billion in the Americas and $102 billion in Europe, the Middle East, and Africa (EMEA) combined.

- With a capitalization of almost $15 trillion, Asia's stock market capitalization is about equivalent in value to that of EMEA (Table 3.1).

- Almost 20,000 companies were listed on Asia's stock markets at end-2012, slightly less than the rest of the world combined. More than 10,000 were listed in the Americas, and 13,300 were listed in EMEA.

- Market liquidity in 2012, measured as the ratio of total turnover to average capitalization, was 0.9 for Asia, compared with 1.2 for the Americas and 0.65 for EMEA.

Asia's stock markets have also become more integrated with the international financial system. Foreign investment in many of the region's stock markets has grown since the Asian financial crisis. Investment has grown exponentially in

TABLE 3.1

Stock Markets around the World: Capitalization at End-2012

Region	Country	Exchange	Amount (Millions of U.S. dollars)	Share of Region (Percent)	Share of World (Percent)
Americas			23,193,460	100.0	42.5
	Brazil	BM & FBOVESPA	1,227,447	5.3	2.2
	Canada	TMX Group	2,058,839	8.9	3.8
	Chile	Santiago SE	313,325	1.4	0.6
	Colombia	Colombia SE	262,101	1.1	0.5
	Mexico	Mexican Exchange	525,057	2.3	1.0
	Peru	Lima SE	102,617	0.4	0.2
	United States	NASDAQ OMX[1]	4,582,389	19.8	8.4
		NYSE Euronext (US)	14,085,944	60.7	25.8
	Others		35,742	0.2	0.1
Asia and Pacific[2]			16,928,860	100.0	31.0
	Australia	Australian SE	1,386,874	8.2	2.5
	China	Shanghai SE	2,547,204	15.0	4.7
		Shenzhen SE	1,150,172	6.8	2.1
	Hong Kong	Hong Kong Exchanges	2,831,946	16.7	5.2
	India	BSE India	1,263,335	7.5	2.3
		National Stock Exchange India	1,234,492	7.3	2.3
	Indonesia	Indonesia SE	428,223	2.5	0.8
	Japan	Osaka SE	202,151	1.2	0.4
		Tokyo SE Group	3,478,832	20.5	6.4
	Korea	Korea Exchange[3]	1,179,419	7.0	2.2
	Malaysia	Bursa Malaysia	466,588	2.8	0.9
	Philippines	Philippine SE	229,317	1.4	0.4
	Singapore	Singapore Exchange[4]	765,078	4.5	1.4
	Thailand	The Stock Exchange of Thailand	389,756	2.3	0.7
		Others	812,116	4.8	1.5
EMEA			14,447,481	100.0	26.5
	Germany	Deutsche Börse	1,486,315	10.3	2.7
	United Kingdom and Italy	London SE Group	3,396,505	23.5	6.2
	Includes France	NYSE Euronext (Europe)	2,832,189	19.6	5.2
		Others	6,732,473	46.6	12.3
World			54,569,801		

Source: World Federation of Exchanges.
Note: EMEA = Europe, the Middle East, and Africa; NYSE = New York Stock Exchange; SE = stock exchange
[1] NASDAQ OMX Nordic Exchange: OMX includes Copenhagen, Helsinki, Iceland, Stockholm, Tallinn, Riga and Vilnius Stock Exchanges.
[2] Total for Asia and Pacific excludes Osaka and National Stock Exchange of India to avoid double counting with Tokyo and Bombay SE, respectively.
[3] Korea Exchange: includes Kosdaq market data.
[4] Singapore Exchange: market capitalization includes domestic listings and a substantial number of foreign listings, defined as companies whose principal place of business is outside of Singapore. Inactive secondary foreign listings are excluded.

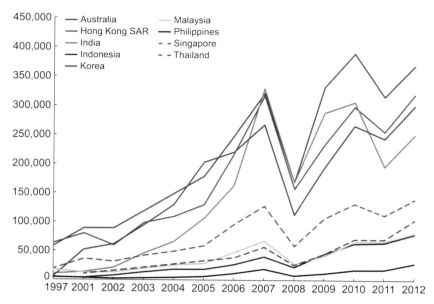

Figure 3.2 Asia and Pacific (Excluding Japan): Outstanding Foreign Investment in Equity Securities, 1997–2012 (*Millions of U.S. dollars*)

Source: IMF staff calculations.
Note: Broken lines denote interpolation of data.

some of the larger markets, which resumed their expansions following the sharp retrenchment during the global financial crisis (Figure 3.2). Meanwhile, cross-listings, including depository receipts from within the region and elsewhere, also expanded as companies sought to tap the region's liquidity. The number of foreign listings in Asia's stock markets tripled between 2002 and 2012, though they are still low, at about 2 percent of the total. This amount compares with 10 percent each in the Americas and EMEA. In turn, emerging market firms, including those from Asia, have sought to access more developed capital markets to benefit from the lower cost of capital, higher valuations, enhanced investor recognition, and better corporate governance, among other reasons.

Although Asia's stock markets have been an important source of funding for the region, their full potential remains to be exploited. One possible reason is the perception that pricing of Asian stocks is more idiosyncratic in nature:

- Speculative activity rather than economic and corporate fundamentals are seen to be driving prices in some of these stock markets. Researchers and the financial press often ascribe sharp drops in Asia's stock markets to the bursting of speculative bubbles (Samuelson 1994; Nam, Park, and Kim 1999), with some of the more recent literature on the topic providing support for this view (Hanim Mokhtar, Nassir, and Hassan 2006; Mei, Scheinkman, and Xiong 2009; Homm and Breitung 2012). Anecdotal evidence suggests that such perceptions of the region's stock markets have prevailed despite analyses showing that the findings are not exclusive to Asia. Evidence of speculative bubbles has also been found in stock prices of advanced economies (West 1987; Homm and Breitung 2012).

- Other related research suggests that the variation in stock returns is larger in emerging markets, appears unrelated to comovement of fundamentals, and is therefore consistent with "noise trading" (Kim and Shamsuddin 2008).[2] In addition to macroeconomic conditions, the literature also contemplates the importance of institutional quality—such as political, legal, regulatory, and governance considerations—for the development of Asia's capital markets (for example, Yartey 2010; Law and Habibullah 2009; Cherif and Gazdar 2010). The evidence also suggests that pricing efficiency in Asian stock markets depends on the level of development as well as on the regulatory framework for transparent corporate governance (Kim and Shamsuddin 2008).

This chapter analyzes the pricing of Asia's stock markets to determine the validity of some of these long-held views. The analysis draws on asset pricing and economic theory, as well as on empirical evidence from the accounting literature. It examines the extent to which well-established systematic international factors and domestic fundamentals influence Asian stock markets as opposed to "idiosyncratic" factors. Specifically, the model does the following:

- It incorporates (1) international factors common to the universe of assets across national boundaries, such as global and regional risks; and (2) domestic economic and financial fundamentals, such as the local business cycle and the financial performance of the corporate sector, to extract the idiosyncratic component in stock returns.

- It subsequently tests for the relationship between this idiosyncratic component and the strength of implementation of securities regulations to represent the role of institutional quality in the pricing of stocks.

The findings corroborate the existing literature on stock market pricing. We find evidence of greater idiosyncratic influences in Asia-Pacific stock markets than in their G7 counterparts, beyond the systematic international factors and local economic and financial fundamentals, which are identified in the analysis. The influence of these international and local factors appears to vary with time, and was most significant during the global financial crisis, when regional developments became the most important factors. Among local factors, forecast earnings appeared to carry the most information for stock pricing, and markedly so during

---

[2] Morck, Yeung, and Yu (2000) find that stock prices tend to move together more in emerging market economies than in advanced economies, and while factors such as market and country size and economic and firm-level fundamentals matter for stock returns, a large residual effect remains and is correlated with measures of institutional development, such as property rights protection. Separately, De Long and others (1989, 1990) find that a reduction in informed trading can increase market-wide noise trader risk.

the global financial crisis. These results suggest that investors may have been seeking more guidance from fundamentals in their pricing decisions during the crisis, in both emerging and advanced economy markets. Separately, asset allocation decisions by foreign investors also appear to have affected stock market volatility and returns in both groups of countries.

We also find a direct and significant connection between market regulation and the importance of idiosyncratic factors. Countries that are better at implementing internationally accepted principles of securities regulation tend to be less subject to idiosyncratic influences in the pricing of their stocks. Thus, improvements in the regulation of securities markets in Asia would likely strengthen investor confidence by ensuring that these markets are operated efficiently and fairly. In turn, this would enhance the role of local stock markets as attractive investment destinations and, thus, as reliable sources of financing. That said, we acknowledge that some of the noise in stock returns may be attributable to other country-specific factors that are not captured in the model.

DATA AND STYLIZED FACTS

The countries in the sample comprise the main emerging market and advanced economies in the Asia-Pacific region (excluding Japan), benchmarked against the G7 countries. The sample countries comprise China, Hong Kong SAR, and Korea (in Northeast Asia); and Indonesia, Malaysia, the Philippines, Singapore, and Thailand (in Southeast Asia); plus Australia and India. The weekly market and earnings data are obtained from Bloomberg and Thomson Reuters I/B/E/S on Datastream. Market capitalization statistics are from Bloomberg and the World Federation of Exchanges (WFE), while annual data on foreign investment and periodic (confidential) information on regulatory implementation are sourced from the IMF.

Broadly speaking, diversified world and regional portfolios have not been the most optimal investments, ex post. In other words, they have not been mean-variance efficient at the asset-allocation-efficient frontier, relative to some individual stock markets (Figure 3.3). For example,

- Asia's stock markets have generally yielded better returns over time relative to their G7 counterparts, but have tended to be more volatile.

- Asia's markets underperformed the G7 during the Asian financial crisis of the late 1990s based on the average risk-return trade-off. Excluding the global financial crisis, they recorded their highest volatility and lowest returns during this period.

- The "peacetime" period immediately before the global financial crisis was the most rewarding for investors. Markets posted their highest returns and were among the least volatile.

- All regions recorded their worst performance during the global financial crisis. Most stock markets posted negative returns (except for India, Malaysia, the Philippines, and Thailand), and many experienced their greatest volatility.

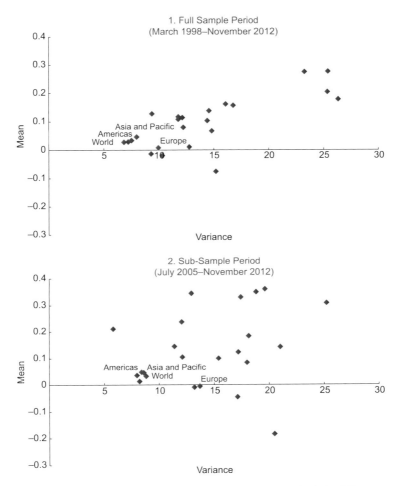

Figure 3.3 Stock Markets around the World: Mean-Variance Analysis of Country, Regional, and World Returns, March 1998–November 2012 (*Weekly U.S. dollar returns, percent*)

Source: IMF staff calculations.

The empirical evidence indicates the following:

- *Stock markets have become more integrated.* As a simple proxy, return correlations between individual and regional stock markets and between individual and world stock markets trended upward during the 15 years to 2012. These correlations tend to be lower for the emerging Asia-Pacific markets compared with the advanced economies in the region and the G7 countries.

- *Foreign investors play a role in influencing stock market volatility and returns.* While there is little relationship between the share of foreign holdings in a country's stock markets and the volatility of returns, asset allocation decisions matter. The analysis finds no relationship between foreign investment in equities as a proportion of average stock market capitalization and the volatility of weekly stock market returns for either the G7 or the Asia-Pacific countries during 2001–12. However, pullout by foreign investors, especially during the global financial crisis period, tended to exacerbate market volatility.

- *Asset allocation decisions by foreign investors have a clear impact on stock market returns.* On average, stock market returns tend to be higher in markets with a higher share of foreign holdings, albeit less obviously so among the G7 markets. For both groups of countries, stock market returns exhibit a strong positive relationship with net foreign portfolio flows.

METHOD

The existing literature suggests that the stock market returns of a country are dependent on local and international factors. We applied Ross's (1976) arbitrage pricing theory in our modeling of individual stock market returns as a factor model in the following generalized form:[3]

$$R_{c,t} = b_{c,0} + b_{c,1}BC_{c,t} + b_{c,2}EPS_{c,t}^{f} + b_{c,3}EPS_{c,t}^{a} + b_{c,4}R_{w,t} + b_{c,5}R_{r,t} + e_{c}, \qquad (3.1)$$

in which

$R_{c,t}$ represents the stock market return for country c at time t.

$BC_{c,t}$ represents the business cycle for country c at time t.

$EPS_{c,t}^{f}$ is the one-year-ahead forecast corporate sector earnings per share (EPS) for country c at time t.

$EPS_{c,t}^{a}$ is the actual (realized) corporate sector EPS for country c at time t.

$R_{w,t}$ is the world stock index return at time t.

$R_{r,t}$ is the regional stock index return at time t.

e_{c} is the idiosyncratic error term, and all the variables are expressed in local currency terms.

In an efficient market, stock prices respond very quickly to incorporate all relevant publicly available information (Fama 1970). Thus, R_{c} should reflect the information contained in the right-hand-side variables, with e_{c} representing relevant pricing information that is not captured in the model. Unfortunately, we are not able to include other emerging market regions for comparison purposes because requisite market data are not available.

---

[3] See Lipinsky and Ong (2014) for a detailed exposition of the model design.

ANALYSIS

The Pricing of Stocks

We run preliminary regressions to determine the most parsimonious form for the relationship between stock market returns and the explanatory variables. First, we apply equation (3.1) to **Dataset 1**, which comprises all independent variables for all countries for July 2005–November 2012. The results show that the systemic regional factor is the most important explanatory variable. Forecast EPS was significant for more countries during the global financial crisis. However, two of the local factors—business cycle and realized EPS—are largely insignificant in explaining stock market returns. The general lack of explanatory power of these variables could mean that much of the related information content may already have been captured by the forecast EPS variable. We also confirm that the individual stock market returns are generally not autocorrelated and are stationary, according to our respective Durbin-Watson and unit root tests. The regression residuals are homoscedastic, according to the White's test results.

Next, we apply equation (3.1) to **Dataset 2**, which comprises *all* independent variables for a *subset* of countries for March 1998–November 2012. The results show that the systemic regional factor remained the most important factor through the extended period. As it was for the global financial crisis period, forecast EPS was significant for more countries during the Asian financial crisis period, suggesting that investors may look for more market guidance during periods of stress.

Based on these findings, we reduce the form of equation (3.1) by omitting two of the largely insignificant local factors. In doing so, we are able to include all countries for the full March 1998–November 2012 period. In this version of the model, the stock market return of a country, c, is generated by a factor model comprising one local factor (forecast EPS) and the two international (world and regional) factors. This relationship is represented as follows:

$$r_{c,t} = b_{c,0} + b_{c,1} EPS_{c,t}^{f} + b_{c,2} R_{w,t} + b_{c,3} R_{r,t} + e_c, \tag{3.2}$$

in which

$EPS_{c,t}^{f}$ is the one-year-ahead forecast corporate sector EPS for country c at time t.

$R_{w,t}$ and $R_{r,t}$ are the world and regional stock index returns, respectively, at time t.

e_c is the idiosyncratic error term, and all the variables are expressed in local currency terms.

The application of Equation 3.2 allows us to use **Dataset 3**, which covers the full March 1998–November 2012 period. The results suggest that although the pricing of Asian stock markets may be more idiosyncratic, the general trends over time are similar to those seen in Asia's G7 counterparts (Annex Table 3.1.1). For example,

- *The findings corroborate the existing literature, which shows that stock market returns in emerging markets are less related to fundamentals and more influenced by idiosyncratic factors.* On average, the adjusted R^2 for Asia's stock markets is much lower than it is for the G7 countries, while the average standard error for Asia is larger than that of the G7 countries by several multiples. Correspondingly, the more developed stock markets in the region (Australia, Hong Kong SAR, Korea, and Singapore) typically show higher adjusted R^2 than that of their regional peers. It is more in line with that of the G7 markets.

- *In general, the influence of international factors on Asia's stock markets has become more significant over time, underscoring the increasing integration across borders.* The systematic regional factors have been relatively more dominant than the world factor at any point in time, supporting the empirical evidence of greater intraregional activity; the importance of regional factors has also increased over time. This outcome is consistent with what has been seen in the G7 markets for some time, where regional factors have consistently been the main pricing influence for stock markets. Within Asia, China's stock markets' growing openness to international influences stands out; all four markets were largely unaffected by world events until the global financial crisis, but have become significantly affected by global developments since its onset.

- *Local developments have been relatively less important in the pricing of Asia's stock markets than world and regional influences.* Any information conveyed by changes in anticipated corporate earnings appears to have had little influence on stock prices in general, both during the Asian financial crisis and "peacetime" periods. This is consistent with the empirical literature, which shows evidence of greater pricing inefficiency during the Asian financial crisis owing to the chaotic financial environment (Lim, Brooks, and Kim 2008). However, this trend changed during the global financial crisis, with information imparted by forecast earnings becoming significant for many more markets. The implication is that investors may be relying more on expert forecasts for guidance during volatile times. The trend is similar for the G7 stock markets.

- *There are few similarities in the pricing of stock markets between the Asian financial crisis period and the global financial crisis period, except for the common lack of "pricing errors" (possible abnormal returns).* Pricing errors reflect, in part, returns that are not accounted for by systematic factors, fundamentals, or idiosyncratic influences. They are captured in the intercept term in equation (3.2). Pricing errors have been significantly different from zero for several Asian markets during "peacetime," most notably for China and India, suggesting that abnormal returns may not have been arbitraged away in the relatively more insulated markets.

The Role of Regulation

The existing empirical evidence points to the importance of institutional factors in the pricing of stocks. In this context, Hsieh and Nieh (2010) argue that certain improvements are needed in Asian countries before greater international financial integration is possible, integration that would lead to the realization of potential benefits of scale, capacity, and liquidity. According to Hsieh and Nieh, areas in need of improvement include regulation, corporate governance, products, and market infrastructure.

We first test for the relationship between the overall strength of regulation and the extent of idiosyncratic influences on stock pricing. We use the International Organization of Securities Commissions' *Objectives and Principles of Securities Regulation* assessments (IOSCO 2003, 2011), conducted during the IMF's Financial Sector Assessment Program (FSAP) missions to the countries in the sample, as a proxy for the strength of securities regulation. Given the infrequency of IOSCO assessments across countries, we regress the standard error of regression from the results of equation (3.2) on individual countries' average IOSCO ratings (see Box 3.1) from the corresponding period, between 2000 and 2012:

$$S_{e,c,t} = a_{c,0} + a_{c,1} IOSCO_{c,t},$$ (3.3)

in which $S_{e,c,t}$ is the standard error of regression for country c at time t; and $IOSCO_{c,t}$ is the average IOSCO rating for country c at time t.

Box 3.1. Deriving a Measure of Effective Securities Regulation

The International Organization of Securities Commissions (IOSCO) is the leading international group of securities market regulators. Its membership comprises regulatory bodies from more than 100 jurisdictions. Each body has day-to-day responsibility for securities regulation and administration of securities laws. The IOSCO *Objectives and Principles of Securities Regulation* ("Principles") sets out a broad general framework for the regulation of securities. Their core aims are to protect investors; ensure that markets are fair, efficient, and transparent; and reduce systemic risk. The scope of the principles includes the regulation of

- Securities markets
- The intermediaries that operate in those markets
- The issuers of securities
- The entities offering investors analytical or evaluative services such as credit rating agencies
- The sale of interests in, and the management and operation of, collective investment schemes.

The methodology for assessing implementation of the IOSCO Principles is designed to provide IOSCO's interpretation of the level of implementation of the principles, and to give guidance on the conduct of a self- or third-party assessment. Two methodologies have been used to date—the first was introduced in 2003 and subsequently replaced by a new one in 2011. As part of the IMF's Financial Sector Assessment Programs (FSAPs), detailed assessments of the implementation of individual IOSCO principles are conducted. Independent experts assign ratings to principles, which are adjudged to be either "implemented," "broadly implemented," "partially implemented," or "not implemented." For this particular analysis, we assign a number to each rating, as follows:

Implemented = 1	Broadly Implemented = 2
Partially Implemented = 3	Not Implemented = 4

For each country, the corresponding numerical rating for each IOSCO principle in a particular assessment is aggregated and then averaged to arrive at the rating that is used in the third regression (equation 3.3).

Sources: IOSCO (2003, 2011).

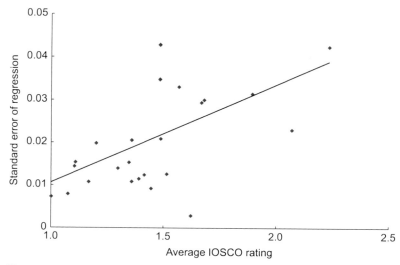

Figure 3.4 Regression Results: Idiosyncratic Influences on Stock Markets and the Effectiveness of Securities Regulation, March 1998–November 2012

$$S_{e,c,t} = -0.012 + 0.023 \cdot IOSCO_{c,t}$$
$$(p = 0.25) \quad (p = 0.00)$$

Adjusted R^2 0.279   Standard error 0.010

Sources: Bloomberg; L.P.; Thomson Reuters I/B/E/S on Datastream; and IMF staff calculations.
Note: IOSCO = International Organization of Securities Commissions.

The regression results point to a significant relationship between idiosyncratic influences in stock pricing and the implementation of securities regulations in individual countries (Figure 3.4). The coefficient for the IOSCO explanatory variable is significantly different from zero at the 1 percent level. The findings imply that countries with better implementation of securities regulations are associated with stock markets that are less subject to idiosyncratic influences. This suggests that some of the noise associated with the regression results for the emerging Asian markets may be attributable to institutional factors, consistent with previous evidence.

The empirical evidence also shows that the quality of regulation affects risk perceptions, and consequently, the cost of financing over the longer term. We group the stock market performance of the Asia-Pacific countries, excluding Japan, and that of the G7 countries in the sample that have undergone FSAPS into four groups roughly equal in size. These range from Group 1, which comprises the countries with the strongest records of implementation of securities regulations (that is, those with the highest average IOSCO ratings), to Group 4, which consists of those with the weakest practices in regulating securities markets. Not surprisingly, the findings confirm that weak regulation tends to be associated

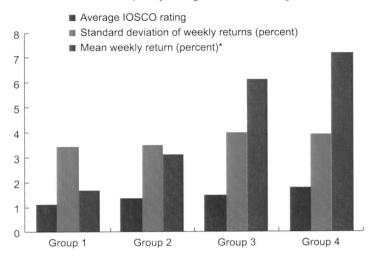

1. Grouped by Strength of IOSCO Rating

■ Average IOSCO rating
■ Standard deviation of weekly returns (percent)
■ Mean weekly return (percent)*

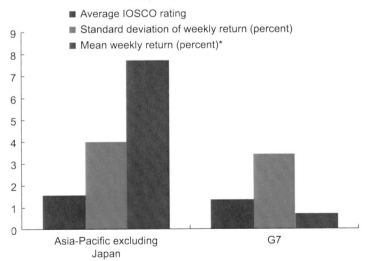

2. Grouped by Country Category

■ Average IOSCO rating
■ Standard deviation of weekly return (percent)
■ Mean weekly return (percent)*

Figure 3.5 Asia-Pacific (Excluding Japan) and the G7 Countries: Securities Regulation and the Risk-Return Trade-Off, March 1998—November 2012

Sources: Bloomberg L.P.; Thomson Reuters I/B/E/S on Datastream; and IMF staff calculations.
Note: IOSCO = International Organization of Securities Commissions.
*Annualized.

with more volatile markets and higher required equity cost of capital, as represented by the actual return (Figure 3.5). As a group, the Asia-Pacific stock markets (excluding Japan) tend to have higher IOSCO ratings (that is, weaker implementation of regulations) relative to the ratings of their G7 counterparts.

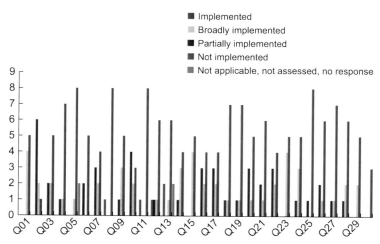

Figure 3.6 Asia-Pacific: Distribution of IOSCO Ratings, 2001–11

Source: IMF staff calculations.

Note: Excludes Japan. Nine assessments applying the 2003 IOSCO methodology were undertaken during this period. IOSCO = International Organization of Securities Commissions.

A closer examination of the nine IOSCO assessments for the Asia-Pacific countries (excluding Japan) over the 2001–11 period shows that securities regulations and their implementation need to be strengthened. The IOSCO principles under the 2003 methodology are grouped into eight categories, specifically, principles relating to the regulator, principles for self-regulation, principles for the enforcement of securities regulation, principles for cooperation in regulation, principles for issuers, principles for collective investment schemes, principles for market intervention, and principles for the secondary market. While good practice securities regulations, as defined under the 2003 IOSCO methodology, had been implemented or broadly implemented in many countries, a wide range of such regulations had also been assessed as being either partially implemented or not implemented depending on the country (Figure 3.6). The assessments reveal that most countries typically require improvements in a few areas, with the biggest weaknesses evident in the areas of operational independence and accountability (Principle 2) and the effective and credible use of powers and implementation of an effective compliance program (Principle 10).

CONCLUSION

In Asia, local stock markets play a key role in financing corporate, and thus, economic, activity. Unfortunately, some of Asia's stock markets have the reputation of being speculative, rather than trading on fundamentals. Going forward, investors must be able to credibly price their investments in the region's stock markets if their asset allocation to the region is to remain stable or to continue to grow.

This chapter assesses the extent to which Asia's stock pricing is based on idiosyncratic factors rather than on systematic risk factors or economic and corporate fundamentals. We design a model that uses international asset pricing and economic theory and that incorporates evidence from the accounting literature. International factors common to the universe of assets, such as global and regional market risks, the local business cycle, and the financial performance of the corporate sector, are applied to extract the "noise" component from stock prices. The G7 countries are used as benchmarks.

Overall, the findings are consistent with the existing literature on the pricing of Asian stock markets. In general, the region's stock returns have tended to be higher than those of the G7 countries against which they are benchmarked, but have also been more volatile. International systemic risk factors and local fundamentals, such as expected corporate earnings, have substantially less explanatory power when it comes to Asian stock prices compared with the power that they have in the G7 markets. The results point to the existence of greater idiosyncratic influences in Asia.

In other aspects, the analysis finds greater commonalities between the emerging market and advanced economies. Regional factors are consistently the most influential pricing variable, which corroborates the research on international market integration. Local developments, such as forecast earnings, had been less useful as an explanatory variable in the past, but became more important for both Asian and G7 markets during the global financial crisis. One possible explanation is that investors may have sought more expert guidance during volatile periods. Foreign investor allocation decisions also significantly influenced the volatility and returns in both the Asia-Pacific and G7 markets.

This analysis demonstrates the role that policy could play in ensuring that noise is reduced in stock pricing. Although we acknowledge that the apparent importance of idiosyncratic influences on Asian markets could also be attributable to specific local fundamental factors that the model may not have adequately captured, the empirical analysis suggests the existence of a significant relationship between the strength of regulation of securities markets and the extent of noise trading in stock markets. This suggests that improvements in local institutions, such as the regulation of securities markets, could enhance the role of Asian stock markets as an attractive investment destination and, thus, as a reliable source of funding for corporate and economic activity in the region.

ANNEX 3.1

ANNEX TABLE 3.1.1

Regression Results: Stock Market Returns, Systematic Factors and Corporate Sector Performance, Part 1: March 1998–June 2005

	Adjusted R^2	Standard Error of Regression	Sum of Squared Residuals	Constant		Return on World Portfolio ($r_{W/C,t}$)		Return on Regional Portfolio ($r_{R/C,t}$)		Change in Forecast Earnings per Share ($e^f_{C,t}$)	
				Coefficient	Probability	Coefficient	Probability	Coefficient	Probability	Coefficient	Probability
Mar 1998–Dec 2000											
G7											
Canada	0.551	0.021	0.064	-0.001	0.539	0.003	0.988	0.842	0.000	0.382	0.055
France	0.820	0.013	0.025	0.001	0.679	0.087	0.335	0.984	0.000	0.331	0.337
Germany	0.785	0.016	0.038	0.000	0.842	-0.300	0.008	1.454	0.000	-0.108	0.524
Italy	0.600	0.021	0.061	0.002	0.417	-0.169	0.239	1.116	0.000	-0.395	0.401
Japan	0.789	0.014	0.029	-0.001	0.454	-0.268	0.000	1.218	0.000	0.085	0.592
United Kingdom	0.721	0.013	0.024	-0.001	0.439	0.094	0.305	0.711	0.000	0.450	0.140
United States	0.994	0.002	0.001	0.000	0.397	-0.039	0.059	1.021	0.000	0.004	0.902
Mean	*0.751*	*0.014*	*0.034*								
Asia and Pacific excluding Japan											
Australia	0.232	0.016	0.037	0.001	0.457	0.251	0.000	0.117	0.027	-0.608	0.055
China Shanghai A	-0.018	0.033	0.155	0.004	0.190	-0.055	0.698	0.033	0.747	-0.037	0.544
China Shenzhen A	-0.016	0.032	0.142	0.004	0.180	-0.057	0.674	0.023	0.811	-0.046	0.431
China Shanghai B	0.045	0.058	0.478	0.001	0.816	0.200	0.419	0.337	0.059	-0.155	0.154
China Shenzhen B	0.019	0.064	0.573	0.002	0.708	0.018	0.946	0.322	0.099	-0.170	0.152
Hong Kong SAR	0.393	0.034	0.167	0.001	0.835	0.707	0.000	0.509	0.000	-0.179	0.587
India	0.043	0.042	0.252	0.000	0.993	0.398	0.028	-0.076	0.562	-0.756	0.031
Indonesia	0.026	0.052	0.379	-0.001	0.769	-0.372	0.021	0.407	0.011	0.010	0.598
Korea	0.157	0.056	0.437	0.000	0.940	-0.012	0.955	0.883	0.000	0.068	0.771
Malaysia	0.090	0.044	0.276	-0.001	0.822	-0.108	0.510	0.553	0.000	-0.329	0.217
Philippines	0.144	0.039	0.219	-0.009	0.011	0.208	0.196	0.244	0.056	-1.838	0.000
Singapore	0.270	0.034	0.167	0.000	0.866	0.311	0.020	0.615	0.000	0.068	0.767
Thailand	0.102	0.050	0.353	-0.005	0.215	-0.013	0.947	0.622	0.000	-0.018	0.218
Mean	*0.114*	*0.043*	*0.280*								

Jan 2001–Jun 2005

G7

Canada	0.610	0.012	0.033	0.001	0.266	0.198	0.013	0.472	0.000	-0.046	0.551
France	0.906	0.009	0.020	0.000	0.614	-0.045	0.473	1.125	0.000	0.035	0.762
Germany	0.847	0.014	0.047	0.000	0.999	0.153	0.114	1.149	0.000	0.004	0.977
Italy	0.802	0.014	0.044	0.000	0.753	-0.032	0.729	1.084	0.000	0.122	0.425
Japan	0.858	0.011	0.026	-0.001	0.075	-0.293	0.000	1.354	0.000	0.041	0.637
United Kingdom	0.896	0.007	0.012	0.000	0.831	0.027	0.584	0.805	0.000	-0.011	0.739
United States	0.997	0.001	0.000	0.000	0.177	-0.070	0.000	1.074	0.000	0.029	0.053
Mean	*0.837*	*0.012*	*0.119*								

Asia and Pacific excluding Japan

Australia	0.240	0.013	0.038	0.001	0.163	0.213	0.000	0.158	0.001	0.132	0.673
China Shanghai A	0.013	0.027	0.169	-0.003	0.099	0.000	0.999	0.172	0.067	0.102	0.627
China Shenzhen A	0.015	0.029	0.188	-0.004	0.026	0.008	0.945	0.175	0.077	0.176	0.428
China Shanghai B	-0.001	0.044	0.437	-0.001	0.666	0.206	0.230	0.014	0.927	0.015	0.965
China Shenzhen B	0.026	0.050	0.572	0.001	0.706	0.104	0.596	0.330	0.056	0.174	0.652
Hong Kong SAR	0.472	0.021	0.097	0.000	0.713	0.536	0.000	0.409	0.000	0.239	0.289
India	0.162	0.028	0.182	0.002	0.231	0.328	0.003	0.304	0.002	0.104	0.762
Indonesia	0.021	0.030	0.210	0.004	0.041	-0.272	0.013	0.286	0.007	-0.005	0.975
Korea	0.287	0.033	0.250	0.003	0.118	0.094	0.450	0.918	0.000	0.009	0.967
Malaysia	0.111	0.020	0.088	0.001	0.564	0.077	0.317	0.235	0.001	0.216	0.386
Philippines	0.031	0.029	0.198	0.000	0.878	0.026	0.817	0.207	0.043	0.292	0.269
Singapore	0.424	0.020	0.090	0.001	0.647	0.366	0.000	0.472	0.000	-0.043	0.760
Thailand	0.117	0.030	0.201	0.003	0.107	-0.029	0.797	0.502	0.000	0.118	0.411
Mean	*0.373*	*0.028*	*0.221*								

(continued)

ANNEX TABLE 3.1 (Continued)

Regression Results: Stock Market Returns, Systematic Factors and Corporate Sector Performance, Part 2: July 2005–November 2012

	Adjusted R^2	Standard Error of Regression	Sum of Squared Residuals	Constant		Return on World Portfolio ($r_{W,t}$)		Return on Regional Portfolio ($r_{R,t}$)		Change in Forecast Earnings per Share ($e^f_{c,t}$)	
				Coefficient	Probability	Coefficient	Probability	Coefficient	Probability	Coefficient	Probability
Jul 2005–Dec 2007											
G7											
Canada	0.586	0.011	0.016	0.001	0.345	0.038	0.687	0.777	0.000	-0.052	0.470
France	0.884	0.007	0.006	0.000	0.942	-0.059	0.527	1.090	0.000	-0.015	0.873
Germany	0.838	0.009	0.009	0.002	0.008	-0.188	0.108	1.212	0.000	-0.099	0.432
Italy	0.798	0.008	0.008	0.000	0.560	0.212	0.049	0.677	0.000	0.070	0.662
Japan	0.852	0.010	0.011	-0.001	0.239	-0.197	0.010	1.012	0.000	0.064	0.710
United Kingdom	0.893	0.006	0.004	-0.001	0.136	-0.016	0.831	0.918	0.000	0.004	0.966
United States	0.990	0.002	0.000	0.000	0.416	-0.198	0.000	1.149	0.000	-0.029	0.014
Mean	*0.834*	*0.007*	*0.008*								
Asia and Pacific excluding Japan											
Australia	0.490	0.012	0.019	0.002	0.161	-0.160	0.111	0.750	0.000	-0.068	0.717
China Shanghai A	0.089	0.034	0.143	0.014	0.000	-0.213	0.480	0.580	0.011	-0.676	0.084
China Shenzhen A	0.055	0.038	0.186	0.016	0.000	-0.501	0.145	0.629	0.016	-0.910	0.042
China Shanghai B	0.019	0.055	0.389	0.014	0.013	-0.210	0.671	0.558	0.135	-0.699	0.277
China Shenzhen B	0.108	0.041	0.215	0.009	0.030	-0.452	0.222	0.927	0.001	-0.400	0.403
Hong Kong SAR	0.562	0.017	0.036	0.002	0.159	0.273	0.072	0.666	0.000	-0.105	0.126
India	0.245	0.026	0.089	0.005	0.062	0.615	0.012	0.316	0.076	0.253	0.279
Indonesia	0.198	0.029	0.106	0.004	0.184	-0.403	0.136	0.889	0.000	0.367	0.341
Korea	0.597	0.018	0.042	0.002	0.275	0.100	0.525	1.057	0.000	-0.059	0.784
Malaysia	0.303	0.016	0.032	0.002	0.134	0.237	0.099	0.362	0.001	0.061	0.752
Philippines	0.351	0.024	0.072	0.005	0.035	0.043	0.844	0.794	0.000	-0.324	0.197
Singapore	0.596	0.014	0.024	0.001	0.644	0.422	0.001	0.541	0.000	0.247	0.248
Thailand	0.217	0.023	0.067	0.001	0.695	-0.315	0.092	0.723	0.000	-0.461	0.136
Mean	*0.295*	*0.027*	*0.109*								

Jan 2008–Nov 2012

G7

Canada	0.772	0.015	0.059	0.000	0.920	0.272	0.001	0.640	0.000	-0.102	0.015
France	0.916	0.011	0.033	-0.001	0.480	-0.197	0.004	1.205	0.000	-0.046	0.494
Germany	0.876	0.014	0.049	0.001	0.377	0.006	0.943	1.022	0.000	-0.122	0.006
Italy	0.800	0.020	0.101	-0.002	0.110	-0.491	0.000	1.491	0.000	-0.070	0.479
Japan	0.880	0.013	0.040	0.000	0.882	-0.117	0.017	1.007	0.000	-0.065	0.051
United Kingdom	0.893	0.011	0.029	0.000	0.640	0.063	0.327	0.842	0.000	0.043	0.443
United States	0.993	0.003	0.002	0.000	0.564	-0.227	0.000	1.183	0.000	0.016	0.039
Mean	*0.876*	*0.012*	*0.045*								

Asia and Pacific excluding Japan

Australia	0.499	0.021	0.109	0.000	0.853	0.813	0.000	0.345	0.000	-0.221	0.027
China Shanghai A	0.188	0.035	0.304	-0.003	0.134	-0.581	0.000	1.008	0.000	0.219	0.285
China Shenzhen A	0.131	0.043	0.461	-0.002	0.506	-0.702	0.000	1.085	0.000	0.113	0.654
China Shanghai B	0.156	0.043	0.459	-0.002	0.444	-0.699	0.000	1.151	0.000	0.154	0.540
China Shenzhen B	0.258	0.035	0.303	0.000	0.963	-0.610	0.000	1.162	0.000	0.266	0.193
Hong Kong SAR	0.795	0.017	0.075	0.000	0.983	0.025	0.708	1.057	0.000	0.201	0.015
India	0.380	0.030	0.226	-0.001	0.532	0.247	0.036	0.622	0.000	0.355	0.029
Indonesia	0.261	0.031	0.248	0.002	0.245	0.075	0.542	0.620	0.000	0.081	0.566
Korea	0.289	0.030	0.224	0.000	0.981	0.166	0.154	0.745	0.000	0.200	0.147
Malaysia	0.387	0.015	0.059	0.001	0.430	-0.096	0.109	0.514	0.000	0.351	0.003
Philippines	0.379	0.026	0.165	0.002	0.179	0.046	0.645	0.687	0.000	0.217	0.279
Singapore	0.685	0.019	0.088	0.001	0.500	0.196	0.008	0.841	0.000	0.234	0.073
Thailand	0.442	0.025	0.157	0.002	0.222	0.077	0.426	0.667	0.000	0.408	0.001
Mean	*0.373*	*0.028*	*0.221*								

Sources: Bloomberg, L.P.; Thomson Reuters I/B/E/S on Datastream; and IMF staff calculations.

REFERENCES

Cherif, Monther, and Kaothar Gazdar. 2010. "Macroeconomic and Institutional Determinants of Stock Market Development in MENA Region: New Results from a Panel Data Analysis." *International Journal of Banking and Finance* 7 (1): 1–21.

De Long, J. Bradford, Andrei Schleifer, Lawrence H. Summers, and Roberg J. Waldmann. 1989. "The Size and Incidence of the Losses from Noise Trading." *Journal of Finance* 44 (3): 681–96.

———. 1990. "Noise Trader Risks in Financial Markets." *Journal of Political Economy* 115 (5): 722–44.

Fama, Eugene F. 1970. "Efficient Capital Markets: A Review of Theory and Empirical Work." *Journal of Finance* 25 (2): 383–417.

Hanim Mokhtar, Suraya, Annuar Md Nassir, and Taufiq Hassan. 2006. "Detecting Rational Speculative Bubbles in the Malaysian Stock Market." *International Research Journal of Finance and Economics* 6: 102–15.

Homm, Ulrich, and Jörg Breitung. 2012. "Testing for Speculative Bubbles in Stock Markets: A Comparison of Alternative Methods." *Journal of Financial Econometrics* 10 (1): 198–231.

Hsieh, Joyce, and Chien-Chung Nieh. 2010. "An Overview of Asian Equity Markets." *Asian-Pacific Economic Literature* 24 (2): 19–51.

International Organization of Securities Commissions (IOSCO). 2003. "Methodology for Assessing Implementation of the IOSCO Objectives and Principles of Securities Regulation," IOSCO Report, Madrid. http://www.iosco.org/library/index.cfm?section=pubdocs&year =2003.

———. 2011. "Methodology for Assessing Implementation of the IOSCO Objectives and Principles of Securities Regulation," FR08/11, Madrid. http://www.iosco.org/about/index .cfm?section=obj_prin.

Kim, Jae H., and Abul Shamsuddin. 2008. "Are Asian Stock Markets Efficient? Evidence from New Multiple Variance Ratio Tests." *Journal of Empirical Finance* 15 (4): 518–32.

Law, Siong Hook, and Muzafar Shah Habibullah. 2009. "The Determinants of Financial Development: Institutions, Openness and Financial Liberalization." *South African Journal of Economics* 77 (1): 45–58.

Lim, Kian-Ping, Robert D. Brooks, and Jae H. Kim. 2008. "Financial Crisis and Stock Market Efficiency: Empirical Evidence from Asian Countries." *International Review of Financial Analysis* 17 (3): 571–91.

Lipinsky, Fabian, and Li Lian Ong. 2014. "Asia's Stock Markets: Are There Crouching Tigers and Hidden Dragons?" IMF Working Paper No. 14/137, International Monetary Fund, Washington.

Mei, Jianping, José A. Scheinkman, and Wei Xiong, 2009. "Speculative Trading and Stock Prices: Evidence from Chinese A-B Share Premia." *Annals of Economics and Finance* 10 (2): 225–55.

Morck, Randall, Bernard Yeung, and Wayne Yu. 2000. "The Information Content of Stock Markets: Why Do Emerging Markets Have Synchronous Stock Price Movements?" *Journal of Financial Economics* 58 (1): 215–60.

Nam, Sang-Koo, Kyung Suh Park, and Yu-Kyung Kim. 1999. "Agenda for Capital Market Reforms in the PRC." In *A Study of Financial Markets, Vol. 4: People's Republic of China.* Manila: Asian Development Bank.

Ross, Stephen A. 1976. "The Arbitrage Theory of Capital Asset Pricing." *Journal of Economic Theory* 13 (3): 341–60.

Samuelson, Paul A. 1994. "The Long-Term Case for Equities and How It Can Be Oversold." *Journal of Portfolio Management* 21 (1): 15–24.

West, Kenneth D. 1987. "A Specification Test for Speculative Bubbles." *Quarterly Journal of Economics* 102 (3): 553–80.

Yartey, Charles Amo. 2010. "The Institutional and Macroeconomic Determinants of Stock Market Development in Emerging Economies." *Applied Financial Economics* 20 (21): 1615–25.

CHAPTER 4

Bond Markets: Are Recent Reforms Working?

Mangal Goswami, Andreas Jobst, Shanaka J. Peiris, and Dulani Seneviratne

MAIN POINTS OF THIS CHAPTER

- Sovereign bond markets in most of emerging Asia have deepened and become more efficient as foreign and institutional investor participation has increased, leading to yield compression without significantly greater volatility in normal times.
- Corporate bond markets have undergone a "quality transition," with a greater diversity of issuance resulting in a widening of access to finance.
- Emerging Asian financial systems are starting to fire up as the corporate bond market develops into an alternative and viable nonbank source of corporate and infrastructure funding (that is, as a second engine next to the banking sector).

INTRODUCTION

It has now been a decade since the Association of Southeast Asian Nations (ASEAN) launched a major effort to develop its domestic bond markets and the larger two Asian emerging market economies—China and India—started to open up their bond markets to foreign investors. That makes it a good time to take stock, see what has been accomplished, and assess whether local bond markets have become an integral element of the financial sector architecture and are able to act as an alternative source of funding ("spare tire") if other parts of the financial system become impaired.[1] An evaluation of progress towards a "twin engine" financial system with both a robust bank lending and corporate debt financing channel is important because much emphasis was placed on developing domestic bond markets in the aftermath of the Asian crisis of the late 1990s. Bond funding was seen as an alternative financing channel to banks, a channel that is less prone to currency and maturity mismatches and less vulnerable to volatile capital flows. More recently, corporate bond markets have been seen as a vehicle for funding the large infrastructure needs of Asian emerging markets, as highlighted in Chapter 8.

---

[1] This chapter builds on a number of related IMF working papers (Gray and others 2011; Felman and others 2011), which were later published in the *Asia-Pacific Journal of Economic Literature*.

The sweeping regulatory reforms and policy initiatives have had a profound impact on the efficiency of local bond markets. Emerging Asian bond markets have successfully managed to overcome the "original sin" problem by shifting from foreign-currency- to local-currency-denominated bond issuance and have extended the maturity of their sovereign debt profiles to reduce vulnerabilities to attendant risks.[2] This chapter considers in depth the determinants of sovereign bond yields from a supply-demand perspective as they act as a benchmark for the pricing of corporate bonds. The key findings are the following:

- ASEAN sovereign bond markets have seen a significant broadening of the investor base, including institutional investors and foreign participants, resulting in a significant rise in liquidity and a reduction in borrowing costs.

- Market deepening and greater foreign participation in ASEAN markets have not led to significant yield volatility in normal times, although sovereign bond yields are susceptible to spikes in global risk aversion.

- The Chinese and Indian sovereign bond markets are large, with high turnover but a captive domestic investor base, and capital account restrictions have limited the role of foreign investors.

Corporate bond markets have grown rapidly in emerging Asia; however, their recent development has been uneven. In most ASEAN countries, the development of corporate bond markets is held back by limited issuance despite rising interest from institutional investors. Chinese and Indian markets, meanwhile, have seen more limited participation by foreign investors alongside gradual institutional reforms. To evaluate the transformation of corporate bond markets in the region, we undertake a firm-level analysis, which reveals that it has become easier for firms to access external finance:

- Emerging Asian corporate bond markets have undergone a "quality transition," marked by repeat issuance and more diversified supply. With lower barriers to entry, smaller issuers are increasingly accessing domestic markets while larger issuers have become more adept at using market funding as part of a broadening of their sources of funding.[3]

- Corporate bond markets are developing into a mature funding channel that corporations can use when other parts of the financial system come under stress and credit supply remains constrained as banks adjust to new regulations on capital, liquidity, and derivatives. However, corporate finance in emerging Asia remains heavily dependent on bank lending. A well-functioning and liquid bond market could help diversify the region's funding sources and enhance the resilience of its financial systems.[4]

---

[2] Eichengreen and Hausmann (1999) introduced the term "original sin" to denote the greater tendency of emerging market countries with weak external positions to borrow in foreign currency as a way to overcome international investors' concerns about higher borrower risk.

[3] However, many of the Asian firms that resort to bond financing prefer private placements since it allows them to save on regulatory costs (for example, registration, prospectus, and disclosure requirements) of public listings.

[4] Also, the cost of borrowing is still the primary determinant of the mode of financing, although maturity and diversification of financing sources are becoming increasingly important considerations.

With the investor base likely to expand as foreign investors devote an increasing portion of their portfolios to emerging market assets, and as demographic changes (and financial liberalization in China) drive regional savings patterns, bond markets in emerging Asia could grow much more rapidly during the coming decade. However, a number of challenges remain to reduce issuance costs and improve liquidity. In particular, derivatives markets that tend to enhance secondary market trading and help hedge risks remain a work in progress. These barriers also tend to drive market activity offshore, which may raise prudential concerns and the risk of spillover from offshore to onshore markets.

Also, the global financial crisis has shown that local currency debt markets in emerging markets are quite susceptible to the vagaries of global shocks. However, the recovery following the crisis was notable, notwithstanding the "taper tantrum" in May 2013 when the Federal Reserve announced its intention to begin tapering its asset purchase program. The tapering of asset purchases by the Federal Reserve since January 2014 has been less disruptive than expected thus far, with investors exhibiting greater differentiation across markets. The latter development places a premium on further market deepening, as well as on maintaining consistent macroeconomic and macroprudential policies.

This chapter examines the reasons for developing bond markets in emerging Asia; sheds light on the depth, liquidity, and pricing of local bonds in Asian emerging markets; and assesses the impact of foreign participation and market development on local currency sovereign spreads. It then focuses on the corporate bond market and other metrics of development, which suggest that a remarkable transformation of ASEAN and emerging Asian corporate bond markets is indeed under way, especially if firm-level data are examined in greater detail. Finally, it reviews the impediments to market development as well as the nexus of the bond and derivatives (and offshore) markets.

WHY DEVELOP BOND MARKETS?

Across the globe, emerging markets have placed great emphasis on developing their bond markets in recent years (IMF 2005). Why have they done so? In large part, because emerging markets have heavy investment requirements, and bond markets play an important role in financing large infrastructure projects. Such projects tend to be risky and take time before they yield returns; however, bond markets can spread these risks over a large number of holders of securities. Moreover, because bond contracts (unlike loans) are designed to be traded, they allow investors to transfer credit risks to others, even before the projects are completed. The combination of these characteristics—the scope for risk sharing and risk shedding, both within and across national boundaries—means that bond markets complement banks, which are constrained by limits on the scope of their cross-border activities and the extent to which they can transform maturities.

Beyond these general principles, there are particular reasons why Asian emerging markets, particularly ASEAN members, have put so much emphasis on developing bond markets since the Asian financial crisis. These reasons stem from the consensus diagnosis of what happened in 1997. According to this view, the Asian crisis can be traced in large part to several underlying problems in national financial systems (Eichengreen 2006):

- *Dependence on bank funding*—Financial systems were extremely bank-centric, which meant that most of the risks were concentrated in the banking system—and there was no alternate channel of intermediation that could be used if the banks once again encountered difficulties.

- *Maturity and currency mismatches*—Borrowing had suffered from a double mismatch, since long-term, domestically oriented investment projects were being funded through short-term, foreign-currency borrowing.

- *Capital account vulnerabilities*—Countries in the region were perceived to be excessively dependent on volatile capital inflows, a situation that struck many observers as ironic since the region had an abundance of domestic savings.

Observers further argued that all three of these problems could be solved by developing domestic bond markets. Vibrant bond markets would create another financing channel, a spare tire that firms could use if banks once again encountered difficulties. And because domestic bonds would be on longer maturity terms and in local currencies, they would eliminate the double mismatch problem. Finally, with more active domestic bond markets, firms could reduce their dependence on foreign capital flows that were very volatile, particularly in Asia.

Based on this diagnosis, emerging Asia has put considerable effort into developing its bond markets (Guonan, Remolona, and Jianxiong 2006). For example, the ASEAN+3, which comprises the ASEAN countries plus China, Japan, and Korea, created the Asian Bond Markets Initiative, which established working groups to study the issues and make recommendations, many of which have been adopted by individual countries. The launch of the Asian Bond Fund-2 in March 2005, a regional local-currency-denominated bond fund, resulted in the introduction of a Pan Asia Bond Index Fund and a Fund of Bond Funds with eight country subfunds open to investment by the public. The Asian Development Bank (ADB) also initiated a study program and created the AsiaBondsOnline database so that researchers and market participants could easily find key information about local currency markets.[5] Meanwhile, the Executives' Meeting of East Asia Pacific Central Banks created pan-Asian bond funds to facilitate regional investment. The Asian Bond Market Forum was set up in September 2010 by the ASEAN+3 countries as a common platform to foster standardization of market practices and harmonization of regulations related to cross-border bond transactions in the region. The 2011 formation of the Credit Guarantee and Investment Facility, a trust fund of the ADB, is expected to support the issuance of corporate bonds.

---

[5] Nonetheless, data problems remain an issue. In some cases, AsiaBondsOnline data differ widely from those available from other sources, such as the Bank for International Settlements (BIS). Also, data for some variables are not available for all countries, hindering ASEAN-wide analysis.

Countries have undertaken structural reforms to foster the development of capital markets. Many have issued new securities regulations in line with the International Organization of Securities Commissions' principles and have adopted more modern legal frameworks that address company and insolvency laws through better protection of creditor rights in the event of bankruptcy. Government debt-management programs have become an important part of the reforms. The infrastructure for payment, custody, and settlement systems has been modernized in many countries.[6] Bond markets have become more transparent with independent vendors collecting and disseminating information on bond trading and bond pricing, facilitating development of the secondary market. The growth in contractual savings institutions has also offered an alternative to bank savings products, helping diversify personal savings into longer-term savings and to promote capital market development. Pension and social security pools with longer-term investment horizons are starting to mobilize domestic savings. As a result, securities valuations have increased correspondingly, accompanied by further diversification and globalization of the investor base.

China and India have also progressively opened their bond markets to qualified foreign investors, though participation remains limited alongside gradual institutional reforms. The Renminbi Qualified Foreign Institutional Investor (RQFII) scheme was introduced in China in 2002, allowing institutional investors who meet certain qualifications to invest in a limited scope of cross-border securities with an initial cap of $4 billion that, by 2013, had been gradually eased and expanded to $150 billion. Under China's RQFII initiated in 2011, investors can apply for quotas to use renminbi they hold offshore to invest directly in domestic Chinese assets, from bonds to stocks to money market funds. The RQFII program had been limited to financial institutions in Hong Kong SAR but was expanded beginning in 2014 to include firms in London, Singapore, and Taiwan Province of China. Gradual interest rate liberalization and financial market infrastructure reforms in China have fostered debt market development, albeit with a number of remaining challenges.[7] The Indian authorities released regulations for foreign institutional investor investment in debt markets in 2005 with a debt cap of only $1.0 billion to $1.5 billion that was progressively increased to $25 billion in government securities and $50 billion in corporate debt in 2013, which includes a sublimit for infrastructure bonds of $25 billion.

---

[6] For example, the Reserve Bank of India uses the Negotiated Dealing System, which was introduced in 2002, as the primary auction platform for government securities. Secondary trading of government securities occurs through over-the-counter, Negotiated Dealing System, or the Negotiated Dealing System–Ordered Matching, which was introduced by the Reserve Bank of India in 2005 and is maintained by the Clearing Corporation of India Limited. In China, the custodianship and settlement of medium-term notes and commercial paper has been moved from ChinaBond to the Shanghai Clearing House.

[7] The regulation of the bond market is fragmented among three government agencies—the central bank, the National Development and Reform Commission, and the China Securities Regulatory Commission. The China Securities Regulatory Commission is pushing ahead with unifying all of the regulators' separate bond-disclosure, credit-rating, investor-protection, and entry standards (Gang 2014).

The Securities and Exchange Board of India has also allowed overseas entities to invest in government securities without any auction mechanism since September 2013, relaxing the debt-allocation norms for foreign institutional investors until overall investment reaches 90 percent of the cap on foreign ownership.

COMPOSITION, DEPTH, LIQUIDITY, AND PRICING DEVELOPMENTS

Since the regional financial crisis of 1997–98, Asian emerging markets have focused considerable attention on developing domestic debt markets to reduce foreign exchange mismatches in their financial systems and to decrease the concentration of credit and maturity risks in banks (CGFS 2007; Turner 2009). Besides building large foreign exchange reserve buffers, much of the effort has gone into local currency bonds since they constitute a significant share of emerging bond markets, especially in Asia (Figure 4.1). The shift from foreign-currency- to local-currency-denominated bond issuance by emerging markets highlights the breakdown of the hypothesis that these economies can typically borrow only in foreign currency, the "original sin" of Eichengreen and Hausmann (1999).

Emerging Asian debt capital markets have grown faster than have many of the mature markets since the turn of the century and are larger than those in other emerging market regions. The rapid growth in Asia's emerging domestic bond markets has been driven by the strong growth performance and favorable longer-term economic prospects for the region, led by China (Figure 4.2). Investments in local currency bonds indeed fetched handsome returns during 2003–12, particularly when considered on a risk-adjusted basis (Figure 4.3). However, the

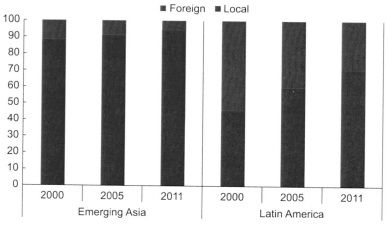

Figure 4.1 The Shift toward Local-Currency-Denominated Bonds (*Currency denomination, percent of total*)

Source: Turner (2012).

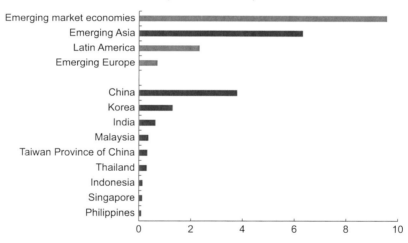

Figure 4.2 International Comparison of Domestic Bond Markets (*Includes government and corporate bonds*)

Source: Bank for International Settlements.

development of bond markets in Asia faced significant headwinds during the global financial crisis, with a sizable retrenchment as gross portfolio inflows fell precipitously, albeit rebounding sharply, particularly to the ASEAN-5 (Figure 4.4).[8]

---

[8] The five largest economies in Southeast Asia that make up the Asean-5 are Indonesia, Malaysia, the Philippines, Singapore, and Thailand.

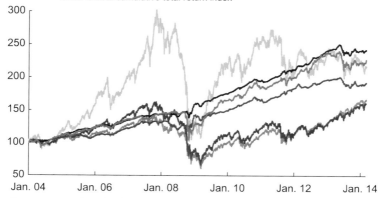

Figure 4.3 High Risk-Adjusted Emerging Market Returns *(Equity and bond market indices, 2004 = 100)*

Sources: Bloomberg, L.P.; and Morgan Markets.
Note: GBI-EM = J.P. Morgan Government Bond Index - Emerging Markets; EMBI = Emerging Markets Bond Index; LCY = Local Currency.

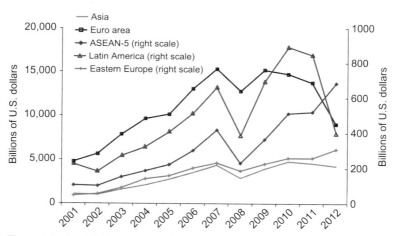

Figure 4.4 Portfolio Investment Liabilities *(Billions of U.S. dollars)*

Sources: IMF, Coordinated Portfolio Investment Survey (CPIS).
Note: ASEAN = Association of Southeast Asian Nations.

Liquidity in the bond markets continues to vary across emerging Asia, but there has been significant financial deepening in many of these markets. The markets in China, Hong Kong SAR, Korea, Malaysia, and Singapore are the most

TABLE 4.1

Domestic Bond Market Liquidity Indicators

| Country | Value Traded ($ billion) | | Turnover Ratio[1] | | Bid-Ask Spread (bps) |
	Government	Corporate	Government	Corporate	Government
China	358	218	0.12	0.15	4.1
Hong Kong SAR	159	11	1.48	0.13	7.3
India	179	40	...	...	1.3
Indonesia	21	2	0.26	0.09	50.0
Japan	11,963	58	1.23	0.07	...
Korea	521	119	0.87	0.13	0.7
Malaysia	84	9	0.46	0.07	3.8
Philippines	39	...	0.49	...	5.4
Singapore	68	...	0.65	...	2.6
Thailand	146	3	0.65	0.06	2.4

Sources: Asian Development Bank, AsianBondsOnline, and *Asia Bond Monitor*.
Note: As of end-2013 or latest available as of 2013:Q3. bps = basis points.
[1]Turnover ratio is defined as value of bonds traded over average amount of bonds outstanding.

liquid (Table 4.1). Debt managers now preannounce the schedule of issuance and consolidate debt into several large liquid benchmark bond issues at certain maturities across the yield curve (which they reopen if additional funding is required). Most emerging Asian economies have established primary dealers for government securities and have taken steps to develop the funding market for repurchase agreements (repos) and securities lending. In Singapore, the primary dealers are required to participate in auctions, make two-way secondary markets, and provide information to the debt manager. Many of the Asian emerging markets have also reformed their market microstructures by introducing modern trading platforms and by upgrading payment and settlement systems. In general, liquidity in corporate bond markets remains significantly below levels in the government bond markets. However, the volume of turnover in the Chinese bond market, especially the corporate segment, has improved substantially since 2005 as a result of the marked increase in the size of the market, although market liquidity remains fickle.

Despite advancements, liquidity in local bond markets dried up during periods of stress, such as the taper episode when expectations of monetary tightening in the United States caused considerable portfolio outflows. Secondary market liquidity in many ASEAN markets is still very much dependent on foreign investors.[9] Trading is often still bunched in certain maturities, leading to market segmentation. This, coupled with a concentration of buy-and-hold investors in domestic bond markets, continues to inhibit liquidity. The 2013 decline in liquidity in some emerging Asian markets, as highlighted by rising bid-ask spreads (Figure 4.5), appears to have contributed to making local bond yields more

---

[9]Although access via offshore derivatives markets, notably by foreign banks, can enhance liquidity, it can also lead to the sudden drying up of liquidity when foreign investors withdraw during periods of heightened global risk aversion.

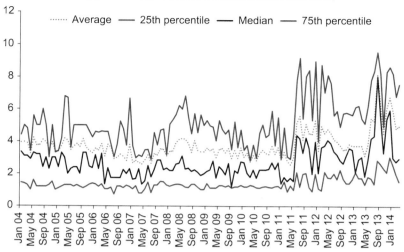

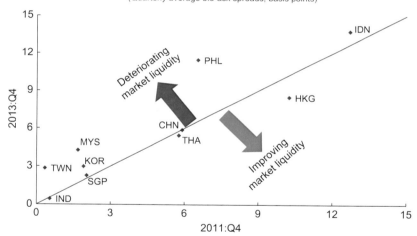

Figure 4.5 Change in Liquidity Patterns in Emerging Asia

Sources: Bloomberg, L.P.; and IMF staff calculations.
Note: CHN = China; HKG = Hong Kong SAR; IND = India; IDN = Indonesia; KOR = Korea; MYS = Malaysia; PHL = the Philippines; SGP = Singapore; THA = Thailand; TWN = Taiwan Province of China.

sensitive to global risk aversion (measured by the VIX)[10] in these markets (IMF 2014), albeit less so than in other emerging markets. The less liquid markets are generally characterized by a narrow investor base, insufficient infrastructure, low

---

[10] VIX is a trademarked ticker symbol for the Chicago Board Options Exchange (CBOE) Market Volatility Index, a popular measure of the implied volatility of S&P 500 index options.

market transparency, and lack of timely information on bond issuers (Gyntelberg, Guonan, and Remolona 2006; ADB 2013a). For example, both Indonesia and the Philippines put in place frameworks for primary dealership and debt management with preannounced issuance schedules, but secondary market liquidity continues to be tenuous, with few players prepared to continuously provide bid/offer quotes. While the role of market makers is central to increasing liquidity and secondary-market trading, it is unclear how the extraterritorial application of new regulations (for example, the Dodd-Frank Act and the Volcker Rule) will affect such activity in the Asian local bond markets. Anecdotal evidence shows that dealers have reduced their inventories ahead of the new regulations, which negatively affected their market-making ability. One key policy initiative has been to ensure that trading data are captured and disseminated but, given that most bond trading is over the counter (OTC), transparent trade data are not always available to all market participants, although that may soon be changing.

The investor base in Asia has become broader and deeper with the emergence of domestic institutional investors (Ghosh 2006). These investors hold a sizable share of the outstanding local currency bonds, led mostly by banks, but other institutional investors such as pension funds, life insurance companies, and mutual funds have also increased their investments in local debt as their assets have grown. Demographic changes, pension reforms, and the larger role played by nonbank financial institutions, including institutional investors, have supported the increase in size and diversity of the investor base (Figure 4.6). Malaysia is a good example, where actively managed publicly mandated or related provident funds provide an important source of retirement savings and liquidity to debt markets (Figure 4.7). In Thailand, contractual savings institutions have become the dominant investors in local currency bonds, partly owing to the incentive provided by the deduction from taxable income of contributions to retirement mutual funds and long-term equity funds. In contrast, investment restrictions on Indian pension and insurance funds that are captive sources of finance for government securities have held back participation of these funds in the corporate bond market. Insurance penetration is also low in India and in many ASEAN countries, including Indonesia, the Philippines, and Vietnam.

Growth in the mutual fund industry throughout Asia has been broad based. Mutual funds have allowed households to hold local currency bonds in more liquid and easily tradable units. Mutual funds tend to trade actively in response to changes in market conditions, thereby bringing additional liquidity to local markets (Turner 2009). Hong Kong SAR and Singapore lead this industry because of their roles as regional financial centers, with more than 50 percent of their assets derived from foreign capital inflows. The rapid growth of mutual funds in other Asian economies such as India, Korea, Malaysia, Thailand, and Taiwan Province of China has been largely dependent on domestic factors, including rising incomes and the broadening of the domestic investor base (Figure 4.8). The mutual fund industry is still stymied by a nascent investment culture in emerging Asia, which is weighed down by the regulatory structure, a lack of independent pricing and valuation, and weak investor education and

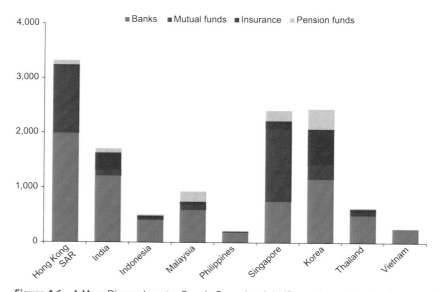

Figure 4.6   A More Diverse Investor Base in Emerging Asia (*Domestic investor base, billions of U.S. dollars*)

Source: Standard Chartered Research.

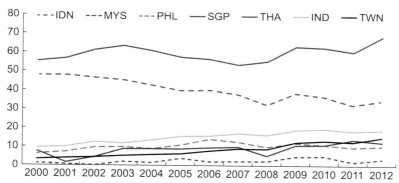

Figure 4.7   Growing Pension Fund Assets (*Percent of GDP*)

Sources: CEIC Data Co., Ltd.; Economist Intelligence Unit; IMF, *World Economic Outlook*; and Investment Company Institute.

Note: IND = India; IDN = Indonesia; MYS = Malaysia; PHL = the Philippines; SGP = Singapore; THA = Thailand; TWN = Taiwan Province of China.

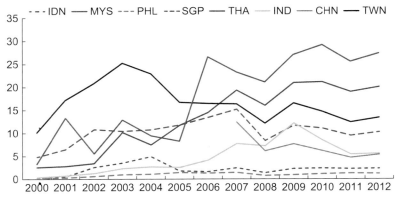

Figure 4.8 Growing Mutual Fund Assets (*Percent of GDP*)

Sources: CEIC Data Co., Ltd.; Economist Intelligence Unit; IMF, *World Economic Outlook*; and Investment Company Institute.

Note: IND = India; IDN = Indonesia; MYS = Malaysia; PHL = the Philippines; SGP = Singapore; THA = Thailand; TWN = Taiwan Province of China.

safeguards. For instance, mutual funds have so far played a limited role in the development of India's corporate bond market, in which 80 percent of the debt mutual funds are owned by corporations with limited retail participation.

The increasing participation of foreign investors has been one of the main structural changes in the Asian domestic debt markets since the global financial crisis (Figure 4.9). The secular increase in the proportion of portfolios allocated to emerging market assets by developed country institutional investors has been underpinned by a more favorable risk-return profile. Foreign participation has largely been through institutional investors such as banks, mutual funds, pension funds, hedge funds, asset management firms (that manage these assets on behalf of pension plans), and sovereign wealth funds (IMF 2014). Assets under management for dedicated emerging market bond funds, particularly local currency bonds, have also risen significantly. Even though the global financial crisis led to a decline in foreign investor demand for emerging market assets, most Asian countries have seen renewed foreign interest and foreign participation that is now above precrisis levels (Figure 4.9).[11] Countries such as China and India, which have traditionally had relatively closed capital accounts, are also gradually easing limits on government securities holdings by qualified foreign institutional investors. This easing will likely attract more long-term institutional investors as well as mutual funds and hedge funds that are sensitive to global risk aversion (IMF 2014). This chapter assesses the impact of foreign inflows on sovereign

---

[11] Available data may understate the importance of foreign investors, since they also use derivatives (including nondeliverable forwards, structured notes, and total return swaps) to take exposures; these derivatives are not easily accounted for.

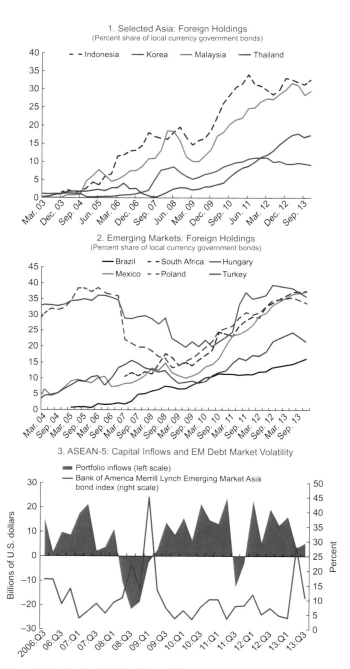

Figure 4.9 Foreign Participation and Sovereign Bond Yields

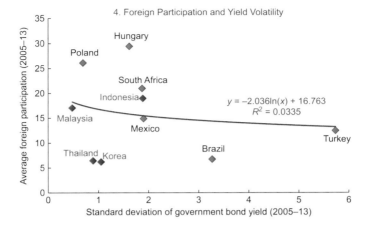

4. Foreign Participation and Yield Volatility

$$y = -2.036\ln(x) + 16.763$$
$$R^2 = 0.0335$$

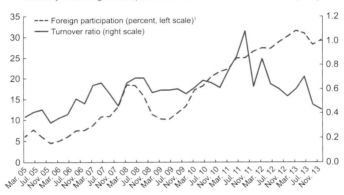

5. Malaysia: Foreign Participation and Government Bond Market Liquidity

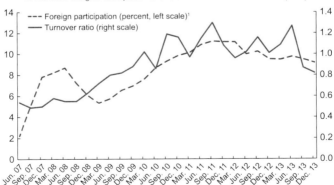

6. Korea: Foreign Participation and Government Bond Market Liquidity

Figure 4.9 *(Continued)*

Sources: Asian Development Bank, AsianBondsOnline; Bloomberg, L.P.; country authorities; IMF, International Financial Statistics database, *Global Financial Stability Report (various issues)*; and IMF staff estimates.

[1] Foreign holdings as a percent of total local currency bonds.

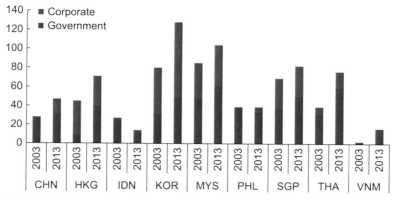

Figure 4.10 Uneven Development of Emerging Market Corporate Bond Markets (*Percent of GDP*)

Source: AsianBondsOnline.
Note: Data for 2013 are as of December 2013 or latest available. CHN = China; HKG = Hong Kong SAR; IDN = Indonesia; KOR = Korea; MYS = Malaysia; PHL = the Philippines; SGP = Singapore; THA = Thailand; VNM = Vietnam.

bond yields and their volatility in emerging Asia, given that global institutional investors are likely to allocate a greater share of their portfolios to emerging markets in the long term, while the unwinding of unconventional monetary policies in advanced economies presents short-term challenges. A preview of the stylized facts suggests rising liquidity and, thus, lower bond yields in emerging Asia as a result of greater foreign participation that does not appear to have been associated with higher volatility except during times of heightened global risk aversion (Figure 4.9).

The development of corporate bond markets in Asia remains uneven (Figure 4.10). Those in Hong Kong SAR, Korea, Malaysia, and Singapore are the largest and most developed, followed by Thailand, while those in Indonesia, the Philippines, and Vietnam have lagged behind (Figure 4.10). The corporate bond market in China has grown rapidly because qualified foreign banks have been allowed to trade and underwrite corporate bonds in the interbank market without the approval of the China Securities Regulatory Commission. The commission also improved access for small and medium-sized businesses by allowing bond issuances of less than 500 million renminbi.[12]

Derivatives markets in the region have grown and internationalized to provide hedging tools for portfolio investors. This development has been driven mostly by very strong growth in OTC markets (BIS 2013). Though difficult to measure, foreign investors' access to Asian capital markets through derivatives instruments (OTC derivatives and structured notes) also boosted capital inflows before the

---

[12] At roughly $4 trillion, China's domestic bond market is the world's fourth largest after the United States, Japan, and France, but its size still lags behind similar markets in advanced economies when compared with the size of the real economy (Noble 2013).

global financial crisis (CGFS 2009). Offshore trading of emerging market currencies has surged, with a significant increase in foreign exchange turnover ratios for many of the emerging Asian countries. This surge has been led by the Chinese renminbi, and trading of emerging market currencies has been positively related to the size of cross-border financial flows (BIS 2013). Of the five main types of derivatives (foreign exchange, interest rate, equity,[13] commodity, and credit), growth has been strongest in the trading of foreign exchange derivatives,[14] followed by exchange-traded equity derivatives[15] and some OTC interest rate contracts (Figure 4.11). Foreign exchange derivatives (outright forwards, foreign exchange swaps, and foreign exchange options) account for a significant part of the total daily turnover. This major contribution of foreign exchange derivatives to the growth in emerging market currencies turnover is consistent with the view that hedging demand and speculation by foreign portfolio investors—who are interested in mitigating the exchange rate risks of their local currency investments or speculating on currency movements—has grown in importance (BIS 2013). However, the following factors have hindered the development of comprehensive derivatives markets:

- Deficiencies in prudential regulation and supervisory oversight (for example, capital rules, disclosure requirements, and accounting rules)
- Operational infrastructure (for example, market trading, clearing, and settlement systems; and sound risk management)
- Limited market participation by domestic and foreign institutional investors, as well as banks

The inadequate environment for derivative trading has stifled progress, particularly for interest-rate derivatives markets, the development of which has been constrained by the insufficient liquidity of the underlying government bond yield curve. Some derivatives instruments, such as forward rate agreements and interest rate futures and options, which are critical for addressing the risk-management issues raised by the growing market determination of interest rates through liquid bond markets, are entirely absent in some countries. Given that OTC derivatives continue to be the largest component of the derivatives sector in Asian capital

---

[13] Stock index futures and stock index options are the most widely traded equity derivatives. Index-based derivatives are usually the first instruments to be developed before options on individual assets are introduced.

[14] This is in contrast to other emerging market regions and mature markets, where interest rate derivatives are more commonly traded than are currency derivatives. Currency derivatives are traded in only a handful of emerging market exchanges; the bulk of the trading occurs in the OTC market. In Asia (excluding Japan), active exchange-based trading of currency derivatives occurs only in Hong Kong SAR, India, Korea, and Thailand. Until recently, most of currency derivatives trading took place offshore.

[15] Stock and equity index derivatives activity is concentrated at the organized exchanges, where equity derivatives are the most liquid among all derivatives products. Contract trading volume continued to expand vigorously in the past few years, which testifies to rising liquidity. Equity index derivatives account for the bulk of the trading.

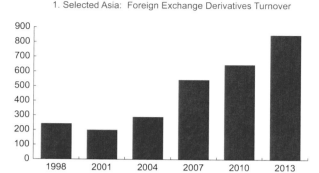

1. Selected Asia: Foreign Exchange Derivatives Turnover

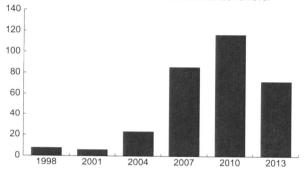

2. Selected Asia: Interest Rate Derivatives Turnover

Figure 4.11 Turnover of Foreign Exchange and Interest Rate Derivatives in Emerging Asia (*Daily averages, billions of U.S. dollars*)

Source: Bank for International Settlements, *Triennial Central Bank Surveys.*
Note: Excludes Japan, Australia, and New Zealand.

markets (excluding Japan), regulatory requirements mandating margin requirements for non-centrally cleared OTC derivatives will likely pose additional challenges to the development of the derivatives market in Asia. Also, market participation of institutional investors in interest rate derivatives markets is fairly constrained, thus encumbering the sufficient supply of counterparty lines.[16]

FOREIGN PARTICIPATION AND BOND YIELDS IN EMERGING ASIA

There has been limited empirical analysis of the determinants of local currency bond market yields in emerging Asia, in general, and even less of the role of foreign investors. Previous studies on emerging markets have generally focused on explaining the determinants of sovereign foreign currency spreads

---

[16] If institutional investors can purchase derivatives, they can hedge risk. However, selling derivatives—as happened with AIG, for example—can clearly lead to problems.

(Gonzalez-Rozada and Levy-Yeyati 2006). Even the empirical evidence of the factors affecting long-term interest rates on government debt in mature markets has focused on domestic fundamentals, with little or no attention paid to foreign participation (Caporale and Williams 2002; Daniel 2008; and Laubach 2009). There is growing evidence, however, that global factors have an increasingly pronounced effect on government securities markets in mature markets. The availability of global funds has made the demand for sovereign securities more dependent on global investors' preferences, although country-specific risk factors may play a smaller role in Group of Seven countries (Kumar and Okimoto 2011). The IMF's (2009) *Global Financial Stability Report* shows that portfolio debt flows, in addition to the standard macrofinancial factors highlighted in the literature, play a significant role in determining bond yields in both mature markets and emerging markets. Agur and Demertzis (2013) find a fundamental shift in local currency bond markets since the global financial crisis. Up to the crisis, these bond markets were mainly driven by domestic interest rates, but postcrisis, the elasticity of local currency bond yields with respect to U.S. Treasury yields has more than quadrupled. In addition, Peiris (2013) estimates that a 1 percentage point increase in foreign participation in local currency bond markets in emerging market economies has reduced bond yields by about 6 basis points, on average, controlling for other factors.

The literature on the determinants of bond yield volatility in emerging markets is even sparser. Early studies using time-series techniques were conducted on bond yield volatility in advanced economies (for example, Borio and McCauley 1996), but subsequent research in this area has generally focused on implied volatility based on option pricing (Brooks and Oozeer 2002). However, derivatives markets in emerging economies are generally not sufficiently developed for information on bond price volatility to be extracted. Previous studies on emerging markets have generally analyzed whether there has been volatility contagion (for example, Andritzky, Bannisters, and Tamirisa 2007) but again focused on determinants of sovereign foreign currency spreads. Azis and others (2013) employ multivariate generalized autoregressive conditional heteroscedastic (GARCH) models to show that significant shock and volatility spillover effects from market volatilities are more influenced by their own price dynamics in emerging Asia; in some other markets (for example, China, Indonesia, Korea, and Malaysia), the direct shock and volatility spillovers from global financial conditions remain significant. However, capital flows cannot be explicitly identified as the likely key transmission channel for contagion and spillovers.[17]

Following Peiris (2013), we estimated a GARCH (1, 1) model of sovereign bond yields in emerging Asian economies during 2000–13 using a comprehensive

---

[17]The IMF's (2014) *Global Financial Stability Report* highlights the importance of accounting for portfolio capital flows in driving bond yields in emerging markets even while controlling for other external factors, such as global risk aversion, where financial deepening can help dampen the sensitivity of local yields to the VIX.

set of macro-financial variables, including foreign portfolio flows. The econometric analysis was based on a standard reduced-form specification for a GARCH model with the following mean equation:[18]

$$Lr_{it} = \alpha_i + \beta_1 Infl_{it} + \beta_2 b_{it} + \beta_3 D_{it-1} + \beta_4 GDP_{it} + \beta_5 USr_{it} + \beta_6 VIX_{it} + \beta_7 FP_{it} + \varepsilon_{it} \quad (4.1)$$

in which Lr denotes nominal yields on the benchmark long-term government bonds for country i for each month t between January 2000 and June 2013; $Infl$ is the inflation rate, b is the fiscal deficit in percent of GDP, D is the level of gross general government debt in percent of GDP, GDP is real expected GDP growth (to control for the country's cyclical position), USr is the U.S. long-term nominal Treasury bond yield (uncovered interest parity), VIX the implied volatility of options on the U.S. S&P 500 index (to control for global risk aversion), and FP is foreign portfolio bond flows as measured by EPFR Global.

Foreign portfolio inflow volatility and the VIX are also introduced in the form of multiplicative heteroscedasticity in the conditional variance equation in the following form:

$$\varepsilon_t \sim N(0, \sigma_t^2)$$
$$\sigma_t^2 = \exp(\varphi + \gamma FPVOL_t + VIX_{it}) + \alpha \varepsilon_{t-1}^2 + \beta \sigma_{t-1}^2 \qquad (4.2)$$

in which σ_t^2 is a measure of volatility of the nominal long-term local currency government bond yield for each sample county. Therefore, the sign on γ provides an estimate of the impact of the contemporaneous foreign portfolio flow volatility in the domestic government bond market on yield volatility, although the magnitude of γ is not comparable across countries given the conditional volatility measure used.[19]

The time series results for monthly data from 2000 show that greater foreign portfolio inflows significantly reduce yields in nearly all emerging Asian countries, controlling for the standard domestic yield determinants in the literature, as well as for U.S. interest rates and global risk aversion (Table 4.2). Overall, both domestic and global factors played nearly equal roles in yield determination in emerging Asia during the past decade but with global factors and capital flows playing a large role during the global financial crisis and "taper" episode, as expected (Figure 4.12). However, capital flow volatility (modeled as a GARCH conditional variance with a simple autoregressive mean equation for

---

[18] The inflation rate was included instead of the short-term nominal policy interest rate (to control for the effects of monetary policy on the bond yield term structure) used by IMF (2009) and Peiris (2013) because it provided a better fit in most countries and the two variables were highly correlated during this inflation-targeting period. The ratio of the current account balance to GDP was also considered but was not a robust explanatory variable when foreign portfolio inflows were included in the specification. It was thus excluded given the focus of the analysis on foreign inflows. In most countries, a high degree of multicollinearity between the budget balance and public debt level was found, as expected; therefore, only the public debt level was included in the final results.

[19] Edwards (1998) uses a similar methodology to estimate the impact of volatility spillovers or contagion in Latin America during the "tequila" crisis.

TABLE 4.2

Determinants of Bond Yields in Emerging Asia								
	Domestic Factors				**External Factors**		**Variance Equation**	
	D	*GDP*	*Infl*	*FP*	*VIX*	*USr*	*FP*	*VIX*
Indonesia	−0.057***	−0.717***	0.157***	−0.726***	0.071***	0.576***	1.115	−0.017
Korea	0.036**	0.239***	0.151***	−0.150*	0.031***	0.567***	−6.874	0.021
Malaysia	0.040***	−0.168***	0.014	−0.042*	0.001	0.355***	−1.608	−0.022*
Philippines	0.093***	−0.110**	0.068*	−0.468***	0.020***	0.768***	2.174	−0.020
Taiwan Province of China	0.118***	0.038**	0.025***	…	0.005***	0.161***	−49.099	−0.006
Thailand	0.021	−0.087**	0.114***	0.032	−0.009*	0.624***	−1.725	−0.009

Source: IMF staff estimates.
Note: D = general government gross debt in percent of GDP; FP = foreign portfolio bond flows; GDP = real GDP growth expectations; Infl = inflation rate; USr = U.S. long-term nominal Treasury yield; VIX = Chicago Board Options Exchange Market Volatility Index.
$^*p < .1; ^{**}p < .05; ^{***}p < .01.$

capital flows) and the VIX do not significantly increase yield volatility in any country (Table 4.2). This result suggests that sovereign bond yields are susceptible to global interest rates and risk aversion over and above the behavior of foreign portfolio flows (possibly related to local-investor portfolio reallocations or an expectations channel) but that foreign portfolio flow volatility and the VIX do not contribute to yield volatility beyond their level impact. The insignificant impact of foreign portfolio flow volatility and the VIX on bond yield volatility reinforces the value of financial deepening emphasized in IMF (2014) by lowering the sensitivity of bond yields to the VIX, because there does not appear to be an additional volatility transmission channel from external factors. Lower inflation, public debt, and deficit levels reduce bond yields, highlighting the importance of maintaining sound domestic fundamentals that can help counteract the potential external spillovers during times of global stress.

A Fundamental Transformation

This section presents the results of a firm-level analysis that reveals that it has become easier for firms to access corporate bond markets.[20] There are many ways to assess the quality of a bond market, but perhaps the most important metric is its usefulness to potential borrowers. For example, a bond market may be irrelevant to most firms because it is highly concentrated, dominated by a handful of large firms that act as price setters, or requires high fixed costs that can only be absorbed by large issues. These high fixed costs limit market access or raise the

[20] The sample includes ASEAN countries with more-developed bond markets (Indonesia, Malaysia, the Philippines, Singapore, and Thailand) as well as China, Hong Kong SAR, India, and Korea. For comparative purposes, Brazil was included as an emerging market benchmark outside Asia.

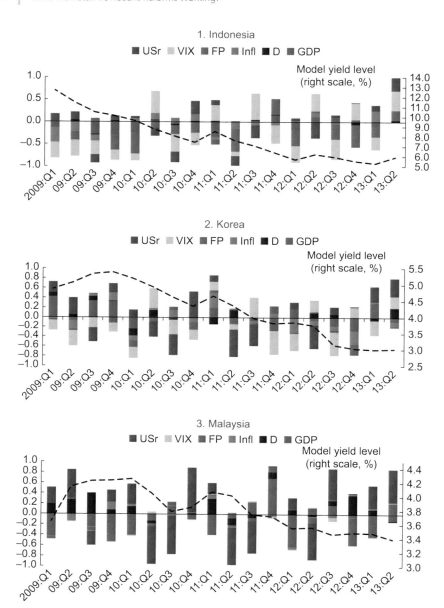

Figure 4.12 Determinants of Sovereign Bond Yields in Emerging Asia

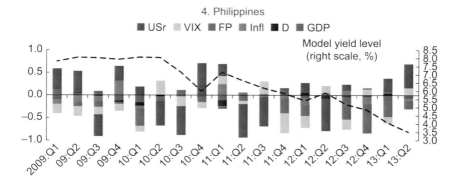

4. Philippines

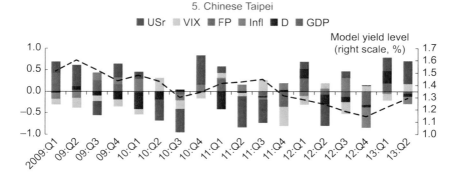

5. Chinese Taipei

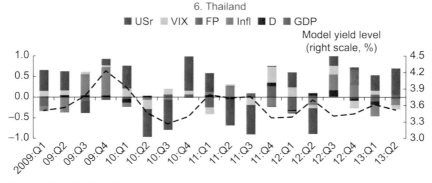

6. Thailand

Figure 4.12 *(Continued)*

Source: IMF staff estimates.

Note: D = general government gross debt in percent of GDP; FP = foreign portfolio bond flows; GDP = real GDP growth expectations; Infl = Inflation rate; USr = U.S. long-term nominal treasury yield; VIX = Chicago Board Options Exchange Market Volatility Index.

cost of capital for smaller firms that have fewer financial resources and insufficient scale. Thus, the usefulness of bond markets could be limited because firms' issues would need to be "significant," defined here as a size that accounts for a large proportion of their balance sheets. The analysis also examines whether the corporate bond market has developed into a "spare tire" that firms can use when other parts of the financial system come under stress.

Firm-Level Analysis

Bond market development can be seen as following an evolutionary pattern. Initially, when the market is at a very early stage, only a few firms will be sufficiently large or financially well regarded (with a long track record and audited public accounts) to issue bonds. Moreover, because there are sizable fixed costs to issuing bonds, and because firms want to establish liquid benchmark issues, initial issuance volumes are normally large relative to firm balance sheets. Over time, however, as markets mature and economies develop, barriers to entry decline, which decreases concentration ratios and the relative significance of individual issuances to both individual issuers and the overall market. Markets will no longer be dominated by a few large issuers, or a few large bond issues, since more and more firms are able to issue and diversify supply ("quantity transition"). In addition, the significance of bond issues will also tend to decline, partly because as issuance becomes routine, firms are likely to issue more frequent smaller amounts rather than occasional large amounts. Moreover, as the administrative costs of issuance decline, minimum amounts will become small relative to the size of growing balance sheets ("quality transition"), especially for firms that access debt markets to support expansionary strategies. The lower administrative costs will also allow smaller firms to access capital markets for funding via bond issuance. In the conceptual representation of an evolutionary pattern (Figure 4.13), the market starts off in the second quadrant, with a high concentration of issuers and a high significance of individual issuance relative to the size of balance sheets. Gradually, as the market develops, it moves into the third quadrant, with low concentration and low significance.

So Much for Theory

What is the evidence for emerging Asia? Some key indicators are provided in Tables 4.3 and 4.4, which show fundamental data on local currency issuance by nonfinancial private sector firms since 2000.[21] The focus of the analysis is on selected ASEAN economies; China, Hong Kong SAR, and Korea as regional

---

[21] Bond issuance (and balance sheet information [total assets]) data were obtained for nine Asian countries comprising five ASEAN countries and four non-ASEAN economies (China, Hong Kong SAR, India, and Korea) as well as Brazil as a global emerging market benchmark. Bond issuance data comprised all local-currency-denominated, nonfinancial private sector transactions during each sample year (2000, 2005, and 2009–13).

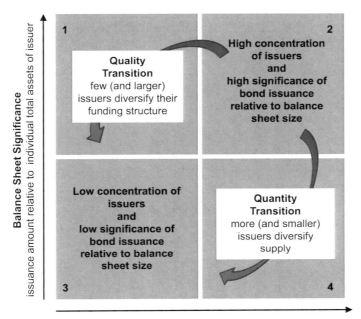

Issuer Concentration

individual assets of issuer relative to total assets of all issuers

Figure 4.13 Bond Market Development Matrix

Source: Felman and others (2011).

benchmarks; and Brazil for comparative purposes.[22] In these markets, some clear progress toward a greater diversity of issuers since 2000 can be seen. The issuance amounts as well as the number of both issues and issuers have been increasing steadily. The average maturity, however, has shortened somewhat in smaller markets but noticeably lengthened in those more developed markets that continued to record high rates of growth, such as Malaysia and Korea.

Pairing the conceptual approach to bond market evolution with relevant concentration metrics supports the broad empirical observations for the region.

---

[22] Issuance by nonoperating financial companies and special purpose vehicles was not considered. Moreover, multiple tranches of issues and issuers for which no balance sheet size could be determined were excluded from the sample. Thus, the issuance volumes for Hong Kong SAR and Singapore in Table 4.3 are understated. Moreover, the sample sizes for Hong Kong SAR, the Philippines, and Singapore became too small for the detailed (deal-based) analysis in Figure 4.14. The total bond issuance between 2003 and 2012 in Hong Kong SAR and Singapore amounted to about $400 billion and $100 billion, respectively (Le Leslé and others 2014). Issuance is predominantly in local currencies (67 percent in Hong Kong SAR; 77 percent in Singapore). In Hong Kong SAR, private sector debt dominates (64 percent), while in Singapore, government and private debt each account for about half of issuance (47 percent and 53 percent, respectively).

TABLE 4.3

ASEAN and Selected Emerging Market Countries: Characteristics of Local Currency Corporate Bond Issuance, 2000–13

	Indonesia	Malaysia	Philippines	Singapore	Thailand	Brazil	China	Hong Kong SAR	India	Korea
	Issuance (In billions of U.S. dollars)									
2000	0.6	3.0	...	1.9	2.7	2.9	1.5	0.2	3.0	37.3
2005	0.4	13.5	0.5	1.4	3.4	5.5	31.1	0.6	2.5	45.5
2009	2.1	11.3	2.2	1.9	8.0	16.6	201.6	2.4	10.7	79.4
2010	1.4	8.2	0.9	5.7	4.1	18.2	182.4	3.4	7.7	41.2
2011	0.8	10.1	1.1	2.6	6.2	21.8	240.0	1.4	5.8	52.0
2012	2.1	18.1	1.6	7.7	6.8	32.2	381.9	1.2	19.9	55.8
2013	2.3	13.0	0.6	3.7	9.7	25.3	464.5	1.3	11.1	93.9
	Average Maturity (In years)									
2000	5.5	4.1	...	4.6	6.0	5.7	4.7	4.1	6.7	3.1
2005	3.9	2.7	5.8	4.3	4.7	6.0	4.7	7.9	6.6	2.9
2009	4.3	1.1	5.4	5.1	4.7	4.6	3.8	9.6	6.0	2.9
2010	4.4	3.8	6.4	5.8	4.6	5.2	2.9	5.9	6.0	3.4
2011	2.9	3.9	6.7	4.7	3.9	5.1	2.9	8.6	5.8	3.8
2012	4.3	6.6	7.6	7.4	5.8	5.4	3.4	9.2	5.5	4.1
2013	4.8	7.1	8.3	4.8	4.6	5.1	2.9	6.1	6.0	5.0

Sources: Bloomberg, L.P.; Moody's KMV; national stock exchanges; Worldscope; and authors' calculations.

Note: The country data are based on the country of domicile of the registered issue. Thus, transactions placed in other jurisdictions for reasons of efficient market access are not attributed to the issuer's country. This is particularly important for the issuance of bonds in Hong Kong SAR by firms from mainland China. These "dim sum bonds" are denominated in Chinese renminbi rather than the Hong Kong dollar.

Figures 4.14 and 4.15 illustrate the interaction of issuer assets (relative to those of other issuers) and the balance sheet significance of issuance in a two-dimensional representation of firm-level data for each sample country. In this way, it is possible to assess whether the presence of new issuers has also resulted in greater economies from bond issuance.

Overall, bond markets throughout the region matured. As illustrated in Figure 4.13, most countries moved toward the third quadrant ("low concentration, low significance"). More specifically, we find the following:

- *Issuance in bond markets has become more diverse.* The concentration of supply in most markets has decreased with the influx of new issuers. Especially in countries that have experienced rapid expansion of their domestic bond markets, such as China and India, concentration—whether measured by issuance (for example, a few large bonds) or by issuers (for example, a few large companies)—dropped to the levels of Hong Kong SAR and Korea, which are home to the most mature bond markets in the region (see Tables 4.3 and 4.4). Moreover, by the end of 2012, the concentration level in China declined to that observed in Brazil, which has one of the largest primary bond markets of any emerging market country. But market concentration in the Philippines (as well as in Malaysia and, to some extent, Thailand if only issuer concentration is considered) remained high.

TABLE 4.4

ASEAN and Selected Emerging Market Countries: Evolutionary Characteristics of Local Currency Corporate Bond Issuance, 2000–12

	Indonesia	Malaysia	Philippines	Singapore	Thailand	Brazil	China	Hong Kong SAR	India	Korea
	Concentration of Issuance Volume									
2000	9.4	4.4	...	...	8.5	7.9	4.9	8.0	7.1	0.3
2005	11.9	7.2	24.8	9.8	3.9	1.8	10.9	1.2	12.1	0.3
2010	7.2	6.8	31.5	5.0	1.8	2.3	11.1	0.4	5.1	0.2
2012	2.6	13.1	20.4	2.7	3.1	1.1	5.9	0.2	7.0	0.2
	Concentration of Issuer Assets									
2000	10.9	22.0	...	...	2.2	5.4	9.9	43.8	9.7	0.7
2005	21.5	9.7	7.1	7.7	7.4	1.9	84.8	8.1	8.1	0.7
2010	15.8	29.5	11.5	6.7	9.0	2.7	38.9	1.6	3.4	0.7
2012	4.7	34.6	22.9	8.8	11.7	2.4	26.8	0.6	3.0	0.6

Sources: Bloomberg, L.P.; Moody's KMV; national stock exchanges; Worldscope; and authors' calculations.

Note: The country data are based on the country of domicile of the registered issue. Thus, transactions placed in other jurisdictions for reasons of efficient market access are not attributed to the issuer's country. This is particularly important for the issuance of bonds in Hong Kong SAR by firms from mainland China. These "dim sum bonds" are denominated in Chinese renminbi rather than the Hong Kong dollar. The concentration measures of each issuer i out of a total of N issuers in each country (based on the issuance amount and total assets reported at the time of issuance) are defined as "market share" using a normalized version of the Herfindahl-Hirschman Index (HHI), which is specified as

$$HHI_{issuer} = \frac{\sum_N^i \left(\frac{total\,assets_i}{\sum_N^i total\,asset_i} \right)^2 - \left(\frac{1}{\sum_N^i total\,assets_i} \right)}{1 - \left(\frac{1}{\sum_N^i total\,assets_i} \right)} \times 100,$$ (1)

and

$$HHI_{issuance} = \frac{\sum_N^i \left(\frac{issuance\,volume_i}{\sum_N^i issuance\,volume_i} \right)^2 - \left(\frac{1}{\sum_N^i issuance\,volume_i} \right)}{1 - \left(\frac{1}{\sum_N^i issuance\,volume_i} \right)} \times 100,$$ (2)

respectively. The higher the value of the HHI, the more concentrated the market.

- *Wider and deeper bond markets have also reduced the significance of new issuance (relative to each issuer's balance sheet size) as funding sources become more diversified.* In many countries (with the exception of Indonesia and Thailand), the balance sheet significance of issuance has significantly declined since 2000. A slower decline in Singapore (similar to that in Brazil) can be explained by the marginal increase of diversity achieved from new issuers (with below-average balance sheet assets) in an already very mature market. In Figure 4.15 (and in Annex Figure 4.1.1, which gives a historical perspective on the market evolution of Indonesia, Malaysia, and Thailand), the center of each ellipse represents the largest density of the joint probability distribution of concentration and significance for each country in 2000 and

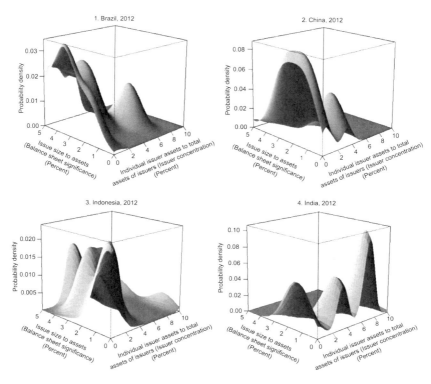

Figure 4.14 ASEAN and Selected Emerging Market Countries: Corporate Bond Issuance Relative to Total Assets Conditional on Issuer Concentration, 2012

2012. The size of each ellipse represents the relative issuance volume (in 2000, Indonesia has two ellipses because it had two distinctive peaks in its probability distribution). After controlling for issuer concentration, Malaysia and Korea show high significance only for many smaller issuers, whereas in Indonesia (and, to a lesser extent, Singapore) issue sizes tend to be more significant even for large issuers (see Figure 4.13). That is, the average issuance volume relative to issuer balance sheets tends to be higher in countries with less developed bond markets and few larger issuers, as the theory would predict. However, this observation might also occur in more mature markets if many smaller issuers with small issue sizes raise the relative importance of larger issuers for the concentration measure (see Table 4.4).

Currently, the state of development, especially in many emerging Asian countries, is encouraging and is not at all far from that in Korea and Brazil—at least as measured by the concentration of issuers and the economic relevance of issuance. A decade ago, only the largest and best-known firms were able to issue bonds, and therefore, their issues dominated local markets. Gradually, however, more firms have been able to issue bonds, thereby creating broader markets. This qualitative progress

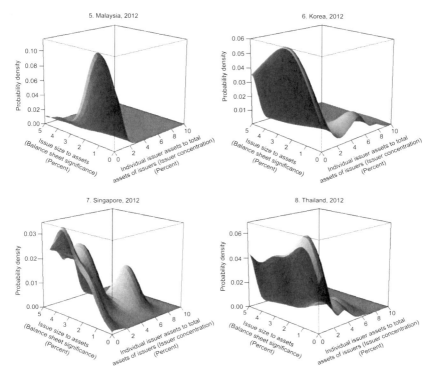

Figure 4.14 (*Continued*)

Sources: Bloomberg, L.P.; Moody's KMV; national stock exchanges; Worldscope; and authors' calculations.

Note: The bivariate density function for each country plots the ratio of the issuance amount over total assets of each issuer (*x*-axis) ("balance sheet significance") and the market share of each issuer's assets relative to total assets of all issuers (*y*-axis) ("concentration of issuers"), which spans the two-dimensional grid of joint probabilities (defined as the integral over the unit square [0,1], *z*-axis) following Jobst (2013). The market share of each issuer is based on a rescaled, normalized Herfindahl-Hirschman Index (HHI), which is specified as

$$\frac{\min\left(HHI_{i,t}, HHI_{i,t} - \min\left(HHI_{N,t}\right)\right)}{\max\left(HHI_{N,t}\right) - \min\left(HHI_{N,t}\right)} \in [0,1], \tag{3}$$

where

$$HHI_{i,t} = \frac{\left(\dfrac{\text{total assets}_{i,t}}{\displaystyle\sum_{N}^{i} \text{total assets}_{i,t}}\right)^2 - \left(\dfrac{1}{N_t}\right)}{1 - \left(\dfrac{1}{N_t}\right)} \times 100, \tag{4}$$

for a total number *N* of issuers *i* in a given year *t*. The closer the value to zero, the less concentrated the respective market based on the size of issuers. The market share of individual issuer assets represents the deal-by-deal representation of the "concentration of issuer assets" as shown in Table 4.3. For Hong Kong SAR and the Philippines, the number of observations was insufficient (due to limited availability of both total assets of issuers and issuance volume). For issuers with multiple issuances, the same issuer concentration is shown relative to the balance sheet significance in the bivariate density functions. The country data are based on the country of domicile of the registered issue. Thus, transactions placed in other jurisdictions for reasons of efficient market access are not attributed to the issuer's country. This is particularly important for the issuance of bonds in Hong Kong SAR by firms from mainland China. These "dim sum bonds" are denominated in Chinese renminbi rather than Hong Kong dollars.

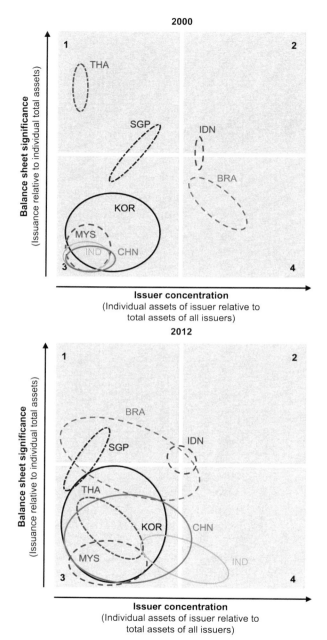

Figure 4.15 ASEAN and Selected Emerging Market Countries: Stylized Concentration of Issuers and Significance of Issuance, 2000 and 2012

Sources: Bloomberg, L.P.; national stock exchanges; Moody's KMV; Worldscope; and author's calculations.
Note: The ellipses show the (stylized) placement of the highest joint incidence of issuer concentration and balance sheet significance for each country based on the bivariate kernel density functions shown in Figure 4.14 and Annex Figure 4.1.1 (for Indonesia, Malaysia, and Thailand). The size of the ellipses indicates the relative size of bond issuance relative to other countries. ASEAN = Association of Southeast Asian Nations; BRA = Brazil; CHN = China; HKG = Hong Kong SAR; IND = India; IDN = Indonesia; KOR = Korea; MYS = Malaysia; PHL= Philippines; SGP = Singapore; THA = Thailand.

has culminated in two critical developments. Two ASEAN-5 countries, Malaysia and Thailand, have decisively entered the third quadrant. However, more progress is needed in diversifying the issuer base in Indonesia and the Philippines, and in ensuring that issuance becomes a more routine method of financing operations.

The New Spare Tire

Amid the depths of the global financial crisis, domestic bond issuance by firms surged. For years, the stock of emerging Asian corporate bonds outstanding had been stagnating relative to Asia's economic growth. But in the second quarter of 2009, the stock of outdated corporate bonds increased by nearly 10 percent quarter-over-quarter in the ASEAN-5 and by more than 20 percent quarter-over-quarter in emerging Asia, excluding China. In the third and fourth quarters of 2009, there was a further large increase. By the end of 2009, ASEAN-5 and emerging Asian local currency corporate bond issuance was higher than the previous peak, reached in 2007, and roughly double the normal level.

This surge was striking for a number of reasons. To begin with, as noted earlier in this chapter, ASEAN-5 firms typically do not rely much on bond issuance for funding. Moreover, the surge took place in the middle of a severe recession, when private sector investment had fallen sharply. So, firms had little need to issue bonds to finance investment projects; they were not initiating projects and they were slowing down the ones that were already under way. Nor were firms forced to issue bonds just to sustain themselves; corporate profitability actually held up reasonably well during the recession.

What explains the issuance boom? The primary factor appears to have been a reaction to changes in bank behavior. Normally, bank-centered financial systems maintain lending ties to their clients, even during difficult times. But this was not a normal downturn. Even though liquidity in the Asian banking systems was ample and capital adequacy was never in doubt, Asian banks nonetheless followed their Western peers and became more cautious after the Lehman Brothers bankruptcy. They tightened their lending standards and reduced their prime lending rates much more slowly and partially than the rate of decline in policy and bond interest rates. Even though sovereign and corporate bond yields widened, they remained below prime lending rates in many markets (Figure 4.16). This allowed many firms to continue to raise funds for new projects, refinance maturing liabilities, or even prefund some borrowing requirements. The relatively lower bond yields and continued corporate bond issuances encouraged firms to turn to the capital markets while reducing their use of bank credit (see Figure 4.17). In fact, adding both bank credit and corporate bond issuance together, total credit to the corporate sector actually declined in the first half of 2009 in the ASEAN-5 countries. So, the bond issuance was not "additional"— firms were *substituting* one form of financing for another. In other words, the domestic bond market acted precisely as reformers had originally hoped it would: it became the "spare tire" that corporations could use if the bank financing channel were to be impaired.

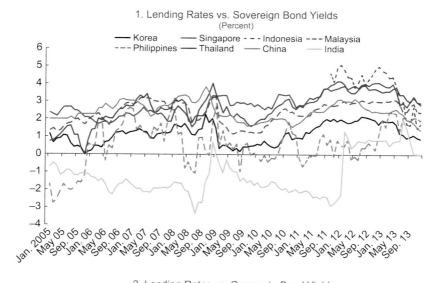

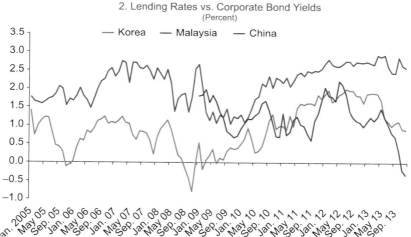

Figure 4.16 Spreads between Lending Rates and Yields

Sources: Asian Development Bank, AsianBondsOnline; Bloomberg, L.P.; CEIC Data Co. Ltd.; Haver Analytics; and IMF staff calculations.

Where was the demand for these bonds coming from? Much of the demand appears to have come from overseas as global risk appetite began to revive with the asset purchases by the Federal Reserve and the stabilization of financial systems in advanced economies, and as prospects in emerging markets began to appear to be better than those in the West. As a result, inflows into emerging

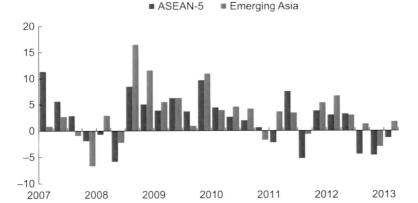

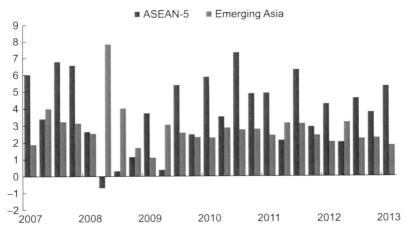

Figure 4.17 ASEAN-5 and Emerging Asia: Local Currency Corporate Bond Issuance and Corporate Lending

Sources: Bank for International Settlements; CEIC Data Co. Ltd.; Haver Analytics; and IMF staff estimates.
Note: ASEAN-5 includes Indonesia, Malaysia, the Philippines, Singapore, and Thailand.

market debt funds resumed in May 2009 and quickly reached levels approaching the peak of the 2005–07 global boom. In short, the ASEAN-5's and emerging Asia's domestic bond markets were able to become a spare tire during the Great Recession—one of Asian policymakers' key original objectives in developing debt markets in the aftermath of the Asian crisis of the late 1990s.

CHALLENGES TO BOND MARKET DEVELOPMENT

Institutional Investor Base

The legal and regulatory framework for nonbank financial institutions should be strengthened. This applies particularly to insurance companies, mutual funds, and pension plans. Full, or at least partial, funding of pension plans—as opposed to pay-as-you-go approaches—would create additional pools of financial capital, potentially expanding and diversifying the investor base.[23] Even in public-led pension systems, outsourcing tranches or a share of funds to private fund managers would be positive, as has been demonstrated in India. In several Asian countries examined in a study by the ADB (2013a), the concentration of the investor base resulted in a sizable portion of local currency bonds held in "buy-and-hold" portfolios. This, in turn, had an adverse effect on market liquidity, constraining trading by the market's largest investors. Although foreign investors, notably hedge funds and banks, are active in trading emerging market local currency bonds, overall trading remains relatively modest. Pension fund portfolio diversification has improved in recent years, but in many Asian countries asset allocations are still heavily concentrated in government securities. Pension funds' asset allocations have been dictated by regulations on their investments that follow rigid criteria set by law or regulatory limits that could be progressively eased. The resulting concentration of exposures in a particular segment of the market has had a negative effect on market liquidity. Development of the mutual fund industry could raise market liquidity and reduce the hold of bank-dominated intermediation. However, the mutual fund industry in Asia generally suffers from lack of an investment culture, instances of fraud, cumbersome or inadequate regulatory structures, improper or inaccurate pricing, and poor investor safeguards (ADB 2013a). From a regulatory perspective, the investment management industry has to have sound governance structures, investment policies, and monitoring frameworks.

Foreign investors continue to face impediments in accessing debt markets in the region. Based on surveys conducted by the ADB (2013b), foreign investors find Singapore, Korea, and Malaysia the easiest markets in which to invest, followed by Thailand. Access to local debt markets in the Philippines and Indonesia is somewhat more difficult. The most challenging countries to gain access to are China and India. In China, for instance, foreign banks, through joint ventures, can trade in bonds and underwrite them on the two regulated bond exchanges. However, these banks mostly remain excluded from underwriting on the interbank market, which is 20 times larger and closed to individual investors (Noble 2013). Access issues could partly explain why Asia's contribution to global GDP far exceeds the global share of investment in Asian emerging markets. This disparity implies that global institutional investors are significantly underweight in

---

[23] Consolidation of the multipillar pension system, with emphasis on the funded component, would be preferable in China.

Asian assets in their investment portfolios. A rough calculation can provide some perspective: for instance, a 1 percent increase in global institutional investors' allocations to Asia would result in capital inflows of about $600 billion, although not all of this would be invested in local currency bonds.

The key impediments facing foreign investors include capital controls, taxation, and weak institutional structures (Table 4.5). Barriers that most directly affect foreign investors include capital controls, investor registration rules, limits and administrative procedures on foreign exchange transactions, availability of foreign exchange hedging instruments, withholding of taxes, and cross-border clearing and settlement systems. Despite some capital account liberalization measures, countries such as China and India allow only licensed foreign institutional investors to hold and trade domestic securities; strict limits are placed on nonresident participation. With the exception of Malaysia and Singapore, most Asian emerging markets impose withholding taxes on interest earned from local bonds by foreign investors. The prospective inclusion of Indian government securities in benchmark indices, such as the JPMorgan Government Bond Index-Emerging Markets Global Diversified Index, can provide significant impetus for inflows into government debt markets and thus reduce yields. At the same time, the exclusion of the Philippines, owing to limited benchmarks and tax issues, hinders the secondary market liquidity of Philippine bonds. Lower foreign participation in corporate bond markets could also be traced to foreign investor concerns about appropriate pricing caused by weak corporate governance, transparency issues, and uncertain bankruptcy and resolution frameworks. For instance, market participants view the recent first default in the corporate bond market and a very public default on a trust loan in China as important steps in addressing moral hazard. The effective pricing of risk requires tolerance for occasional losses or haircuts on interest-bearing financial instruments, such as corporate bonds or wealth management products, without a formal principal guarantee. More generally, across emerging Asia, defaults need to be resolved more predictably via bankruptcy proceedings rather than treated as idiosyncratic events to be dealt with through a sharing of losses among stakeholders largely independent of their position in the capital structure of the borrower.

Financial Infrastructure

After more than a decade of reform, market infrastructure in emerging Asia compares favorably to that in other emerging markets in several ways:

- *Transparency*. All OTC markets in the region, with the sole exception of corporate bond markets in Singapore, have posttrade transparency, mainly as a result of trade reporting obligations imposed by regulatory authorities. As a result, transparency in these markets is aligned with international best practices.

- *Dematerialization of securities and central securities depositories*. Dematerialization (or at least immobilization) of securities has become common practice, facilitating the trading of securities as well as trade settlement.

TABLE 4.5

Accessibility, Taxation, Funding, and Hedging

	China	Hong Kong SAR	Korea	India	Indonesia	Malaysia	Philippines	Singapore	Thailand
Holding and buying local bonds	Limited	Yes	Yes	Limited	Yes	Yes	Custodian	Yes	Limited
Nonresident access	Via QFII	Yes	Yes	Via QFII	Yes	Yes	Yes	Yes	Yes
Foreign exchange restrictions	Yes	No	No	Yes	Yes	Very Few	Yes	No	Yes
Withholding tax (nonresident)	Only crop	No	Yes	Yes	Yes	No	Yes	No	Only crop
Capital gains tax (nonresident)	No	No	Yes	Yes	Only crop	No	Only crop	No	Only crop
Funding and hedging instruments									
Developed repo markets	Yes	Yes	Yes	Yes	Limited	Yes	No	Yes	Limited
OTC Instruments									
IR swaps	Yes	Yes	Yes	Yes	Yes	Yes	Yes	Yes	Yes
Foreign exchange swaps	Yes	Yes	Yes	Yes	Yes	Yes	Yes	Yes	Yes
Foreign exchange forwards	Yes	Yes	Yes	Yes	Yes	Yes	Yes	Yes	Yes
Exchange-traded instruments									
IR futures	No	Yes	Yes	No	No	Yes	No	Yes	No
Foreign exchange futures	No	No	Yes	No	No	No	No	No	No
Liquid NDF market	Yes	No	Yes	Yes	Moderate	Moderate	Moderate	No	No
Up to 12 months	Yes	–	Yes	Yes	Moderate	–	Moderate	–	–
Up to 5 months	Limited	–	Yes	Moderate	ILLiquid	–	Limited	–	–

Source: ADB (2013b).

Note: IR = interest rate; NDF = non-deliverable forward; OTC = over the counter.

Malaysia and the Philippines have already moved from scrip to a dematerialized system of representation of securities. In Singapore corporate bonds are not required to be dematerialized. In Indonesia not all corporate bonds are dematerialized, and in Thailand both government and corporate debt are legally required to be issued in paper form. In all three countries, however, immobilization has, to a large extent, eliminated the risk of paper securities. However, book-entry systems for government and corporate bonds remain fragmented among different depositories at the local level.

- *Clearing and settlement risks.* In all ASEAN-5 countries, wholesale trading usually takes place on a delivery-versus-payment basis, reducing counter-party risk. The implementation of delivery-versus-payment has helped reduce settlement risk; that is, the risk that the seller of securities delivers but does not receive payment for the securities, or vice versa.

However, some consolidation of depository and settlement systems in ASEAN-5 countries would increase market efficiency. Central securities depositories promote efficiency by reducing the number of securities accounts and connections required by investors or traders. Central securities depositories also economize on the cash settlement leg.[24] Thailand has a book-entry system for both government and corporate bonds that is centralized in a single central securities depository; Malaysia also has a central securities depository, which captures unlisted bonds issued by both firms and the government. Thus, some countries could explore further consolidation of book-entry systems. In addition, except for transactions with listed corporate bonds in Malaysia, clearing and settlement of transactions with government and corporate bonds does not involve a central clearing counterparty. While not yet a global standard, consideration could be given to moving toward clearing fixed-income markets through central clearing counterparties to minimize settlement risks. Given that the viability of these entities depends on the existence of a minimum trading volume, ASEAN-5 countries might wish to analyze the convenience of central clearing counterparties in a regional context.

Cross-border investors face an additional settlement risk. Settlement of a domestic bond normally involves payment in a local currency. Nonresident investors buying or selling domestic bonds will normally need to purchase or sell local currency. As a result, cross-border investors are exposed to the settlement risk of the foreign exchange trade, in addition to the settlement risk of the bond trade itself. Thus, a key problem for foreign investors is the timing difference between the securities and cash movements, and this difference in timing is compounded by the fact that most foreign exchange deals in the ASEAN-5 countries are transacted against the U.S. dollar, which settles after Asian business hours. Thus, there would likely be a major benefit from a cross-country clearing and settlement arrangement.

Some standardization of market infrastructure across ASEAN-5 countries, in line with the Joint Ministerial Statement of the 17th ASEAN Finance Ministers' Meeting in 2013, by regional finance ministers, would also help promote more intraregional intermediation. Currently, each country has its own market infrastructure; there are no cross-border infrastructure linkages for trading, clearing, custody, or settlement. Furthermore, only local central securities depositories, in Malaysia and Singapore, have links with international central securities

---

[24] For instance, if an investor sells a government bond and invests the proceeds in a corporate bond, a single central securities depository means that the cash flows can net out.

depositories.[25] The absence of integrated market access and trade processing is a challenge for the region because it increases transaction costs and might deter cross-border investment.[26] The 17th ASEAN Finance Ministers' Meeting in April 2013 encouraged the ASEAN financial regulators and ASEAN exchanges to continue working for the development of an integrated ASEAN capital market. The group also agreed to establish a cross committee to develop a blueprint for the establishment of clearing, settlement, and depository linkages (ASEAN Secretariat 2013). It must be acknowledged, however, that this is a common challenge in many regions that are striving toward greater integration, including the European Union.

The final report of the Asian Bond Markets Initiative Group of Experts (ADB 2010) discusses the development of a cross-border arrangement to address the foreign exchange risk of cross-border bond transactions. It provides a comparative analysis of the benefits of different options for such regional arrangements, in particular assessing the benefits of an Asian international central securities depository in comparison with a central securities depository linkage. It also includes a feasibility study for these two options. A key finding from this study is that multiple legal and regulatory barriers would need to be removed for any option to be operationally feasible. Now, a development plan that combines both government and market efforts is needed.

In the ASEAN-5 region, central clearing counterparties exist in the context of markets operated by the exchanges. However, in most of the Asia and Pacific region, bond trading is mainly over the counter and is settled on a bilateral basis, without the intervention of a central clearing counterparty. The benefits of a central clearing counterparty in managing counterparty risk are clear, but the implementation costs are significant. Central clearing counterparties have sizable fixed costs; thus, a minimum settlement volume is needed to make them economically feasible. In the context of each domestic market in the ASEAN-5, such costs might outweigh the benefits. A stronger business case might exist, however, for a regional market. Thus, when considering a regional central securities depository, Asian countries may also find it useful to consider the implementation of a regional central clearing counterparty.

Cash and Derivatives Market Nexus

Progress in enhancing liquidity and foreign participation in local currency sovereign bond markets provides an opportunity to support the complementary development of both the corporate bond and derivatives markets. A deep and liquid cash sovereign bond market is the cornerstone for all other asset prices, including corporate bonds and various types of derivatives. For example, a deep local currency

---

[25] A task force comprised of the central banks of Indonesia, Malaysia, and Thailand, the Hong Kong Monetary Authority, and Euroclear was created in June 2010 to explore gradual harmonization based on a common platform.

[26] As with a single national central securities depository, links between central securities depositories in different countries (or the introduction of an international central securities depository) reduce the need for multiple securities accounts and simplify cash management.

sovereign bond market makes it easier to price corporate bonds based on issuers' credit. Once a high-volume cash bond market is established, separate trading of registered interest and principal securities and interest rate swaps is easily started. Then, with the advancement of a secondary market, all the cash flow components needed for financial engineering would become available. Hence, structured finance products that are essential for infrastructure finance in emerging Asian countries would become available. Eventually, with two reasonably liquid interest rate swaps markets, there would be room for basis swaps between interest rates in different currencies. These are the tools essential for hedging currency and duration mismatches. Overall turnover in both foreign exchange and interest rate derivatives has increased significantly in emerging Asia but remains low by advanced economy standards.

Laws and regulations governing the derivatives market need to be revised. Although derivatives contracts in mature markets are structured under tried and tested norms of market practice and governed by a highly developed legal regime, statutory barriers and uncertainty surrounding legal and accounting requirements specific to the creation, trading, and enforcement of derivatives have inhibited the development of derivatives markets in Asia and the Pacific. In many instances, legal codes and accounting rules are silent on all or certain types of derivatives, fail to identify the regulatory jurisdiction over derivatives, or make derivatives contracts unenforceable. Also, restrictive cash market regulation, such as occasional limits on short selling, or limited securities lending such as occurs in Indonesia, the Philippines, and Thailand, have inhibited derivatives trading.

ASEAN-5 countries face challenges in developing local derivatives markets and ensuring their balanced growth in support of local bond markets. While several countries have made large strides in developing the enabling legal environment, regulatory obstacles in other countries hinder capital market development. Example of these obstacles include transaction taxes as well as restrictions on various instruments, on short selling, and on parties to transactions. Appropriate regulation and supervision of institutions active in derivatives markets reduces counterparty risk, discourages trading activity detrimental to market integrity, and minimizes potential threats to financial stability. In addition, problems of limited asset supply have resulted in liquidity-induced market risks such as difficulties in executing securities margin requirements. Liquid collateral, including pricing benchmarks, ensures efficient price formation of derivatives markets in the initial stage of development. Increasingly, however, the depth and liquidity of cash markets themselves have, to some extent, come to depend on the presence of similarly well-developed derivatives markets.

Dealing with Offshore Activity

The rise of foreign interest in domestic bonds has another important ramification—growing offshore activity. Offshore trading of emerging market currencies has continued to rise since the global financial crisis, notably for the Chinese renminbi, the Indian rupee, the Indonesian rupiah, and the Korean won.

International investors could be an important driver of the growing demand for emerging market currencies for hedging and speculation (Ehlers and Packer 2013). In some countries, offshore sovereign bond issuances are significant. The Philippines is one example, where even local currency bonds, such as global peso notes, have been issued offshore. Foreign investors often gain exposure to emerging markets by using various "access products," such as OTC derivatives, structured securities, or offshore special purpose vehicles. Modes of access include innovative financial instruments such as nondeliverable forwards and other derivatives instruments. Examples of the latter include foreign exchange currency swaps and options. Partly as a result of these activities, derivatives transactions with emerging market assets as an underlying reference have exploded since 2010.

Aside from the obvious benefit of ensuring that counterparty risk is focused on a few familiar, developed market financial institutions, investors stay offshore mainly because of impediments or costs to entering. These impediments include the following:[27]

- Limits on access to funding on domestic markets
- Clearing and settlement protocols and custody arrangements, such as custody controls, directed settlement, and rules on sub-custody[28]
- Minimum holding periods

Does any of this matter? Yes, for several reasons. Controls and taxes that drive activity offshore thereby reduce liquidity onshore, impairing price discovery. In other words, they reduce efficiency. They also reduce transparency. For example, national authorities will find it difficult to monitor market developments with much of the activity taking place beyond their jurisdictions, in relatively opaque OTC markets. Indeed, a significant proportion of bonds owned by the domestic financial sector may actually be held on behalf of foreign investors—typically by onshore banks—through derivatives structures.

A shift toward offshore activity may also raise prudential concerns. Offshore markets may be less regulated, and in any case will not be regulated by the home authorities. Moreover, even though controls that aim to isolate domestic markets from those offshore might exist, inevitably firms find ways to arbitrage between the two. As a result, developments in markets offshore can be transmitted onshore. In that case, compensating policy action might prove difficult because national authorities might not have much information on the genesis or the nature of the underlying shock.

For all these reasons, over time it may be beneficial to try to bring such markets onshore. One way to do so would be by reducing or eliminating withholding

---

[27]The nature and extent of impediments differ widely from country to country. For example, Malaysia has none of the impediments listed. In fact, Malaysia has made its bond market internationally accessible via international central securities depositories (Euroclear and Clearstream) to enable foreign investors to settle securities transactions without opening a local custodian account.

[28]The cost of appointing a local custodian can make cross-border investments unattractive.

taxes. Such a measure, however, would raise difficult issues of equity and efficiency. For example, if nonresidents are exempted from withholding tax, practices could emerge such as "coupon washing," whereby bonds are sold during the
coupon payment period—perhaps via repo or securities lending—to investors
paying low or zero withholding tax. Alternatively, resident investors might begin
to direct purchases through offshore routes to avoid or reduce the cost of withholding tax. However, abolishing the withholding tax on bonds for all, residents
and nonresidents alike, might create a distortion favoring bond markets over
equity markets.

CONCLUSION

Local debt markets in emerging Asia have made significant progress since 2000.
Market development reforms and the opening up of markets to foreign investors
have helped overcome the "original sin" problem and lengthened debt maturities
while enhancing liquidity and market depth. Importantly, corporate bond markets served as a "spare tire" during the global financial crisis, as intended, while
the banking system was deleveraging. Meanwhile, the recent corporate issuance
boom attests to the development of a "twin engines" financial system. However,
corporate bond market liquidity has lagged behind sovereign markets in most of
emerging Asia because of weaker foreign participation, as well as concerns about
corporate governance and resolution frameworks.

However, greater foreign participation has not only enhanced sovereign debt
market liquidity, it has also made yields more vulnerable to changes in global risk
aversion. Emerging market assets—in particular local debt markets—came under
heavy selling pressure following the Federal Reserve's announcement of a tapering
plan in June 2013. The prospect of higher interest rates, lower global liquidity,
and the growth slowdown in emerging Asia, led by China and India, resulted in
net outflows of capital along with a deterioration of trading and liquidity conditions. Such concerns were concentrated in the emerging market economies with
relatively high external (current account deficit) and domestic (inflation) imbalances. With more flexible exchange rates, policymakers allowed exchange rates to
take the brunt of the adjustments along with higher yields. This episode of stress
also showed that the domestic investor base (local pensions, mutual funds, and
insurance firms) can play a critical role as a shock absorber, highlighting the
importance of further financial deepening.

Asian capital markets have broadened and deepened since the global financial
crisis, but the following reform efforts are still needed:

- On pricing benchmarks, most sovereigns have developed the local currency
  government yield curve (also the credit curve) but liquidity across the maturity spectrum remains fragmented.

- Market liquidity has improved as the investor base has become more diverse,
  with a notable increase of foreign investors in local currency bonds. Markets
  could deepen even further if market makers were to take on a more active

role. Secondary market liquidity in most local currency bond markets has been hampered by the limited progress made in funding markets, such as developing the repo and securities lending markets.

- Market access has eased through progressive capital account liberalization, but impediments remain because of tax treatment and remaining capital controls.

- The physical market infrastructure (clearing, settlement, and custody) supporting Asian local bond markets has developed significantly but mainly in the larger markets. The infrastructure could benefit from the economies of scale of a regional link. Other impediments to improving the infrastructure include an embryonic legal and regulatory framework for nonbank financial institutions, weak corporate governance, inadequate information provision (including pricing transparency), the lack of hedging instruments, and the absence of a robust framework for asset-backed securitization. Additional barriers that affect both foreign and domestic investors include limited foreign exchange and interest rate hedging instruments, which require regulatory and legal frameworks related to derivatives markets.

ANNEX 4.1

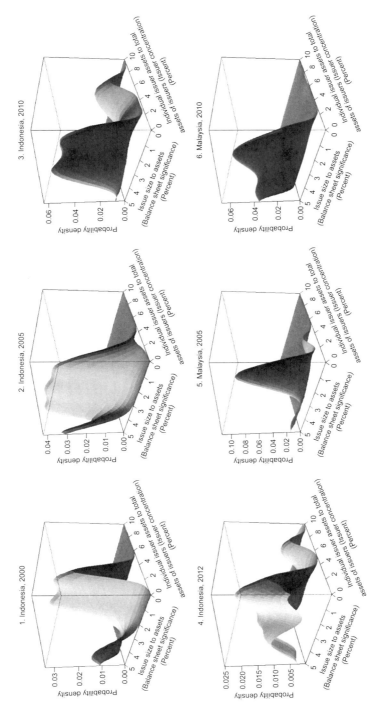

Annex Figure 4.1.1 Indonesia, Malaysia, and Thailand: Corporate Bond Issuance Relative to Total Assets Conditional on Issuer Concentration, 2000–2012

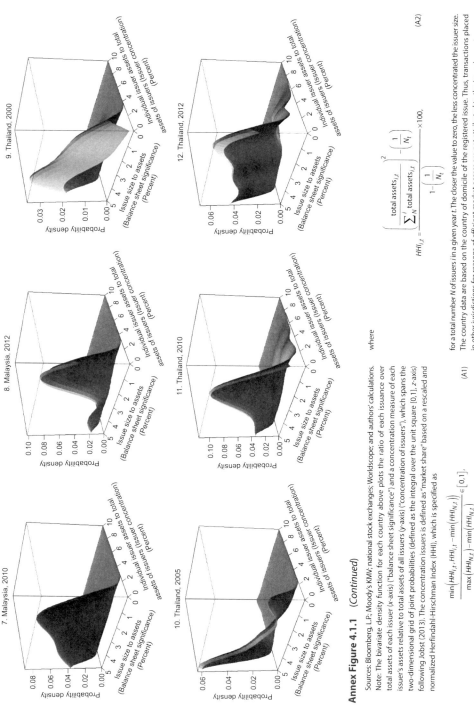

Annex Figure 4.1.1 *(Continued)*

Sources: Bloomberg, LP; Moody's KMV; national stock exchanges; Worldscope; and authors' calculations.

Note: The bivariate density function for each country above plots the ratio of each issuance over total assets of each issuer (x-axis) ("balance sheet significance") and a concentration measure of each issuer's assets relative to total assets of all issuers (y-axis) ("concentration of issuers"), which spans the two-dimensional grid of joint probabilities (defined as the integral over the unit square [0,1], z-axis) following Jobst (2013). The concentration issuers is defined as "market share" based on a rescaled and normalized Herfindahl-Hirschman Index (HHI), which is specified as

$$\frac{\min\left(HHI_{i,t}, HHI_{i,t} - \min\left(HHI_{N,t}\right)\right)}{\max\left(HHI_{N,t}\right) - \min\left(HHI_{N,t}\right)} \in [0,1], \tag{A1}$$

where

$$HHI_{i,t} = \frac{\left(\dfrac{\text{total assets}_{i,t}}{\sum_N' \text{total assets}_{i,t}}\right)^2 - \left(\dfrac{1}{N_t}\right)}{1 - \left(\dfrac{1}{N_t}\right)} \times 100, \tag{A2}$$

for a total number N of issuers i in a given year t. The closer the value to zero, the less concentrated the issuer size. The country data are based on the country of domicile of the registered issue. Thus, transactions placed in other jurisdictions for reasons of efficient market access are not attributed to the issuer's country.

REFERENCES

Agur, Itai, and Maria Demertzis. 2013. "Leaning against the Wind and the Timing of Monetary Policy." *Journal of International Money and Finance* 35 (C): 179–94.

Andritzky, Jochen R., Geoffrey J. Bannister, and Natalia T. Tamirisa. 2007. "The Impact of Macroeconomic Announcements on Emerging Market Bonds." *Emerging Markets Review* 8 (1): 20–37.

ASEAN Secretariat (Association of Southeast Asian Nations Secretariat). 2013. "Joint Ministerial Statement of the 17th ASEAN Finance Ministers' Meeting." Bandar Seri Begawan, Brunei Darussalam, April 3–4.

Asian Development Bank (ADB). 2010. "Asian Bond Markets Initiative Group of Experts Report." Asian Development Bank, Manila.

———. 2013a. *Asian Bond Market Monitor.* Manila: Asian Development Bank.

_____. 2013b. "Foreign Holdings in LCY Government Bonds." *AsianBondsOnline.* Manila: Asian Development Bank.

Azis, Iwan J., Sabyasachi Mitra, Anthony Baluga, and Roselle Dime. 2013. "The Threat of Financial Contagion to Emerging Asia's Local Bond Markets: Spillovers from Global Crises." Working Paper on Regional Economic Integration No. 106, Asian Development Bank, Manila.

Bank for International Settlements (BIS). 2013. *Locational Banking Statistics, International Financial Statistics.* Basel: Bank for International Settlements. http://www.bis.org/statistics/bankstats.htm.

Borio, Claudio E. V., and R. McCauley. 1996. "The Economics of Recent Bond Yield Volatility." BIS Economic Paper No. 45. Bank for International Settlements, Basel.

Brooks, Chris, and M. Currim Oozeer. 2002. "Modelling the Implied Volatility of Options on Long Gilt Futures." *Journal of Business Finance and Accounting* 29 (1&2): 111–37.

Caporale, Guglielmo M., and Geoffrey Williams. 2002. "Long-Term Nominal Interest Rates and Domestic Fundamentals." *Review of Financial Economics* 11 (2): 119–30.

Committee on the Global Financial System (CGFS). 2007. *Financial Stability and Local Currency Bond Markets.* CGFS Papers No. 28. Basel: Bank for International Settlements. http://www.bis.org/publ/cgfs28.htm.

———. 2009. "Capital Flows and Emerging Market Economies." CGFS Paper No. 33. Basel: Bank for International Settlements. http://www.bis.org/publ/cgfs33.htm.

Daniel, L. 2008. "Foreign Investors Participation in Emerging Market Economies' Domestic Bond Markets." *Bulletin Digest No. 173.* Banque de France, Paris.

Edwards, Sebastian. 1998. "Interest Rate Volatility, Contagion and Convergence: An Empirical Investigation of the Cases of Argentina, Chile and Mexico." *Journal of Applied Economics* 1 (May): 55–86.

Ehlers, Torsten, and Frank Packer. 2013. "FX and Derivatives Markets in Emerging Economies and the Internationalisation of Their Currencies." *BIS Quarterly Review* (December). Bank for International Settlements, Basel.

Eichengreen, B. 2006. "The Development of Asian Bond Markets." In *Asian Bond Markets: Issues and Prospects.* BIS Papers 30. Basel: Bank for International Settlements.

———, and R. Hausmann. 1999. "Exchange Rates and Financial Fragility." In *New Challenges for Monetary Policy, Conference Proceedings.* Kansas City, Kansas: Federal Reserve Bank of Kansas.

Felman, Joshua, Simon Gray, Mangal Goswami, Andreas Jobst, Mahmood Pradhan, Shanaka J. Peiris, and Dulani Seneviratne. 2011. "ASEAN5 Bond Market Development: Where Does It Stand? Where Is It Going?" IMF Working Paper No. 11/137, International Monetary Fund, Washington.

———. 2014. "ASEAN5 Bond Market Development: Where Does It Stand? Where Is It Going?" *Asia-Pacific Journal of Economic Literature* 28 (1): 60–75.

Gang, Xiao. 2014. Press Conference on Financial Reform. Second session of 12th National People's Congress (NPC), March 11 (Beijing).

Ghosh, Swati. 2006. *East Asian Finance: The Road to Robust Markets.* Washington: World Bank.

Gonzales-Rozada, Martin, and Eduardo Levy-Yeyati. 2006". "Global Factors and Emerging Market Spreads." Working Paper No. 552, Inter-American Development Bank. Washington.

Gray, Simon, Joshua Felman, Andreas A. Jobst, and Ana Carvajal. 2011. "Developing ASEAN5 Bond Markets: What Needs to Be Done?" IMF Working Paper No. 11/135, International Monetary Fund, Washington.

Guonan, Ma, Eli Remolona, and He Jianxiong. 2006. "Developing Corporate Bond Markets in Asia: A Synopsis of the Kunming Discussions." In *Developing Corporate Bond Markets in Asia*, BIS Papers, No. 26. Basel: Bank for International Settlements.

Gyntelberg, Jacob, Ma Guonan, and Eli Remolona. 2006. "Developing Corporate Bond Markets in Asia." In *Developing Corporate Bond Markets in Asia*, 13–21. Basel: Bank for International Settlements.

International Monetary Fund (IMF). 2005. "Development of Corporate Bond Markets in Emerging Market Countries." *Global Financial Stability Report.* Washington: International Monetary Fund, September.

———. 2009. "Annex 1.9. Methodologies Underlying Assessment of Bubble Risks." *Global Financial Stability Report.* Washington: International Monetary Fund, October.

———. 2014. "How Do Changes in the Investor Base and Financial Deepening Affect Emerging Market Economies?" *Global Financial Stability Report.* Washington: International Monetary Fund, April.

Jobst, Andreas A. 2013. "Multivariate Dependence of Implied Volatilities from Equity Options as Measure of Systemic Risk." *International Review of Financial Analysis* 28 (June): 112–29.

Kumar, Manmohan S., and Tatsuyoshi Okimoto. 2011. "Dynamics of International Integration of Government Securities' Markets." *Journal of Banking and Finance* 35 (1): 142–54.

Laubach, Thomas. 2009. "New Evidence on the Interest Rate Effects of Budget Deficits and Debt." *Journal of European Economic Association* 7 (4): 858–85.

Le Leslé, Vanessa, Franziska Ohnsorge, Minsuk Kim, and Srikant Seshadri. 2014. "Why Complementarity Matters for Stability—Hong Kong SAR and Singapore as Asian Financial Centers." IMF Working Paper No. 14/119, International Monetary Fund, Washington.

Noble, Josh. 2013. "China Bond Market Emerges from the Shadows." *Financial Times*, October 23. http://www.ft.com/intl/cms/s/0/4f0950da-3b98-11e3-87fa-00144feab7de .html#axzz2w2PaGqUu.

Peiris, Shanaka J. 2013. "Foreign Participation in Local Currency Bond Markets of Emerging Economies." *Journal of International Commerce, Economics and Policy* 4 (3): 1350016-1–1350016-15.

Turner, Philip. 2009. "How Have Local Currency Bond Markets in EMEs Weathered the Financial Crisis?" Presentation prepared for the 2nd International Workshop on Implementing G8 Action Plan, Frankfurt, Germany, November 12–13.

———. 2012. "Weathering Financial Crisis: Domestic Bond Markets in EMEs," BIS Papers chapters, in: Bank for International Settlements (ed.), Weathering Financial Crises: Bond Markets in Asia and the Pacific, volume 63, pages 15–34, Bank for International Settlements.

PART II

Where Is Asia Going?

CHAPTER 5

Is Asia Still Resilient?

Phakawa Jeasakul, Cheng Hoon Lim, and Erik Lundback

MAIN POINTS OF THIS CHAPTER

- Asia was less affected by the global financial crisis than were other regions because of its lower external and financial vulnerabilities. Asia had learned an important lesson during its own financial crisis in the late 1990s: good economic management is necessary, but not sufficient, to prevent a financial crisis.

- The market turmoil surrounding the U.S. Federal Reserve's tapering announcements in mid-2013 led to a repricing of global risk premiums. This episode provided the first test case of whether Asia could remain resilient in the face of more volatile external conditions following the global financial crisis.

- For the most part, Asian economies that did not binge on the easy global financing conditions after the global financial crisis were relatively unscathed by the "taper tantrum." By contrast, countries that did releverage and had higher domestic imbalances were hit by sudden stops and sharp asset price corrections.

- Nevertheless, underlying financial and economic fundamentals have shifted since the global financial crisis. A quantitative analysis comparing more recent conditions with those before the global financial crisis suggests that Asia has become less resilient. Causes include growing domestic imbalances from rapid credit growth and elevated house prices, higher leverage in the household and corporate sectors, and deteriorating external positions.

- To maintain its standing in the world as an engine of growth, Asia must proactively implement policies to guard against vulnerabilities while pushing ahead with structural reforms.

RESILIENCE DURING THE GLOBAL FINANCIAL CRISIS

Asia proved to be remarkably resilient in the face of the global financial crisis. The scale of capital outflows and the collapse in real activity in late 2008 were of the same magnitude as those experienced during the height of the Asian financial crisis in the late 1990s. This time, however, the outcome for Asia was markedly different. No full-blown financial crisis or sharp destructive external adjustments occurred. Asia was relatively resilient and able to preserve economic and financial stability even as the euro area encountered its worst economic and financial crisis in history and other major advanced economies, including the United Kingdom and the United States, struggled to regain their footing. The economies of several Asian countries, such as China and Indonesia, continued growing throughout the global financial crisis. And the economies of those Asian countries that experienced an initial steep decline in output, such as Korea, Malaysia, and Singapore, posted swift and robust recoveries.

Asia was resilient because of relatively low financial and external vulnerabilities, the result of a decade of financial and structural reform following the Asian financial crisis (Annex Table 5.1.1). In particular, the Asian financial crisis experience prompted many countries in Asia, including those less directly affected by the crisis, to embark on ambitious financial sector reform agendas. New laws and institutions were introduced to fill identified gaps in the regulatory and supervisory framework. Failed institutions were closed, while the remaining viable banks were recapitalized and their legacy nonperforming loans removed and sold to restore profitability. Risk-management policies, including rules on corporate governance and disclosure, were revamped with stiffer penalties set for unsafe and unsound banking practices, and supervisory authorities were given expanded powers to intervene and conduct regular examinations. Policymakers in Asia were also early adopters of what is now referred to as "macroprudential instruments." These include loan-to-value and debt-service-to-income restrictions, as well as limits on credit growth and on currency and maturity mismatches, all of which are aimed at mitigating systemic risk from excessive financial imbalances.[1]

At the same time, the private sector, including banks and firms, deleveraged and strengthened their balance sheets.[2] Rapid balance sheet restructuring was reflected in sharp declines in banks' provision of credit to the private sector, particularly in Indonesia, Malaysia, and Thailand. Financial institutions gradually cleaned up their balance sheets, improved risk management, and became more prudent in their risk taking and lending. Likewise, private firms undertook substantial deleveraging, enhanced corporate governance, and became more conservative in undertaking investment, which eventually restored corporate profitability, and strengthened transparency and competitiveness.

Another important reform was a shift toward policies to contain external vulnerabilities. Before the Asian financial crisis, currency pegs encouraged one-way bets that favored foreign currency borrowing, especially in Korea and some Association of Southeast Asian Nations (ASEAN) countries. When it became clear that the pegs were no longer sustainable as capital flowed rapidly out of the region, substantial balance sheet mismatches at banks and firms made the fallout from the devaluation that followed especially severe. In the aftermath of the Asian

---

[1] For an analysis of macroprudential tools and usage, see IMF (2013b). Lim and others (2011) provide a comprehensive overview of global country experiences, including Asian countries.

[2] Gourinchas and Obstfeld (2012) identify the rapid buildup of leverage as a key precursor to financial crises in emerging market and advanced economies.

financial crisis, Asia reduced its vulnerability to contagion and sudden stops of capital flows by more closely monitoring external borrowing and net open foreign exchange positions while accumulating foreign reserves.[3] These efforts allowed greater exchange rate flexibility.

These structural reforms reduced Asia's financial and external vulnerabilities and enabled the region to quickly recover and sustain strong output performance during the global financial crisis. On a weighted average basis, Jeasakul, Lim, and Lundback (2014) find that the drop in output in Asia in the immediate period after the global financial crisis was 3.8 and 1.4 percentage points less than it was in Europe and the Western Hemisphere, respectively; they also find that the recovery period was shorter by about 5.4 and 5 quarters, respectively. As a result, the cumulative output loss in Asia was 21 and 16 percent of annualized 2008:Q3 GDP less than it was in the other two regions, respectively. The study showed that initial financial and external conditions at the time of the global financial crisis were critical to explaining differences in the resilience of economies. In particular, indicators used to capture the degree of financial and external vulnerabilities were statistically and economically significant when tested against output performance.[4]

The results indicate that the combination of *financial factors* (modest credit growth, limited reliance on noncore funding, and improved bank asset quality and capitalization) and *external factors* (reduced external debt, strengthened current account balances, and significant accumulation of foreign reserves) could explain 60 to 84 percent of the difference in the cumulative output loss between Asia and Europe, and 49 to 65 percent of the difference between Asia and the Western Hemisphere (Figure 5.1). Standard macroeconomic variables such as inflation, public debt, and the fiscal balance were also included in the analysis, but were not found to be significant in explaining cross-country differences. This is not to say that macroeconomic fundamentals did not matter in explaining output performance.[5] Macroeconomic fundamentals in Asia were sound going into the global financial crisis, but this was also true for many of the countries at

---

[3] Aizenman, Pinto, and Sushko (2012) examine episodes of financial sector booms and contractions, and conclude that the effects on the real economy from abrupt financial contractions are mitigated by buffers of foreign reserves.

[4] Output performance is defined as the cumulative real GDP loss or gain from the 2013:Q3 level through 2010:Q4. Economic resilience minimizes the output loss for each country as estimated in a series of bivariate regressions $y_i = \alpha + \beta x_i + \varepsilon_i$, in which y_i is output performance in country i and x_i is an indicator capturing the degree of financial or external vulnerabilities in country i before the global financial crisis. Other definitions, measuring the depth of the output decline from precrisis peak to trough, or the length of time it takes for output to recover to the 2008:Q3 level, were also used with qualitatively similar results.

[5] In a related study, Park, Ramayandi, and Shin (2013) analyze factors explaining output performance in countries that have experienced a currency crisis. They find that basic macroeconomic conditions such as inflation and GDP growth before a crisis can explain output performance. However, their focus is on comparing the experiences during the Asian and global financial crises of the five Asian economies that were hit the hardest during the Asian financial crisis, and not on the differences in output performance between Asia and other countries and regions.

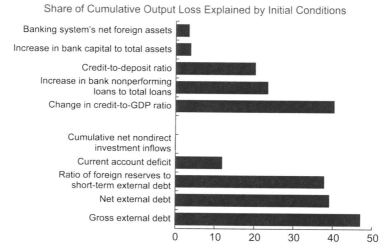

Figure 5.1 The Relative Importance of Financial and External Vulnerabilities in Explaining Differences in Output Performance between Asia and Other Regions (*Share of cumulative output loss explained by initial conditions*)

Source: IMF staff estimates.
Note: For each region, the share of cumulative output loss (relative to Asia) explained by a particular initial condition is calculated as its estimated output loss (relative to Asia) divided by its actual output loss (relative to Asia). Then, the shares of individual regions are aggregated and weighted by regional GDP. The estimated output loss is based on the bivariate regression analysis.

the epicenter of the crisis. Asia and many of the advanced economies shared common attributes: low inflation, fiscal surpluses or small deficits, and public debt that was generally below 60 percent of GDP (with the exception of Japan). These indicators were not exceptionally more favorable in Asia compared with the rest of the world. Thus, while credible and consistent macroeconomic policies were necessary to support a stable economy, they alone are not sufficient to explain cross-country differences in resilience during the global financial crisis.

Another important factor contributing to Asia's resilience was its regional dynamism and, in particular, China's strong economic performance. Asia is one of the most dynamic and fastest growing regions in the world, with trade and supply chains that help individual economies sustain each other's growth momentum. China's robust growth and appetite for commodities was a boon to regional growth and to commodity exporters such as Australia, Indonesia, and Malaysia. Rough estimates suggest that Asian economies on average gained 1.2 percentage points for each additional percentage point increase in the growth of its partners.

EMERGING MARKET STRESS IN 2013 AND EARLY 2014

After several years of easy monetary and financial conditions following the global financial crisis, emerging markets came under stress again between mid-2013 and early 2014 (Figure 5.2). In testifying to Congress in May 2013, Federal Reserve

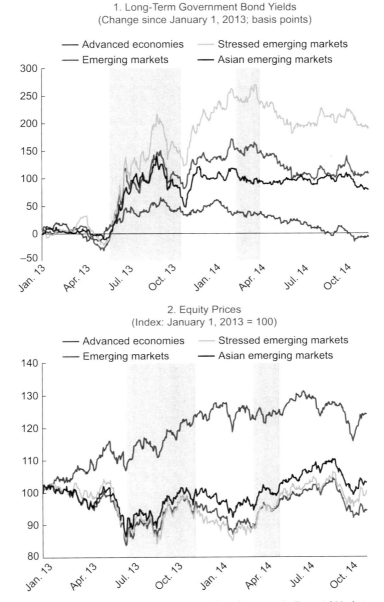

1. Long-Term Government Bond Yields
(Change since January 1, 2013; basis points)

— Advanced economies — Stressed emerging markets
— Emerging markets — Asian emerging markets

2. Equity Prices
(Index: January 1, 2013 = 100)

— Advanced economies — Stressed emerging markets
— Emerging markets — Asian emerging markets

Figure 5.2 Selected Economies: Divergent Developments in Financial Markets
Sources: Bloomberg, L.P.; and IMF staff calculations.

Chairman Bernanke raised the possibility of the Federal Reserve tapering its purchases of Treasury and agency bonds. The announcement sent financial shock waves to many emerging markets and triggered sharp corrections in emerging market asset prices and exchange rates, as well as a reversal in capital flows (Sahay and others 2014).[6] Market reaction was indiscriminate in the first few weeks of volatility as investors abruptly revised their expectations of future interest rate hikes in anticipation of an earlier-than-expected tightening of monetary policy by the Federal Reserve.[7] Subsequent market reaction was more differentiated, and countries with larger external financing needs and macro-financial imbalances—such as Brazil, India, Indonesia, South Africa, and Turkey—came under greater pressure. For example, India and Indonesia, respectively, saw a 140 and 280 basis point increase in their bond yields and 15 percent depreciation in their exchange rates between May and September 2013. Indonesia also suffered significant reserve losses because it initially used foreign exchange interventions (partly directed toward meeting the foreign currency needs of the oil and gas state-owned-enterprise) to limit the rupiah's depreciation. Emerging Asia as a whole, however, was less affected than were other emerging markets, and the rise in long-term rates and decline in equity prices were somewhat smaller. Markets calmed after the Federal Reserve announced a delay in tapering in September 2013 and provided assurances that tapering would be conditional on the recovery of the U.S. economy.

However, during January and February of 2014, global market volatility reemerged. The main contributing factors were lingering concerns about tapering; country-specific imbalances; and idiosyncratic factors, such as Argentina's debt litigation proceedings and signs of slowing growth in China. This time, market reaction was quick to differentiate, and India and Indonesia, which were seen to have taken more comprehensive policy actions to address domestic imbalances since the 2013 taper tantrum, were relatively unscathed compared with other emerging markets. India's and Indonesia's long-term bond yields stabilized, their exchange rates strengthened, and stock prices recovered strongly. By comparison, some other emerging markets, including Argentina, Kazakhstan, and Ukraine, experienced relatively large declines in reserves and sizable exchange rate pressures. Brazil, Turkey, and South Africa, which had tightened monetary policy in response to the earlier bout of volatility, saw bond yields increase but not to the degree seen in the earlier bout. Market turbulence subsided after advanced economies—especially the United Kingdom and the United States—showed signs of economic recovery. Credit risks declined and risk appetite returned. Financial markets in advanced economies rallied, which increased asset prices and compressed spreads relative to emerging market high-yield bonds and equities. Capital inflows to emerging markets resumed in April 2014.

---

[6] See IMF (2014c) and Sahay and others (2014) for an analysis of the impact of the Federal Reserve's tapering announcements on emerging market asset prices and capital flows, and the different reactions across countries.

[7] Systemic liquidity mismatches appeared to have amplified the price reactions. Large increases in nonresident holdings of local currency debt coincided with a decline in liquidity conditions in secondary markets, which can create larger market price fluctuations during periods of outflows even if the outflows are small. See the IMF's October 2014 *Global Financial Stability Report* (IMF 2014a).

FUNDAMENTALS DO MATTER

The 2013–14 stress episodes show, once again, that economic and financial fundamentals matter in ensuring countries' resilience to shocks. No single fundamental matters for all countries at all times, given that markets appear to focus on different fundamentals at different times (Sahay and others 2014). Typically, however, countries with large external financing needs, low growth prospects, financial vulnerabilities, and rising public deficit or high inflation become easy targets (Figure 5.3).[8] In Asia, both India and Indonesia were struggling with current account deficits, relatively low reserves, and persistent inflation in the period leading up to the tapering announcement. Indonesia had also seen a period of accelerating credit growth and rising credit-to-deposit ratios. In India, credit growth had been weak, but the overhang of corporate debt, rising nonperforming and restructured loans, and persistent large fiscal deficits raised concerns—and at a time when potential growth appeared to be slowing because of structural bottlenecks.

Both countries took measures starting in the summer of 2013 to address domestic imbalances. Indonesia raised interest rates, scaled back its intervention, and allowed the rupiah to adjust to market conditions. It also implemented measures to increase liquidity and ease pressures on the exchange rate, including the following:

- Holding biweekly auctions of foreign exchange swaps with resident banks, and allowing derivatives positions held by banks to be passed on to the central bank through the swap auctions

- Extending the maturities of U.S. dollar term deposits offered by the central bank

- Relaxing the rules on foreign exchange purchases by exporters to encourage repatriation

- Shortening the minimum holding period of central bank bills to increase market liquidity

Indonesia also strengthened macroprudential measures and embarked on fiscal consolidation, including cutting energy subsidies. India raised interest rates and took additional actions by relaxing the limits on foreign direct investment and external borrowing, introducing capital flow measures, increasing gold import duties, and tightening fiscal policy.

These efforts paid off, and as the policies started to take effect and gain credibility, the Indian rupee and the Indonesia rupiah recovered, and the Indian stock market reached an all-time high in late 2013. That upward trend continued in 2014. Indeed, capital flows to emerging Asia as a whole were, as noted by the Institute of International Finance (2015), well sustained in 2014, helped by

---

[8]The analysis of factors explaining cross-country experiences during 2013 and early 2014 is very much ongoing, but there is agreement that external vulnerabilities and macro imbalances (in particular, current account deficits, high inflation, and fiscal imbalances) have been key in setting countries apart. See, for example, IMF (2014b) and Mishra, Moriyama, and N'Diaye (2014).

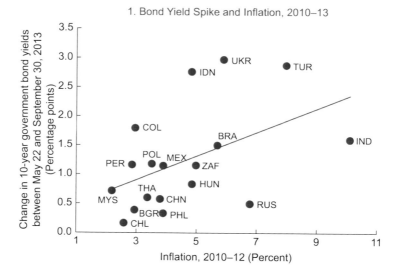

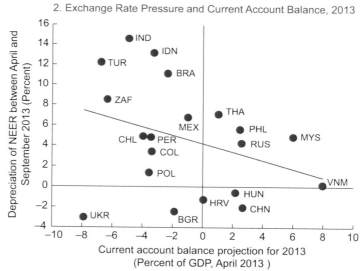

Figure 5.3 Emerging Market Economies: Market Reactions and Macroeconomic Fundamentals

Sources: IMF, Information Notice System and World Economic Outlook database; and IMf staff calculations.
Note: BRA = Brazil; BGR = Bulgaria; CHL = Chile; CHN = China; COL = Colombia; HRV = Croatia; HUN = Hungary; IND = India; IDN = Indonesia; MYS = Malaysia; MEX = Mexico; PER = Peru; PHL = Philippines; POL = Poland; RUS = Russia; ZAF = South Africa; THA = Thailand; TUR = Turkey; UKR = Ukraine; VNM = Vietnam; NEER = nominal effective exchange rate.

strengthened fundamentals, although the region experienced a phase of volatility late in the year triggered by changes in global risk appetite and the oil price slump. These sustained capital flows were due to generally strong regional growth, corrective policies, the election of pro-reform governments in India and Indonesia,

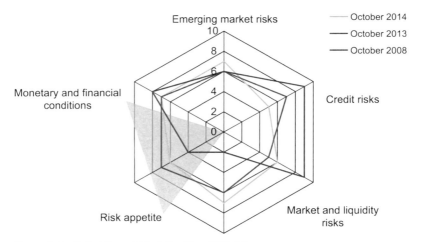

Figure 5.4 Global Financial Stability Map, 2008–14

Sources: IMF, *Global Financial Stability Reports* (2008, 2013a, 2014a).

Note: Away from center signifies higher risks, easier monetary and financial conditions, or higher risk appetite.

and a return to a functioning administration in Thailand—all of which sup-ported market sentiment.[9] Still, the favorable sentiment toward Asia was to some extent a reflection of the region's relative position rather than of the absolute strength of underlying fundamentals and policies.

RISING VULNERABILITIES AND NEW CHALLENGES

Although Asia easily withstood the market turmoil in 2013–14, the experience nevertheless revealed that vulnerabilities have been rising. A bird's-eye view pro-vided by the *Global Financial Stability Report*'s global financial stability map (Figure 5.4) shows that, although credit risks in advanced economies have declined since 2008, emerging market risks have risen in step with global risk appetite. Monetary and financial conditions were loose in 2014 compared with conditions in 2008, but they became tighter than in 2013. This is consistent with a closer look at Asia, where financial, external, and macroeconomic developments since 2008 appear to have moved the region to a more vulnerable position.

Financial Developments

- *Credit growth*—Credit growth has accelerated significantly since 2008 com-pared with the period before the global financial crisis, when the ratio of outstanding credit to GDP actually declined in several countries (Figure 5.5). In particular, China, Hong Kong SAR, Malaysia, Singapore, and Thailand have gone from moderate to strong credit growth. To some extent, this robust credit growth reflects desirable financial deepening and market

---

[9] See Institute of International Finance (2015). The conclusions are based on estimates for the whole of 2014.

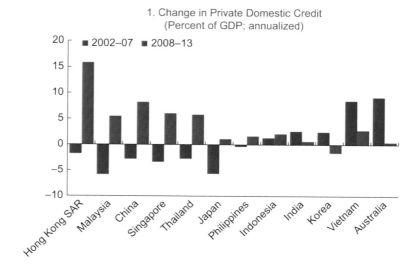

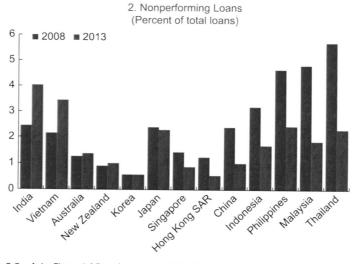

Figure 5.5 Asia: Financial Developments, 2002–13

development in these economies. However, rapid credit growth also raises concerns—especially for low-income households and small and medium-sized enterprises—if most of the credit is channeled to the property sector and household and corporate balance sheets are stretched.

- *Household debt*—Household debt has increased sharply in China, Indonesia, Singapore, and Thailand, where the household-debt-to-GDP ratio has jumped by 50 percent or more since 2008. Debt levels in Malaysia and Thailand are above 60 percent of GDP. Although some of the risk is

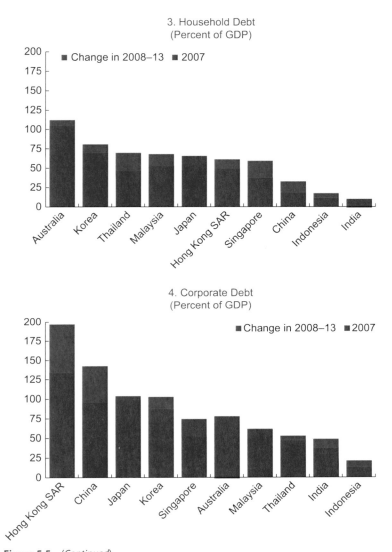

3. Household Debt
(Percent of GDP)

4. Corporate Debt
(Percent of GDP)

Figure 5.5 (*Continued*)

Sources: Bank for International Settlements, Credit to Private Sector data; IMF, *International Financial Statistics*, Financial Soundness Indicators database, and World Economic Outlook database; and IMF staff calculations.

mitigated by increased household wealth, leveraged households are likely to be more susceptible than are nonleveraged households to an unexpected or faster tightening of global monetary and financial conditions, sharp corrections in house prices, or a slowdown in domestic growth.

- *Corporate debt*—Corporate debt has increased by more than 40 percent in China, Hong Kong SAR, Indonesia, and Singapore since 2008. This rise is modest in comparison with the spike in leverage observed in the mid-1990s.

Nevertheless, there is reason to be concerned about already highly leveraged and weaker companies being increasingly exposed to shocks, in, for example, India and Indonesia (IMF 2014c, 2014d). In China, the buildup of debt is concentrated in a "fat tail" of highly leveraged large firms, mostly in real estate and construction. State-owned enterprises' leverage ratios also have edged up. In Korea, risks are concentrated in a few vulnerable industries including construction, shipbuilding, and transportation, as a result of profitability pressures, liquidity risks, and high leverage.

- *Bank balance sheets*—One bright spot is Asian banks, which tend to be well capitalized and liquid, and where supervision is broadly strong (see Chapter 11). Total capital levels have increased across many countries although they remain below those in other regions. Banks are mostly funded by retail deposits, and the ratio of loans to deposits has actually declined slightly since the period before the global financial crisis, limiting concerns about dependence on potentially destabilizing noncore funding. Overall, the ratio of nonperforming loans to total loans has declined, though not by nearly as much as during the period before the global financial crisis, when many Asian countries were repairing bank balance sheets. Banks' profitability has improved as growth has boosted non-interest revenues, but the acceleration in credit growth of the past few years could pose asset quality issues down the road.

- *Nonbank lending*—Across Asia, nonbank lending, which is lightly regulated, has increased substantially. This activity is most evident in China, where nonbank financial intermediation doubled between 2010 and 2013, fueling a real estate market boom in major cities (see Chapter 2). Nonbank lending has also increased in other countries, such as Korea, Malaysia, and Thailand, where lending by specialized and nonbank financial institutions has contributed a large portion to the rise in household debt.

External Developments

- *Current account*—Current account surpluses have narrowed since the global financial crisis, and some countries are in deficit (Figure 5.6). Indonesia has gone from surplus to deficit partly because of a significant terms-of-trade shock, notwithstanding some improvement due to weaker domestic demand and a more competitive exchange rate. In India the current account deficit has narrowed thanks to direct measures aimed at curbing gold imports, weak domestic demand, and some revival in exports, but is still in deficit. Current accounts in other Asian countries are still fairly strong overall. Lower surpluses partly reflect the relative strength of the region's economies, as well as its progress in shifting away from an export-driven to a consumption-based growth model.

- *External debt*—The decline in current account surpluses, however, has been accompanied by an increase in external debt, especially in China, India, and Malaysia. In addition, some of the increased borrowing, notably in China,

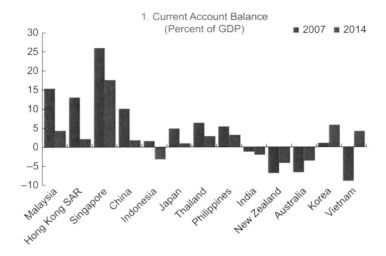

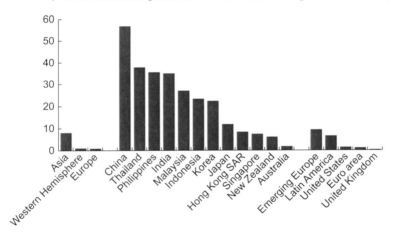

Figure 5.6 Asia: External Developments, 2007–14

Sources: IMF, *International Financial Statistics* and World Economic Outlook database; and IMF staff calculations.

Indonesia, and the Philippines, has been of shorter maturities, making the countries more vulnerable to sudden stops. India also appears to be increasingly financing its current account deficit with debt flows, including in the form of nonresident Indian deposits and external commercial borrowing by leveraged Indian firms. In Indonesia, firms are resorting to external borrowing because domestic lending rates have increased and external spreads have declined, leading to rapidly rising private external debt (including by state-owned enterprises).

- *Reserves*—Asian countries still have large foreign reserves as buffers against capital flow volatility. Thanks to recent policy actions to address vulnerabilities, India, Indonesia, and other Asian emerging markets were able to weather the bout of global financial volatility in January 2014 with only limited use of their reserves to counter currency pressures. Indeed, for most Asian countries, reserves ended up higher in 2014 than they had been a year earlier, with the main exceptions being Indonesia and Thailand (IMF 2014d). Still, the foreign reserves coverage of short-term external debt is below levels in effect before the global financial crisis.

Macroeconomic Developments

- *Fiscal positions*—With a few exceptions, fiscal positions in the region have weakened relative to historical benchmarks because the fiscal policy responses in the wake of the global financial crisis have not been fully unwound (Figure 5.7). Medium-term fiscal risks could be large because of federal contingent liabilities in the form of loan guarantees, insured deposits, and other obligations. Although fiscal deficits in India and Vietnam are fairly sizable, for emerging Asia as a whole, fiscal balances are strong and debt levels appear manageable, and not a cause for near-term concern.

- *Inflation*—Inflation is generally low, and contained inflation expectations provide welcome monetary policy space. The exceptions are India and, to a lesser extent, Indonesia. India's high and persistent inflation remains a policy concern and is projected to decline only gradually. In Indonesia, inflation expectations appear well anchored despite a recent uptick in prices following a subsidized fuel price hike.

- *Growth outlook*—The growth outlook for Asia is solid, but with clear downside risks, and supply-side constraints appear to have reduced potential output. The October 2014 *World Economic Outlook* (IMF 2014b) and *Regional Economic Outlook: Asia and Pacific* (IMF 2014d) pointed to financial dislocations associated with higher global interest rates and protracted weak growth in advanced and emerging market economies as the main downside risks to the outlook. Advanced economies, in particular, may face low potential output growth and "secular stagnation," given that robust demand growth has not yet emerged despite a prolonged period of very low interest rates and increased risk appetite in financial markets. Geopolitical tensions, including turmoil in the Middle East and international tensions surrounding the situation in Russia and Ukraine, could also disrupt trade and financial flows. These tensions could take a toll on market confidence, with adverse effects on growth. In the near term, slower growth in China is seen as a healthy development, but the region could be adversely affected if the slowdown is more acute than expected, or if growth-supporting policies in Japan are not as effective as envisaged. Overall, Asia is expected to continue to drive the global economic engine, but it may do so at a slower pace. *World Economic Outlook* forecasts for real GDP growth in emerging Asia

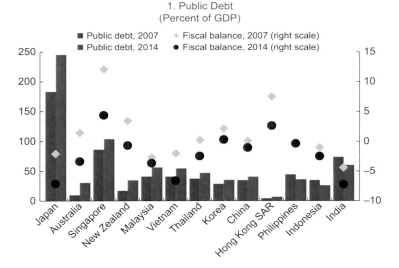

1. Public Debt
(Percent of GDP)

2. Emerging Asia: Real GDP Growth from World Economic Outlook (Percent)

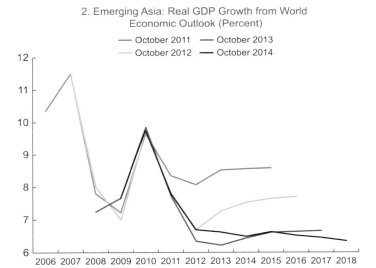

Figure 5.7 Asia: Macroeconomic Vulnerabilities, 2006–18

Sources: IMF, World Economic Outlook database; and IMF staff calculations.
Note: Each vintage graph shows actual numbers up to the previous year and projections thereafter.

have been gradually pared down since 2011 even though potential growth in Asia is still higher than it is in other regions.[10] The reasons behind the lower growth prospects vary across economies, and include deceleration or a leveling off of total factor productivity growth in key Asian economies

---

[10] Based on comparison of outer year forecasts in the World Economic Outlook database for April 2009 and 2014.

(ASEAN, with an exception of the Philippines); a rebalancing of growth away from investment; less dependence of the economy on credit (China); and supply bottlenecks in infrastructure, power, and mining (India).

These developments suggest that Asia has become less resilient to shocks than it was before the global financial crisis. On the *financial* front, although bank balance sheets appear strong, risks have increased because of accelerated credit growth. This growth has come through nonbank lending and through substantially higher levels of household and corporate debt. *External* positions still appear to be relatively strong, and large reserves are providing buffers. However, current accounts have deteriorated and external debt, including shorter-maturity debt, has increased in several countries. Also, *macroeconomic* vulnerabilities have increased because fiscal positions have weakened and growth prospects have been revised down, even though the growth outlook is still solid.

Resilience: How Would Asia Fare Today Given a Global-Financial-Crisis-Sized Shock?

Given these developments, how resilient is Asia today, compared with its resilience during the global financial crisis period? In other words, what would be the impact on output performance today if Asia were hit by shocks similar in size to the shocks during the global financial crisis? Applying the methodology used by Jeasakul, Lim, and Lundback (2014) to financial and external conditions at end-2013, the analysis finds that Asia looks less resilient today compared with during the global financial crisis period (Table 5.1). There would be a larger output loss of some 6½ to 8½ percent of GDP compared with the loss witnessed following the global financial crisis if Asia were to be hit by similar shocks (Table 5.1).

The rise in both financial and external vulnerabilities has contributed to this estimated reduced resilience to shocks comparable to those of the global financial crisis. The rapid expansion in private sector credit explains the bulk of the cumulative decline in output loss, roughly an estimated 7 percentage points of GDP.[11] The estimated cumulative effects of higher external debt and lower current account surpluses (or higher deficits) explain about 1 to 2½ percentage points of GDP. Nevertheless, the current deterioration in macro-financial conditions in Asia is nowhere near the scale seen in the period leading up to the 1997–98 Asian financial crisis for the crisis countries. Moreover, current conditions in Asian countries would still lead to a better outcome for Asia today compared with other regions during the global financial crisis. The results of this analysis suggest that Asia is still in a strong position, but that emerging vulnerabilities, fueled by cheap and plentiful money since the global financial crisis, have made it more susceptible to shocks. The 2013–14 episodes were a first test of Asia's resilience since the global financial crisis.

---

[11] Estimated effect from bivariate regression, 2008:Q3 annualized real GDP (Table 5.1).

TABLE 5.1.

Estimated Impact on Output Performance Using End-2013 Initial Conditions and Shock Equivalent to Global Financial Crisis

	Initial Conditions				Estimated Impact on Output Performance[1]
	Asian financial crisis countries	All Asia			
	Before Asian financial crisis	Before Asian financial crisis	Before global financial crisis	End-2013	Cumulative output gain (percent of GDP)
Change in ratio of credit to GDP	4.6	1.9	−1.6	4.4	−7.0
Increase in bank nonperforming loans to total loans	...	...	−7.0	−0.6	−1.3
Banking system's net foreign assets	−7.3	−0.4	7.8	3.6	−0.6
Increase in ratio of bank capital to total assets	...	...	1.1	0.8	−0.1
Credit-to-deposit ratio	142.5	105.5	88.2	86.0	0.3
Cumulative net nondirect investment inflows	4.2	0.5	0.9	4.5	−2.7
Gross external debt	40.8	23.3	16.2	23.3	−2.5
Net external debt	...	...	−5.4	5.5	−2.0
Current account deficit	4.5	0.4	−5.4	−1.3	−1.5
Ratio of foreign reserves to short-term debt	72.6	109.4	440.9	385.7	−1.0
Preferred multivariate specifications:[2]					
Net external debt					−8.3
Ratio of foreign reserves to short-term debt					−7.4
Gross external debt					−6.7

Source: IMF staff estimates.
[1]The difference in estimated cumulative output gain following a global shock between the global financial crisis and end-2013.
[2]Multivariate regressions are based on change in the ratio of credit to GDP, increase in bank nonperforming loans to total loans, credit-to-deposit ratio, and one of the following external vulnerability indicators: gross external debt, net external debt, and ratio of foreign reserves to short-term external debt.

CONCLUSION

Asia proved to be remarkably resilient during the global financial crisis when many advanced economies around the world succumbed to a financial and economic meltdown. This strength reflected the lessons learned from the Asian financial crisis of the late 1990s. That crisis triggered wide-ranging financial and structural reforms that led to stronger banks, improved corporate governance, more sustainable current account balances, and a stockpile of foreign reserves to cushion a sudden reversal of capital inflows. The active use of macroprudential policies well before they were recognized as an essential component of the financial stability toolkit, and the overhaul of Asia's financial regulation and oversight framework, forced positive changes in risk taking by households and firms. In addition, Asian economies benefited from being part of a fast-growing region with momentum from trading partner growth. These conditions helped the region recover quickly from the global crisis after an initial decline in output.

The financial market turmoil in 2013–14 was the first test of Asia's resilience since the global financial crisis. Although the turmoil was not caused by the kind of broad and massive global shocks that triggered the global financial crisis, the experience of Asian economies demonstrated once again that economic and financial fundamentals matter, and that strong policies—both preventive and remedial—pay off. Across the world, countries with larger external financing needs and macro-financial imbalances came under greater pressure. Asia withstood the test well, but it was clear that, for the first time since 2008, rising vulnerabilities weighed on market sentiment. This chapter's quantitative comparison of current macro-financial conditions with those prevailing before the global financial crisis suggests that Asia's domestic imbalances have grown. The influx of cheap money from abroad has encouraged rapid credit growth, which has, in turn, resulted in more leveraged household and corporate sectors, elevated house prices, and higher external debt. Supply-side constraints, including those caused by infrastructure bottlenecks, have also dampened growth prospects.

Asia remains the world's engine of growth, but in the future, it may well have to adjust to rates of economic growth lower than those reached during the boom before the global financial crisis. Making the transition to this "new normal" will be a challenge that policymakers in Asia will no doubt rise to meet. However, policymakers will need to summon the political will to push ahead with structural reforms to deliver sustainable growth while at the same time strengthening fiscal and macroprudential policies to contain systemic risks, and provide the room to take countercyclical measures, should the need arise.

ANNEX 5.1

ANNEX TABLE 5.1.1

Financial Sector Reforms Following the Asian Financial Crisis

Indonesia

Amendments to the banking law

- Modified requirements regarding bank secrecy
- Ended restrictions on foreign ownership of banks
- Enabled the Indonesian Bank Restructuring Agency to transfer assets and to foreclose on a nonperforming debtor

Strengthening the prudential and regulatory framework

- New regulations regarding loan classification, loan provisioning, and the treatment of debt restructuring operations
- New liquidity management reporting requirements: Banks required to submit liquidity reports twice monthly for their global consolidated operations, including the foreign currency liquidity profile and actions that the bank intends to take to cover any liquidity shortfall or absorb any liquidity surplus
- New regulations to tighten rules for connected lending
- Disclosure of financial statements: Banks required to publish their financial statements quarterly, beginning April 1999

Banks resolution framework

The Deposit Insurance Corporation (Lembaga Penjamin Simpanan) Law of 2004 established a coordination committee comprising the Ministry of Finance, the Bank of Indonesia, and the Lembaga Penjamin Simpanan to determine the policy for the resolution and handling of a failing bank that is expected to have a systemic effect

Korea

Reforms of institutional arrangements, based on Presidential Commission on Financial Reform in 1997

- Significantly strengthened the independence of the Bank of Korea
- Consolidated financial sector supervision in a single Financial Supervisory Commission and unified supervisory authority (the Financial Supervisory Service), separate from the government
- Legislation to grant the Financial Supervisory Commission power to license and delicense financial institutions, as well as to supervise specialized and development banks
- Merged deposit insurance protection agencies into the new Korea Deposit Insurance Corporation, which was provided with powers and funds to pay back deposits in failed institutions and, if necessary, to provide recapitalization funds to banks
- Established a Financial Restructuring Unit within the Financial Supervisory Commission to oversee and coordinate the restructuring of the financial sector

Strengthened prudential standards and supervision procedures

- New loan classification standards and provisioning rules under which loans more than three months overdue are classified as substandard; general provisioning requirement increased.
- Regulations to require provisioning for securities losses and to discontinue the inclusion in Tier 2 capital of all provisions for nonperforming loans
- Loan classification and provisioning guidelines to take into account a borrower's future capacity to repay in classifying and provisioning loans
- Strengthened prudential supervision and regulation of foreign exchange operations by commercial and merchant banks, including requiring short-term assets to cover at least 70 percent of short-term liabilities, and long-term borrowing to cover more than 50 percent of long-term assets
- Banks to maintain overall foreign currency exposure limits per counterparty, including foreign currency loans, guarantees, security investments, and offshore finance
- A maturity ladder approach requiring banks to report maturity mismatches for different time brackets, and with limits on mismatches
- Limits on exposures to single borrowers and groups, and tightened regulations for connected lending
- Full foreign ownership of merchant banks allowed

(continued)

ANNEX TABLE 5.1.1

Financial Sector Reforms Following the Asian Financial Crisis (*Continued*)

Malaysia

Measures to strengthen the financial sector introduced in 1998

- Stricter loan classification and provisioning standards: Classification standards to be brought to best practice standards; 20 percent provisioning requirement against uncollateralized portions of substandard loans; off-balance-sheet items incorporated in the loan classification and provisioning system
- Tightened rules for accounting interest in suspense, such that banks would be required to reverse unpaid interest out of income and record it in the interest-in-suspense account
- Tighter capital adequacy framework: Increased risk-weighted capital adequacy requirements of finance companies from 8 percent to 10 percent; minimum capital for finance companies increased from 5 million ringgit to 300 million ringgit; compliance with capital adequacy requirement required each financial quarter
- Single borrower limit reduced from 30 percent to 25 percent of capital funds
- Aggregate statistics on nonperforming loans, provisions, and capital positions for all financial institutions to be published monthly by the Bank Negara Malaysia
- All institutions to report and publish key indicators of financial soundness on a quarterly basis; banks required to report on the ratio of nonperforming loans broken down into substandard, doubtful, and loss; loans by sectors on a quarterly basis
- More intensive and rigorous supervision of banks through monthly stress tests by Bank Negara Malaysia and a requirement for similar exercises by individual institutions on the basis of parameters set by Bank Negara Malaysia
- A prudentially based framework for assessing bank liquidity risks was introduced, effective August 2, 1998
- Bank Negara Malaysia facilitated the merger program of finance companies on market-based criteria

Ten-Year Financial Sector Masterplan for 2001–10

- Bank merger program designed to take advantage of economies of scale and to determine an exit strategy for the weakest banks; domestic banks given broad flexibility to form their own merger groups
- Changes to regulation and supervision in line with best practices, including implementing risk-based supervision with more focused supervisory attention for weak institutions, refined calculation of risk weightings for capital adequacy, implementation of a system of incremental enforcement action, and early warning system

Philippines

Broad financial sector reform program

- Raised minimum capital requirements for banks, and phased out lower capital requirements for certain universal banks
- Banks required to make a general loan-loss provision of 2 percent and specific loan-loss provisions of 5 percent for loans specifically mentioned, and 25 percent for secured substandard loans
- The Bangko Sentral ng Pilipinas required banks to start marking to market their trading securities portfolio
- All banks listed on the Philippine Stock Exchange instructed to publicly disclose detailed information on a quarterly basis, including the level of nonperforming loans, and the ratio of nonperforming loans to the total loan portfolio
- Consolidated supervision of financial conglomerates
- Stricter licensing guidelines for establishing banks, focusing on the statement of income and expenses; evidence of asset ownership; and in the case of a foreign bank, certification by the home supervisory authority that it agrees with the proposed investment
- Changed focus of supervision activities from compliance-based and checklist-driven assessments of banks' condition to a forward-looking and risk-based framework
- Improved rating methodologies. The capital adequacy, asset quality, management quality, earnings, sensitivity to market risk (CAMELS) rating system revised, including to ensure that the composite rating will never be better than the bank's individual factor rating for capital adequacy
- External auditors of banks required to report to the Bangko Sentral ng Pilipinas all matters that could adversely affect the financial condition of their clients, any serious irregularity that may jeopardize the interests of depositors and creditors, and any losses incurred that substantially reduce the bank's capital

ANNEX TABLE 5.1.1

Financial Sector Reforms Following the Asian Financial Crisis (*Continued*)

Addressing recognition and resolution of weak banks

- Intensified bank monitoring of selected banks
- Measures to improve the ability of the Philippine Deposit Insurance Corporation to act as the receiver of banks, including selling assets of distressed banks to pay for the administration costs related to receivership, and faster approval by the Monetary Board of a proposed liquidation
- Prompt corrective action and explicit procedures for bank capital shortfalls

Later measures

- Memorandum of Agreement between the Securities and Exchange Commission and the Bangko Sentral ng Pilipinas (2001)
- Anti-Money Laundering Act (2001)

Thailand

Revamping of the prudential framework

- Tightening of loan classification, with loans being classified into five categories
- Establishment of strict rules on interest accrual
- Provisioning requirements gradually tightened to bring them in line with international best practice
- Rules for classification and provisioning of restructured loans set clear incentives for banks and finance companies to actively initiate restructuring of nonperforming loans
- New regulation requires collateral for loans larger than a certain size to be independently appraised

Strategy to restructure and rehabilitate the financial system

- Established the Financial Sector Restructuring Agency to deal with suspended finance companies, replacing the Bank of Thailand and the Ministry of Finance temporarily as decision maker on all matters related to financial sector restructuring
- Amended the Commercial Banking Act and the Finance Company Act to empower the Bank of Thailand to request capital reductions, capital increases, or changes in management in troubled commercial banks and finance companies
- Established an asset management company to deal with assets of finance companies that had their operations suspended, or impaired assets in any financial institution in which the Financial Institutions Development Fund had acquired shares (intervened) and assumed management control
- Amended the Bank of Thailand Act to empower the Financial Institutions Development Fund to lend to these institutions with or without collateral, raise the fee charged to financial institutions whose depositors and creditors were protected, and make explicit the government's financial support of the Bank of Thailand

Sources: IMF (1999); and Financial Sector Stability Assessment reports for Financial Sector Assessment Programs undertaken in the countries.

REFERENCES

Aizenman, Joshua, Brian Pinto, and Vladyslav Sushko. 2012. "Financial Sector Ups and Downs and the Real Sector: Up by the Stairs and Down by the Parachute." University of California Santa Cruz Department of Economics Working Paper 689, Santa Cruz, California.

Gourinchas, Pierre-Olivier, and Maurice Obstfeld. 2012. "Stories of the Twentieth Century for the Twenty First." *American Economic Journal: Macroeconomics* 4 (1): 226–65.

Institute of International Finance. 2015. *Capital Flows to Emerging Markets Report,* The Institute of International Finance, Washington.

International Monetary Fund (IMF). 1999. *Financial Sector Crisis and Restructuring: Lessons from Asia.* Occasional Paper 188. Washington: International Monetary Fund.

———. 2008. *Global Financial Stability Report: Assessing Risks to Global Financial Stability,* Washington, October.

———. 2013a. *Global Financial Stability Report: Making the Transition to Stability,* Washington, October.

———. 2013b. "Key Aspects of Macroprudential Policy." IMF Policy Paper, Washington, June.

———. 2014a. *Global Financial Stability Report: Risk Taking, Liquidity, and Shadow Banking— Curbing Excess while Promoting Growth.* Washington, October.

———. 2014b. *World Economic Outlook: Legacies, Clouds, Uncertainties.* Washington, October.

———. 2014c. "India: 2014 Article IV Consultation." *IMF Country Report No. 14/57.* Washington.

———. 2014d. *Regional Economic Outlook: Asia and Pacific.* Washington, April.

Jeasakul, Phakawa, Cheng Hoon Lim, and Erik Lundback. 2014. "Why Was Asia Resilient? Lessons from the Past and for the Future." *Journal of International Commerce, Economics and Policy* 5(2).

Lim, Cheng Hoon, Francesco Columba, Alejo Costa, Piyabha Kongsamut, Akira Otani, Mustafa Saiyid, Torsten Wezel, and Xiaoyong Wu. 2011. "Macroprudential Policy: What Instruments and How to Use Them? Lessons from Country Experiences." IMF Working Paper No.11/238, International Monetary Fund, Washington.

Mishra, Prachi, Kenji Moriyama, and Papa N'Diaye. 2014. "Impact of Fed Tapering Announcements on Emerging Markets." IMF Working Paper No. 14/109, International Monetary Fund, Washington.

Park, Donghyun, Arief Ramayandi, and Kwanho Shin. 2013. "Why Did Asian Countries Fare Better during the Global Financial Crisis than during the Asian Financial Crisis?" In *Responding to Financial Crisis: Lessons from Asia Then, the United States and Europe Now,* edited by Changyong Rhee and Adam S. Posen. Washington: Asian Development Bank and Peterson Institute for International Economics.

Sahay, Ratna, Vivek Arora, Thanos Arvanitis, Hamid Faruqee, Papa N'Diaye, and Tommaso Mancini-Griffoli. 2014. "Emerging Market Volatility: Lessons from the Taper Tantrum." IMF Staff Discussion Note No. 14/09, International Monetary Fund, Washington.

CHAPTER 6

The Future of Asia's Financial Sector

Rina Bhattacharya, Fei Han, and James P. Walsh

MAIN POINTS OF THIS CHAPTER

- As incomes in Asia continue to rise rapidly, they are likely to be accompanied by a further rapid deepening of the region's financial sectors.
- Demographics could have a large impact on this process as countries with rapidly rising dependency ratios see declining savings rates, and those with falling dependency ratios see increased savings.
- Asian financial systems are bank dominated, and for the most part, not particularly complex. But net interest margins can be expected to decline across much of the region, a phenomenon generally associated with rising complexity as banks seek to raise profits through nontraditional activities and increased competition for deposits spurs faster financial innovation.
- Asian financial systems are also likely to become more integrated with the rest of the world, and especially with each other.

INTRODUCTION

For the next few decades, Asia's economic growth is expected to lead the world—just as it has for the past generation. What does this mean for the future of the region's financial sector? How will a region with highly diverse financial systems evolve? What can we say about the future of finance in Asia based on the experience of other countries?

As discussed in Chapter 2, Asia's financial systems today are relatively large, but not particularly complex or integrated with the rest of the world. This chapter discusses what might cause those factors to change and how Asia's financial systems are likely to look in the years ahead.

SIZE

Asia's already large financial systems can be expected to grow even larger. Over time, financial market development and economic growth both influence and support each other. A well-functioning financial sector plays a vital role in facilitating and sustaining economic growth (see, for instance, the literature survey by Zhuang and others [2009]). The financial sector plays this role in various ways, for example, by facilitating investment to raise potential growth, by providing incentives to save, or by reducing transaction costs (Bencivenga and Smith 1991; De Gregorio and Guidotti 1995; and Aziz and Duenwald 2002). An efficient financial system can also improve the efficiency and quality of investment (for instance, Greenwood and Jovanovich 1990; Ansari 2002). But causality can also run the other way: as Asian consumers grow wealthier and as companies grow larger and more sophisticated, demand for financial services such as mortgages, credit cards, and instruments to hedge duration, interest rate, and foreign exchange risks will also rise. In all likelihood, both forces are at play in Asia.

A cross-country panel data model (Box 6.1) sheds light on the relationship among macroeconomic factors, demographics, and legal and institutional developments and the growth of the financial sector. The main results are summarized in Table 6.1 and discussed in this chapter.

Box 6.1. A Model of Financial Size

The size of the financial sector (as a percentage of GDP) is defined as total banking sector assets plus stock market capitalization plus the outstanding stock of domestic private and public debt securities. Following Chinn and Ito (2006) and Ayadi and others (2013), the econometric model is specified as

$$FS_{i,t} - FS_{i,t-1} = \beta_0 + \beta_1 FS_{i,t-1} + \beta_2 X_{i,t} + \varepsilon_{i,t} \qquad (6.1)$$

in which FS is the size of the financial sector (as a percentage of GDP), and X is a vector of control variables.[1] To avoid the endogeneity problem and remove the impact of short-term cyclicality, the model is specified as growth-over-level regressions with nonoverlapping periods.

In particular, the lagged size of the financial sector is included in each regression. Log GDP per capita is included to control for wealth effects. Inflation is incorporated as the annual growth rate of the GDP deflator.

Three different measures are used for capital account openness. The first measure is an indicator proposed by Lane and Milesi-Ferretti (2006, 2007), which consists of the aggregate of gross external assets and liabilities (as defined in the International Investment Position of the Balance of Payments) measured as a percentage of nominal GDP in U.S. dollars. Two other measures were also considered—the Chinn-Ito and Quinn indices. Following Chinn and Ito (2006) and Ayadi and others (2013), the analysis includes trade openness, measured by total trade as a percentage of GDP, and the growth of government debt (as a percentage of GDP) to capture the impact of trade flows and fiscal policy on financial development, respectively.

Data availability limited the sample period to 2003–11. The initial sample of countries included the S-29[2] plus other Asian countries with 2012 nominal GDP of $150 billion or more.

---

[1] The dependent variable of equation (6.1) is actually the growth of the financial sector size as a percentage of the current-period GDP, that is, $FS_{i,t} - (GDP_{i,t-1} / GDP_{i,t}) FS_{i,t-1}$. Explanatory variables X include (the log of) GDP per capita in purchasing-power-parity dollars, a measure of capital account openness, inflation, an interaction term between capital account openness and inflation, trade openness, growth of government debt, the dependency ratio, measures of legal development, and interaction terms between capital account openness and legal development measures.

[2] S-29 includes Australia, Austria, Belgium, Brazil, Canada, China, Denmark, Finland, France, Germany, Hong Kong SAR, India, Ireland, Italy, Japan, Korea, Luxembourg, Mexico, the Netherlands, Norway, Poland, Russia, Singapore, Spain, Sweden, Switzerland, Turkey, the United Kingdom, and the United States.

Box 6.1. (*continued*)

However, two economies—Luxembourg and the regional hub of Hong Kong SAR—turned out to be outliers and were dropped from the sample.[3] The final sample included 38 economies.

The data were drawn from a number of sources. For the size of financial sector, data for total banking sector assets,[4] stock market capitalization, and outstanding domestic private and public debt securities were obtained from the IMF's International Financial Statistics database; Bloomberg, L.P.; and the Bank for International Settlements' Statistics database, respectively. Macroeconomic data including purchasing-power-parity GDP per capita, the GDP deflator, trade openness, and growth of government debt were obtained from the IMF's World Economic Outlook database. The measures of capital account openness, namely, the Lane and Milesi-Ferretti measure, Chinn-Ito index, and Quinn index, were obtained from Lane and Milesi-Ferretti (2006, 2007), Chinn and Ito (2002), and Quinn (1997), respectively. Finally, the dependency ratios were drawn from the World Population Prospects database of the United Nations, and the measures of legal and institutional development were drawn from the International Country Risk Guide database published by the PRS Group.

Following Chinn and Ito (2006) and Ayadi and others (2013), equation 6.1 was estimated using fixed-effect panel regressions with cross-section and time fixed effects. Time fixed effects were also included to control for possible time-specific exogenous shocks.

---

[3] The sizes of the financial sectors in Luxembourg and Hong Kong were both greater than 1,500 percent of GDP during the sample period, much higher than the other countries in the sample.

[4] Total banking sector assets are defined as claims on central banks, plus net claims on government, plus domestic private credit, plus foreign assets.

Convergence

In general, poor countries tend to show more rapid income growth than do rich countries. Poor countries can adopt technologies and import capital goods from rich countries, allowing their incomes to converge to rich-country levels (Figure 6.1, panel 2). Because rich countries tend to have large financial systems relative to the size of their economies, and poor countries tend to have shallower financial systems, we would expect that as poor countries become richer, their financial systems would grow even faster. That is, they would experience financial deepening.

The results of the empirical model provide support for convergence. Lagged purchasing-power-parity GDP per capita has a significantly negative impact on financial sector growth, implying that the richer a country is, the more slowly its financial system tends to grow (Figure 6.1). Similarly, countries with relatively large financial sectors tend to show slower growth in their financial sectors even when controlling for income per capita. That is, financial systems tend to grow faster in lower-income countries, but even when controlling for this effect, relatively small financial systems tend to converge toward larger ones. Thus, financial systems in Asia's lower-middle-income economies, such as the Philippines and India, can be expected to grow more rapidly in the medium term than can the region's richer countries, especially the advanced economies.

TABLE 6.1

Determinants of the Growth of Financial Sector Size

Dependent Variable: Growth of Financial Sector Size (Percent of GDP)
Sample Countries over 2003–11

	I	II	III
Lag of financial sector size	−0.3***	−0.4**	−0.4**
	(0.1)	(0.2)	(2.5)
Log GDP (based on purchasing power parity per capita)	−46.1*	−52.0*	−97.2**
	(21.9)	(29.1)	(42.9)
Inflation	0.9	0.2	2.6**
	(0.8)	(0.5)	(1.3)
Capital account openness (Lane and Milesi-Ferretti measure)	0.3*		
	(0.2)		
Capital account openness (Chinn-Ito index)		−19.7	
		(20.0)	
Capital account openness (Quinn index)			1.0
			(1.0)
Interaction (Inflation × Capital account openness)	−0.0*	−0.6**	−0.0**
	(0.0)	(0.3)	(0.0)
Dependency ratio	−3.8***	−5.3***	−5.9***
	(1.0)	(1.4)	(1.7)
Trade openness (Total trade/GDP)	0.4	0.4*	0.4*
	(0.3)	(0.2)	(0.2)
Bureaucratic quality (BQ)	37.2***	3.1	5.3
	(13.6)	(13.0)	(19.4)
Law and order	−7.0	5.4***	−6.6
	(4.7)	(1.2)	(18.9)
Interaction (Capital account openness × BQ)	−0.1**	13.4**	−0.2
	(0.1)	(6.4)	(0.3)
Constant	642.5**	797.7**	1279.2**
	(280.8)	(364.2)	(576.8)
Cross-section fixed effects	Yes	Yes	Yes
Time fixed effects	Yes	Yes	Yes
Number of cross-section units	38	36	34
Total panel observations	326	308	286
Adjusted R^2	0.7	0.7	0.7

Sources: Chinn and Ito (2006); Lane and Milesi-Ferretti (2006, 2007); Quinn (1997); IMF, World Economic Outlook database; UN, World Population Prospects database; and IMF staff estimates.
Note: Sample countries include Australia, Austria, Belgium, Brazil, Canada, China, Chile, Colombia, the Czech Republic, Denmark, Finland, France, Germany, Hungary, India, Indonesia, Ireland, Israel, Italy, Japan, Korea, Malaysia, Mexico, the Netherlands, Norway, the Philippines, Poland, Portugal, Russia, Singapore, South Africa, Spain, Sweden, Switzerland, Thailand, Turkey, the United Kingdom, and the United States. Heteroscedasticity robust standard errors are provided in the parentheses.
*$p < .1$; **$p < .05$; ***$p < .01$.

Capital Account Openness

As shown by Chinn and Ito (2006), capital account openness can be beneficial for financial sector growth when a country is equipped with well-developed legal systems and institutions. Capital account openness thus intuitively seems to be a factor that might affect financial sector development. Three measures of capital account openness, namely, the international investment position (IIP), Chinn-Ito index, and Quinn index, are included in the baseline regressions in Table 6.1. These three measures reflect different ways of thinking about capital account openness. The Quinn and Chinn-Ito measures, though compiled from different

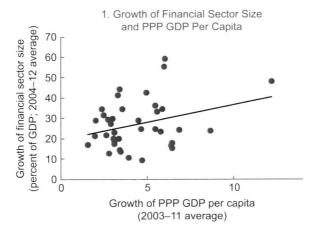

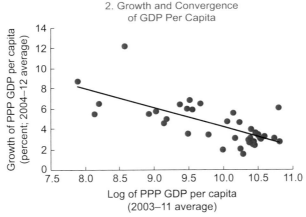

Figure 6.1 Growth of Financial Sector Size and Income Convergence

Sources: Bank for International Settlements; Banking Statistics database; Bloomberg, L.P.; IMF, International Financial Statistics database; IMF, World Economic Outlook database; and IMF staff calculations.

Note: Sample countries include Australia, Austria, Belgium, Brazil, Canada, China, Chile, Colombia, Czech Republic, Denmark, Finland, France, Germany, Hungary, India, Indonesia, Ireland, Israel, Italy, Japan, Korea, Malaysia, Mexico, Netherlands, Norway, the Philippines, Poland, Portugal, Russia, Singapore, South Africa, Spain, Sweden, Switzerland, Thailand, Turkey, the United Kingdom, and the United States. PPP = purchasing power parity.

data, focus on the legal framework for capital account transactions (de jure openness), whereas the IIP looks at the total stock of foreign assets and liabilities held by nonresidents, and is thus a data-based de facto proxy for capital account openness. The results of the regressions are shown in columns I–III of Table 6.1, using each measure successively.

When measured by the IIP, capital account openness has a significantly positive impact on the growth of the financial sector. Comparisons are not straightforward, but in general, Asian economies tend to have relatively low IIPs.[1] This is particularly true among Asia's emerging economies, which are relatively closed. However, both China and India, along with other countries, have increasingly opened their capital accounts.[2] As companies in the region globalize, domestic savers are able to invest more freely abroad, and as Asian companies grow more sophisticated and global, larger capital flows (Chapter 10) and greater integration with the rest of the world should occur.[3] Given the large infrastructure needs of Asia's emerging market economies, the need for more open capital accounts is expected to grow, which is likely to accelerate financial sector growth. Furthermore, a higher degree of trade openness is also likely to increase the growth of the financial sector, as suggested by the regression results.

Inflation

Many observers (for example, Boyd, Levine, and Smith 2001) have noted that high inflation can discourage financial intermediation and adversely influence the development and growth of the banking sector and equity markets. Table 6.1 shows that higher inflation is associated with slower financial sector growth once capital account openness is controlled for. Intuitively, countries with higher inflation and more open capital accounts are likely to experience more capital flight, slowing financial development. In countries such as India and Indonesia, where inflation is relatively high and where capital accounts are being liberalized, bringing down inflation could help bolster stronger financial deepening in the future.

Demographics

Another key change that will affect Asia in the medium and long term is demographics. Demographic trends vary widely across Asia. The region includes some of the world's most quickly aging countries, such as Japan and Korea, and others on the cusp of enjoying a "demographic dividend," where the working-age population is rising as a share of the total population, stimulating growth of the labor force and, all else equal, of the economy.

Dependency ratios affect saving rates, which in Asia is likely to be a significant issue (Heller 2006). Household survey studies, such as those by Chamon and Prasad (2008) and Chamon, Liu, and Prasad (2010), have also shown that higher dependency ratios are associated with lower saving. Lower saving, in

---

[1] In 2011, Japan and Korea both had IIPs below 200 percent of GDP, compared with 318 percent of GDP in the United States and 527 percent of GDP among all non-Asian advanced economies. Hong Kong SAR and Singapore, however, had IIPs of 2,212 and 1,576 percent of GDP, respectively—higher than any non-Asian advanced economy.

[2] Under the Lane and Milesi-Ferretti measure, China shows up as relatively open, but once the large international reserves at the People's Bank of China are taken into account, the ratio is lower.

[3] Both Chinese and Indian corporations have already become large buyers of foreign companies, with Chinese outward foreign direct investment reaching $73 billion in 2013, and Indian foreign direct investment reaching $18 billion.

turn, should imply slower financial deepening, as is confirmed in the regression analysis in Table 6.1.[4]

Thus, the rapid aging expected in many Asian countries, including China, the largest economy in the region, will likely act as a drag on financial deepening. However, in countries where dependency ratios are expected to decline, such as India and Indonesia, the rising number of working-age people saving for retirement could act as a spur to financial deepening.

Institutional Development

The relationship between financial sector growth and legal and institutional development has been widely studied. Work by La Porta and others (1997) shows that financial sector development is stronger within more developed institutional frameworks that protect and are better able to match the needs of investors. Chinn and Ito (2006) find that a higher level of financial openness spurs equity market development only if development of the legal system attains a specific threshold. Other studies have built upon these conclusions by showing that strong legal institutions, good democratic governance, and adequate implementation of financial reforms can have a significantly positive impact on financial development only when they are collectively present.

The specification in Table 6.1 follows Chinn and Ito (2006), including three indicators of legal and institutional development: the level of corruption, the quality of the bureaucratic system, and law and order. The interaction terms between each of these three indices and capital account openness are also included to control for the potential complementarities discussed in the literature.

Depending on which measure of capital account openness is used, the quality of the bureaucracy and law and order appear to have substantial and positive impacts on the growth of the financial sector. These results are consistent with other studies.

Institutional development has a particularly significant relationship with development of equity markets. Regardless of the stage of development of the rest of the financial sector, countries with higher law and order ratings tend to have more rapid growth in equity market capitalization. This relationship is reinforced by capital account openness; presumably countries with better governance and more open capital accounts see even stronger growth in equity markets because foreign investors more willingly enter the market.

Other Factors

Finally, some variables that might be expected to be related to financial sector growth do not appear to support deepening once the other variables in the specification are taken into account. Chinn and Ito (2006) and others suggest that

---

[4] The main specification in the regression analysis includes the total dependency ratio as measured by the number of people under age 15 and those over age 64, divided by the number of people between ages 15 and 64.

liberalization in goods markets is a precondition for liberalization of financial markets. Because trade openness is an area in which emerging markets in general—and Asia in particular—do quite well by international comparison, it might be expected to be a significant factor, but regression results do not strongly support this hypothesis. Why this is the case is not clear, though one reason could be Asia's tightly regulated financial sector in many countries, which has impeded the impact of Asia's relatively liberal environment for goods trade.

Similarly, the growth of government debt does not appear to be tied to the overall growth of the financial sector (Table 6.1). Fiscal pressures that lead to a rapid increase in government debt might have negative effects on financial markets because rapid growth in debt might crowd out private investment or raise the level of inflation. Countries with larger stocks of public debt tend to have less efficient financial sectors than do countries with lower levels of public debt (Ayadi and others 2013). These hypotheses are consistent with the Indian experience. In other cases, prudent fiscal policies over time have meant that government debt markets are relatively small, making it more difficult to diversify domestic capital markets and establish benchmark interest rates.

COMPLEXITY AND DOMESTIC INTERCONNECTEDNESS

The complexity of Asia's financial systems mirrors their size. The financial centers of Hong Kong SAR and Singapore, along with advanced economies such as Australia, Japan, Korea, and New Zealand, have financial systems as complex as any in Europe or North America. However, emerging market financial systems tend to be less complex, and this holds true in Asia (Chapter 2).

Bank lending tends to dominate financial sectors in emerging Asia, and the largest share of this bank lending is at relatively short maturities. Equity markets are large, but, as discussed in Chapter 4, they tend to be highly volatile. However, despite the rapid growth of corporate bond markets in recent years, long-term debt options tend to be more limited. In many countries, bond markets, even for public debt, tend to be relatively illiquid, and the lion's shares of issuers tend to be highly rated companies, especially publicly traded companies. In addition to these supply problems, demand is also an issue. Emerging Asia tends to have fewer local long-term buy-and-hold investors than do advanced economies, because it has relatively small pension funds and insurance companies. In addition, in many countries in emerging Asia, pension funds and insurance companies are publicly owned, with regulations that complicate their participation in private sector debt markets, especially at higher risk ratings. Many Asian emerging markets also lack the infrastructure of financial data, credit expertise, and incentives needed to catalyze lending to small firms or innovative start-ups (Sheng, Ng, and Edelmann 2013).

Whether this pattern will change in Asian emerging markets will depend on, among other things, the relative returns from bank lending versus other kinds of investment. During the past decade, net interest margins in Asia have been rising albeit slowly (Figure 6.2, panel 1), which has limited the incentives for banks to

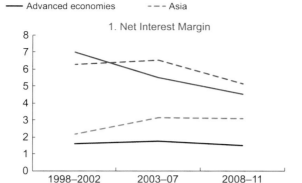

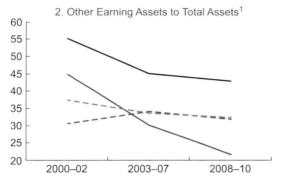

Figure 6.2 Net Interest Margin and Composition of Bank Assets (*Percent*)

Source: World Bank, Global Financial Development database.
Note: Central and Eastern Europe includes Bosnia and Herzegovina, Croatia, FYR Macedonia, Romania, and Turkey. Latin America and the Caribbean includes Brazil, Chile, Colombia, Costa Rica, Mexico, and Paraguay. Advanced economies include Austria, Belgium, Finland, France, Germany, Greece, Ireland, Italy, the Netherlands, Portugal, Spain, and the United States. Asia includes Australia, China, Hong Kong SAR, India, Indonesia, Japan, Malaysia, the Philippines, Republic of Korea, Singapore, Sri Lanka, and Thailand.
[1]Does not include Australia, Hong Kong SAR, the Philippines, Singapore, or Sri Lanka, as data were not available.

diversify their asset portfolios and seek higher returns from nontraditional banking activities. This growth focus on traditional lending is also visible in banks' sources of income; the share of banks' total income contributed by trading and other nontraditional activities has declined in recent years (Figure 6.2, panel 2).

However, these conditions are likely to change in the medium term. As the global economy recovers and advanced economies unwind their highly accommodative monetary policies, interest rates are likely to rise. The higher global cost of capital will put pressure on net interest margins, improving the relative trade-off of moving into unconventional and more complex activities.

Foreign investors are another potential source for such diversification. But foreign participation tends to be greatest in open and liquid markets. Asian markets often are not as open to foreigners as are markets in other emerging regions (Chapter 2), and poor liquidity and other factors tend to discourage foreign participation (Chapters 4 and 5).

Domestic factors will matter as well. In many Asian countries, net interest rate margins are likely to come under modest downward pressure due to competition among lenders for business and for deposits. In countries such as Malaysia and Indonesia, where most loans are at floating rates, competition for higher-quality borrowers could be particularly strong. The continued deepening of equity markets and development of local currency bond markets also will offer increasingly varied options for the large and high-quality borrowers who form the most stable segment of bank lending in most countries today. As banks compete for this business, lending margins are likely to fall. The liability side of balance sheets also will matter. In markets in which retail deposits form the backbone of bank financing, as in Asia's emerging markets, competition for deposits will erode net interest margins from below, pushing banks to become more innovative in measuring risk, pursuing new lines of business activity, and developing new products for savers.

Regulatory changes also may have an impact. For example, meeting the Basel III liquidity coverage ratio requirement is expected to lead to intensified competition for stable retail deposits. This competition will likely put greater pressure on interest margins in countries such as Australia—even taking into account that Australia, with a system dominated by four major banks, has a relatively concentrated, and thus in theory less competitive, banking sector. In China, rates on bank deposits have generally been lower than returns on alternative products, such as wealth management products purchased by retail investors, and on other items, often offered by banks, that are purchased by larger corporate borrowers. As deposit rates are liberalized, bank deposit rates can be expected to converge with rates on these alternative products, potentially putting pressure on margins. The regional hubs of Hong Kong SAR and Singapore may prove to be important exceptions to the regional trend of declining net interest margins. This is due to both economies' global reach and opportunities to expand their lending activities in profitable emerging markets.

Across the region, this potential squeezing, or at least stabilization, of net interest margins will be a strong incentive for Asian banks to move away from traditional banking toward more complex and riskier business activities and financial instruments. Indeed, there is a strong and negative relationship between net interest margin and the importance of non-interest-earning assets as a share of total assets (Figure 6.3, panel 1). Cross-country annual data from 42 countries covering the period 2000–11 show this correlation; moreover, the correlation between net interest margin and other earning assets to total assets, and between net interest margin and other interest-bearing liabilities to total liabilities, are statistically significant (Table 6.2).

However, a key result of this process is likely to be a push by banks into higher-risk loan segments, raising the stakes for regulators, an issue discussed in Chapter 11. As banks' reliance on non-interest income increases (that is, as their business models become more complex), so does their reliance on wholesale funding. The importance of interbank markets also increases. (Figure 6.3, panels 2–4). More competition for deposits also may spur more rapid growth in nonbank financial institutions and shadow banking, which could complicate the task for regulators who will have to supervise a more diffuse financial system.

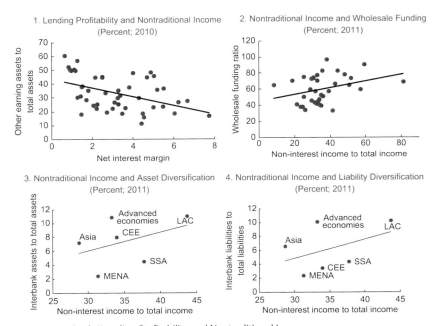

Figure 6.3 Banks' Lending Profitability and Nontraditional Income

Sources: Bankscope; World Bank, Global Financial Development database; IMF, International Financial Statistics database; and IMF staff calculations.

Note: Central and Eastern Europe (CEE) comprises Bosnia and Herzegovina, Bulgaria, Croatia, Hungary, Latvia, Lithuania, FYR Macedonia, Poland, Romania, and Turkey. Latin America and the Caribbean (LAC) comprises Brazil, Chile, Colombia, Costa Rica, El Salvador, Mexico, and Paraguay. Advanced economies comprise Austria, Belgium, Cyprus, Estonia, Finland, France, Germany, Greece, Ireland, Italy, Luxembourg, Malta, the Netherlands, Portugal, the Slovak Republic, Slovenia, Spain, and the United States. Middle East and North Africa (MENA) comprises Algeria and Pakistan. Sub-Saharan Africa (SSA) comprises Kenya, Mauritius, South Africa, and Uganda. Asia comprises Indonesia, Japan, Malaysia, the Philippines, and Thailand.

TABLE 6.2

Correlation with Net Interest Margins	
Variable	**Correlation Coefficient**
Other earning assets to total assets	−0.3 (−3.9)[***]
Other interest-bearing liabilities to total liabilities	−0.5 (−8.2)[***]

Sample Period: 2000–11
Number of Observations: 210

Sources: Bankscope; World Bank, Global Financial Development database; and IMF staff calculations.
Note: *, **, and *** denote that the correlation coefficients are statistically different from zero at the 10 percent, 5 percent, and 1 percent significance levels, respectively.

TABLE 6.3

Correlation with Non-Interest Income to Total Income	
Variable	Correlation Coefficient
Ratio of wholesale funding to total liabilities	0.4 (4.6)***
Ratio of interbank assets to total assets	0.3 (3.8)***
Ratio of interbank liabilities to total liabilities	0.1 (2.1)**
Sample period: 2000–11 Number of observations: 210	

Sources: IMF, International Financial Statistics database; World Bank, Global Financial Development database; and IMF staff calculations.
Note: *, **, and *** denote that the correlation coefficients are statistically different from zero at the 10 percent, 5 percent, and 1 percent significance levels, respectively.

The same factors that will drive Asian financial systems toward greater complexity also will likely lead to systems with greater domestic interconnectedness. As banks move toward more nontraditional activities, they are likely to look for cheaper alternative sources of market funding—wholesale or interbank—to finance these activities. Indeed, cross-country data show a positive and statistically significant correlation between the ratio of non-interest income to total income on the one hand, and the ratios of wholesale funding to total liabilities and of interbank assets (or liabilities) to total assets (or liabilities) on the other (Table 6.3). Some of this market funding is likely to come from other financial institutions. Thus, as financial systems in Asia become more complex, domestic financial institutions are likely to become increasingly interconnected. Furthermore, in the longer term, Basel III liquidity requirements, and in particular the need to meet the net stable funding ratio requirement, may encourage borrowers to look more to institutional investors, such as pension funds and insurance companies, to fund their longer-maturity projects.

INTERNATIONAL INTERCONNECTEDNESS

As shown in Chapter 2, Asian financial systems are less connected to the rest of the world than are financial systems in other regions. As Asian financial systems grow larger and more complex, international interconnectedness will also rise. In fact, various studies suggest that many of the same factors that drive financial sector deepening are also associated with greater international connectedness. Chief among these factors is income. Aizenman and Noy (2009) find that a $1,000 increase in GDP per capita is associated with an increase in the IIP of 0.1–0.3 percentage point of GDP. Larger financial systems also tend to be more globally interconnected.[5]

---

[5] However, this may partly be due to the statistical artifact that larger IIPs by necessity mean larger financial systems because foreign assets and liabilities will be held or issued by financial institutions.

Countries with more openness toward goods trade also tend to become more financially interconnected. Aizenman and Noy (2009) find that a one standard deviation increase in the trade openness index is associated with a 9.5 percent increase in de facto financial openness. One reason this occurs is that greater trade openness by necessity deepens financial connections with the rest of the world. These interconnections increase the cost of enforcing financial repression, thereby reducing the effectiveness of financial repression as an implicit tax on capital flows and increasing the de facto financial openness. In the future, as GDP per capita and trade openness are expected to continue rising in Asia, particularly in emerging Asia, economies such as China and India are likely to have higher degrees of financial openness given that they are already finding it difficult to maintain financial repression.

Stock market liberalizations, privatization of state-owned companies, and other steps toward financial liberalization are also associated with greater international interconnectedness. During the 1990s, the privatization of state-owned enterprises in central and eastern Europe and other regions led to a large jump in capital inflows. In East Asia, foreign investors' purchases of local banks in financial distress tripled the share of foreign-controlled banking assets from 2 percent in 1994 to 6 percent in 1999. Countries with larger stock market capitalization also tend to have more international interconnectedness, likely due to the greater attractiveness to foreign investors of more liquid and diversified equity markets in recipient countries. The presence of institutional investors also is closely linked to international interconnectedness.[6] Here, too, financial liberalization and capital account liberalization reinforce each other by reducing the effectiveness of financial repression, leading to less market distortion and better capital allocations.

In addition, the demographic shifts, especially changes in dependency ratios, that affect saving rates in both advanced and emerging markets are associated with greater global interconnectedness. In Asia, where dependency ratios, on average, are lower than they are in other regions or in advanced markets, rising dependency ratios are thus likely to spur higher saving rates. Investing this larger savings pool domestically will likely drive down the rate of return on capital, particularly relative to that in the emerging markets with low capital levels. As a result, capital will tend to flow to countries where it can earn higher returns.

These capital inflows can be expected to particularly benefit Asia's rapidly growing economies with young populations, such as Indonesia and India. Faster growth in these economies should create more potential opportunities for investors than there will be in the region's slower-growing advanced and emerging market economies. Integration of the region's faster-growing economies will also accelerate because of gravity effects. In general, cross-border investments tend to flow from countries to their own neighbors, where information and some

---

[6] With institutional investors, however, endogeneity concerns are particularly pronounced because these investors focus on the kind of liquid, transparent markets that already tend to be well developed and reasonably open.

transaction costs tend to be lower. Thus, as Asia's savings look for higher returns, they can be expected, on average, to concentrate more in the region itself than in the rest of the world, especially given the large infrastructure needs of the region's rapidly growing economies with young populations.

WHAT DOES THE FUTURE LOOK LIKE?

How might Asia's financial sectors evolve? As discussed elsewhere in this chapter, numerous factors will influence the size and structure of Asian financial markets in the future. Extrapolating the model laid out in Table 6.1 provides some insight into how these factors will affect Asia's financial sectors and what the future might look like. First and foremost is the relationship with economic growth. As incomes in emerging Asia rise, the process of catch-up that has allowed them to grow rapidly in recent years can be expected to continue. However, higher incomes will lead to slower growth rates, so the pace of convergence should decline. The degree to which growth will cause most Asian emerging markets to narrow the gaps with developed economies will vary. For example, by 2030, growth alone could raise the size of Vietnam's banking sector by about 13.5 percentage points of GDP. But growth should have a smaller effect on Asia's richer economies. For example, Japan should see only a marginal further deepening of its financial sector resulting from economic growth, with banking sector assets rising only by about 3 to 4 percent of GDP by 2030. This is because Japan already has mature financial markets and its income growth per capita is expected to be relatively slow and from a high base.

Figure 6.4 puts these results into context. Panel 1 presents the projections for four selected countries: China, India, the United Kingdom, and the United States. Panel 2 shows the regional averages for emerging and advanced Asian and non-Asian economies. The effects, however, are relatively small for emerging markets. Considering the rapid growth in emerging market banking sectors in recent decades, this relatively unimpressive expectation of future growth is somewhat surprising. One reason for the low average forecast is the historical frequency of financial crises. The emerging market crises of the 1990s slowed or reversed the growth of emerging market banking sectors, pulling down the historical average growth rate, and affecting these forecasts. Because the quality of regulation and supervision has improved, and macroeconomic fundamentals are broadly better in Asia's emerging market economies today than they were in the 1990s, we should expect to see fewer homegrown crises in the future.

In addition, other macroeconomic and social factors are likely to have a significant impact. Chief among these are rising dependency ratios. Financial sector growth will be further weighed down by the rising share of retirees in the population and the accompanying drawdown of their savings. According to projections from the UN's World Population Prospects database (the 2012 Revision) and the IMF's World Economic Outlook database (the April 2014 Update), the dependency ratios in most Asian countries are expected to rise during 2012–20

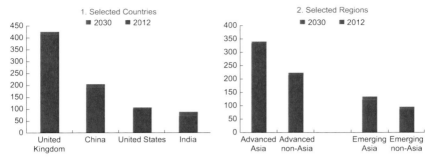

Figure 6.4 Effect of Income Growth on Financial Sector Size *(Financial sector size as a percentage of GDP)*

Source: IMF staff calculations.

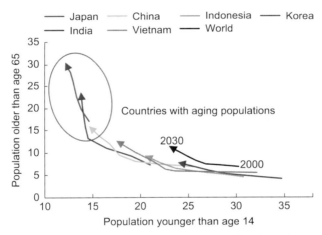

Figure 6.5 Asia Demographic Change *(Percent of total population, 2000–30)*

Sources: United Nations; and IMF staff calculations.

(Figure 6.5),[7] and purchasing power parity GDP per capita will rise in all countries. These negative effects will be significant in many countries, especially in Japan and Korea. But Vietnam will also see large increases in the share of the population older than the working age.

China is an unusual case for both macroeconomic and social reasons. Banking assets as a share of GDP are already higher than they are in the United States. They are comparable to those in Germany. This partly reflects a postcrisis credit

---

[7] Except India, Indonesia, Malaysia, and the Philippines, where dependency ratios are projected to decline slightly over this period.

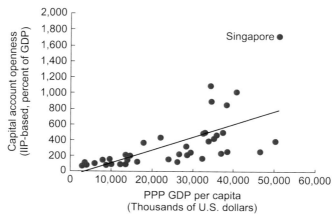

Figure 6.6 Capital Account Openness and Purchasing Power Parity (PPP) GDP per Capita *(2003–11 average)*

Sources: Lane and Milesi-Ferretti (2006, 2007); and IMF, World Economic Outlook database.
Note: Sample countries include Australia, Austria, Belgium, Brazil, Canada, China, Chile, Colombia, the Czech Republic, Denmark, Finland, France, Germany, Hungary, India, Indonesia, Ireland, Israel, Italy, Japan, Korea, Malaysia, Mexico, the Netherlands, Norway, the Philippines, Poland, Portugal, Russia, Singapore, South Africa, Spain, Sweden, Switzerland, Thailand, Turkey, the United Kingdom, and the United States. IIP = international investment position.

boom that can be expected to unwind gradually during the next few years. In the future, income per capita is still expected to grow at a fast rate, which can be expected to boost the size of the financial sector, whereas the rapid pace of aging can be expected to weigh it down. With the relative importance of these factors unclear, the overall direction of China's financial sector is uncertain. Nonetheless, it will certainly remain the largest financial sector in Asia.

Capital account openness will be another key factor in determining the future financial landscape of Asia. Capital account openness, at least as measured by the de facto IIP measure discussed elsewhere in this chapter, is linked with GDP per capita (Figure 6.6). Within Asia, countries at broadly similar levels of income differ widely in their openness by IIP, and thus the extent to which further opening is likely to occur is difficult to project. But using Australia, a relatively open advanced economy, as a model, calculations based on the regression results in Table 6.1 show the effect of further liberalization on the size of Asian financial sectors. If relatively open Asian economies, such as Malaysia, were to become as open by 2020 as Australia is today, the size of the financial sector would increase by an average of 13 percentage points of GDP. For less open countries, the effect is even larger. Indonesia's current IIP, for example, is 80 percent of GDP compared with Malaysia's 230 percent. If Indonesia were to rise to Australia's level (unlikely in such a short time frame), the size of the financial sector would increase by about 46 percentage points of GDP. For economies that are even more closed than Indonesia's, such as India's, the effect would be even larger. Although, again, such a rapid increase in IIP is unlikely in such a short period.

China is, again, an unusual case. China's capital account is relatively open in de facto terms, at about 109 percent of GDP in 2011, but this is partly due to its very large stock of central bank international reserves. Excluding these reserves tells a somewhat different story. China is on the low end of openness compared with other Asian emerging markets.[8] A lifting of China's restrictions on both inward and outward investment can be expected to lead not only to an increase in inflows as foreign investors gain greater access to Chinese assets, but also to potentially substantial outflows, as Chinese savings kept currently within the country would be able to be invested abroad. These outflows could be substantial (Bayoumi and Ohnsorge 2013). China's capital account openness would thus provide domestic financial firms with more opportunities to diversify and expand their foreign portfolios while also allowing domestic savers to invest in a wider range of assets.

Other variables are more difficult to forecast. Governance indicators, like capital account openness, are highly correlated with income. As the incomes of Asian countries rise, it can be expected that bureaucratic quality and law-and-order indicators also will improve, further spurring the development of Asian financial markets. Indeed, these improvements should help strengthen the deepening of equity markets—one of Asia's key deficiencies, as improving governance, higher incomes, and continued capital account liberalization reinforce one another.

As discussed, this large growth in the size of Asian financial sectors will be accompanied by a rise in complexity and interconnectedness. The eventual normalization of global interest rates, the impact of global regulatory reforms (see Chapter 11), declining interest margins, and other factors should spur more innovation among financial institutions, including nonbank entities, and lead to increasing complexity within Asia's financial systems. This process is likely to go farthest in markets in which net interest margins have already been falling, such as Malaysia and Korea. In countries where there is less competition, deposit growth is more robust, but in countries where financial repression is more effective because of closed capital accounts, this process is likely to go more slowly.

Finally, Asia's large and increasingly complex financial systems can be expected to further integrate with the rest of the world. While these linkages are currently smaller than they are in many other regions, diversification of Asia's large savings pools, further liberalization of domestic equity and bond markets, and especially Asia's rising income levels, should lead Asian countries' financial linkages to each other and to the rest of the world. With these linkages, Asia's financial systems will more closely resemble the region's deep internal and external trade relationships. And as with trade, this integration should be expected to increase intraregional linkages.

---

[8] In China, IIP assets and liabilities, less official reserves, were about 64 percent of GDP at end-2013. In Indonesia, the total was 75 percent, while in Malaysia and Thailand it exceeded 120 percent.

CONCLUSION

Asia's financial sector growth can be influenced by many macroeconomic and social factors, particularly income and demographics. The rising income in this region has been accompanied by rapid financial sector growth since 2002. The size of financial sectors in the region's lower-middle-income countries can be expected to converge in the medium term to the size of those in the richer economies, especially the advanced economies. Another key factor that will affect Asia's financial sector in the medium and long terms is demographics. Higher dependency ratios in many Asian countries, especially the advanced economies, tend to be associated with less savings, and in turn, imply slower financial deepening. Other factors that might affect Asia's financial sector growth, such as inflation, capital account openness, and legal and institutional development, are likely to be linked with income.

Asia's financial sectors are mostly bank dominated. The financial centers of Hong Kong SAR and Singapore, along with the advanced economies in the region, have financial systems as complex as any in Europe and North America. However, the financial sectors in the region's emerging markets tend to be less complex and dominated by banks. Because net interest margins can be expected to decline across the region, Asian banks will have strong incentives to move away from traditional banking toward more complex business activities and financial instruments, leading to more complex and interconnected financial sectors in the region.

In the future, Asia's financial sectors can be expected to be more integrated with the rest of the world and especially with each other, as banks search for profits through more complex business activities and financial instruments. In addition, this process could be accelerated as Asia's large savings pools become more diversified, domestic equity and bond markets become more liberalized, and most important, income levels rise further.

REFERENCES

Aizenman, J., and I. Noy. 2009. "Endogenous Financial and Trade Openness." *Review of Development Economics* 13 (2): 175–89.

Ansari, M. I. 2002. "The Impact of Financial Development, Money, and Public Spending on Malaysia National Income: An Econometric Study." *Journal of Asian Economics* 13 (1): 72–93.

Ayadi, R., E. Arbak, S. B. Naceur, and W. P. De Groen. 2013. "Determinants of Financial Development across the Mediterranean." MEDPRO Technical Report No. 29, Mediterranean Prospects, European Commission.

Aziz, J., and C. Duenwald. 2002. "Growth-Finance Intermediation Nexus in China." IMF Working Paper No. 02/194, International Monetary Fund, Washington.

Bayoumi, T., and F. Ohnsorge. 2013. "Do Inflows or Outflows Dominate? Global Implications of Capital Account Liberalization in China." IMF Working Paper No. 13/189, International Monetary Fund, Washington.

Bencivenga, V. R., and B. D. Smith. 1991. "Financial Intermediation and Endogenous Growth." *Review of Economic Studies* 58 (2): 195–209.

Boyd, J. H., R. Levine, and B. D. Smith. 2001. "The Impact of Inflation on Financial Sector Performance." *Journal of Monetary Economics* 47 (2): 221–48.

Chamon, M., and E. Prasad. 2008. "Why Are Saving Rates of Urban Households in China Rising?" IMF Working Paper No. 08/145, International Monetary Fund, Washington.

Chamon, M., K. Liu, and E. Prasad. 2010. "Income Uncertainty and Household Savings in China." IMF Working Paper No. 10/289, International Monetary Fund, Washington.

Chinn, Menzie D. and H. Ito. 2002. "Capital Account Liberalization, Institutions and Financial Development: Cross Country Evidence." NBER Working Paper No. 8967, National Bureau of Economic Research, Cambridge, Massachusetts.

———. 2006. "What Matters for Financial Development? Capital Controls, Institutions, and Interactions." *Journal of Development Economics* 81 (1): 163–92.

De Gregorio, J., and P. E. Guidotti. 1995. "Financial Development and Economic Growth." *World Development* 23 (3): 433–48.

Greenwood, J., and B. Jovanovich. 1990. "Financial Development, Growth and the Distribution of Income." *Journal of Political Economy* 98 (5): 1076–1107.

Heller, P. S. 2006. "Is Asia Prepared for an Aging Population?" IMF Working Paper No. 06/272, International Monetary Fund, Washington.

La Porta, R., F. Lopez-de-Silane, A. Shleifer, and R. W. Vishny. 1997. "Legal Determinants of External Finance." *Journal of Finance* 52 (3): 1131–50.

Lane, P. R., and G.-M. Milesi-Ferretti. 2006. "The External Wealth of Nations Mark II: Revised and Extended Estimates of Foreign Assets and Liabilities, 1970–2004." *Journal of International Economics* 73 (2): 223–50.

———. 2007. "Europe and Global Imbalances." *Economic Policy* 22 (51): 519–73.

Quinn, D. 1997. "The Correlates of Change in International Financial Regulation." *American Political Science Review* 91 (3): 531–51.

Sheng, A., C. S. Ng, and C. Edelmann. 2013. *Asia Finance 2020*. Hong Kong SAR: Oliver Wyman and Fung Global Institute.

Zhuang, J., H. Gunatilake, Y. Niimi, M. E. Khan, Y. Jiang, R. Hasan, N. Khor, A. S. Lagman-Martin, P. Bracey, and B. Huang. 2009. *Financial Sector Development, Economic Growth, and Poverty Reduction: A Literature Review*. ADB Economics Working Paper No. 173, Manila: Asian Development Bank.

CHAPTER 7

Hong Kong SAR and Singapore as Asian Financial Centers— Complementarity and Stability

Vanessa le Leslé, Franziska Ohnsorge, Minsuk Kim, and Srikant Seshadri

MAIN POINTS OF THIS CHAPTER

- Hong Kong Special Administrative Region (SAR) and Singapore have evolved into Asia's preeminent international financial centers (IFCs).
- Their historical growth paths have thus far been largely complementary, with each tending to specialize in different asset markets and financial services, and each focusing on different parts of Asia.
- These complementary evolutionary paths, if maintained, may also carry significant benefits for regional and global financial stability.
- Hosting large financial institutions with complex, fluid business models in both economies calls for the maintenance of strong regulatory and supervisory cooperation between Hong Kong SAR and Singapore. Such cooperation could also play a significant role in enhancing Asian financial integration—both regionally and globally.

INTRODUCTION

Asian financial centers are frequently viewed through the lens of a "race for dominance" among a few well-established cities such as Hong Kong SAR, Singapore, and Tokyo, as well as other potential contenders like Seoul and Shanghai. Indeed, an extensive literature looks at the development of these financial centers from that perspective. This chapter, however, suggests that an alternative consideration— regional and global financial stability—also matters when looking at the evolution of these centers. Rather than asking what each financial center needs to do to make itself stronger or "dominant," the chapter asks if the patterns of coexistence of financial centers in Asia have a bearing on regional or global financial stability. To answer this question, the analysis explores different scenarios with a global shock propagation model, using well-known network analysis methods. The exercise takes as given that Singapore and Hong Kong SAR are the two main international financial centers in Asia, and looks at how their coexistence might affect regional and global financial stability because they are both, indeed, significantly more internationalized than are their Asian peers. The point is not to rule out the emergence or reemergence of other financial centers. Rather, with the world as it is today, we document not only how these two centers complement each other— geographically and through product specialization—but also suggest that this complementarity may better serve to stabilize the global financial system.

Keeping the focus on global and regional stability, both cities host a large number of global systemically important banks (G-SIBs), and need to maintain appropriate licensing, regulatory, supervisory, and resolution mechanisms. Supervising and regulating large financial institutions in a global web of financial markets and supervisors raises particular challenges explored in the later sections of this chapter. For instance, the two centers face the challenge of maximizing coordination with home supervisors and ensuring domestic regulatory requirements are in place that meet the highest international standards. And, they must do this without hampering global cooperation or generating regulatory arbitrage.

BACKGROUND ON HONG KONG SAR AND SINGAPORE AS INTERNATIONAL FINANCIAL CENTERS

Parallels and Differences

From trading hubs to financial hubs. The historical parallels and differences between Singapore and Hong Kong SAR are well documented and can be traced back to their days as trade hubs (Ng Beoy Kui 1998; Huat, Lim, and Chen 2004; Pauly 2011). Both cities enjoyed important strategic locations on major trade routes, between the South China Sea and the Indian Ocean for Singapore, and as a privileged location in Northeast Asia and a gateway to China for Hong Kong SAR. Both were traditionally large trade and trans-shipment centers until the 1970s. Continuing growth in trade was accompanied by rapid improvements in infrastructure and growth in banking facilities. The two financial systems have developed on complementary trajectories with limited overlap and competition.

Asian Dollar Market. The creation of the Asian Dollar Market (ADM) was central to the development of Singapore. The rapid expansion of the Eurodollar market created pressures for an Asian city to host a market for the U.S. dollar to broaden its time zone coverage. Singapore began such a market in 1968, when the ADM was first introduced, and the government provided incentives and preferential tax treatment for the development of the Asian Currency Units to support the ADM. Hong Kong SAR initially continued to impose a moratorium on banking licenses and maintain the 15 percent withholding tax on interest income from foreign currency deposits. However, once the moratorium was lifted in 1978, Hong Kong SAR began to take a more active presence in debt markets. Both cities proceeded with a series of liberalization measures to open up their financial sectors to foreign banks and other financial institutions.

China. Hong Kong SAR has benefited from access to China's vast internal market. Many policy changes to China's financial sector were initially piloted in Hong Kong SAR, including the various quota regimes that govern portfolio flows to and from China, as well as attempts to encourage the international use of the renminbi. In this respect, Hong Kong SAR resembles other international financial centers with large domestic economies, such as New York.[1] The introduction of "H shares," which allowed companies incorporated in mainland China to be traded on the Hong Kong Stock Exchange, helped foster financial links between Hong Kong SAR and China.

Growing Asian bond markets. Hong Kong SAR and Singapore both benefit from the broader growth of Asian credit. Before the global financial crisis, Asian bond markets were relatively small, illiquid, and not very diversified, with a primary focus on sovereign and financial issuers. Since 2008, the market has grown 2.4 times (from $200 billion to $480 billion), reflecting a shift in Asia from heavy surpluses (both external and internal surplus, and excess savings) to a greater reliance on markets to fund growing demand. Both consumption and investment have caused this shift.[2] Primary issuance by Asian borrowers is growing, and most credit securities are now allocated to Asian investors, reflecting a rebalancing of the investor base into the region.

Government policies. Singapore developed as an IFC with the support of active government policies. The government fostered and maintained Singapore's position in the global financial market through internationally competitive tax structures and by promoting a well-regulated financial system. A robust financial center is considered central to the city's economic future. The Monetary Authority of Singapore (MAS), which is tasked with multiple policy roles, oversees the entire financial system and ranks among the best globally in regulation and supervision.[3] By comparison, Hong Kong SAR's success as an IFC has been characterized as largely "laissez-faire," with financial sector growth generally left to market forces (Ng Beoy Kui 1998; Huat, Lim, and Chen 2004; Pauly 2011). For instance, when the public pension fund (Mandatory Provident Fund) was launched in 2000, its management was left to the private sector, unlike in Singapore, where the Central Provident Fund is largely managed by the government.

Government support. Authorities in both jurisdictions have introduced measures to encourage the development of debt markets. They have done this by improving clearing infrastructure via a settlement, central clearing, and custodian system (for example, the Central Moneymarkets Unit in Hong Kong SAR); promoting exchange fund notes in the retail market; expanding the profits tax

---

[1] The importance of China for Hong Kong SAR is discussed further in other sections of this chapter.
[2] Primary issues from Asian issuers are growing, and the majority of credit securities are now allocated to Asian investors, reflecting a rebalancing of the investor base into the region.
[3] See IMF (2013), "Singapore Financial System Stability Assessment" (FSSA). MAS has the following responsibilities: monetary policy and sustainable economic growth, foreign reserves management, maintaining financial stability, and fostering a sound financial center. In addition, MAS is in charge of microprudential and macroprudential supervision of all financial intermediaries, and acts as the resolution authority.

concession scheme; and streamlining regulations on issuing and listing debt securities. Hong Kong SAR and Singapore both took measures to establish a full benchmark yield curve, with a greater range of tenors, and expanded markets from government debt to corporate debt. Singapore also participated in the implementation of cross-border securities offering standards by the Association of Southeast Asian Nations (ASEAN), together with Malaysia and Thailand.[4] Issuers offering equity and plain debt securities in multiple jurisdictions within ASEAN will only need to comply with a single set of disclosure standards for prospectuses, bringing about greater efficiency and cost savings to issuers. Neither Hong Kong SAR nor Singapore has market entry requirements, restrictions on remittances, capital gains taxes on listed equities, or capital gains taxes on fixed-income securities for nonresident participants in bond markets.

Competition or Complementarity?

Singapore and Hong Kong SAR seem to complement each other, since they typically provide financial services to clients in two distinct geographic regions. Hong Kong SAR tends to concentrate on markets in China, Taiwan Province of China, and Korea, whereas Singapore's clients are mainly, but not exclusively, from India and Southeast Asia.

Market specialization. This differentiation is mirrored at the product level, given that the two IFCs display complementary product expertise. Aside from foreign exchange trading and fund management, competition between the two in other areas, such as the derivatives market and off-shore lending, is limited. Hong Kong SAR and Singapore offer different derivatives products, and there is a distinct difference in the geographical distribution of their respective offshore lending activities (Figures 7.1 and 7.2).

Important foreign exchange markets. Both Hong Kong SAR and Singapore are important foreign exchange markets (Figure 7.1) despite not having major currencies of their own (unlike London, New York, and Tokyo). Their financial expertise and robust infrastructure have facilitated the trading of hard currencies necessary to support trade growth in the region. Hong Kong SAR's currency board exchange rate arrangement with the U.S. dollar since October 1983 has promoted its currency's use as a proxy for the U.S. dollar in futures and option hedging. On a global scale, however, foreign exchange markets in both Singapore and Hong Kong SAR remain significantly smaller than those in the United Kingdom and the United States.

Renminbi. The development of the renminbi business has mostly profited Hong Kong SAR, which has become the premier offshore hub for renminbi trading, settlement, financing, and wealth management. According to the Hong Kong Monetary Authority (HKMA), for Hong Kong SAR in 2013, renminbi trade settlement amounted to RMB3,841 billion in 2013, and the stock of

---

[4]The ASEAN Disclosure Standards Scheme aims to facilitate fund-raising activities as well as to enhance investment opportunities within ASEAN capital markets.

Asia's equity markets have grown rapidly but remain mid-sized, both by capitalization …

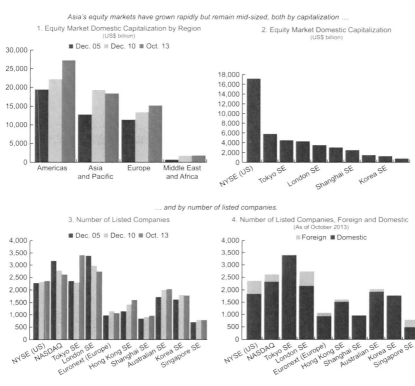

1. Equity Market Domestic Capitalization by Region
(US$ billion)

2. Equity Market Domestic Capitalization
(US$ billion)

… and by number of listed companies.

3. Number of Listed Companies

4. Number of Listed Companies, Foreign and Domestic
(As of October 2013)

Although Hong Kong SAR and Singapore are important foreign exchange markets in Asia, they are mid-sized by global standards.

Both Singapore's and Hong Kong SAR's asset management businesses have grown rapidly.

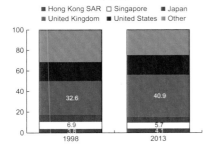

5. Geographical Distribution of Forex Market Turnover
(Percent)

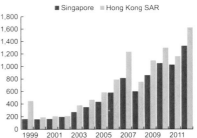

6. Aggregate Assets under Management
(US$ billion)

Figure 7.1 Business Lines

Sources: Bank for International Settlements Triennial Bank Survey (2013); Hong Kong SAR Securities and Futures Commission; Monetary Authority of Singapore; and World Federation of Exchanges (2011).
Note: SE = stock exchange

Hong Kong SAR and Singapore are important equity and bond markets in the region, but mid-sized global players. Hong Kong SAR has larger international equity issuance, Singapore larger bond issuance.

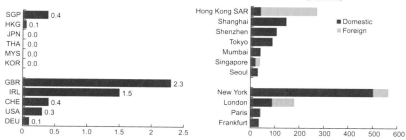

1. International Bond Issuance in Major IFCs (2003–12)
(US$, trillions)

2. IPOs in Asian Financial Centers
(US$, billions)

Hong Kong SAR's international bond issuance is mainly and increasingly by Mainland Chinese issuers. Despite recent diversification, Singapore's international bond issuance remains mainly by Korea and Hong Kong SAR issuers.

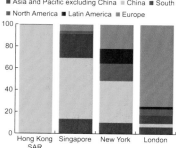

3. International Bond Issuance (2003–07)
(Percent of total international issuance)

4. International Bond Issuance (2008–12)
(Percent of total international issuance)

International IPO issuance in Hong Kong SAR is also mainly by Mainland Chinese issuers but has recently become more diversified. Issuance in Singapore is by now also mainly by non-Chinese North Asia and Pacific issuers (including a few large deals by issuers from Hong Kong SAR).

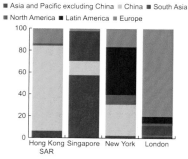

5. International IPO Issuance (2003–07)
(Percent of total international issuance)

6. International IPO Issuance (2008–12)
(Percent of total international issuance)

Figure 7.2 Geographic Distribution of Issuers

Sources: Dealogic; IMF (2014); World Federation of Exchanges (2011); and authors' estimates.
Note: CHE = Switzerland; DEU = Germany; GBR = the United Kingdom; HKG = Hong Kong SAR; IFC = international financial center; IPO = initial public offering; IRL = Ireland; JPN = Japan; KOR = Korea; MYS = Malaysia; SGP = Singapore; THA = Thailand; USA = the United States.

outstanding renminbi bonds was ¥310 billion at the end of 2013.[5] The total issue size of the renminbi sovereign bond market has risen substantially since the first issue in 2009, reaching ¥8 billion in 2010 and ¥23 billion in 2013. Renminbi lending by banks in Hong Kong SAR also expanded, with outstanding renminbi loans amounting to ¥116 billion at the end of 2013. The range of renminbi financial instruments and products has expanded to include renminbi shares, currency futures, and exchange-traded funds accessing the A-share market. All of these activities are supported by a sustained pool of liquidity, with renminbi customer deposits and outstanding certificates of deposit issued by banks totaling ¥1,053 billion at the end of 2013.

Competition for renminbi business. Hong Kong SAR is currently the main hub for conducting renminbi operations. Singapore, like London, aims to increase its market share, especially as the renminbi market continues to grow. The development of renminbi business in Singapore was given a boost when the People's Bank of China appointed ICBC Singapore as Singapore's renminbi clearing bank in February 2013. This catalyzed growth of renminbi activities in Singapore,[6] particularly in trade financing.[7] In December 2013, Singapore Exchange Ltd and Hong Kong Exchanges and Clearing Ltd signed a memorandum of understanding to leverage each other's strengths and capture more of Asia's growth. This collaboration will cover new technology, regulation, and joint product development. The yuan-denominated products covered could be bonds, commodities, equities, or currencies.

Bond markets. Hong Kong SAR and Singapore are both mid-sized international bond markets, smaller than Ireland, London, Luxembourg, and the United States, despite a fivefold expansion in bond issuance in Hong Kong SAR and a tenfold expansion in Singapore since 1995. Issuance is predominantly in local currencies (67 percent in Hong Kong SAR; 77 percent in Singapore). In Hong Kong SAR, private sector debt dominates (64 percent), while in Singapore government and private debt each account for about half of issuance (47 percent and 53 percent, respectively).[8] Singapore is one of the most international bond markets in Asia, with more than a quarter of total annual issuance from foreign entities. Foreign entity issuers consist mainly of supranational agencies, corporations, and financial institutions. Since 2005, Singapore has been part of several main benchmark bond indices.[9]

---

[5] HKMA, International Financial Center section, 2013 Annual Report.

[6] According to an April 28, 2014, SWIFT press release, Singapore overtook London as the top renminbi offshore clearing center after Hong Kong SAR.

[7] According to a December 3, 2013, Society for Worldwide Interbank Financial Telecommunication press release, Singapore was ranked first, outside of China and Hong Kong SAR, in the use of renminbi for trade finance as of October 2013.

[8] In Singapore, property-related companies dominate private corporate debt issuance, followed by government-related companies (airlines, telecom, transportation, banking). Comparable data for Hong Kong SAR are not available.

[9] Citigroup's World Government Bond Index, HSBC Asian Local Bond Index, and JPMorgan World Government Bond Index.

Equity markets. The Hong Kong SAR and Singapore stock exchanges remain smaller than those of their global peers, but are strong in Asia, with 4.8 percent and 1.2 percent, respectively, of the world aggregate equity market domestic capitalization (and 16.4 percent and 4.8 percent, respectively, if compared with the equity market capitalization of Asian countries). Capitalization of the Hong Kong SAR Stock Exchange is almost four times that of the Singapore Exchange.

Rapid growth. The market capitalization of Singapore's securities market increased more than 20-fold in 20 years (from $34 billion in 1990 to $770 billion in 2013). This growth was fueled by an influx of offshore banking activities and foreign capital, by the liberalization of the Central Provident Fund (whereby savings could be used to invest in equities), and by a relaxation of listing requirements. Hong Kong SAR's stock market capitalization is much larger, with $3 trillion as of November 2013, ranking right behind the main European, Japanese, and U.S. stock exchanges. Half of the companies listed in Hong Kong SAR come from China, illustrating the degree to which Hong Kong SAR benefits from economic developments in China. As of October 2013, there were 1,602 listed companies in Hong Kong SAR, with a market capitalization of HK$23.4 billion.

Growing fund management. Growth within the Asia and Pacific region, especially in China, has supported the fund management industries in Hong Kong SAR and Singapore. Both IFCs have played an active role in the international investment of local savings, and in managing offshore money on behalf of investors based overseas. As a result, Singapore's and Hong Kong SAR's assets under management have grown rapidly (almost sixfold and fourfold, respectively) since 1999, including mutual funds, hedge funds, private equity, and real estate investment trust funds.

Asset management hubs. Two-thirds of the top 50 global fund management companies have established a presence in Hong Kong SAR and Singapore. Hong Kong SAR hosts the largest number of fund managers and the largest pool of hedge fund assets ($87 billion as compared with $63 billion in Singapore), including assets that are invested in Asia. Hong Kong SAR is also the premier offshore renminbi business center. Assets under management are predominantly invested overseas and broadly equally divided between stocks and bonds. Asia and Pacific markets were a major destination of investment, accounting for 70 percent of assets for Singapore and 80 percent of assets for Hong Kong SAR.

Openness. The fund management industry is quite international in both cities. Singapore mainly serves as a conduit for funds that come from abroad and are reinvested abroad. Some 80 percent of the assets managed by the 600 fund management firms in Singapore originate outside of the country, mostly in Asia; 86 percent of these assets are then invested elsewhere.[10] Because Singaporean banks have limited exposures, financial stability risks linked to the potential failure of an asset manager would mostly carry reputational risks for the financial center. The favorable tax and legal framework underpins the attractiveness of Singapore.

---

[10] Asian-Pacific markets were the major destination of investment, accounting for 70 percent of assets for Singapore and 80 percent of assets for Hong Kong.

In both Hong Kong SAR and Singapore, excellent market infrastructure, financial expertise, a favorable tax environment, the absence of exchange restrictions, and the establishment of a robust Code on Unit Trusts and Mutual Funds also attract foreign fund managers.

UNTANGLING DRIVERS OF GROWTH

This section looks at the underlying factors behind the growth of Hong Kong SAR and Singapore since the global financial crisis. Hong Kong SAR, for example, has traditionally enjoyed a large and growing volume of initial public offerings (IPOs) and bond issuances from China. But is the postcrisis growth largely due to Hong Kong SAR's geographical advantage as the "gateway to China," or does it also reflect gains in Hong Kong SAR's own competitiveness, such as the quality of relevant institutions and infrastructure? More generally, to what extent have Hong Kong SAR and Singapore benefited from the favorable mix of foreign issuers concentrated in the quickly recovering Asian emerging economies? How much have they benefited from their inherent competitiveness as IFCs? How do the experiences of Hong Kong SAR and Singapore differ from each other and from the experiences of their Western competitors—New York and London?

Constant market share method. This analysis used the constant market share method to examine these questions. In its original trade context, the basic intuition underlying this approach is that a country's export growth can be attributed to the following two distinct factors: (1) changes in the composition of the country's export destinations and products (*structural effect*), and (2) changes in the country's share of world exports under the assumption that the composition of destinations and products is held fixed (*competitiveness effect*). The analysis used the same approach to analyze growth in the volume of foreign IPOs and bond issuances within an IFC. In this setting, the structural effect captures the change in foreign issuer mix of the IFC, while the competitiveness effect measures the change in the share of world IPOs (or bonds) issued in the IFC.[11]

Different drivers. The constant-share market analysis[12] indicates similar drivers for both Hong Kong SAR and Singapore: Competitiveness gains were the main driver of postcrisis growth in IPO issuance, while structural effect was more important for international bond issuances.

IPOs. Since 1998, the volume of international IPOs in the two Asian IFCs increased significantly (Table 7.1). The gain in competitiveness contributed substantially in both IFCs, but Hong Kong SAR's growth benefited more from the change in the shares of foreign issuers (232 percent) than did Singapore (93 percent). IPOs from China rose by more than sixfold in Hong Kong SAR, accounting for almost the entire share of international IPOs in Hong Kong SAR during 2003–07. Singapore benefited primarily from a gain in competitiveness

---

[11] Seade, Wei, and Wu (2010) use a similar method to analyze the sources of IFCs' growth in different financial service markets.

[12] The approach follows Jiminez and Martin (2010).

TABLE 7.1

Decomposition of International IPO Growth in Major IFCs				
Percent	Real Growth Rate	Structural	Competitiveness	First-Time Issuance
From 1998–2002 to 2003–07				
Hong Kong SAR	424	232	192	0
Singapore	1,595	93	718	784
New York	−113	−23	−89	−1
London	203	−26	146	83
From 2003–07 to 2008–12				
Hong Kong SAR	10	−8	3	15
Singapore	38	−12	49	0
New York	0	12	−13	1
London	−39	−19	−23	3

Sources: Dealogic; and IMF staff calculations.
Note: IFC = international financial center; IPO = initial public offering.

(718 percent) and a large amount of issuances from first-time issuers (784 percent), coming mostly from emerging Asian countries. Postcrisis, Hong Kong SAR and Singapore continued to grow, albeit at a much slower pace. Hong Kong SAR experienced a sharp decline in Chinese IPOs, which dropped by 26 percent. Large first-time issuances, in contrast, contributed about 15 percent to Hong Kong SAR's growth, more than offsetting the negative structural shock. The bulk of these first-time IPOs came from North American and Western European countries, which, together with the competitiveness effect of 3 percent, provide an indication that Hong Kong SAR's growth stems from the city's own competitiveness rather than just a "gateway-to-China" effect. Similarly, in Singapore, the mix of foreign issuers concentrated among emerging Asian countries actually had a negative contribution of 12 percent to Singapore's growth relative to the world, while the contribution from improvement in competitiveness more than offset that effect.[13]

Bonds (Precrisis). The results from international bond markets offer a markedly different overall picture (Table 7.2). From 1998–2002 to 2003–07, international bond issuances in Singapore more than doubled, or grew by 44 percent relative to world growth. The competitiveness effect contributed about 13 percent and the structural effect contributed −22 percent to this growth. The overall growth, however, was mainly driven by issuances from first-time issuers, mostly from emerging Asian countries, suggesting that the locational advantage could have played a relatively larger role than the gain in competitiveness. Meanwhile, Hong Kong SAR experienced an 8 percent decline of issuances, or −76 percent relative to world growth, largely driven by a loss of competitiveness (−112 percent). The negative impact was mitigated by the first-time issuances from a few Asian

---

[13] Whereas the gain in competitiveness played a key role for Hong Kong SAR and Singapore in the postcrisis period, New York and London both lost competitiveness. New York benefited from a large increase in IPOs from emerging market economies in its region, including Brazil and Mexico.

TABLE 7.2

Decomposition of International Bond Issuance Growth in Major IFCs				
Percent	Real Growth Rate	Structural	Competitiveness	First-Time Issuance
From 1998–2002 to 2003–07				
Hong Kong SAR	–76	7	–112	30
Singapore	44	–22	13	53
New York	306	94	183	30
London	38	20	14	4
From 2003–07 to 2008–12				
Hong Kong SAR	261	234	27	1
Singapore	134	65	68	1
New York	91	8	80	3
London	12	9	3	0

Sources: Dealogic; and IMF staff calculations.
Note: IFC = international financial center.

issuers and from the United Kingdom, suggesting that Hong Kong SAR also mainly benefited from the growing funding needs of the region.

The structural effect played a more important role during the postcrisis period. In Singapore, issuances increased by 134 percent, of which about 65 percentage points can be attributed to the change in the composition of issuers toward Asian countries, notably China, and about 68 percent to Singapore's own gain in competitiveness. Hong Kong SAR's growth (261 percent) was predominantly driven by the structural effect and in particular by the fast growth in China-originated issuances that represented about 90 percent of total international issuances after the crisis.[14]

COEXISTENCE OF HONG KONG SAR AND SINGAPORE AS INTERNATIONAL FINANCIAL CENTERS

Micro efficiency versus financial stability. As argued elsewhere in this chapter, Hong Kong SAR and Singapore have complemented each other in Asia by specializing in different markets and clientele. In principle, the existing specialization can have implications in two dimensions: efficiency (limited competition, or inability to fully exploit possible scale economies in the provision of financial services, causing possible "micro" inefficiencies) and stability (destabilizing

---

[14] While the "gateway-to-China" effect was the central driver behind Hong Kong SAR's growth, and to a lesser extent Singapore's growth, the relative growth in New York during the postcrisis period mainly reflected a sustained increase in competitiveness. London, however, benefited relatively more from the structural effect, in part resulting from a large increase of issuances from some of the European countries, such as Switzerland and Sweden, which are considered to be safe havens.

competition leading to increased transmission of financial shocks). This section reviews the implications of the existing business model of the two centers for financial stability, setting aside the question of efficiency.

Shock propagation exercise. The probabilistic shock propagation model (used recently in the 2012 IMF "Spillover Report") is founded on a network of bilateral exposures between country pairs, and is a useful tool for this exercise.[15] The model is a thought experiment consisting of multiple rounds of deleveraging. Investors who face losses in one market may need to deleverage in others. As funding in the second set of markets also dries up, investors in those also decide to deleverage, including from third markets and so on. (See Box 7.1.)

Data and scenarios. To illustrate the role of the two financial centers in Asia clearly, a stylized hypothetical network was constructed with only three regions: Asia (including Hong Kong SAR, Singapore, China, and eight other Asian countries), a global financial center that links Asia to the rest of the world (the United Kingdom or the United States), and the rest of the world.[16] Three scenarios were considered (for a graphical illustration, see Annex 7.1).

1. Hong Kong SAR and Singapore continue their specialized, and complementary, business models: Hong Kong SAR intermediates all exposures to China, whereas Singapore intermediates those to the rest of Asia. This scenario is a highly stylized representation of the current geographical complementarity between the two cities.

2. Hong Kong SAR and Singapore begin competing for the same business in Asia: both countries intermediate the rest of the world's financial exposures to Asia.

3. One of the two (here, purely for illustrative purposes, Hong Kong SAR) supplants the other as the sole financial center in Asia.

Random shocks. Figure 7.3 shows the propagation of a random shock anywhere in the network for each of the three scenarios. If both Hong Kong SAR and Singapore were to remain specialized financial centers in Asia (the dotted red curve) or even if one of them were to shrink (the black curve), global shocks would propagate more slowly than if both of them were competing in the same markets and for the same clientele (the blue curve). This is based on the following rationale: Because of their widely dispersed exposures, financial centers act as shock propagators. Two financial centers competing for the same business would each establish exposures to the same set of partner countries. As a result, these

---

[15] In contrast to the work of the 2012 IMF "Spillover Report," however, this analysis uses a stylized, hypothetical network rather than an actual network of bilateral data.

[16] The actual network of Bank for International Settlements or Coordinated Portfolio Investment Survey exposures is, of course, much richer, with an abundance of exposures between countries. However, many of these exposures are small and would have been a distraction to the focus of the exercise about the role of Hong Kong SAR and Singapore. Therefore, the analysis concentrated on a hypothetical network that abstracts from any links between the two countries and countries outside the region. In a stylized form, this represented the geographical differentiation discussed elsewhere in this chapter.

Box 7.1. Shock Propagation Model

Mechanics of the shock propagation model. An initial shock can hit any particular country in the network at random. The likelihood of a particular country being hit by an initial shock depends on the country's interconnectedness: the more interconnected a country, the more likely it is to be a source of shocks. Once the first (source) country is hit by an initial shock, it responds by cutting exposures, that is, eliminating links to partner countries in the network. Once struck by the initial random shock, the source country's financial system is assumed to be more likely to cut larger exposures than to cut smaller exposures. This deleveraging transmits the shock to the source country's partner countries, which now face a similar decision, triggering another round of deleveraging and contagion. Once a link has been severed, it cannot be reestablished and cannot be severed again. Each of these rounds of deleveraging is called a "step" in the experiment, and the exercise allowed as many steps as were needed for all countries in the network to be affected. This probabilistic exercise was repeated a thousand times. Strictly speaking, the steps have no time dimension because several steps could, in principle, collapse into one if financial systems are able to react instantaneously. In practice, however, deleveraging may well take time, so a few steps may afford policymakers time to respond.[1]

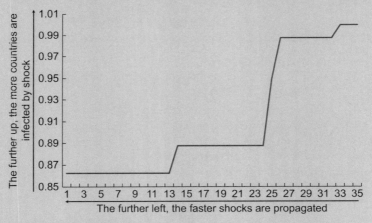

Figure 7.1.1   Shock Propagation Curve (*Share of countries affected in each step*)

Source: IMF staff calculations.

Interpreting shock propagation results. This exercise assumes that a link is severed. In principle, a link could, of course, be reduced rather than severed. Defining the degree of reduction, however, introduces an additional layer of assumptions. To keep the conceptual exercise simple and clear, assumptions that are not strictly necessary for the thought experiment are avoided. This does imply, however, that the results can only be interpreted with regard to *speed of contagion* rather than *size of the impact*. For example, Figure 7.1.1 shows the number of steps on the horizontal axis and, on the vertical axis, the share of countries affected in each of these steps.[2] The line is a "shock propagation curve." The further to the right or the lower the shock propagation curve, the longer it takes for contagion to reach a particular proportion of countries or the fewer the countries affected in each step, that is, the slower the shock propagation.[3]

---

[1] In the model, the shock generates a change in the network by cutting individual links. In practice, the network may change more broadly in response to the shock.

[2] Since the hypothetical network is unweighted, all links that exist are assumed to be of equal size. In this figure, the share of countries is not weighted by the number of their total links.

[3] The shock propagation curves are highly nonlinear because the network contains two distinct regions. For example, when a shock leaves Asia, reaches the global financial center, and jumps to the rest of the world, it suddenly causes an impact in a large number of countries.

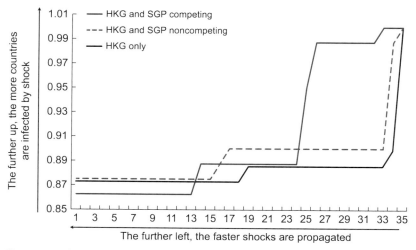

Figure 7.3 Shock Propagation Curve: Random Shock (*Share of countries affected in each step*)

Source: IMF staff calculations.

Note: HKG = Hong Kong SAR; SGP = Singapore.

partner countries would subsequently have a higher probability of receiving a global shock from either Hong Kong SAR or Singapore than they would have had if they were linked to only one of the two.

Shocks originating in China. The next experiment assumed that the initial shock originated in China specifically, rather than in a random location in the network (see Figure 7.4). In this exercise, the shock propagation curves for Hong Kong SAR and Singapore represent the following scenarios: specialized complementary centers (dotted red) and only one of the two (black) separate. A shock in China travels faster through a network in which there is only one Asian financial center (black curve) than in a network with two specialized financial centers (dotted red curve). This is because a single Asian financial center would provide a direct channel from China—the source of the shock—to the rest of Asia. In contrast, Singapore as a second financial center could buffer a shock from China that was immediately transmitted to Hong Kong SAR and, hence, slow the contagion to the rest of Asia. For the same reasons as in the case of random shocks, either scenario would slow contagion more than would two competing financial centers (blue curve).

Capital account liberalization in China. The final experiment considered a scenario of capital account liberalization in China. The assumption was that Hong Kong SAR becomes the only financial center for China. Of course, alternatively, Shanghai might become the only financial center for China, with Hong Kong SAR's financial market role withering once capital controls were removed. For this scenario, the only important element is that the source of the shock—China—is now home to a financial center in its own right. In Figure 7.5, for reference, two shock propagation curves from the previous experiment are shown

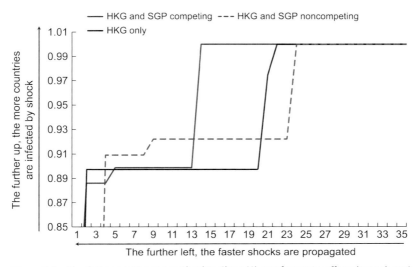

Figure 7.4 Shock Propagation Curve: Shock in China (*Share of countries affected in each step*)

Source: IMF staff calculations.
Note: HKG = Hong Kong SAR; SGP = Singapore.

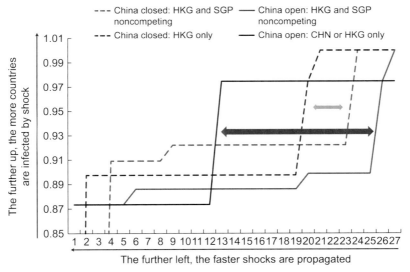

Figure 7.5 Shock Propagation Curve: Shock in China (*Share of countries affected in each step*)

Source: IMF staff calculations.
Note: CHN = China; HKG = Hong Kong SAR; SGP = Singapore.

in dotted lines: a dotted red for the scenario of Hong Kong SAR and Singapore as specialized financial centers and a dotted black for a scenario in which only one of them survives as the Asian financial center. The distance between these curves (indicated by a light green arrow) illustrates the degree to which the presence of the second, specialized, complementary financial center stabilizes the financial network by slowing contagion from shocks in China. Next, consider a merging of Hong Kong SAR into China as China's opens its capital account. The two continuous lines in the figure indicate the shock propagation curves for an open China. Again, the gap between the two continuous curves (dark green arrow) indicates the degree to which the presence of Singapore would slow the propagation of shocks in China. This gap is substantially wider. Hence, as China opens its capital account and integrates into the global financial network, Singapore's presence becomes increasingly stabilizing to the financial network by providing a buffer between China as the source of shocks and the rest of Asia.[17]

These results suggest that the stabilizing role of additional financial centers depends on the nature of the additional financial centers. Here, financial centers have many links and hence are able to propagate shocks widely. Additional financial centers would only serve to stabilize the network if they were different from existing financial centers, in particular, if they served as additional buffers between the source of shocks and other financial centers or countries.

Put together, these experiments suggest that the current complementarity between the two jurisdictions' business models may be an important consideration from the standpoint of regional and global financial stability. And as China integrates into the global financial system, the importance of maintaining this complementarity increases. As mentioned earlier, competition may foster other standard considerations of micro efficiency. While not seeking to disregard such micro considerations, it is worth noting that there is an inherent tension in favoring outright competition in an industry that is broadly thought to have economies of scale. The main insight we seek to convey from these shock propagation studies is that excessive competition may also engender destabilizing levels of complexity and interconnectedness in the network, and the presence of two "specialized" Asian financial centers may better balance the micro benefits from economies of scale with the macro benefits of stability.

REGULATORY AND SUPERVISORY ISSUES

Presence of Foreign Financial Institutions

Gateway. Foreign financial market participants typically use Hong Kong SAR and Singapore as access points to the rest of Asia. The two cities are considered to be hubs that offer robust expertise and infrastructure and diversified financial entities and services, as well as strong legal, regulatory, and supervisory frameworks. A characteristic both IFCs share is the strong presence of foreign banks, including G-SIBs, many of which are incorporated as branches rather than as subsidiaries. The presence of these G-SIBs has resulted in large cross-border exposures,

---

[17]This is consistent with other authors' findings. For example, Hooley (2013) cautions that, as China integrates into the global financial network, the global financial system becomes more vulnerable to financial shocks originating in China.

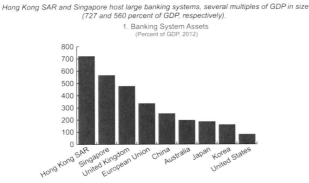

Hong Kong SAR and Singapore host large banking systems, several multiples of GDP in size (727 and 560 percent of GDP, respectively).

1. Banking System Assets
(Percent of GDP, 2012)

Banking systems are very open, both to the United Kingdom and to the United States ...

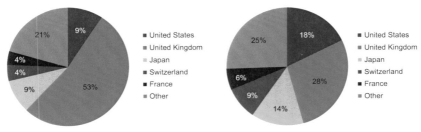

2. Claims of Foreign Banking Sector on Hong Kong SAR
(Percent)

3. Claims of Foreign Banking Sector on Singapore
(Percent)

... partly as a result of the predominance of foreign banks (especially their branches) in both financial systems.

4. Hong Kong SAR: Share of Licensed Banks

5. Singapore: Share of Commercial Banks

Figure 7.6 Banking Systems

Sources: Australia October 2012 Financial Sector Assessment Program; Bank for International Settlements, preliminary international banking statistics (consolidated foreign claims ultimate risk), 2013:Q2; European Banking Federation; Haver Analytics; Hong Kong Monetary Authority; Korean Financial Statistics Information System Monthly Bulletin; Monetary Authority of Singapore; and The CityUK.

Note: The largest four foreign banks account for one half of the banking system assets. Commercial banks account for 77.8 percent of the financial system assets. About half of the foreign banks offer retail services and accept retail deposits.

especially to the United States and the United Kingdom, and banking system assets that are several multiples of GDP (Figure 7.6). These interconnections represent the "plumbing" of the networks examined elsewhere in this chapter.

Business models. Foreign banks operate using several business strategies, depending on their group and regional preferences. To simplify, two business models dominate: (1) deposit-led retail and commercial banking, in which banks operate on a stand-alone basis collecting local deposits first and then lending locally or regionally; and (2) an investment-led model, in which banks are typically branches of large foreign banks, and fund projects that are primarily financed by the parent company or by funds directly raised in capital markets. Across Asia, and in Hong Kong SAR and Singapore in particular, HSBC, Standard Chartered Bank (SCB), and Citigroup have become strong local deposit-taking institutions, similar to the first model. Many European and other American G-SIBs follow the second model.

Foreign G-SIBs. Three foreign banks stand out in their size and importance for both Hong Kong SAR and Singapore: HSBC Group and SCB from the United Kingdom, and Citigroup from the United States. In aggregate, they hold 23 percent of bank assets in Singapore and, together with Bank of China, they hold 53 percent in Hong Kong SAR. These three institutions illustrate the fact that global banks implement their global strategic choices in Asia out of geographic convenience and to leverage business specialization, by using primarily, but not exclusively, Singapore as a platform for non-Japan, non-China Asia, and Hong Kong SAR as a hub for China and Northeast Asia. Similarly, fixed-income trading and asset management are often executed out of Singapore, while equities and investment banking tend to be done in Hong Kong SAR. HSBC is a Hong Kong SAR subsidiary, with a branch in Singapore, in line with the HSBC's stated model and preference for subsidiaries. SCB operates as a subsidiary in Hong Kong SAR, and incorporated a subsidiary in Singapore in October 2013 to house its retail banking operations, but the bank continues to have other operations under its branch. Citibank has both a subsidiary and a branch in Singapore. The incorporation status of individual banks has implications for the extent of supervisory powers available to home and host authorities. Although capital regulations may not apply to branches (requirements for "branch capital" are relatively rare), many other prudential risk-management requirements often apply to both branches and subsidiaries. In both Hong Kong SAR and Singapore, standards, such as liquidity requirements, are applied across the board to all authorized institutions, subsidiaries, and branches. Home and host supervisory responsibilities and cooperative arrangements often reflect proportionality considerations.

Importance of Sound Financial Regulation in IFCs

Regulation of IFCs has become an increasingly important factor in financial center competition since the global financial crisis. Two concurrent trends have emerged:

- **Tolerance of policymakers for unregulated products and markets has waned.** The financial crisis reiterated the need to make financial systems more resilient and provided a strong impetus globally to strengthen regulatory frameworks. Financial centers not compliant with international rules are faced with peer pressure, stigmatization, and reputational damage. Well-regulated financial centers with sound prudential requirements and effective mechanisms for supervisory intervention may be considered to be safe havens, particularly in times of crisis.

- **Tension is rising between greater convergence of regulation and national fragmentation.** The recent emergence of more harmonized regulatory standards at the global level and greater policy coordination may narrow the scope for regulatory competition. However, full consistency in the drafting and implementation of global rules has not yet been achieved. Sharp divergences in regulatory and supervisory standards—particularly between financial centers—may increase risks of regulatory arbitrage, and therefore, implicitly or explicitly, generate destabilizing competition to the detriment of global stability.

Opting for a strict approach. A robust regulatory framework is widely viewed to be an element of competitiveness for global financial centers. Both Hong Kong SAR and Singapore have demonstrated their interest in robust regulations and a high degree of transparency in the financial sector, as essential elements in their status as IFCs. The two jurisdictions have a strong track record in their timely adoption, and strict implementation, of the global regulatory agenda.

Regulatory Cooperation, Priorities, and Challenges

Membership in key regional and global forums. In addition to their membership in the Basel Committee on Banking Supervision and the Financial Stability Board, MAS and HKMA actively participate in several regional forums to promote financial stability in Asia and improve the collective voice of the region in international standard-setting bodies.[18] These forums include (1) the ASEAN Capital Markets Forum, which focuses on projects to harmonize standards in capital market regulations in ASEAN; (2) ASEAN+3, which coordinates initiatives between ASEAN and China, Japan, and Korea;[19] and (3) Executives' Meeting of East Asia Pacific Central Banks (EMEAP) to support regional financial stability and development and to discuss financial and monetary stability, bond market development, payment and settlement systems, and banking supervision. In addition, Singapore hosts the IMF's Training Institute for Asia, the Chiang Mai Initiative Multilateralization's independent surveillance unit, and the ASEAN+3 Macroeconomic Research Office. HKMA took the lead on the implications of global financial reforms for Asia as Chair of the EMEAP Monetary and Financial Stability Committee.

Business model review. The emergence of various sets of structural measures, such as initiatives proposed in the United States (Volcker rule), the United

---

[18] For initiatives led by Hong Kong SAR, see HKMA, 2012 annual report. MAS co-chaired the Basel Committee on Banking Supervision Core Principles Group, which delivered the revised Core Principles for Effective Banking Supervision in September 2012 and currently chairs the Macroprudential Supervision Group.

[19] These initiatives include promotion of financial stability through the Chiang Mai Initiative Multilateralization, and development of the bond market through the Asian Bond Markets Initiative.

Kingdom (Independent Commission on Banking, also known as "Vickers"), and the European Union (Liikanen proposals), may be one incentive, among other regulatory and macroeconomic changes, prompting banks to review their business models, geographic footprints, and operational structures.[20] While it is too early to assess the full impact of these combined changes, some banks are reportedly considering moving assets to markets where funding is readily available and cheaper, and are also likely to book and net derivatives where they trade the underlying assets. Asian financial centers could benefit from attracting EU and U.S. banks' activities, especially in asset and private wealth management, and possibly in derivatives. Should more complex assets be transferred to Hong Kong SAR and Singapore, a robust regulatory framework that minimizes regulatory arbitrage and fosters solid supervision would be critical.

Challenges of hosting G-SIBs. As noted elsewhere in this chapter, foreign G-SIBs have been central to the development of the two financial centers by connecting them to the G-SIBs' sophisticated and large home jurisdictions, and allowing the transfer of staff, technology, and know-how. This helped deepen overall sophistication and credibility and created a critical mass. At the same time, the presence of G-SIBs may bring some externalities worth monitoring and possibly regulating. For instance, in the case of Hong Kong SAR and Singapore, externalities may include the following:

- *Size*—Even if the portion of assets (or revenues) of G-SIBs associated with Hong Kong SAR and Singapore is small compared with those of the rest of the G-SIBs' assets, they could still be meaningful relative to these jurisdictions' total banking assets, GDP, and reserves.[21]

- *Interconnectedness*—G-SIBs have strong connections with each other and with other financial sector participants. The failure of one G-SIB could amplify and propagate systemic shocks. As hosts to G-SIBs, Hong Kong SAR and Singapore need to be particularly guarded against such vulnerabilities in their respective self-interests, in the interests of preserving complementarity, and for greater regional and global stability.

- *Complexity for supervision and resolution*—Large foreign banks often have complex business models, geographic footprints, and organizational structures. Properly supervising these sophisticated cross-border groups is a challenging task that requires joint surveillance from both home and host authorities.

---

[20] European Commission January 2014 proposal for a regulation of the European Parliament and of the Council on structural measures improving the resilience of EU credit institutions. Section 619 of the Dodd-Frank Wall Street Reform and Consumer Protection Act of 2010, which created a new section 13 of the U.S. Bank Holding Company Act of 1956. Section 4 of the Financial Services (Banking Reform) Act 2013, which inserts Part 9B (sections 142A – 142Z1) into the Financial Services and Markets Act 2000.

[21] The HKMA and MAS participate in crisis management groups for G-SIBs that are sizable in Hong Kong SAR and Singapore. HKMA participates in nine such groups and MAS participates in seven.

- *Systemic importance*—G-SIBs have relative systemic values that vary depending on whose perspective is being considered (for example, from home and host authorities or from the banking group). A group like HSBC, for instance, would likely be considered of systemic importance for the United Kingdom, Hong Kong SAR, and Singapore. From HSBC's point of view, it is possible that operations in Singapore would be considered to be less systemic for the group than would be operations in the United Kingdom or Hong Kong SAR. SCB would also be viewed as systemically important for the two Asian jurisdictions, but might not be for its home country, since its U.K. activities are quite small. Based on the elevated contribution that Singapore and Hong Kong SAR make to the bank's revenues, SCB is likely to label both centers as systemic.

- *Leakages*[22]—Domestic regulations may not always apply to foreign banks operating locally. The perimeter of application would depend on the form of incorporation of the banks (branch or subsidiary), giving greater powers to home and host authorities, respectively.[23]

Regulatory responses thus far. In addition to opting for a strict regulatory approach for domestic banks and maintaining a strong track record as already noted, the two centers have already adopted measures to mitigate the risks associated with foreign banks and hedge funds:

- *Foreign banks*[24]—HKMA and, to a larger degree, MAS, impose strict standards, comparable to those applicable to domestic banks. These standards apply to (1) licensing and access to retail deposits, which may require local incorporation; and (2) prudential requirements. For instance, in Singapore, full and wholesale branches have to observe a minimum asset maintenance ratio of 35 percent and 15 percent, respectively. In addition, a separate set of asset maintenance requirements under the Deposit Insurance Act covers insured deposits. Foreign branches also must comply with stringent liquidity requirements (they typically hold minimum liquidity assets equivalent to 16 percent of their qualifying liabilities), and must maintain minimum cash balances. MAS enjoys resolution powers, and can impose corrective and remedial actions on branches. In Hong Kong SAR, the existing liquidity requirements apply, and the new liquidity coverage ratio (for Category 1 banks) and liquidity maintenance ratio (for Category 2 banks) will apply to foreign bank branches. A proposed new resolution regime would extend to branches of foreign banks, and existing supervisory intervention powers for banks extend to branches already.

---

[22] See Aiyar, Calomiris, and Wieladek (2012) for an illustration of leakages from macroprudential policy in the United Kingdom.

[23] Even though requirements such as capital rules may not apply to branches, branches are subject to other prudential requirements, including liquidity requirements, corporate governance requirements with respect to management, and inspections by host authorities.

[24] Measures are detailed in the Singapore FSSA (IMF 2013), Box 2 on "Supervision and Resolution of Foreign Branches."

- *Hedge funds*—Hedge funds are also subject to closer scrutiny. In line with the United States, where stricter registration and reporting requirements have been imposed on hedge funds by Dodd-Frank, MAS now requires asset and hedge fund managers operating in Singapore (including foreigners) to either hold a capital markets license or be registered. Similarly, both Hong Kong SAR and the United Kingdom are tightening the regulation and surveillance of hedge funds.

Outlook for future regulatory responses. The hosting of G-SIBs in Hong Kong SAR and Singapore is an opportunity, but also calls for intensified supervision and cross-border cooperation. Authorities' active participation in foreign banks' colleges of supervisors and crisis management groups is essential to identifying and developing robust and actionable resolution strategies for foreign G-SIBs active in Hong Kong SAR and Singapore.

CONCLUSION

Complementarity. Using network analysis tools, we posited that financial system stability would be enhanced if Hong Kong SAR and Singapore both existed as financial centers *and* acted in a complementary fashion to one another across geographic clientele and asset markets. Indeed, this framework closely matches how they have developed thus far. The main insight we seek to convey is that excessive competition may engender destabilizing levels of complexity and interconnectedness in the network, and the presence of two "specialized" Asian financial centers may better balance the micro benefits from economies of scale with the macro benefits of stability.

    Credibility. If Hong Kong SAR and Singapore are to continue playing their stabilizing roles, they will need to preserve sound financial systems. Doing so will require effective regulation, intensive supervision, and strong fiscal and external buffers. It would benefit both centers, and Asia at large, if the two jurisdictions were to collaborate on enhancing Asia's connectivity and address infrastructure regulations affecting Asia and identify common themes and solutions for financial markets.

    Strategic challenges. Hong Kong SAR's financial depth, intensive social and professional networks, and sheer depth of soft institutional structures create comparative advantages. At the same time, these advantages require the jurisdiction to strike a balance between servicing the financial needs of China and reaping the related opportunities, while preserving and further growing its international character and ability to define its policies to support its own financial services sector for a broader clientele. Singapore is characterized by a small domestic market, which is dominated by a few large banks. Without a base similar to the one that Hong Kong SAR has with China, Singapore's banks need to continue to develop long-term, risk-based regional strategies. To attract foreign interest and continue to benefit from further innovation, Singapore needs to deepen its debt and stock markets as well as its insurance and asset management sectors. Singapore is expected to continue to be considered a "safe haven" in South and Southeast Asia. However, Singapore may also have to venture beyond this region, to new geographic and product growth drivers.

Meeting the region's needs more effectively. Many emerging Asian economies appear to have low degrees of financial integration, both with the world and with other Asian countries. A low degree of financial integration or openness tends to be mirrored by a lack of financial sector depth. This is where Hong Kong SAR and Singapore could help boost financial integration. For instance, the two jurisdictions could help link Asia and niche regional centers to global financial centers, which could improve economic growth and financial resilience in Asia. Finally, the prospective development of pan-Asian banking groups may mitigate some of the volatility associated with hosting groups from the United States and Europe, and further enhance the voice of Asia in the global regulatory and policy agenda.

ANNEX 7.1

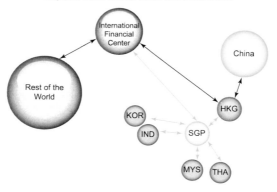

1. Hong Kong SAR is the Financial Center for China, Singapore is the Financial Center for the Rest of Asia

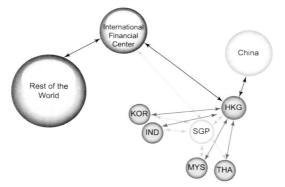

2. Hong Kong SAR and Singapore are Competing Financial Centers for Asia

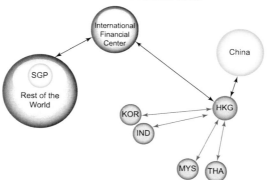

3. Hong Kong SAR Becomes the Dominant Financial Center for China and the Rest of Asia

Annex Figure 7.1.1 Connections and Shocks

Note: Since the hypothetical network is unweighted, all links are assumed to be of equal size. In the figures presented here, the size of the circles is illustrative. HKG = Hong Kong SAR; KOR = Korea; IND = India; MYS = Malaysia; Singapore; THA =Thailand.

REFERENCES

Aiyar, S., C. Calomiris, and T. Wieladek. 2012. "Does Macropru Leak? Evidence from a UK Policy Experiment." Bank of England Working Paper No. 445, London.

Hong Kong Monetary Authority. *2012 Annual Report.* Hong Kong SAR: Hong Kong Monetary Authority.

———. 2013. "Financial Infrastructure in Hong Kong." Background Brief No. 4, February, Hong Kong SAR.

———. 2014. "An Effective Resolution Regime for Financial Institutions in Hong Kong," Consultation Paper, January, Hong Kong SAR.

Hooley, John. 2013. "Bringing down the Great Wall? Global Implications of Capital Account Liberalization in China." *Bank of England Quarterly Bulletin* 53 (4): 304–16.

Huat, Tan Chwee, Joseph Lim, and Wilson Chen. 2004. "Competing International Financial Centers: A Comparative Study between Hong Kong and Singapore." Paper prepared for Saw Centre for Financial Studies and ISEAS Conference, November.

International Monetary Fund. 2012. "Spillover Report." International Monetary Fund, Washington.

———. 2013. "Singapore Financial System Stability Assessment." IMF Country Report No. 13/325, Washington, October.

———. 2014. "People's Republic of China–Hong Kong Special Administrative Region Financial System Stability Assessment." IMF Country Report No. 14/130, Washington, April.

Jiminez, N., and E. Martin. 2010. "A Constant Market Share Analysis of the Euro Area in the Period of 1994–2007." *Banco de España Economic Bulletin* 2–16.

Monetary Authority of Singapore. 2012. *Singapore Bond Market Guide.* Singapore: Monetary Authority of Singapore.

———. 2013. "Financial Stability Review," December. Singapore.

Ng Beoy Kui. 1998. "Hong Kong and Singapore as International Financial Centres: A Comparative Functional Perspective." Nanyang Technological University, Singapore.

Pauly, Louis W., 2011. "Hong Kong's International Financial Centre: Retrospect and Prospect," Report for the Savantas Policy Institute, February 5.

Seade, J., X. Wei, and Y.-T. Wu. 2010. "The Competitiveness of Financial Services in Hong Kong: Rising Tide or Competitive Gain?" In *Hong Kong as an International Financial Centre for China and for the World*, edited by J. Seade, P. Lin, Y. Ma, and others, 179–200. Hong Kong: Lingnan Research Monograph.

PART III

Challenges Ahead

Asia's Demographic Changes and Infrastructure Needs: How Can the Financial Sector Address These Challenges?

DING DING, W. RAPHAEL LAM, AND SHANAKA J. PEIRIS

MAIN POINTS OF THIS CHAPTER

- Asia's financial sector has a key role to play in addressing the challenges associated with the region's changing demographics and large infrastructure investment needs.

- Enhancing financial innovation and integration in the region could facilitate intraregional financial flows and mobilize resources from the aging savers in industrialized Asia to finance infrastructure investment in emerging Asia.

- Strengthening financial ties within the region as well as with global financial markets, alongside appropriate prudential frameworks, could also help diversify the sources of finance and reduce the cost of funding in emerging Asia.

- Financial deepening could help ease potential overheating from the scaling up of infrastructure investment and, hence, achieve more balanced growth in the region.

INTRODUCTION

This chapter explores the potential role of Asia's financial sector in addressing the region's main challenges: changing demographics and large infrastructure investment needs. Diverse demographic trends across Asia are likely to affect aggregate savings and, thereby, intraregional financial flows in the long term. Population aging in the advanced Asian economies, and in several emerging Asian economies

The authors are grateful to Fei Han, Yitae Kim, Jerry Schiff, Alison Stuart, Chikahisa Sumi, and participants at the IMF Asia and Pacific Department seminar and the joint IMF/Hong Kong Monetary Authority seminar for helpful comments. This chapter is partially based on IMF Working Paper 14/126 (Ding, Lam, and Peiris 2014).

as well, could affect returns on asset classes and change the structure of the region's financial markets. In an aging society, how to address downward pressures on savings and ensure adequate returns through diversification to high-growth emerging Asian assets remains a challenge. In some other emerging Asian economies, however, the share of the working-age population is expected to continue to rise in the coming decades and could bring higher growth and savings. However, despite their favorable demographic and growth prospects, emerging Asian economies export capital and suffer from underdeveloped infrastructure. This situation is partly related to these economies' shallow financial systems, which constrain growth prospects. Mobilizing financial resources for infrastructure investment to harness emerging Asia's so-called "demographic dividend" through financial deepening and innovation remains a key challenge.

Aging trends within Asia are expected to become more diverse, exacerbating the long-term challenge of downward pressure on aggregate savings. Population aging is a looming issue in China and in advanced Asia, including Japan and Korea. This trend results from a sharp drop in fertility rates and an increase in life expectancies, which can be attributed to higher incomes and medical advances (Figure 8.1). Overall, Asia is facing a demographic shift that will see a large segment of its population age significantly during the next half century. As a result, aggregate savings are likely to decline, with people running down their savings during retirement. Aggregate savings is one of the key channels through which population aging affects capital flows and financial markets (IMF 2010). Examples of these effects include reductions of external surpluses, declining asset prices, and higher risk aversion. At the same time, public saving could also come under pressure from rising pension and aging-related expenses. Access to a wider

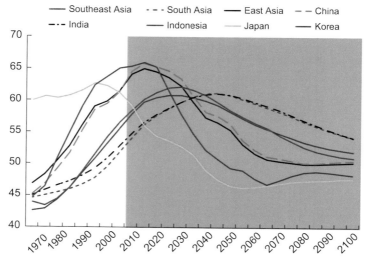

Figure 8.1   Working-Age Population Ratio in Asia (*Percent*)

Source: The United Nations *World Population Prospects 2012.*

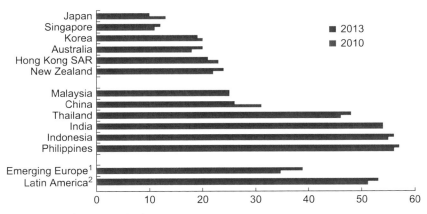

Figure 8.2 Infrastructure Ranking

Source: International Institute for Management Development, *World Competitiveness Online*.

Note: A lower ranking indicates a better score out of sample countries. There were 58 countries in the sample in 2010 and 60 countries in 2013.

[1] Emerging Europe = Bulgaria, Croatia, the Czech Republic, Estonia, Hungary, Latvia, Lithuania, Poland, Romania, Russia, the Slovak Republic, Slovenia, Turkey, and Ukraine.

[2] Latin America = Argentina, Brazil, Chile, Colombia, Mexico, Peru, and Venezuela.

array of financial instruments with superior risk-return characteristics in emerging Asian economies could entice aging Asian savers to reduce home bias and investments in low-return, advanced economy assets.

Meanwhile, several emerging Asian economies with favorable demographic transitions will face the challenge of mobilizing resources to finance infrastructure investment. Despite favorable demographic transitions that would raise growth potential, emerging Asian countries such as India, Indonesia, and the Philippines continue to suffer from underdeveloped infrastructure. Although infrastructure in these economies has improved during the past decades, investment has fallen short of the pace of rapid economic and population growth. In the *World Competitiveness* database published by the International Institute for Management Development (IMD 2014), emerging Asia generally scores lower in the infrastructure category than do its advanced peers in the region and remains in the higher half in the global rankings (Figure 8.2) This is particularly true for electricity generation and road networks.[1] With rising public debt constraining public infrastructure investment in emerging Asia, inadequate infrastructure could be partly related to limited private sector participation and a lack of long-term capital market financing (ADB 2013). These infrastructure deficits are estimated to have impeded growth. For instance, the drop of infrastructure investment in Indonesia from 5–6 percent of GDP in the early 1990s to 2–3 percent in the past decade has limited growth by as much as 3 to 4 percentage points of GDP (Tahilyani, Tamhane, and Tan 2011). Meeting the infrastructure gap solely with fiscal spending would significantly add to the fiscal burden, eventually posing greater risks to growth.

---

[1] A higher ranking indicates a lower score out of the sample countries.

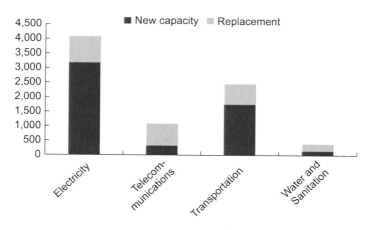

Figure 8.3 Estimated Infrastructure Needs in Developing Asia (*Billions of U.S. dollars*)
Source: Asian Development Bank (2009).

Estimates of the adequacy of infrastructure usually rely on the stock of infrastructure relative to income, urbanization, population density, and the economic structure across countries. In this regard, the greatest infrastructure gap or shortfall in emerging Asia appears to be electricity generation (Figure 8.3). The median electricity generating capacity in the region is approximately 90 percent of the median for Latin America (IMF 2010). Road networks seem most in need of upgrading in Bangladesh, Myanmar, Mongolia, and the Philippines. And, despite the rapid spread of telephones and mobile phones in the region in the past decade, emerging Asia continues to lag behind Latin America in its stock of telecommunications infrastructure. How to finance this vast infrastructure investment is a key challenge for the region's policymakers.

Financial deepening and innovation in the region may change the way in which policies are developed to address these long-term challenges. In designing such policies, policymakers would need to consider the implications of rapid financial growth and innovation. Should further financial sector development help address these challenges, policymakers could focus on the following:

- *Financial innovation and integration in the region*—Financial innovation and integration could improve the allocation of savings and strengthen domestic resilience to external shocks. With sound prudential frameworks and pricing of risks, financial innovation and a more integrated financial market across Asia would help channel large savings in the aging economies to the financing of infrastructure gaps in emerging Asia, while achieving higher yields in return. At the same time, an integrated financial sector across Asia would increase countries' abilities to share risks. Risk sharing captures the degree to which countries succeed in insuring each other against shocks. The newly industrialized Asian economies (Hong Kong SAR, Korea, Singapore, Taiwan

Province of China) share substantial risks with the United States, but much less with emerging Asian economies. Intraregional risk sharing is low, in general, within Asia (IMF 2011).

- *Improve financial deepening by improving domestic financial inclusion and capital market development*—Financial deepening could help harness the increased savings from the rising working-age population in emerging Asia, which could be intermediated to finance infrastructure investment in these economies. At the same time, greater financial inclusion could raise financial savings and allow households better access to credit. Addressing the impediments to developing corporate bond markets and an institutional investor base, as highlighted in Goswami and others (2014), will be critical to channeling savings from greater financial inclusion and from advanced Asian economics to infrastructure investment in emerging Asia.

- *Greater financial integration*—Financial integration can help channel savings to the most productive investment opportunities across the region. However, it also comes with the potential cost of amplifying shock propagation and synchronization in the region (IMF 2014b), as well as making portfolio flows and asset prices more sensitive to global "push" factors, and posing challenges to financial stability (IMF 2014a). In particular, if regional financial integration involves freer capital accounts and greater foreign participation in financial markets, policymakers will need to be vigilant and strengthen regional safety nets and international policy cooperation. They will also need to implement appropriate macroprudential policies.

The rest of the chapter presents stylized facts about Asia's demographic changes and infrastructure gaps; presents empirical evidence on how demography could affect saving rates; uses a dynamic general equilibrium model to illustrate the macroeconomic impact of certain financial sector developments and discusses their potential benefits when the region is faced with demographic and infrastructure financing challenges; and discusses the role of the financial sector in addressing these challenges and the plausible policy implications; then offers conclusions.

ASIA'S MAIN CHALLENGES

Asia has experienced a demographic shift during the past half century, with diverse trends across countries. Advanced economies in Asia have mostly faced aging populations. The elderly dependency ratios have increased by 4–21 percentage points since 1980, most notably in Hong Kong SAR, Japan, and Korea. Population aging is modest for emerging Asian economies with the exceptions of China and Thailand (Table 8.1; Figure 8.4). The divergence in the region is likely to be more evident in the next few decades, with a few economies aging rapidly (China, Japan, and Korea), while other emerging economies continue to face demographic dividends as the youth population enters the labor force. Examples of the latter include Cambodia, India, Indonesia, Lao P.D.R., Malaysia, and the Philippines. As the working-age population increases in an economy,

TABLE 8.1

Age Dependency Ratios (*Ranked by net change 1985–2012*)

	1981–85		2008–12		Net Change 1985–2012	
Emerging Asia	**Elderly**	**Youth**	**Elderly**	**Youth**	**Elderly**	**Youth**
Thailand	6.4	61.6	12.5	29.4	6.1	−32.2
China	8.8	52.5	11.2	27.2	2.4	−25.3
Bhutan	5.3	78.3	7.2	45.6	2.0	−32.8
Indonesia	6.4	70.7	8.2	40.4	1.8	−30.3
India	6.3	68.4	7.6	47.9	1.3	−20.5
Malaysia	6.2	66.5	7.3	47.2	1.1	−19.4
Cambodia	5.2	72.2	5.9	50.6	0.7	−21.7
Bangladesh	6.9	85.2	7.1	49.5	0.2	−35.7
Myanmar	7.4	69.4	7.4	37.5	0.0	−32.0
Philippines	5.9	86.9	5.9	58.6	0.0	−28.2
Brunei Darussalam	5.1	66.7	5.0	37.6	−0.1	−29.1
Vietnam	8.9	72.2	8.5	34.2	−0.3	−38.1
Lao P.D.R.	6.9	84.2	6.3	57.2	−0.6	−26.9
Average	*6.6*	*71.9*	*7.7*	*43.3*	*1.1*	*−28.6*
Advanced countries						
Asia:						
Japan	14.3	33.2	34.9	20.9	20.6	−12.4
Korea	6.4	49.3	15.2	23.1	8.7	−26.2
Hong Kong SAR	10.0	34.5	16.8	15.6	6.8	−19.0
Singapore	7.3	36.4	12.2	24.0	4.9	−12.5
Australia	15.3	36.8	19.8	28.2	4.5	−8.6
New Zealand	15.7	39.8	19.4	30.9	3.7	−8.9
Average	*11.5*	*38.4*	*19.7*	*23.8*	*8.2*	*−14.6*
Outside Asia:						
Germany	22.0	24.8	30.6	20.4	8.6	−4.3
United Kingdom	23.1	30.5	25.0	26.3	1.9	−4.1
United States	17.6	33.2	19.4	30.1	1.8	−3.1
Average	*20.9*	*29.5*	*25.0*	*25.6*	*4.1*	*−3.8*

Sources: United Nations *World Population Prospects 2012*; and IMF staff calculations.

a notable rise in income per capita is experienced. The relationship, however, tapers off when income per capita reaches a certain threshold (Figure 8.4).

Demographic change could affect Asian economies in several ways. First, the demographic transition affects labor force participation, which in turn affects growth potential. Second, for rapidly aging economies, fiscal positions could come under pressure from rising pension and other aging-related spending. Third, aggregate saving could also fall with population aging, because people run down their savings during retirement. Investment could also fall as capital stock shrinks in tandem, and the interplay of investment and saving would affect capital flows and financial markets. Asset returns could be affected as risk appetite changes because an elderly population tends to favor less risky investment. Financial product structures may also change in response to age-related demand.

Aggregate saving is one of the channels through which demographic change affects capital flows and financial markets. The demographic transition in Asia is often identified as a factor contributing to high saving rates. Studies by Park and Shin (2009) and Horioka and Terada-Hagiwara (2011) show a strong relationship

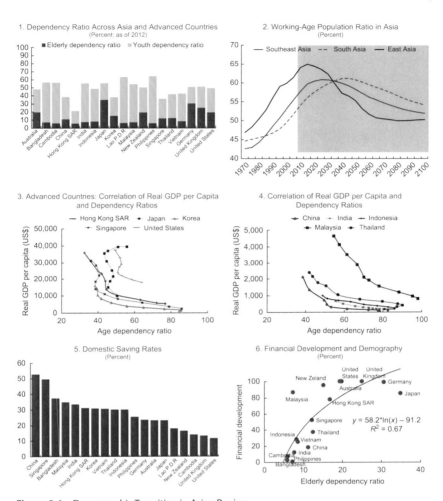

Figure 8.4 Demographic Transition in Asian Region

Note: Financial development measured by the penentration ratio of the use of public and private registries in credit market.

between demography and saving rates, in light of the life hypothesis.[2] Domestic saving rates appear to have increased as dependency ratios (the population ages 65 or older and ages 14 or younger to the total population) declined during the

---

[2] Previous empirical analyses find an important role for demographic variables on saving rates based on the life-cycle hypothesis, such as Modigliani (1970), Feldstein and Horioka (1980), Chinn and Prasad (2003), Park and Shin (2009), Hung and Qian (2010), and Chinn and Ito (2008). A higher proportion of elderly in the population is often associated with lower saving rates given that the elderly typically finance their living expenses by drawing down savings. Similarly, higher youth dependency in the population will typically be associated with greater consumption given limited earning income, posing a negative impact on the overall domestic saving rates. The elderly also see less need for precautionary saving, because they assume that younger relatives will provide them with care and financial assistance. This suggests that higher elderly and youth dependency in the population would generally be associated with lower saving rates.

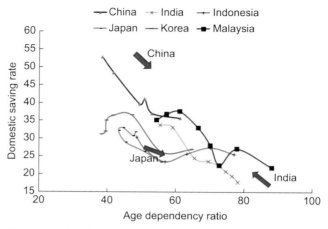

Figure 8.5 Correlation of Domestic Savings and Dependency Ratios, 1985–2012 (*Percent*)

Source: World Bank, *World Development Indicators.*

period 1960–2012 (Figure 8.5). The negative relationship tends to hold, although with a weaker correlation, for other advanced economies outside Asia. In particular, the dependency ratio decreased until recently in most emerging Asian economies (the youth were growing up while fertility rates declined), whereas domestic saving rates increased.

In addition, demographic change could also shape financial sector development, which is a key determinant of saving. Population aging in China and advanced Asian economies will reduce aggregate risk appetite given that the elderly tend to be more risk averse in their savings. Households' financial needs in these economies will require stable returns on saving and more customized wealth management products and services. In economies enjoying the demographic dividends of higher growth and saving rates, financial sector development and innovation would help channel those savings toward higher returns and diversification. Financial frictions and borrowing constraints in these economies may encourage the need for precautionary saving. If that happens, domestic saving rates would increase for a given level of income. Financial integration and deepening would reduce such constraints and the precautionary savings motive while providing more saving options (for example, bank deposits, wealth management products, real estate through mortgages) with higher expected returns. As a result, financial development may affect economies differently, depending on the specific phase and condition of the financial markets. Empirical evidence is ambiguous (Chinn and Prasad 2003).

The impact of infrastructure on growth has been extensively studied, with most studies finding that improvement in a broad range of infrastructure categories tends to lead to faster and more balanced growth. In addition to economic returns, infrastructure investment generates large social returns in the form of stronger economic activity, improved health and education outcomes, and diminished inequality. There is also solid evidence, supported by empirical analysis, that better infrastructure improves productivity growth. For example, Canning and Pedroni (2008) use cross-country data to show that infrastructure positively contributes to long-term economic growth despite substantial variations across countries. And, using cross-country data from 1980 to 2010, Seneviratne and Sun (2013) find that better infrastructure, both in quantity and quality, could improve income distribution and reduce inequality.

Although the benefits of improving infrastructure are well understood, mobilizing financial resources for infrastructure investment has been challenging in many countries. Historically, given the public goods nature of infrastructure investment, the provision of investment has been almost entirely in the public domain in Asia and elsewhere, including in advanced economies. The large sunk costs and long construction periods often associated with infrastructure projects also make it less attractive to private investors, forcing the public sector to bear the main financing responsibility, using both on- and off-balance-sheet instruments. However, in the past, public debt levels in many emerging Asian economies, including India, Indonesia, and the Philippines, have not provided sufficient fiscal space to scale up infrastructure spending. In China, for example, local governments were one of the major drivers behind the infrastructure investment boom in recent decades (Walsh, Park, and Yu 2011). They have been actively involved in mobilizing financing for infrastructure projects through public guarantees—implicit and explicit—for bank loans, and in some cases, direct subsidies for infrastructure special purpose vehicles to boost their profits and credit ratings. In addition, the dominance of commercial banks in most emerging Asian economies also means they are the largest source of infrastructure funding. However, bank liabilities are generally short term, while infrastructure projects have long payback periods (20–30 years). This tends to exacerbate maturity mismatches and impede long-term infrastructure finance.

Government financing and provision of infrastructure alone may not be sufficient to address Asia's infrastructure gap. ADB 2009 estimates Asia's total infrastructure investment needs to be $8 trillion over 10 years, or about 4 percent of the region's GDP per year. This proportion is almost equivalent to the average of the current total public investment level in industrialized Asia, and half of that in emerging Asia (Figure 8.6). The scope for sustained increases in public investment in a particular country also depends crucially on the prospects for debt sustainability and other short-term financing considerations. In recent years, although several governments across the region have stepped up their allocation to infrastructure as part of the fiscal stimulus packages developed in response to the 2008–09 global financial crisis, their ability to sustain elevated levels of infrastructure investment may be limited by other demands on budgets and on a shrinking fiscal space.

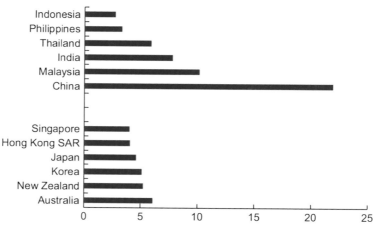

Figure 8.6 Public Investment as a Percentage of GDP, 2010

Source: IMF *World Economic Outlook.*

The challenge of infrastructure investment financing in emerging Asia may become more pressing, given the region's rising population and large infrastructure gap. Whether this financing gap can be met in the long term by an increase in emerging economies' own savings remains an open question. In the meantime, changing demographics in Asia may prompt further intraregional financial integration. As advanced Asia ages further, demand will grow for access to a wider array of financial instruments with superior risk-return characteristics located in emerging Asian economies. In particular, infrastructure projects in emerging Asia could provide high yield but steady long-term returns, making them appealing to advanced Asia's investors, such as pension funds. As discussed in the next section, further financial integration, combined with domestic financial deepening, may help emerging Asian economies address their infrastructure investment challenges.

THE MACROECONOMIC IMPACT OF FINANCIAL DEEPENING AND INTEGRATION

The Impact of Demographic Changes

This section first analyzes the impact of population aging on domestic saving rates using reduced-form panel estimations. The estimation provides an analysis of the determinants of savings for 12 to 15 Asian economies. The analysis includes Australia, Bangladesh, Brunei Darussalam, Cambodia, China, Hong Kong SAR, India, Indonesia, Japan, Korea, Lao P.D.R., Malaysia, the Philippines, Singapore, Thailand, and Vietnam. These economies are further separated and grouped into different categories in the specification to test for robustness and for any differences among Asian emerging, advanced, and frontier economies. Other advanced economies outside Asia, such as Germany, the United Kingdom, and the United

States, are included for reference and robustness checks. The reduced-form panel estimations features follow:

- *Sample period*—Since the focus is on long-term trends, the analysis uses annual data from 1960 to 2012 where data are available. Averages over a multiyear interval (for example, 1960–65, 1965–70, 2001–07, and 2008–12) are also included to mitigate cyclical effects and account for possible structural breaks around the global financial crisis.

- *Data*—Data are obtained from various sources, including the IMF's International Finance Statistics, the World Bank's World Development Indicators, the United Nations Population Projections, and Heston, Summers, and Aten's Penn World Tables Version 7.1.

- *Specification*—The specification is as follows:

$$
\begin{aligned}
SGDP_{i,t} = \beta_{0i} &+ \beta_1 AGE_{EL_{i,t}} + \beta_2 AGE_{YO_{i,t}} + \beta_3 ADV \times AGE_{EL_{i,t}} \\
&+ \beta_4 ADV \times AGE_{YO_{i,t}} + \beta_5 GGDP_{i,t} + \beta_6 LNPCGDP_{i,t} \\
&+ \beta_7 LN(PCGDPSQ_{i,t} + \beta_8 CREDITGDP_{i,t} \\
&+ \beta_9 CREDITGDP\_SQ_{i,t} + \beta_{10} FD_{i,t} + \beta_{11} X_{i,t} + \gamma D_t + \varepsilon_{i,t}
\end{aligned}
$$

SGDP is the gross domestic saving rate in country i at time t in real terms; AGE_{EL} and AGE_{YO} refer to the dependency ratios of the elderly (ages 65 or older) and youth (ages 14 or younger) obtained from the Penn World Tables. *GGDP* refers to the real growth rate in the domestic economy, and *LNPCGDP* is the log GDP per capita in local currency units. CREDITGDP is the credit to the private nonfinancial sector as a ratio to nominal GDP. *FD* is an indicator of financial development, proxied by bank access and financing constraints, available from the World Development Indicators. X is a vector of control variables (such as real interest rates and inflation), and D refers to the time dummy variables for each year or for each five-year interval. Institutional or legal developments and availability of social security could also be important factors determining saving rates (Ayadi and others 2013; Chamon and Prasad 2007), which would be partly captured in the cross-sectional and annual dummy variables.

The specification also includes an interaction term on aging and additional terms to assess the nonlinear impact on savings. Population aging may affect savings differently in advanced and emerging economies. A dummy variable equal to 1 for advanced economies is interacted with the elderly and youth dependency ratios to see if the aging impact on saving varies across the two groups of economies. At the same time, since the level of GDP per capita and the credit-to-GDP ratio may have nonlinear effects on saving rates, the specification also includes quadratic terms (*LN(PCGDPSQ)* and *CREDITGDP_SQ*) with separate coefficients.[3]

---

[3]The regression uses lagged terms on the explanatory variables to mitigate potential endogeneity problems. An alternative would be to use the non-overlapping periods for the saving rate and the explanatory variables as in Chinn and Ito (2008) and Ayadi and others (2013).

The empirical results of the estimation are presented in Table 8.2. A summary of the main results follows:

- *A higher dependency ratio in the population tends to be associated with lower domestic savings across most specifications.* The impact of elderly and youth dependency on domestic savings tends to be negative and statistically significant. The adverse impact is also notably higher for elderly dependency than for youth dependency (about three to four times higher) in both

TABLE 8.2

Panel Regression Estimation Results

Dependent Variable: Domestic Saving As a Percentage of GDP	(1)	(2)	(3)	(4)	(5)	(6)
Constant	−213.4	−2.9	−8.1	38.7	33.9	55.3
	(772.5)	(29.5)	(31.6)	(31.7)	(27.7)	(29.2)
Elderly dependency ratio	**−0.71**	**−0.31**	**−0.54**	**−0.64**	**−0.76**	**−0.90**
	(0.4)	(0.4)	(0.2)	(0.2)	(0.4)	(0.5)
Youth dependency ratio	−0.22	**−0.21**	**−0.15**	**−0.16**	**−0.19**	**−0.22**
	(0.4)	(0.1)	(0.1)	(0.1)	(0.1)	(0.1)
Elderly dependency ratio × Dummy advanced economies	-	-	-	-	0.12	0.59
					−(0.2)	(0.5)
Youth dependency ratio × Dummy advanced Economies	-	-	-	-	**−0.17**	**−0.22**
					(0.1)	(0.1)
Ln (real GDP per capita)	32.35	**14.52**	**11.90**	0.93	2.53	−1.03
	(157.4)	(6.4)	(7.1)	(7.3)	(6.7)	(7.2)
Ln (real GDP per capita squared)	−0.83	**−1.02**	**−0.75**	−0.06	−0.15	0.03
	(8.1)	(0.4)	(0.4)	(0.5)	(0.4)	(0.5)
Ln (private sector credit to GDP)	**0.19**	**0.01**	0.00	**0.06**	**0.01**	**0.02**
	(0.0)	(0.0)	(0.0)	(0.0)	(0.0)	(0.0)
Ln (private sector credit to GDP squared)	**−0.02**	**−0.05**	−0.03	−0.05	**−0.01**	**−0.01**
	(0.1)	(0.0)	(0.4)	(0.4)	(0.0)	(0.0)
Real growth	0.21	**0.20**	**0.12**	**0.15**	**0.19**	**0.22**
	(0.1)	(0.0)	(0.0)	(0.0)	(0.0)	(0.0)
Real interest rate	−0.59	**−0.58**	−0.20	**−0.41**	**−0.37**	**−0.54**
	(0.4)	(0.2)	(0.2)	(0.2)	(0.2)	(0.2)
Inflation rate	−0.02	−0.01	−0.01	−0.01	−0.01	−0.01
	(0.1)	(0.0)	(0.0)	(0.0)	(0.0)	(0.0)
Openness in financial development	0.02	**−0.04**	**0.04**	**0.03**	**0.02**	**0.01**
	(0.0)	(0.0)	(0.0)	(0.0)	(0.1)	(0.0)
Control variables: Cross-section dummy	Y	Y	Y	Y	Y	Y
Country groups	Advanced Asia	Emerging Asia	All	All Asia	All	All Asia
Number of country groups	5	9	15	14	15	14
Adjusted R^2	0.89	0.87	0.65	0.72	0.77	0.80

Source: Authors' estimates.

Note: Numbers in parentheses denote standard errors of estimated coefficients. Numbers in bold denote 10 percent significance level. Interactive term refers to the dummy variable for advanced countries multiplied by the respective age-dependency ratios. Country group "all" includes emerging and advanced Asia, as well as selected member countries of the Organisation for Economic Co-operation and Development. "All Asia" includes Asian emerging and advanced economies.

advanced and emerging Asia. For instance, a 1 percentage point increase in the elderly dependency ratio would reduce domestic savings by 0.3–0.9 percentage point, while the same increase in the youth dependency ratio would only reduce domestic savings by 0.1–0.2 percentage point.

- *Moreover, the negative correlation between youth dependency and domestic savings tends to be higher for advanced economies.* The coefficients on interacting terms (specifications 5 and 6) suggest that the negative impact of youth dependency on the saving rate appears mainly in advanced countries. This could be related to higher spending on children in advanced countries— spending that focuses more on education and human capital.

- *Per capita income and the demand for private credit tend to have nonlinear impacts on domestic savings.* The nonlinear effect is similar to the findings in other studies and supported by the stylized facts shown in Figure 8.4. Higher per capita income is associated with higher savings, but the domestic savings rate begins to decline as income per capita reaches a certain threshold. The nonlinear effect also applies to credit demand. Other factors, such as real GDP growth and higher risk premiums, affect savings in an expected manner, but inflation rates do not seem to have a significant effect on savings rates.

- *Financial development, measured by openness in financial markets, tends to play a role in domestic savings, though the magnitude is small.* The coefficients are, in most cases, positive and statistically significant.

To complement the empirical estimations, the analysis examines the macroeconomic impact of the expected demographic transitions across countries in Asia, especially the impact on savings and capital flows, using a dynamic structural general equilibrium model. The changing demographics in the region call for a strengthening of financial integration for better risk sharing and capital allocation, as well as an increase in investment in infrastructure to meet the growing demand from the rising population in emerging Asia. In this context, the exercise illustrates that more balanced growth can be achieved through further financial development in the region. Because demographic changes and infrastructure investment would affect all agents in the economy, several examples are presented to indicate the benefits of better household financial inclusion, lower corporate riskiness, and lower sovereign risk premiums. The analysis uses the IMF's Global Integrated Monetary and Fiscal model (GIMF) to study the macroeconomic impact of the projected demographic changes and infrastructure investment in Asia and the potential benefits of financial sector development. The GIMF is a multiregional dynamic structural general equilibrium model with optimizing behavior by households and firms and full intertemporal stock-flow accounting.[4] Frictions in the form of sticky prices and wages, real adjustment costs, and liquidity-constrained households, along with finite planning

---

[4] For the theoretical structure of the GIMF model, see Kumhof and others 2010.

horizons of households, mean monetary and fiscal policy have important roles in economic stabilization. In the exercise the model is calibrated to contain four regions: China, other emerging Asia, industrialized Asia, and the rest of the world. Because the model allows for dynamic interaction across sectors and regions, scenarios can be designed to incorporate the different demographic changes and investment needs across the region.

The projected demographic changes in Asia would have different macroeconomic effects across the region, especially on savings and investment. According to the 2010 United Nations *World Population Prospects*, the working-age population in emerging Asia is projected to rise by about 25 percent by 2030, continuing its upward trend from the early 2000s, albeit at a slower rate (Table 8.3).[5] In Asia's advanced economies, the working-age population is projected to decrease by 9 percent in the next two decades. China's working-age population is projected to peak about 2020.[6] In the GIMF, the changing working-age populations in different regions are introduced as labor supply shocks. Moreover, as the empirical analysis shows, the elderly and youth dependency ratios tend to have negative impacts on domestic saving rates in Asia, after controlling for other factors. Because the GIMF does not allow for an explicit incorporation of the age of agents or their retirement decisions, the analysis imposes the impact of demographics on saving as estimated in the GIMF in addition to the labor supply shocks.[7] The combination of labor supply shocks and shocks to household savings rates allows the impact of the changing demographics on both labor supply and households saving behavior to be captured.

GIMF model simulations suggest that demographic factors in emerging Asia are likely to be supportive of growth in the coming decades. The model simulations show that the increasing working-age population growth in emerging Asia could add 1.5 percentage points to the region's long-term annual real output and 0.7 percentage point to its gross savings as a share of GDP (Figure 8.7) by 2020. The interplay between savings and investment would also have a significant impact on the dynamics of current accounts and, thereby, on both interregional and intraregional capital flows. In emerging Asia, the increase in savings tends to outweigh the increase in investment, leading to a rise in annual current account surpluses. In advanced Asia, the decline in savings tends to outweigh the decline in investment, which would lead to an increase in the real interest rate and capital inflows. (However, in practice, emerging markets are likely to continue to receive net capital inflows given their relatively high growth rates and real interest rates).

---

[5] In our analysis, the working-age population is defined as ages 20–64. Data can be downloaded from http://esa.un.org/wpp/.

[6] Although the elderly dependency ratio in China is projected to more than double by 2030, the youth dependency ratio is expected to decline sharply. As a result, China's working-age population ratio will only decline from 65 percent in 2010 to 63 percent in 2030.

[7] We assume that a 1 percent increase in the working-age population ratio will increase the savings rate by 0.3 percent in emerging Asia and by 0.5 percent in advanced Asia.

TABLE 8.3

Asia Demographic Changes
(Cumulative growth in percentage points)

	2000–10			2010–20				2020–30			
	Population	Working-Age Population	Working-Age Population Ratio	Population	Working-Age Population	Working-Age Population Ratio	Implied Savings Rate Change	Population	Working-Age Population	Working-Age Population Ratio	Implied Savings Rate Change
China	5.7	14.7	8.5	3.5	4.7	1.2	0.4	0.4	−2.6	−3.0	−0.9
Other Emerging Asia[1]	15.4	24.4	7.8	12.5	18.3	5.2	1.6	9.2	12.0	2.6	0.8
Industrialized Asia[2]	3.9	2.0	−1.9	2.1	−3.1	−5.2	−2.6	0.0	−6.0	−6.0	−3.0

Source: United Nations; IMF staff estimates
[1] Other Emerging Asia = India, Indonesia, Malaysia, the Philippines, Thailand, and Vietnam.
[2] Industrialized Asia = Australia, Japan, Korea, Hong Kong SAR, New Zealand, and Singapore.

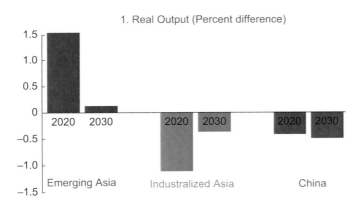

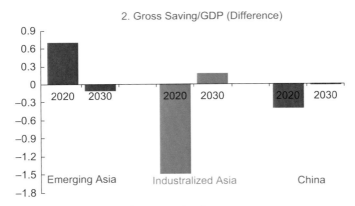

Figure 8.7 The Impact of Demographic Changes

Source: Authors' estimates based on the simulations of the Global Integrated Monetary and Fiscal model.

Although gross savings in emerging Asia would increase because of the rising working-age population, such savings would probably be insufficient to finance the region's immediate infrastructure investment needs, given the estimated size of the infrastructure gap. The decrease in the interest rate spread between emerging Asia and advanced Asia, owing to the demographic changes, is unlikely to have a material impact on intraregional financial flows. More needs to be done to enhance regional financial integration to facilitate a more efficient allocation of resources across countries.

The Benefits of Financial Deepening and Integration

The baseline scenario considers the expected demographic changes and rising investment in Asia during the next decade. The simulation assumes an increase in investment of 2 percent of GDP per year for the next 10 years in emerging Asia, with public and private investment each contributing half.[8] Different policy instruments are available to increase public infrastructure investment. The domestic options—financed by domestic debt or the sale of state assets—include reallocating public expenditure, implementing tax policy measures, and relaxing fiscal targets. The external options consist mostly of external borrowing. In the GIMF, because fiscal policy is governed by specific rules that allow it to respond flexibly to the business cycle while containing the government debt-to-GDP ratio, the augmented public investment spending would be financed by a combination of revenue measures and domestic and external borrowing.

Long-term output would increase under the baseline scenario but would crowd out private demand and widen trade deficits. The model simulation suggests that emerging Asia's long-term annual output would increase by 3–4 percentage points, but private demand would be replaced by public demand and the region's trade deficit would widen. The persistent positive output gaps and inflationary pressure would also lead to tighter monetary policy.[9] In this regard, the question of how to mobilize domestic and external financing resources to ease the impact of the expansionary shock is a key policy challenge. The analysis uses the GIMF to illustrate that enhancing financial deepening and integration in emerging Asia could help mobilize savings in the region and potentially lower infrastructure financing costs. In particular, the analysis illustrates the benefits of financial development in three scenarios representing the three important agents in the economy: households, firms, and the sovereign. The three scenarios, explained in more detail below, are (1) household financial inclusion, that is,

---

[8]The scenario of a 2 percent increase in investment as a share of GDP is for illustrative purposes. Although the need to increase infrastructure investment in emerging Asia, partly through public investment, is widely recognized, there is no consensus on the optimal level of infrastructure investment, the financing scheme, or the efficiency of the investment.

[9]In the GIMF, the central bank uses an inflation-forecast-based interest rate rule. The central bank varies the gap between the actual policy rate and the long-term equilibrium rate to achieve a stable target rate of inflation over time. Under this framework, the monetary policy stance tends to tighten when there is a positive output gap or inflation gap and vice versa.

improving household access to financial markets in emerging Asia; (2) lowering the sensitivity of the external finance premium to corporate leverage (or net worth); and (3) reducing emerging Asia's external borrowing premium, possibly through financial integration.

Household financial inclusion scenario—This scenario assumes that the share of liquidity-constrained households in emerging Asia declines from 50 percent in the baseline scenario to 25 percent, the level that is applicable in advanced Asia. If more households have access to financial instruments, and thus the ability to smooth consumption intertemporally, the private sector will have a greater ability to offset the expansionary fiscal shock, and the private sector will be less subject to crowding out. A larger domestic saving pool would also improve the economy's ability to mobilize savings to finance large investment needs and reduce pressure on public finance. Model simulations suggest that, with improved financial inclusion, a more sustainable and balanced growth path can be achieved. The positive output gap resulting from the increase in labor supply and public investment is slightly less than in the baseline scenario, but there is much less inflationary pressure and the need for monetary tightening is less. The region also imports less compared with the baseline scenario.

Corporate riskiness scenario—This scenario shows the effects of a persistent decrease in the riskiness of emerging Asia's corporate borrowers that reduces the corporate finance premium by 1 percentage point. The decrease in the corporate finance premium originates from the lower sensitivity of "external" spreads to corporate leverage, which effectively reduces the borrowing cost faced by firms. Thus, there is an immediate decrease in the cost of capital. Therefore, business investment, such as in private infrastructure, increases. A lower cost of capital also raises profitability, leading to higher dividends and an increase in household wealth. This effect is particularly important if there is private sector involvement in infrastructure investment. Lower costs also lead firms to increase production and demand more labor, which pushes up wages.

Sovereign risk premium scenario—This scenario assumes a 1 percentage point decrease in emerging Asia's sovereign risk premium. A sustained fiscal expansion (as assumed in the baseline scenario) tends to increase the cost of capital and crowd out private investment. If financial integration could lower external borrowing premiums for the region (discussed in the next section), public investment would rely more on foreign funding, thereby reducing pressure on the domestic economy. Similar to the financial deepening scenario, inflation and the real interest rate would not increase as much as in the baseline scenario, and there would be less monetary tightening.

The simulation results suggest that better access to finance and lower financing costs would allow emerging Asia to scale up infrastructure investment with lower macroeconomic and fiscal risks. As shown in Figure 8.8, interest rate and inflation increases (indicators of aggregate demand pressures) would be less than in the baseline scenario, while long-term growth benefits would remain largely unaffected. Moreover, a deeper domestic investor base and lower financing costs also would create fiscal space and enhance fiscal sustainability. The next section

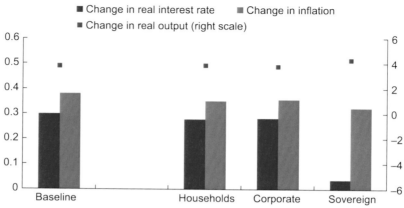

Figure 8.8 Simulation Impact of Financial Sector Development in Emerging Asia (*Percent*)
Source: Authors' estimates.

discusses the possible ways to bring about these benefits and the policy implications of doing so.[10]

HOW TO ENHANCE FINANCIAL DEEPENING AND INTEGRATION IN ASIA

Financial sector development can play an important role in addressing the challenges of demographic change and infrastructure investment needs in Asia. Financial sector development broadly consists of financial integration and financial deepening, through which economies across Asia develop closer financial linkages and firms and households have greater inclusion in and better access to financial markets.

Relative to its trade integration, Asia's degree of financial integration, both with the world and the region, is low. Asia's financial integration could be more effective, particularly its intraregional integration. Asian economies currently benefit less from risk sharing than do advanced economies. Controlling for a broad set of structural and cyclical factors, including trade integration, relative GDP growth, interest and exchange rate movements, and exchange rate volatility, the degree of financial integration of many Asian economies is below the level predicted by the model for all economies. The exceptions are the financial centers of Hong Kong SAR and Singapore. In several cases, financial integration falls

---

[10] Results show the peak level impact on the real interest rate and inflation and the average impact on real output over the next decade after the initial shocks. The households scenario assumes the share of liquidity-constrained households in emerging Asia declines from 50 percent to 25 percent; the corporate scenario assumes the corporate borrowing premium declines by 1 percentage point; and the sovereign scenario assumes the sovereign risk premium declines by 1 percentage point.

below the norm for Latin America and emerging Europe (IMF 2011). Risk sharing captures the degree to which countries succeed in insuring each other against shocks— perfect risk sharing implies no further potential gain from redistributing risk.[11] Greater risk sharing in Asia could help reduce its susceptibility to external shocks and lower sovereign risk premiums.

One way to enhance risk sharing is to strengthen the quality of financial integration by further developing financial markets and increasing harmonization and coordination.[12] Indeed, policies can amplify the benefits from risk sharing at minimal risk of financial contagion and excessive volatility. Such policies include developing harmonized market standards and rules, building common trading rules and platforms, and harmonizing accounting standards and securities regulation. These policies, in turn, will deepen regional markets, increase participation of institutional investors, and encourage Asia-wide portfolio investment. Recent capital market reforms and the Asian Bond Market Initiative, for example, have already led to a notable diversification of sources of financing and an expansion of the investor base (Goswami and others 2014). Combining these initiatives with ongoing efforts to promote convergence in macroeconomic policy objectives can help ensure that the benefits of financial integration are maximized for Asia. Examples of efforts to promote convergence include regional surveillance, peer review, policy discussions, and, ultimately, greater regional policy coordination and safety nets.

As noted previously, a component of financial deepening is greater financial inclusion. Financial inclusion could help harness the increased saving from population growth in Asia, which, in turn, could be used to finance the region's infrastructure investment. Increasing households' and small and medium-sized enterprises' access to finance in Asia could be facilitated by diverse savings products, credit bureaus, and better collateral and contract enforcement (Table 8.4). The impediments to developing the corporate bond markets and institutional investor base highlighted by Goswami and others (2014) and discussed earlier in this chapter will be critical to channeling financial savings realized from greater inclusion in the region into infrastructure.

Financial integration and deepening could potentially reduce the external borrowing premium and its sensitivity to domestic balance sheet considerations. The degree of financial integration within Asia is low, in part reflecting capital account restrictions in a number of countries in the region (Pongsaparn and Unteroberdoerster 2011). However, Asia as a whole is a net capital exporter. A large amount of Asia's capital outflows go to the government debt market in the United States and Europe and, in turn, Asia receives foreign direct investment and portfolio inflows that typically have a higher rate of return than do the sovereign bonds. Foreign portfolio inflows tend to significantly reduce sovereign bond yields as shown in Goswami and others 2014. Thus, greater

---

[11] Typically, risk sharing compares how growth in the marginal utility of consumption differs across countries, which is indicative of how much risk is shared.

[12] However, risk sharing should not be expected to contain the most extreme of shocks.

TABLE 8.4

Selected Indicators of Financial Inclusion			
	Households with Access to Banks (percent)	**Adult Population Not Using Formal Financial Services (millions/percent)**	**SMEs Lacking Access to Loans from Financial Institutions (millions/percent)**
East Asia and Pacific	42	876 / 51–75	140–170 / >59
South Asia	22	612 / 51–75	60–70 / >59
Middle East and North Africa	42	136 / 26–50	12–15 / >59
Sub-Saharan Africa	12	326 / 75–100	26–30 / >59
Latin America and the Caribbean	40	250 / 51–75	11–12 / 40–59
Central Asia and Eastern Europe	50	193 / 26–50	5–7 / 20–39
High-income countries	90	60 / 0 –25	10–12 / <20

Source: Consultative Group to Assist the Poor and World Bank, *Financial Access 2010.*

regional portfolio flows (or integration) would be expected to reduce sovereign risk premiums, particularly in emerging Asia. However, deepening the debt market by encouraging greater participation by regional investors might increase asset price sensitivity to global and regional financial conditions. At the same time, a broader domestic investor base can prevent asset prices from over-shooting or undershooting in response to sales or purchases by foreigners that are driven by external factors (IMF 2014a). Therefore, the size of direct participation of foreign investors in local-currency bond markets warrants close monitoring and needs to be balanced with broad financial system development policies. Mizen and Tsoukas (2012) also find that the external finance premium measured by corporate bond spreads of Asian firms was more sensitive to leverage and risk of bankruptcy during the Asian crisis of 1997–98 than it was during the global financial crisis. This suggests that bond market deepening in the region, partly in response to the Asian crisis (Goswami and others 2014), may have played a role. Lower sovereign and corporate spreads would be an important channel through which financial integration and deepening could help finance infrastructure in emerging Asia. This includes aging Asia, where the returns would still be greater than they would be through investing domestically or in other advanced economies.

Financial product structures will also need to adapt to demographic change and infrastructure financing. Aging societies will demand financial products that provide inflation protection and allow the drawdown of savings, such as annuities. Markets in such products remain underdeveloped in Asia, partly because of limited diversification of systemic risks. Government policy can help these markets develop by addressing the duration and inflation risks. Building on the deepening of sovereign bond markets in emerging Asia as outlined in Goswami and others 2014—including the introduction of Treasury Inflation-Protected Securities and Separate Trading of Registered Interest and Principal of Securities—could facilitate public infrastructure investment, while also helping develop a benchmark to price financial innovations in the provision of private infrastructure finance.

Public-private partnerships (PPPs) offer an alternative provision mechanism to public investment, provided they are properly structured. PPPs have become a popular vehicle for providing infrastructure given that sound infrastructure projects that address clear bottlenecks are likely to have relatively high economic rates of return. Also, the private sector can be made responsible for constructing the infrastructure, providing the principal services related to it, and tailoring asset design specifically to this purpose. To the extent that these infrastructure services are supplied directly to final users, charging is both feasible and, from an efficiency standpoint, desirable. However, experience suggests that effective implementation of PPP projects and, more generally, increasing private sector involvement in the provision of infrastructure, requires coordinated action on many fronts, including strong legal and institutional frameworks and a well-informed decision-making process.

PPPs have specific characteristics such as long duration, varied risk-return characteristics, and complex structures that make capital markets better able to finance infrastructure—especially the corporate bond market. As to project financing through banks in Asia, new Basel III capital requirements mandate that banks hold more capital against long-term finance typical in PPPs. Moreover, the large size of investments would run up against banks' single borrower limits, even with syndication, given the infancy of takeout financing and securitization.[13] Although raising adequate equity finance tends to be one of the most challenging aspects of infrastructure project financing and PPPs, Asia's relatively deep stock markets,[14] as well as growing private equity firms, make it less of a binding constraint (ADB 2013). However, once the construction phase is over and an infrastructure project is generating a steady stream of revenue over a long horizon, it might be suitable to package the financing as long-term bonds that are sold to investors.[15] In some Asian markets, bonds issued by infrastructure-related companies already constitute a substantial share of total bonds outstanding. For example, in Malaysia, 40 percent of bonds outstanding are issued by infrastructure-related firms. Developing the infrastructure bond market in the region can help draw nontraditional investors into the financing of infrastructure projects.

However, several obstacles must be overcome before investors can be encouraged to purchase infrastructure bonds:

- *Shortage of regional infrastructure asset class*—Although a substantial pool of funds in the region is ready to be invested in infrastructure projects, a regional infrastructure asset class that meets the requirements of investors is

---

[13] Long-term syndicated bank lending to Asia from outside the region has also been affected by the global financial crisis and continued deleveraging of European banks, although a number of Asian banks have stepped up cross-border lending, particularly Australian, Singaporean, and Japanese banks.

[14] The share of stock market capitalization as a percentage of GDP in most Asian countries is comparable to the countries' total banking sector assets, with debt securities markets coming in a distant third. This contrasts with many advanced economies, where the banking sector continues to dominate financial intermediation

[15] The revenue stream from infrastructure tends to be less sensitive to the economic cycle and is generally inflation protected, too.

absent, particularly in advanced Asia. Assisting emerging Asian economies in structuring bond financing for the brown-field phase in infrastructure projects could create additional supply.

- *Low credit ratings*—Another hurdle is that infrastructure projects tend to be given credit rating that are too low to be of interest to institutional investors, particularly the pension funds in aging advanced Asia. Traditionally, governments have provided guarantees to ameliorate the situation, but doing so carries a fiscal risk. Another way to improve the credit rating of infrastructure bonds is to make subordinated debt tranches available to raise the credit rating of the senior tranches of the debt to investment grade. The securitization of infrastructure assets can allow banks to offload some of their long-term risk in infrastructure loans and help promote the development of a bond market. This would also allow banks to conserve their capital under the Basel III rules. However, securitization would require well-developed bond and derivatives markets, which usually go hand in hand, as outlined in Goswami and others 2014, to provide liquidity and minimize risk. It would also involve having a regulatory framework that allows for the securitization of revenue streams while ensuring some "skin in the game," as well as functioning markets for distressed assets including well-functioning bankruptcy laws and resolution frameworks.

Promoting a long-term investor base would help build up a stable source of finance for infrastructure projects. The role of long-term institutional investors (for example, pension funds, mutual funds, and life insurance) has increased (Table 8.5, IMF 2014a), offering a natural financier for infrastructure projects. Also, infrastructure assets offer pension funds some measure of protection against inflation, while pension funds offer financing in domestic currencies. However, the main drawback of pension funds as a source of infrastructure project financing is that they tend to lack the expertise to evaluate and invest in complex and heterogeneous infrastructure assets. A more common way for institutional investors to gain exposure is by participating directly in an unlisted fund. Unlisted funds are set up by management companies on behalf of institutional investors to provide these investors with exposure to infrastructure projects without having to develop in-house expertise. Data from ADB 2013 show that, as of 2013, there were 88 unlisted infrastructure funds investing in Asia, with a total of $22 billion committed. That total is growing. Institutional investors can also buy debt linked to infrastructure projects through bond funds that invest in such projects. This investment is done mostly through mezzanine debt. Another option is to purchase debt that is issued by project operators and securitized by the revenue stream from infrastructure projects.

CONCLUSION

In conclusion, we find that further financial integration and market deepening in Asia would allow the region to mobilize financial resources for greater benefit. As discussed in Obstfeld 2009, financial opening could benefit the emerging economies that pursue it through better risk sharing with the rest of the world

TABLE 8.5

Amount of Institutional Investor Assets (*Millions of U.S. dollars*)

	Insurance	Pension Funds	Mutual Funds
Hong Kong SAR	13,933	79,640	1,237,624
India	306,513	74,760	114,489
Indonesia	57,719	16,354	21,532
Malaysia	54,647	185,369	96,293
Philippines	14,639	9,456	3,566
Singapore	142,872	190,165	1,328,540
Korea	655,087	367,028	267,582
Thailand	47,000	18,860	72,546
Vietnam	0	3,453	137

Source: Standard Chartered Research.

and the alleviation of capital scarcity. Because the share of the working-age population appears to be at a stark transition point in many Asian countries, there is a greater need to enhance financial integration and deepening to cope with the higher dependency ratio that will reduce domestic savings and growth. Well-executed and well-structured infrastructure projects—particularly PPPs in emerging Asia—could provide pensioners in advanced Asia with high-yielding, long-term returns. In addition, demographic transitions are likely to intensify incentives for capital flows to emerging Asia, where labor resources remain abundant. Financial innovation and integration could provide individuals and pension funds with access to a broader array of financial products tailored to the needs of an aging society. This, alongside greater financial inclusion and financial market deepening, could reduce the cost of capital in emerging Asia. Together, these changes could help spread the benefits of financial integration across the region. The simulations suggest that raising the infrastructure investment-to-GDP ratio by 1 percentage point in emerging Asia will raise annual output by 2 to 3 percentage points in the long term.

At the moment, the degree of *financial* integration, both within Asia and between Asia and the rest of the world, is relatively low, especially when compared with Asia's high degree of *trade* integration. Several barriers may have limited financial integration and the channeling of savings to the most productive investment opportunities across the region. For instance, financial inclusion is relatively low in emerging Asia, capital account and investment restrictions remain in place in many countries, and the development of debt capital markets that would be an ideal vehicle for private infrastructure finance has been uneven (Goswami and others 2014). However, deepening debt markets by encouraging greater regional flows might increase asset price sensitivity to global and regional financial conditions (IMF 2014a). That said, a broader long-term domestic investor base can reduce the susceptibility to external factors and finance infrastructure at lower costs if it is supported by appropriate financial instruments, macroprudential policies, and regional cooperation.

Asia's financial sector has a key role to play in the transformation of the region's real economy by helping address the key challenges of demographic change and infrastructure needs. As its population becomes increasingly urban and middle class, Asia needs to shift from its current manufacturing- and export-driven growth model to more vibrant and diverse markets. A healthy and dynamic financial sector can serve the social and economic needs for this transformation, and support a successful and sustainable new growth model.

REFERENCES

Asian Development Bank (ADB). 2009. *Infrastructure for a Seamless Asia*. Manila: Asian Development Bank and Asian Development Bank Institute.

———. 2013. "Asia Bond Monitor." November, Manila.

Ayadi, R., E. Arbak, S. Ben Naceur, and W. de Groen. 2013. "Determinants of Financial Development across the Mediterranean." MEDPRO Technical Report No. 29, Center for European Policy Studies, Brussels.

Canning, D., and P. Pedroni. 2008. "Infrastructure, Long-Run Economic Growth and Causality Tests for Cointegrated Panels." *Manchester School* 76 (5): 504–27.

Chamon, M., and E. Prasad. 2007. "Why Are Saving Rates of Urban Households in China Rising?" IZA Discussion Paper No. 3191, Bonn, Institute for the Study of Labor.

Chinn, M., and H. Ito. 2008. "A New Measure of Financial Openness." *Journal of Comparative Policy Analysis* 10 (3): 309–22.

Chinn, M., and E. Prasad. 2003. "Medium-Term Determinants of Current Accounts in Industrial and Developing Countries: An Empirical Exploration." *Journal of International Economics* 59 (1): 47–76.

Consultative Group to Assist the Poor (CGAP), and the World Bank Group. 2010. *Financial Access 2010: The State of Financial Inclusion through the Crisis*. Washington: World Bank.

Ding, D., R. Lam, and S. Peiris. 2014. "Future of Asia's Finance: How Can It Meet Challenges of Demographic Change and Infrastructure Needs?" IMF Working Paper No. 14/126, International Monetary Fund, Washington.

Feldstein, M., and C. Horioka. 1980. "Domestic Saving and International Capital Flows." *Economic Journal* 90 (358): 314–29.

Goswami, M., A. Jobst, S. Peiris, and D. Seneviratne. 2014. "Bond Markets: Are the Recent Reforms Proving to Be Effective?" In *Future of Asia's Finance: How Can It Meet Challenges of Demographic Change and Infrastructure Needs?* Washington: International Monetary Fund.

Heston, A., R. Summers, and B. Aten. 2012. "Penn World Table Version 7.1." Center for International Comparisons of Production, Income and Prices at the University of Pennsylvania.

Horioka, C., and A. Terada-Hagiwara. 2011. "The Determinants and Long-Term Projections of Saving Rates in Developing Asia." Working Paper No. 17581, National Bureau of Economic Research, Cambridge, Massachusetts. http://www.nber.org/papers/w17581.

Hung, J., and R. Qian. 2010. "Why Is China's Saving Rate So High? A Comparative Study of Cross-Country Panel Data." Congressional Budget Office Working Paper 2010-07, Washington, Congressional Budget Office.

International Institute for Management Development (IMD). 2014. *World Competitiveness Yearbook 2014*. Lausanne, Switzerland: International Institute for Management Development.

International Monetary Fund (IMF). 2010. *Regional Economic Outlook: Asia and Pacific*. Washington, October.

———. 2011. *Regional Economic Outlook: Asia and Pacific*. Washington, October.

———. 2014a. "How Do Changes in the Investor Base and Financial Deepening Affect Emerging Market Economies?" In *Global Financial Stability Report*. April. Washington: International Monetary Fund.

———. 2014b. *Regional Economic Outlook: Asia and Pacific*. Washington, April.

Kumhof, M., D. Laxton, D. Muir, and S. Mursula. 2010. "The Global Integrated Monetary and Fiscal Model GIMF–Theoretical Structure." Working Paper No. 10/34, International Monetary Fund, Washington.

Mizen, P., and S. Tsoukas. 2012. "The Response of the External Finance Premium in Asian Corporate Bond Markets to Financial Characteristics, Financial Constraints and Two Financial Crises." *Journal of Banking and Finance* 36 (11): 3048–59.

Modigliani, F. 1970. "The Life Cycle Hypothesis of Saving and Intercountry Differences in the Saving Ratio." In *Induction, Growth, and Trade*, edited by W. A. Eltis, M. F. G. Scott, and J. N. Wolfe. Oxford: Oxford University Press.

Obstfeld, M. 2009. "International Finance and Growth in Developing Countries: What Have We Learned?" *IMF Staff Papers* (56) 1: 63–111.

Park, D., and K. Shin. 2009. "Saving, Investment, and Current Account Surplus in Developing Asia." Economics Working Paper Series No. 158, Asian Development Bank, Manila.

Pongsaparn, R., and O. Unteroberdoerster. 2011. "Financial Integration and Rebalancing in Asia." Working Paper No. 11/243, International Monetary Fund, Washington.

Seneviratne, D., and Y. Sun. 2013. "Infrastructure and Income Distribution in ASEAN-5: What Are the Links?" Working Paper No. 13/41, International Monetary Fund, Washington.

Tahilyani, N., T. Tamhane, and J. Tan. 2011. "Asia's $1 Trillion Infrastructure Opportunity." Insights & Publications, March, McKinsey & Company, Mumbai.

United Nations. 2010. "World Population Prospects: The 2010 Revision." United Nations, New York.

Walsh, J., C. Park, and J. Yu. 2011. "Financing Infrastructure in India: Macroeconomic Lessons and Emerging Market Case Studies." Working Paper No. 11/181, International Monetary Fund, Washington.

CHAPTER 9

ASEAN Financial Integration: Harnessing Benefits and Mitigating Risks

GEERT ALMEKINDERS, ALEX MOURMOURAS, JADE VICHYANOND, YONG SARAH ZHOU, AND JIANPING ZHOU

MAIN POINTS OF THIS CHAPTER:

- The 10 member countries of the Association of Southeast Asian Nations (ASEAN)[1] have performed very well during the past decade, with growth averaging more than 5 percent a year. The region is receiving ample foreign direct investment, but financial integration of most ASEAN economies lags behind that of other emerging market economies.

- Further liberalization of interregional and intraregional flows of goods, services, and capital could be beneficial for growth, the creation of jobs, and inclusion in ASEAN. Most ASEAN countries are still at a relatively early stage of development and have large infrastructure gaps. In light of this, the planned further opening up of ASEAN economies can be expected to unlock growth-enhancing cross-border flows of capital, when taken in the context of reform commitments establishing the ASEAN Economic Community (AEC) by 2015, other regional and bilateral free trade agreements, and the Trans-Pacific Partnership, which continues to be under discussion.

- ASEAN countries are, for the most part, taking a cautious approach toward further liberalization and integration. Experience elsewhere shows that financial liberalization can exacerbate prevailing domestic financial sector vulnerabilities and heighten external vulnerabilities and risks. However, while erring on the side of caution may have benefits, delays to further financial integration could hold back growth and job creation. Therefore, the ongoing work to foster a consensus on a detailed road map to ASEAN financial integration should be intensified. Actions to minimize potential

The authors are grateful for helpful discussions and comments from Vivek Arora, Sanchita Basu Das, Pek Koon Heng, Heedon Kang, Hoe Ee Khor, Kenneth Koh, Jerry Schiff, Chikahisa Sumi, Shinji Takagi, and participants at a seminar in the IMF's Asia and Pacific Department.

[1] Brunei Darussalam, Cambodia, Indonesia, Lao P.D.R., Malaysia, Myanmar, the Philippines, Singapore, Thailand, and Vietnam.

adverse effects should complement this work. Accordingly, individual countries should address financial sector vulnerabilities and strengthen policy frameworks to make them more resilient to shocks. Reinforcing bilateral, regional, and global financial safety nets can also play an important role.

INTRODUCTION

ASEAN is a diverse group of 10 fast-growing countries at very different stages of economic and financial development. Their populations are young and growing and have high saving rates. But investment needs are also large, related to advancing urbanization and the region's growing middle class as well as the need to increase connectivity and provide hard and soft infrastructure. The region has witnessed an increase in trade and capital flows, both within the region and in relation to the rest of Asia and the world. ASEAN financial integration has also progressed. Direct investment has risen, cross-border banking linkages have deepened, and foreign participation in ASEAN capital markets has increased. Financial integration in ASEAN could gather steam in the years ahead, including through the establishment of the AEC in 2015 (Box 9.1). If properly phased and sequenced, and with adequate safeguards put in place, the prospect of greater ASEAN financial integration brings with it the promise of greater financial inclusion and faster real convergence in incomes per capita. These advancements could help reduce poverty and ameliorate the strong migration incentives in the region that are generated by large wage disparities.

This chapter takes stock of ASEAN's financial integration and its prospects. More financial integration of ASEAN with other capital-abundant Asian countries, especially the "plus three" (China, Japan, and Korea), can be expected to trigger large capital flows. Strong pull forces could potentially drive large capital flows and financial integration as the less-open ASEAN member countries liberalize their capital accounts and financial sectors, resulting in important benefits for ASEAN countries' growth and development. The chapter also reviews the AEC agenda for possible impediments to closer financial integration, including insufficient real and financial infrastructure in some countries.

Coming out of the Asian financial crisis of the late 1990s, ASEAN countries have made great strides in strengthening their macroeconomic frameworks and their external positions. Theory and experience from other geographic regions suggest that some ASEAN countries' current account balances can be expected to become more volatile when the region's financial integration gathers pace and barriers to cross-border flows are gradually removed. As larger current account deficits are financed by a mix of capital flows, risks will rise. The resulting increased macroeconomic volatility will need to be managed at the individual country, regional, and global levels. The bouts of volatility of cross-border capital flows since May 2013 related to the actual and prospective unwinding of unconventional monetary policies in advanced economies serve as a reminder that the region's financial architecture is still a work in progress. In view of this, and given

Box 9.1. ASEAN and the ASEAN Economic Community 2015: A Brief Chronology

The Association of Southeast Asian Nations (ASEAN) is home to more than 610 million people, of whom about 100 million live below the poverty line. In its early days, ASEAN's primary focus was reducing geopolitical tensions in the region. In 2003, ASEAN leaders decided to establish an ASEAN Economic Community (AEC) by 2020. The target date for the AEC was subsequently moved up five years. Amid growing concerns about the ASEAN region's perceived loss of competitiveness to China and India, there was a strong desire to enhance the region's role against the backdrop of a proliferation of free trade agreements between ASEAN and its trade partners. Accordingly, in 2007, ASEAN leaders agreed on a blueprint for an integrated AEC by 2015.

The AEC has set four main targets: (1) fostering a single market and production base with a free flow of goods, services, investment, and skilled labor, and freer flow of capital within ASEAN; (2) developing a highly competitive economic region nurturing fair competition, consumer protection, intellectual property rights, and infrastructure development; (3) attaining equitable economic development by strengthening small and medium-sized enterprises; and (4) achieving ever greater integration into the global economy. The AEC Blueprint lays out 176 priority actions, including nine related to the free flow of financial services, strengthening ASEAN capital market development and integration, and allowing greater capital mobility. An AEC scorecard mechanism was introduced in 2008 to monitor progress in achieving the milestones laid out in the blueprint and to track the priority actions undertaken by ASEAN member states, both individually and collectively.

Key initiatives to support ASEAN financial integration

Key initiatives taken to date include the following:

- *The Master Plan on ASEAN Connectivity*—In 2010, ASEAN leaders adopted the *Master Plan on ASEAN Connectivity*. The plan's objective is to facilitate the establishment of the AEC by 2015 by enhancing intraregional connectivity in areas such as trade, investment, tourism, and development. ASEAN Connectivity comprises three main elements: (1) enhancing *physical connectivity* by improving transportation, information and communication technology, and energy infrastructure; (2) improving *institutional connectivity* by setting up procedures to facilitate international transactions of goods, services, and the cross-border movement of skilled workers; and (3) strengthening *people-to-people connectivity* through sociocultural initiatives such as education and tourism within ASEAN. While improving intra-ASEAN connectivity would bring significant benefits, it also poses important challenges, including cross-border crime, illegal immigration, and environmental degradation.
- *Cross-border collaboration enhancements*—Several initiatives have been taken to enhance cross-border collaboration among the various capital markets in ASEAN, including the following efforts to build capacity and infrastructure:
  - The Working Committee on Capital Account Liberalization monitors the implementation of priority actions to achieve freer flow of capital in the region in line with the AEC Blueprint.
  - The ASEAN Capital Markets Forum focuses on the harmonization of domestic laws and regulations and the development of market infrastructure with a view to integrating the region's equities markets.

Box 9.1. (*continued*)

- ○ In April 2010, ASEAN central bank governors endorsed the creation of the Working Committee on Payment and Settlement Systems, which focuses on policy, legal frameworks, instruments, institutions, and market infrastructure.
- ○ In April 2011, ASEAN central bank governors endorsed the creation of the Task Force on the ASEAN Banking Integration Framework, which aims to achieve ASEAN-wide banking sector liberalization by 2020. The Working Committee on Financial Service Liberalization focuses on further liberalization of the banking and insurance sectors.
- ○ The ASEAN Capital Markets Infrastructure Blueprint was developed in 2013. Accordingly, the Working Committee on Capital Market Development aims to enable ASEAN issuers and investors to access cross-border ASEAN equity and bond markets through integrated access, clearing, custody, and settlement systems and arrangements.

Initiatives to strengthen regional economic surveillance and crisis management

To complement the integration initiatives, considerable progress has been made in setting up regional institutions to enhance information sharing, improve economic surveillance and crisis management, and provide a regional safety net, including the following:

- The ASEAN Integration Monitoring Office was established in 2010 to enhance the ASEAN Secretariat's monitoring capacity for tracking progress of regional economic integration.
- The Chiang Mai Initiative Multilateralization (CMIM), established in March 2010 among the ASEAN+3 countries, is a multilateral currency swap arrangement that replaced the preexisting Chiang Mai Initiative's network of bilateral swap lines.
- A crisis prevention facility, the CMIM Precautionary Line, has been introduced.
- An independent regional macroeconomic surveillance unit—the ASEAN+3 Macroeconomic Research Office (AMRO)—has been operating in Singapore since 2011.
- In their New Delhi communiqué of May 2013, the ASEAN+3 Ministers of Finance and Central Bank Governors called for an "effective cooperative relationship with the International Monetary Fund (IMF) and other multilateral financial institutions in the areas of surveillance, liquidity support arrangements, and capacity development."

Further progress in advancing regional surveillance and strengthening crisis management institutions, including their analytical capacity and cooperation with the IMF, is high on ASEAN's agenda. In this regard, recent initiatives have included information sharing on macroprudential policies and capital flow management measures. Initiatives have also been taken to expand the scope of integration to other partners in Asia, including through the ASEAN+3 initiative and the Regional Comprehensive Economic Partnership (ASEAN+6, comprising ASEAN countries plus Australia, China, India, Japan, Korea, and New Zealand). The U.S.–ASEAN Expanded Economic Engagement initiative, agreed to in late 2012, calls for expanding trade and investment and engaging with regional institutions.

existing financial sector vulnerabilities in some of the low-income ASEAN countries, policymakers have been taking a cautious approach in moving forward with further financial and capital account liberalization. As they move further along with this process, ASEAN countries should continue to strengthen their macroeconomic frameworks and financial systems. They can rely on substantial quantities of international reserves and other buffers, including bilateral credit lines and regional financial safety nets (for example, the Chiang Mai Initiative Multilateralization), which could help their resilience to risk-on, risk-off cycles in capital flows.

This chapter briefly takes stock of growth and trade integration in ASEAN and assesses the state of ASEAN financial integration to date. This stocktaking is followed by a discussion of the benefits of further liberalization and regional integration in ASEAN. The chapter goes on to review policy measures at the national, ASEAN, and regional levels that would help promote further safe financial development and financial integration, including in the context of ASEAN countries' commitment to establishing the AEC.

GROWTH, TRADE INTEGRATION, AND FINANCIAL INTEGRATION IN ASEAN

ASEAN countries have performed very well during the past decade. Since the turn of the century, ASEAN-wide economic growth has averaged 5¼ percent a year (weighted average), and the economies of the individual member countries have expanded by 5¾ percent a year, on average (Table 9.1). The success of most ASEAN member states has been associated with a long-standing export-oriented development strategy. As a consequence—with the exception of Indonesia, Myanmar, and the Philippines—ASEAN countries boast large trade openness, with the sum of imports and exports of goods and services exceeding 100 percent of GDP. The downside of this large trade openness was visible when the slump in international trade in 2008–09 triggered by the global financial crisis caused growth to slow in ASEAN. But this was followed by a pronounced rebound when international trade recovered (Figure 9.1).

Intra-ASEAN trade has grown rapidly, but there is scope for further regional trade liberalization with potentially important benefits for growth and employment:

- Intra-ASEAN trade has almost quadrupled since 2000, to $630 billion in 2013. Excluding Singapore, whose large gross trade flows can cloud underlying trends in the other member countries, intra-ASEAN trade now accounts for 23 percent of total ASEAN trade, up from 21 percent in 2000 (Figure 9.2). ASEAN countries' intraregional trade remains considerably smaller than does intraregional trade in the European Union (EU) (50 percent of total trade). Studies indicate that nontariff measures may be holding back the growth of regional trade in ASEAN (Basu Das and others 2013; World Bank 2014). The gradual removal of these nontariff

TABLE 9.1

ASEAN Countries: Selected Economic Indicators

	Indonesia	Malaysia	Philippines	Singapore	Thailand	Brunei Darussalam	Cambodia	Lao P.D.R.	Myanmar	Vietnam
GDP in 2013 (billions of U.S. dollars)	870	313	272	298	387	16	16	11	57	171
Population in 2013 (millions)	248.0	29.9	97.5	5.4	68.2	0.4	15.1	6.8	51.0	89.7
GDP per capita in 2013 (U.S. dollars)										
Headline	3,510	10,457	2,791	55,182	5,676	39,659	1,028	1,594	1,113	1,902
Purchasing power parity basis (2012)[1]	4,272	14,775	3,803	53,266	8,459	45,979	2,150	4,335	3,989	3,133
Poverty in 2012 (percent of population)										
Below two dollars per day	13.0	0.2	13.8	n.a.	0.7	n.a.	15.1	24.8	n.a.	13.5
Below national poverty line	12.0	1.7	26.5	n.a.	13.2	n.a.	20.5	27.6	n.a.	20.7
Income inequality (Gini coefficient)										
2000	29.7	37.9	46.1	43.4	42.8	n.a.	41.9	32.6	n.a.	37.6
2012 (or latest available year)	38.1	46.2	43.0	41.2	39.4	n.a.	36.0	36.7	n.a.	35.6
Growth (percent)										
2010–12 (average)	6.3	6.1	6.0	7.9	4.8	2.3	6.8	8.0	6.2	6.0
2013	5.8	4.7	7.2	3.9	2.9	-1.8	7.4	8.0	8.3	5.4
Inflation (percent, period average)										
2010–12 (average)	4.8	2.2	3.9	4.2	3.4	0.2	4.1	5.9	4.6	12.3
2013	6.4	2.1	2.9	2.4	2.2	0.4	3.0	6.4	5.7	6.6
Fiscal balance (percent of GDP)										
2010–12 (average)	-1.2	-4.0	-1.1	7.0	-1.1	17.8	-3.6	-1.8	-3.9	-3.5
2013	-2.1	-4.6	-0.1	6.2	-0.2	16.8	-2.7	-5.6	-1.6	-5.6
Public debt (percent of GDP)										
Public debt in 2010	26	54	43	97	43	1	29	62	50	48
Public debt in 2013	26	58	39	103	46	2	28	61	40	52
Of which: external debt	14	23	18	...	6	0	32	43	19	21

Current account balance (percent of GDP)									
2013	−3.3	3.9	3.5	18.3	−0.6	31.5	−8.5	−27.7	−5.4	5.6
Gross reserves at end-2013									
Level (billions of U.S. dollars)	99.4	134.9	83.2	273.1	167.3		3.6	0.7	5.5	26.0
In months of imports	5.8	6.8	11.9	6.2	7.7	6.1	3.6	1.2	3.5	2.3
Trade openness in 2013 (imports plus exports in goods and services in percent of GDP)									
Total trade	48	154	53	358	144	115	141	112	53	163
Intra-ASEAN merchandise trade	11	38	9	70	26	35	27	60	22	23
FDI inflows during 2010–12 (average, percent of GDP)									
Total	4.2	6.3	1.1	29.1	6.9	0.7	2.1	2.8	1.2	3.3
From within ASEAN[2]	0.7	1.2	0.3	2.7	1.7	…	1.0	…	0.6	0.6
Portfolio inflows during 2010–12									
Total	2.7	9.8	6.7	9.3	5.4	0.0	0.2	2.4	0.0	0.4
From within ASEAN	0.8	1.7	0.5	1.7	0.7	0.0	0.0	0.2	0.0	−0.2
Private credit in 2013									
Growth (percent)	20	10	16	54	10	7	27	36	66	13
Private credit (percent of GDP)	36	134	36	173	121	31	45	39	15	97
Number of banks in 2012[3]	119	27	49	124	30	8	35	32	10	47
Of which: foreign and joint banks	24	19	15	119	14	5	12	21	0	6

Sources: Bankscope; CEIC Data Co. Ltd.; country authorities; IMF, *2014 Coordinated Direct Investment Survey*, *2014 Coordinated Portfolio Investment Survey*, *Direction of Trade Statistics* September 2014, *World Economic Outlook* October 2014; World Bank, *World Development Indicators* 2014; and IMF staff calculations.

Note: ASEAN = Association of Southeast Asian Nations; FDI = foreign direct investment; n.a. = not available.

[1] Constant 2005 international U.S. dollars, except for Lao P.D.R. and Myanmar data from *World Economic Outlook* (nominal purchasing power parity GDP/population).

[2] Excluding services.

[3] Data for Vietnam refer to 2011.

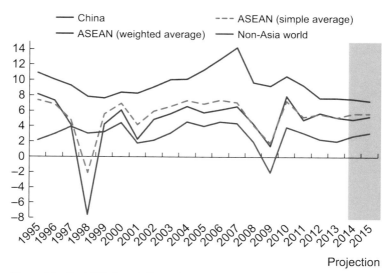

Figure 9.1 Real GDP Growth (*Percent*)

Sources: IMF, *World Economic Outlook*, October 2014; and IMF staff calculations.
Note: ASEAN = Association of Southeast Asian Nations.

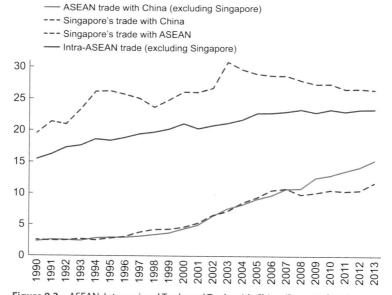

Figure 9.2 ASEAN: Intraregional Trade and Trade with China (*Percent of total merchandise trade*)

Source: IMF, *Direction of Trade Statistics*, September 2014; and IMF staff calculations.
Note: ASEAN = Association of Southeast Asian Nations.

Figure 9.3 ASEAN-5: Intraregional Exports by Category *(Percent of total exports in each category)*

Sources: UN Comtrade; and IMF staff calculations.

measures, consistent with the Strategic Schedule in the AEC 2015 Blueprint, could provide renewed impetus to the creation of a single ASEAN market for goods and services. China's rising importance as a trading partner for ASEAN countries reflects increasing trade in intermediate goods as ASEAN countries and China integrate to form supply chain networks (IMF 2010).

- There are also signs that regional trade within ASEAN has become increasingly oriented to final consumer goods (Figure 9.3). This, together with a large and vibrant domestic market and a growing middle class, appears to provide the region with a potential source of resilience to global demand shocks. For instance, Cubero and others (2014) find that, besides global demand, intraregional demand is an important driver of growth in most ASEAN-5 countries (Indonesia, Malaysia, the Philippines, Singapore, and Thailand). This outcome applies less to Indonesia, which has a lower trade-to-GDP ratio and sends the bulk of its commodity-heavy exports outside ASEAN.

Typically, a country's degree of financial integration tends to increase with its degree of trade integration. However, as noted by Pongsaparn and Unteroberdoerster (2011), compared with the rest of the world, most Asian economies' rapid expansion into global trade has not been matched by a commensurate increase in their degree of financial integration. This is particularly the case for ASEAN economies, for which the main channel of financial

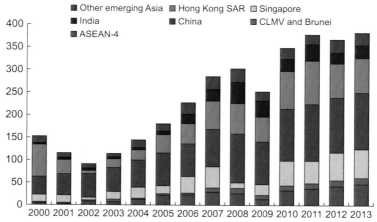

Figure 9.4 Emerging Asia: Nominal Foreign Direct Investment Inflows, 2000–13 (*Billions of U.S. dollars*)

Source: United Nations Conference on Trade and Development.
Note: ASEAN = Association of Southeast Asian Nations. CLMV = Cambodia, Lao P.D.R., Myanmar, and Vietnam. Other emerging Asia comprises Bangladesh, Bhutan, Korea, Macao SAR, Mongolia, Nepal, Sri Lanka, Taiwan Province of China, and Timor-Leste.

integration is through foreign direct investment (FDI) flows. Pongsaparn and Unteroberdoerster (2011) estimate a model that relates the degree of financial integration, measured by countries' ratio of capital flows to GDP, to a set of country characteristics including trade integration, relative GDP growth, interest and exchange rate movements, and exchange rate volatility. They consider a panel of 90 advanced and emerging markets. Except for the financial centers of Hong Kong SAR and Singapore, the degree of financial integration of many Asian economies is below the level predicted by the model for all economies, and in several cases falls behind the norm for Latin America and Eastern Europe.

FDI is generally regarded as a desirable form of capital inflows. In addition to capital, FDI can bring improved technology, generating knowledge spillovers that can result in total factor productivity growth in recipient countries. Moreover, though net FDI flows to emerging and developing countries do exhibit fluctuations, they have consistently been positive during the past three decades (Park and Takagi 2012). Recent trends and the outlook for FDI flows to ASEAN are favorable:

- FDI flows to ASEAN amounted to a record high of $125 billion in 2013, up 7 percent from 2012 (Figure 9.4). Moreover, at almost 9 percent of world FDI inflows, ASEAN's share of total global FDI is back to the level it reached during the boom years preceding the Asian financial crisis of the late 1990s (Figure 9.5).

- The trend of rising FDI inflows, in U.S. dollar terms and in relative terms, applies equally to the group of ASEAN-4 countries (Indonesia, Malaysia, the Philippines, and Thailand), Singapore (which continues to receive half of all FDI inflows into ASEAN), and the CLMV countries (Cambodia,

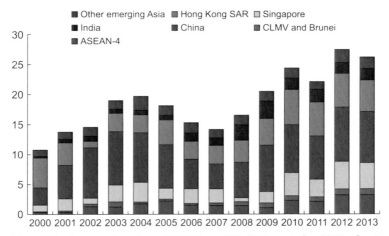

Figure 9.5 Emerging Asia: Share of FDI Inflows, 2000–13 (*Percent of world FDI inflows*)

Source: United Nations Conference on Trade and Development.
Note: ASEAN = Association of Southeast Asian Nations. CLMV = Cambodia, Lao P.D.R., Myanmar, and Vietnam. FDI = foreign direct investment. Other emerging Asia comprises Bangladesh, Bhutan, Korea, Macao SAR, Mongolia, Nepal, Sri Lanka, Taiwan Province of China, and Timor-Leste.

Lao P.D.R., Myanmar, and Vietnam) and Brunei Darussalam, which together now account for about 11 percent of FDI inflows into ASEAN.

- Several factors may be helping to make ASEAN an attractive investment destination. Manufacturing wage costs in ASEAN have been declining relative to China, owing to divergent demographics and exchange rate movements. The favorable trend in relative wage costs is expected to continue, reflecting stronger labor force growth in ASEAN. Geopolitical considerations and ASEAN's growing middle class could also drive more FDI into ASEAN. The U.S.-ASEAN Expanded Economic Engagement initiative calls for expanding trade and investment and engaging with regional institutions. Last, ASEAN's commitment to form a single market and production base can be expected to reduce trade and investment barriers and provide economies of scale.

- The World Bank (2014) finds that foreign ownership restrictions are still common in ASEAN countries, particularly in the services sector. Relaxing these restrictions could give rise to substantial productivity-enhancing FDI inflows and provide an impetus to the structural transformation and convergence of the emerging market and frontier economies in ASEAN.

The level of banking integration in ASEAN is rising, but from a low base, and global banks have a bigger footprint in ASEAN than do regional banks:

- Bank for International Settlements (BIS) locational banking statistics indicate that BIS reporting banks' cross-border exposure to Asia and ASEAN-5 countries in U.S. dollar terms increased during 2012–13. Meanwhile, deleveraging from the euro area and Eastern Europe continued, and banks' cross-border assets in Latin America were flat in 2012–13. BIS reporting

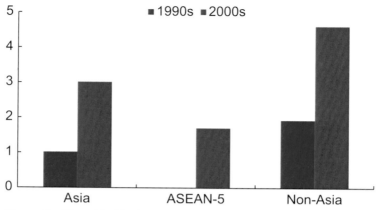

Figure 9.6 Bilateral Banking Integration

Source: Duval and others (2014).
Note: ASEAN = Association of Southeast Asian Nations. Calculated as period medians of the median country pairs in each group, expressed as a percentage of the total external position with the world.

banks' cross-border liabilities have, for the most part, changed little during 2012 and 2013. Relative to GDP, the value of BIS reporting banks' cross-border assets trended upward in relation to Malaysia, Thailand, and Indonesia in 2012–13. It remained mostly flat in Singapore and the Philippines.

• Bilateral banking integration is particularly low in ASEAN. ADB 2013 reports that foreign banks accounted for 18 percent of total commercial bank assets in Malaysia, the Philippines, and Thailand in 2009. The share of ASEAN-based banks in Malaysia, at 8.5 percent, was the highest among the three member states. The share was 0.4 percent in the Philippines and 3.7 percent in Thailand. Based on detailed country-by-country BIS data, Duval and others (2014) calculate that the level of bilateral banking integration in Asia has continued to lag behind the rest of the world. Their calculations echo the ADB's (2013) finding that bilateral banking integration is particularly low among ASEAN-5 countries (Figure 9.6).

Banks are likely to be the leaders of ASEAN financial integration, given the opportunities provided by the deleveraging of European banks and the prospects of the AEC. They also remain key to financial intermediation in the region. Singapore, as one of the largest financial centers in the world, plays a dominant role in regional financial integration. Malaysian banks have also expanded abroad significantly.

Cross-border portfolio investment inflows to ASEAN countries have been rising. However, as noted by Pongsaparn and Unteroberdoerster (2011), relative to GDP, cross-border portfolio investment in Asia and other emerging markets has remained well below that of the euro area. Moreover, the bulk of Asia's portfolio investment has remained interregional (that is, with economies outside the region), especially after adjusting for the role of Hong Kong SAR and Singapore

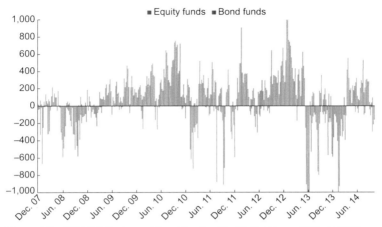

Figure 9.7   ASEAN-5: Equity and Bond Funds—Weekly Net Flows, 2008–14 (*Millions of U.S. dollars*)

Source: EPFR Global, accessed through Haver Analytics.
Note: Includes exchange-traded fund flows and mutual fund flows.

in intermediating inflows from outside the region. In contrast, portfolio investment in the euro area is mostly intraregional.

As was the case with other emerging market economies, ASEAN economies experienced a strong pickup in portfolio investment during 2010–12, following the temporary retreat caused by the global financial crisis. Advanced economies' unprecedented liquidity-easing measures undertaken to mitigate the effects of the global financial crisis were a key contributing factor to the acceleration of portfolio flows to ASEAN countries. ASEAN-5 economies may have received a relatively larger share of these inflows by virtue of the ongoing progress in developing local currency bond markets, the Asian Bond Markets Initiative, and the linking of stock markets in Malaysia, Singapore, and Thailand. Data on inflows in equity and bond funds for ASEAN-5 countries show that overall portfolio flows surged in the first four months of 2013 (Figure 9.7). After that, expectations of a reduction in the U.S. Federal Reserve System's monetary stimulus ("tapering") ignited capital outflows from the ASEAN-5 countries and many other emerging markets. An improvement in global risk appetite in the second quarter of 2014 caused capital flows to improve again.

Price measures also suggest that financial integration in ASEAN, while increasing, has some way to go. Cross-border interest rate and bond yield differentials have narrowed in recent years (see Figures 9.8 and 9.9). However, these differentials remain substantial, even after controlling for exchange rate movements (ADB 2013). Comovements in ASEAN interest rates and bond yields have increased since 2010, but these comovements may also reflect increasing integration with the global market or improving fundamentals (such as lower inflation rates and differentials and improved sovereign credit ratings). Increased comovements in equity market returns, even after controlling for global factors, suggest that stock markets are more integrated than are money and bond markets.

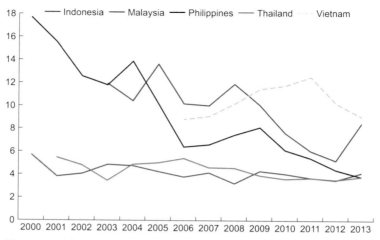

Figure 9.8   Selected ASEAN Countries: 10-Year Bond Yields (*Percent*)

Source: Haver Analytics.

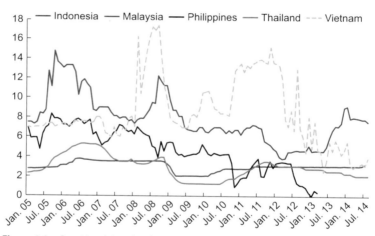

Figure 9.9   One-Month Interbank Interest Rate (*Percent*)

Source: CEIC Data Company Ltd.

TOWARD FURTHER FINANCIAL INTEGRATION IN ASEAN

Most ASEAN countries are still at relatively early stages of development and have large infrastructure gaps. Further liberalization of interregional and intra-regional flows of goods, services, and capital could be beneficial for growth, job creation, and living standards of poorer segments of the population in ASEAN. Accordingly, the AEC is working to create a common market with "free move-ment of goods, services, investment, skilled labor, and freer flow of capital"

(ASEAN 2008, 5). This is seen as a multiyear process, with each country, for the most part, moving at its own pace. Consistent with the "ASEAN Way" (ASEAN's regional multilateralism based on the ideals of noninterference, informality, consultation and consensus, minimal institutionalization, non-use of force, and nonconfrontation) this means that individual ASEAN member countries can take steps toward further financial sector liberalization and capital account liberalization if and when they believe they are ready. This readiness could be a function of several factors, including adequately strengthening relevant policy frameworks and institutions, as well as achieving broadly favorable domestic economic and financial conditions. Although this flexible approach could make for a long, drawn-out process, it does ensure ownership and incentive compatibility. This is important given that considerable risks involved in further opening up the financial sector and the capital accounts have been visible around the world and are by now well documented. Various ASEAN working groups have been meeting regularly to review progress made by individual member countries and discuss next steps. For instance, the 27th meeting of the Working Committee on Capital Account Liberalization was held in Myanmar in February 2014. This gathering coincided with a meeting of the Working Committee on Capital Market Development, also in Myanmar. Given the documented risks of further liberalization, the diligence of these groups is commendable.

ASEAN Financial Sector Liberalization: What Is at Stake?

In theory, financial integration can bring important benefits to a country and a region. ASEAN countries' financial systems remain, for the most part, bank centered, particularly in the countries at earlier stages of economic development. However, the role of insurance companies, investment funds, and pension funds is growing, particularly in Malaysia and Singapore. Financial integration can spur the development of the financial sector and product innovation. These advancements can boost growth, employment, and financial inclusion—including in the poorer regions of higher-income ASEAN members—by enhancing financial institutions' competitiveness and efficiency. Financial integration can also help facilitate the development of larger, deeper, and more liquid markets, which can lower the cost of capital, improve resource allocation, enhance diversification of risks, lengthen the maturity of financing, and improve trading and settlement practices. It could also impose greater discipline on governments, banks, and nonbank corporations, and make the economy more resilient to shocks.

For ASEAN, an important aspect of financial integration will be that the less financially developed economies will have the opportunity to catch up with the more developed ones. Table 9.2 highlights the wide divergence in financial development among ASEAN countries. In most, the outstanding stock of credit to the private sector remains below 50 percent of GDP. These countries would stand to gain the most from increased financial integration. At the same time, these countries also currently have the highest credit growth. As discussed extensively in

TABLE 9.2

Credit to the Private Sector						
	Private Sector Credit (Percent of GDP)				GDP Per Capita (U.S. dollars)	Credit Growth (Percent)
	1990	2000	2010	2013	2013	2010–12 (Average)	2013
Indonesia	46	20	28	36	3,510	23	20
Malaysia	105	137	120	134	10,457	11	10
Philippines	18	42	30	36	2,791	15	16
Singapore	84	96	130	173	55,182	14	16
Thailand	83	108	97	121	5,676	15	10
Brunei Darussalam		50	41	31	39,659	−1	7
Cambodia		6	28	45	1,028	27	27
Lao P.D.R.		14	22	39	1,594	41	36
Myanmar			5	15	1,113	59	66
Vietnam		35	115	97	1,902	18	13
China	87	122	130	136	6,747	17	15
India	35	36	54	57	1,505	18	15
Japan	126	117	107	115	38,491	0	5
Korea	122	129	154	156	24,329	5	3

Sources: CEIC Data Company Ltd.; Haver Analytics; and IMF staff estimates.

Chapter 7 of Schipke (2015), financial innovation and development in frontier economies and emerging market economies—when poorly supervised or unregulated—can, in some cases, negatively affect macroeconomic stability. State-owned banks continue to have a significant presence in several ASEAN countries, and often have ties to state enterprises. Some economies also engage in directed credit operations as part of their development strategies, which can impose quasi-fiscal liabilities and impinge on the profitability of private banks. The Asian financial crisis of the late 1990s highlighted the critical vulnerabilities to which rapid (and inadequately supervised) growth in banking and capital markets can give rise. Poor risk management, overexposure to cyclical economic activities, weak governance, and directed and connected lending are only some of the potential hazards. These problems and associated risks can be exacerbated as cross-border linkages grow, and could ultimately prove costly to output, international reserves, and public finances in the event of a crisis.

If managed well, ASEAN financial integration can play a key role in raising living standards in ASEAN's frontier and emerging markets by spurring financial development and deepening. By contributing to the creation of ASEAN-wide financial markets, financial integration would help overcome the present fragmentation of national financial sectors caused by national regulations and standards (for example, bank supervision, rating agencies, credit bureaus, and securities commissions). The lack of mutual recognition and common disclosure requirements is also standing in the way of the creation of a common market. In this regard it is important to note that the AEC Blueprint calls for regulatory harmonization and the strengthening of policy coordination among member states. The experience in the EU during the global financial crisis underscores that it is equally important to take a regional approach to financial stability. In particular, a supranational oversight framework may be necessary in a single market for financial services, and such a framework needs to be supported by a single resolution regime with a common backstop (for example, deposit insurance).

ASEAN Financial Sector Liberalization: Reform Initiatives

The ASEAN nations continue to move toward achieving greater regional financial integration. For example, in 2013, the securities regulators of Malaysia, Singapore, and Thailand signed a memorandum of understanding to establish and implement a framework for cross-border trade of collective investment schemes. Details of the broader integration framework are being worked out. The AEC Blueprint identifies freer capital movements and financial integration as two key elements. However, it is brief on specifics such as the desirable degree of financial integration and the necessary legal, institutional, and regulatory requirements for achieving financial integration (ASEAN 2008). The ADB (2013) lays out the state of thinking among ASEAN countries on the steps needed to achieve a certain degree of financial integration during the next 10 years.

One key objective identified is that the ASEAN region should nurture globally competitive banks. Commercial banks remain by far the most important type of financial institution in ASEAN. Given that banks headquartered in ASEAN countries ("ASEAN banks"), on average, remain rather small on an international scale, this objective, referred to as the "ASEAN banking framework," would give market access preference to ASEAN banks over other banks. By virtue of this preference, large globally competitive ASEAN banks could develop over time with a customer base large enough to support their growth, allowing theses banks to take the lead in ASEAN finance in the future. They would also be able to obtain a foothold in global banking through mergers and the acquisition of smaller banks.

The report concludes that full banking integration, such as the "single passport" system in the EU, would be too ambitious for ASEAN for the next 10 years. Instead, it proposes steps for partial banking integration over a 10-year period, with different timelines for each ASEAN member state. This partial integration would be supported by an institutional approach based on regulatory harmonization and the strengthening of policy coordination among the ASEAN member states, in line with the principles set out in the 2008 AEC Blueprint.

In addition to preferential market access for ASEAN banks, the strategy proposed (ADB 2013) includes the following elements:

- *A two-track approach for banking integration*—This approach would be supported by regional harmonization of regulations. Accordingly, member states should immediately start phasing out most of the remaining restrictions on wholesale banking, while delaying the completion of the liberalization of cross-border retail banking (deposit taking).

- *A three-dimensional framework*—Comprised of equal access, equal treatment, and equal environment, this framework would guide the long process of financial services liberalization in ASEAN. Accordingly, ASEAN member states should agree on a set of minimum conditions that ASEAN banks must meet to be named a Qualified ASEAN Bank and be eligible to enter into the banking sectors of other member states. These conditions should include minimum capital adequacy requirements, consolidation require-ments and authority for consolidated supervision, restrictions on large exposures, and minimum accounting and transparency requirements. A similar principle of mutual recognition has also governed the EU's "single bank license" approach, in which a bank licensed in an EU member state is also authorized to open branches in other EU countries, without any other formalities or requirements.

The proposals in ADB 2013 identify key elements of a framework for financial integration in ASEAN. But several issues still need to be addressed, including those identified below:

- The ADB report suggests that "a carefully planned market integration process can help more ASEAN-based banks develop faster than their non-ASEAN-based counterparts" (ADB 2013, 8). This slower integration pro-cess could potentially reduce the efficiency and competitiveness gains from banking integration.[2] It could also create too-big-to-fail problems that many countries, especially the United States and countries in Europe, have found to be costly to their citizens and difficult to resolve.

- One or more member countries may want to delay, for economic or political reasons, the opening up of their markets to banks from other ASEAN coun-tries. This desire could make it very difficult to agree on a comprehensive set of minimum conditions that ASEAN-based banks must meet to be eli-gible to enter into the banking sectors of other member states. One com-monly mentioned solution could be for two or more countries to move ahead with opening their markets for each other's banks. Other ASEAN countries could then join these front-runners at a later stage. This is often called the "2+x" approach.[3] The 2+x approach is consistent with the "ASEAN Way." It is incentive-compatible and would allow the front-runners to start reaping some of the benefits from increased financial inte-gration, albeit on a smaller scale than they would in an ASEAN-wide move. The first two movers could trigger action on the part of the other ASEAN members to catch up.

- Not only do the member states, on an ASEAN-wide basis or on a 2+x basis, need to agree to facilitate qualified ASEAN banks' access to their banking markets, qualified ASEAN banks and local banks should be treated equally by host country supervisors. The harmonization of banking regulation

---

[2] Empirical research shows that the presence of foreign banks is in general associated with increased efficiency and competition in local banking sectors, as well as lower net interest margins, reduced excessive profits, and lower cost ratios (for example, Claessens and van Horen 2014).
[3] ASEAN (2008, 11) calls it the "ASEAN minus x" approach.

should start with licensing requirements and extend to cover (1) bank accounting standards and disclosure requirements, (2) minimum capital requirements, (3) risk management, (4) prompt corrective action and resolution methods for failed banks, (5) restrictions on large exposures, and (6) anti-money laundering and consumer protection regulations.

- Clarity is also needed regarding the institutional setup and legislative process at the regional level to ensure effective cross-border supervision and resolution.

- The choice of organizational structure for cross-border banking groups has not been addressed explicitly. Fiechter and others (2011) conclude that one size does not fit all when it comes to choosing between subsidiaries and branches. Home authorities typically prefer a cross-border bank structure with stricter firewalls across parts of the group (the subsidiary model) when their banks expand into weaker, riskier country markets. Host authorities might also prefer the subsidiary model if conditions in their countries are better than those in the home country, to shield local subsidiaries from the parent's potential problems. In contrast, countries with underdeveloped financial systems and weak economies may prefer regional or global banks to enter via branches that can facilitate credit services based on the parent's strength. The quality of supervision, adequacy of information-sharing systems, and systemic importance of the affiliate for home and host financial systems also play a role in home and host preferences.

- The modalities for collaboration between national authorities and the private sector need to be worked out. The success of financial integration hinges on active cooperation between public and private sector players. It is mostly up to national authorities to design and roll out policy reforms. However, successful implementation requires close collaboration with financial institutions and other private agents.

ASEAN Financial Sector Liberalization: Lessons from Europe

What lessons can be drawn from the European experience in establishing a single market in banking? ASEAN nations are in many ways very different from the EU countries. Unlike the EU countries, ASEAN countries have a variety of exchange rate regimes (Table 9.3). ASEAN nations are also more diverse in the stages of their economic and financial development, their political systems, and their cultural backgrounds. Europe's recent history and its devastation from the two world wars set it apart from Asia as well, and serve to explain the desire for political unity. Despite these important differences, the EU's experience in creating a single market for banking and the weaknesses in its approach, as exposed by the stress episodes during 2008–12, could offer some lessons for ASEAN.

Achieving banking integration will require strong political commitment from all ASEAN nations. It is important that ASEAN leaders clearly spell out the objective of banking integration and how each ASEAN member state, large or

TABLE 9.3

De facto Exchange Rate Arrangements, April 30, 2014	
Indonesia	Floating arrangement
Malaysia	Other managed arrangement
Philippines	Floating arrangement
Singapore	Stabilized arrangement
Thailand	Floating arrangement
Brunei Darussalam	Currency board with the Singapore dollar
Cambodia	Other managed arrangement
Lao P.D.R.	Crawl-like arrangement
Myanmar	Other managed arrangement
Vietnam	Stabilized arrangement

Source: IMF, 2014 *Annual Report on Exchange Arrangements and Exchange Restrictions.*

small, will benefit. It is equally important for leaders to clearly grasp the potential contagion and spillover risks brought on by integrated banking markets, as well as the transition and operational risks, especially for the less developed ASEAN countries. Once these risks are identified, strong policy frameworks at national and regional levels would need to be put in place to manage them properly.

Progress toward banking integration would need to be supported by sound institutional and legislative frameworks. The plan to establish a single market for ASEAN banking would need to specify (1) the minimum regulatory requirements for entry, (2) permissible banking activities that are consistent with the current stage of ASEAN development and growth objectives, (3) regional arrangements for effective cross-border bank supervision and resolution, and (4) new regional institutions that would set standards and rules and enforce national compliance with regional rules.

A harmonized set of core regulatory rules is necessary to ensure the efficient functioning of the single market. A level playing field would be difficult to ensure when rules, supervisory practices, and resolution regimes differ substantially at the national level. EU members were able to maintain considerable flexibility in the interpretation and enforcement of common EU directives, which led to wide divergences in national banking regulations. Different national rules and regulations resulted in competitive distortions and encouraged regulatory arbitrage. In particular, for cross-border financial groups, such regulatory differences went against efficient group approaches to risk management and capital allocation, and made the resolution of cross-border financial institutions even more difficult.

However, regulatory harmonization and regional coordination, as implemented in Europe and proposed by the AEC Blueprint, may not be sufficient to ensure the financial stability of a single market. The financial stability arrangements for the single market in Europe were strongly based on national financial stability frameworks. When the crisis hit Europe in 2008, the initial policy response was handicapped by the absence of robust national, and more importantly, EU-wide crisis management frameworks. The lack of ex ante and ex post burden-sharing agreements led to national ring fencing and increased EU financial market segmentation, thus reversing the progress achieved toward EU financial integration.

An ASEAN-wide framework for banking oversight may be necessary to sustain a single market for banking services. The EU crisis has shown that national decisions, even well-intended ones, can have region-wide repercussions for financial stability. Following the example of the Single Supervisory Mechanism introduced in Europe in November 2014, the future ASEAN supervisor could be responsible for the oversight of the systemic ASEAN banks. The effectiveness of a single supervisor would need to be safeguarded by giving it powers to maintain general oversight over all banks and to intervene in any bank it deems necessary. Its governance and its "will to act" would need to be robust, including by ensuring that "nationality dominance" is avoided and that a regional perspective is consistently maintained.

An effective cross-border bank resolution framework for the banks headquartered in ASEAN countries would be another critical element of an ASEAN banking integration framework. At a minimum, ASEAN nations should be advised to strengthen their bank resolution frameworks by adopting best international practices and the Financial Stability Board initiatives. When ASEAN markets for banking and financial services become fully integrated, it may be necessary to put in place a single resolution mechanism that includes a single resolution agency and a common deposit guarantee scheme, with common backstops. But as revealed by the ongoing discussion of banking union in Europe, political resistance may arise, since a single resolution mechanism may involve burden sharing, with net resources flowing from the countries with strong financial systems to those with weaker ones.

ASEAN Capital Account Liberalization: What Is at Stake?

In addition to financial sector liberalization, there is ample scope for further capital account liberalization to spur the development of ASEAN countries. Despite high overall savings in the region, investment needs are huge, including for infrastructure. Rapid urbanization and the growth of the ASEAN middle class requires improved infrastructure in urban communities, including amenities, utilities, and links between production locations and centers of domestic consumption. There is a growing need for more (and cheaper) infrastructure finance to be provided by banks and nonbank intermediaries alike, even as banks adjust their business models in response to changes in global regulatory standards.[4] Closing the large education gap will also require resources. The ADB (2012) calculates that the region needs $0.6 trillion during the next 10 years. Recently, ASEAN policymakers raised the figure to about $1 trillion (for example, Purisima 2014).

---

[4] Banks are the dominant providers of finance in ASEAN and generally rely on demand deposits for funding. They tend to focus on commercial and household lending. Maturity transformation is essential in banking, and banks would be involved more in financing long-term, risky infrastructure projects if these projects were profitable, taking into account risk, externalities, and the local public good aspects of many such projects.

Capital flows from within and outside the region could supplement domestic savings generated in individual ASEAN countries. The removal of restrictions on capital outflows from ASEAN countries could also contribute to reducing the "roundtripping" of regional savings whereby capital is moved from one ASEAN country to another ASEAN country, but indirectly, through financial centers in advanced economies outside ASEAN. For instance, owing to the fungibility of capital, some of the funds invested abroad by ASEAN central banks as they greatly expanded their holdings of official reserves after 1997–98 may have returned to the region in the form of interregional portfolio investments. The gradual relaxation of restrictions on capital outflows from ASEAN countries would likely lead to increased intraregional capital flows, in part by virtue of the commonly observed "home bias" whereby investors invest a relatively large share of their portfolios in their home countries and home regions because of familiarity and information advantages.

The pickup in cross-border financial activity in recent years, both with the rest of Asia and within ASEAN, is a testament to the pull forces driving capital flows into ASEAN. Increased ASEAN integration and openness could, in theory, unleash large flows of investment goods from capital-abundant sources, including China, Japan, and Korea, and from elsewhere within ASEAN (for example, Singapore and Malaysia). The large potential for such flows is discussed and analyzed further in the context of a simple growth model in Almekinders and others (2015). If financial integration within ASEAN and with the rest of the world is incomplete, large differences in GDP per capita (and hence output per worker) can persist, and real convergence can be slow, reflecting long-lasting differences in capital-to-labor ratios. Financial integration can help accelerate economic growth by facilitating capital deepening. Countries at early stages of development should receive the largest inflows, with large potential gains for growth, real convergence, and poverty reduction.

In the simplest case, in which there are no adjustment costs to investment and no legal barriers or informational or other impediments to international capital mobility, capital would quickly move across borders until risk-adjusted rates of return are equalized internationally. In reality, the size of capital flows depends critically on the removal of remaining barriers and the establishment of complementary public factors of production. Raising total factor productivity, as reflected in a country's institutional development (for example, well-defined and respected private property rights, including for intellectual property, a good business climate, and so forth), is a powerful pull force for capital flows.

The simple neoclassical view of real convergence underscores the potential benefits of removing capital controls but omits the dangers lurking in improperly sequenced, rash liberalizations. The problems are well known from an extensive literature on financial crises. Among these problems is "original sin" (borrowing in foreign currency and at short maturities to finance long-lived projects) followed by sudden stops of foreign capital from emerging markets. In this case, self-insurance is an appropriate policy response. Among other things, self-insurance can involve the accumulation of international reserves and the implementation of taxation measures to internalize Pigovian externalities (Aizenman 2009; Jeanne and Korinek 2010) and the incomplete labor insurance markets present in many recipient countries (Mourmouras and Russell 2013).

The IMF's institutional view on this issue (IMF 2012, 2013a) acknowledges the benefits of capital flow liberalization—higher efficiency in resource allocation, technological improvement, higher investment, and better consumption smoothing—while also emphasizing the risks of capital flows, including higher volatility and increased vulnerability to capital account crises. These risks are magnified for countries that are still lagging in financial and institutional development. This is an important lesson: economic development requires more advanced financial systems, which go hand in hand with greater capital flows. Accordingly, the IMF's view on capital flows stresses that the benefits from capital flow liberalization are greatest when financial and institutional development is adequate and the macroeconomic situation is sound. There is no presumption that full liberalization is appropriate for all countries at all times.

Consistent with this approach, the ASEAN capital account integration agenda is properly gradualist in nature, emphasizing the correct sequencing of liberalization and the putting in place of regulatory safeguards to protect individual countries from capital flow volatility. The ADB (2013) defines capital account liberalization as a process of dismantling legal and administrative impediments to the freedom with which economic agents can transfer ownership claims across national borders. The wide divergence among ASEAN economies observed in the area of financial sector development extends to capital account openness. One way to compare countries' openness and assess the scope for increasing it is to look at the various de jure indices of capital account openness used in the empirical literature (Box 9.2).[5]

As discussed in Chapter 10, Asian countries have had diverse experiences with capital flows since 1995, illustrating that, while the scope to remove capital account restrictions is clear, there is no guarantee that doing so will lead to a significant increase in net capital inflows. Net capital flows to ASEAN countries have been large at times, including for many years before the Asian financial crisis of 1997–98. However, on average over the period 2000–12, notwithstanding rising FDI and portfolio inflows discussed in the previous sections, only four ASEAN countries (Lao P.D.R., Cambodia, and, to a lesser extent, Vietnam and Myanmar) were net capital recipients. Remarkably, despite large infrastructure needs and development potential, Indonesia, the Philippines, and Thailand were net capital exporters, with average current account surpluses of about 2 percent

---

[5] In all cases, a higher value of the index denotes a higher degree of capital account openness. A common characteristic of these indices is that the primary source of information for the indices is the IMF's *Annual Report on Exchange Arrangements and Exchange Restrictions* (IMF 2014). The report provides a wealth of detailed information. But it does not accompany this detail with any form of summary or bottom-line characterization of a country's overall degree of openness or restrictiveness. The IMF also does not produce an index of its own.

Box 9.2. De Jure Indices of Capital Account Openness in ASEAN Countries

The Quinn-Toyoda and Schindler indices of capital controls focus on capital account restrictions (see Vargas 2014). In contrast, the Chinn-Ito index (Chinn and Ito 2008) measures four categories of restrictions on external transactions: (1) the presence of multiple exchange rates, (2) restrictions on current account transactions, (3) restrictions on capital account transactions, and (4) requirements regarding the repatriation of export proceeds.

A comparison over time of the evolution of the Chinn-Ito index suggests that Singapore has maintained a high degree of financial openness since the early 1980s (Figure 9.2.1). Restrictions introduced about the time of the Asian financial crisis were quickly unwound. ASEAN-4 countries (Indonesia, Malaysia, the Philippines, and Thailand) maintain only a few restrictions on the buying and selling of domestic securities by nonresidents. This comparative lack of restrictiveness is reflected in relatively high de facto financial openness, measured, for instance, by the level of actual cross-border portfolio flows. However, some restrictions apply to capital account transactions by residents. Moreover, in the aftermath of the Asian financial crisis and the global financial crisis, ASEAN-4 countries introduced or intensified some restrictions on current account transactions, including those involving the repatriation of export proceeds and verification procedures for service payments.

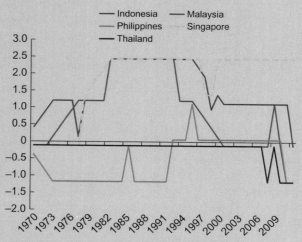

Figure 9.2.1 Chinn-Ito Index for ASEAN-4 and Singapore
Source: Updated from Chinn and Ito (2008).

According to the Chinn-Ito index, as a result of a package of liberalization measures phased in from 2001 onward, Cambodia was the second most financially open economy in ASEAN in 2011. However, capital flows mostly take the form of foreign direct investment and official grants. Portfolio inflows remain limited (low de facto financial openness) given that the relevant domestic financial markets are still being developed. Similarly, Lao P.D.R., Vietnam, and Myanmar have historically displayed relatively low financial openness. Perhaps reflecting their limited exposure to volatile portfolio flows, the CLMV countries (Cambodia, Lao P.D.R., Myanmar, and Vietnam) did not tighten their capital account restrictions with the onset of the global financial crisis (Figure 9.2.2). It should be noted that

Box 9.2. (*continued*)

Myanmar's 2012 liberalization and unification of the exchange rate is not yet reflected in the Chinn-Ito index shown in Figure 9.2.1.

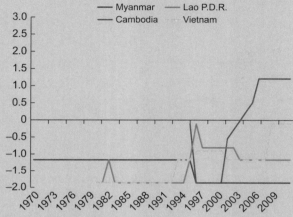

Figure 9.2.2 Chinn-Ito Index for CLMV

Source: Updated from Chinn and Ito (2008).

A comparison with other emerging market economies suggests that the ASEAN-4 countries are not as open in de jure classifications of capital account openness. Figure 9.2.3 shows the three de jure indices for 2005, the latest year for which all three indices are available. All are scaled to a common zero-to-one range, where a larger number represents a higher level of capital control openness. The bars rank the countries by their scores on the Quinn-Toyoda index. The three indices show a substantial correlation and all put the ASEAN-4 countries among the emerging market economies with less open capital accounts.

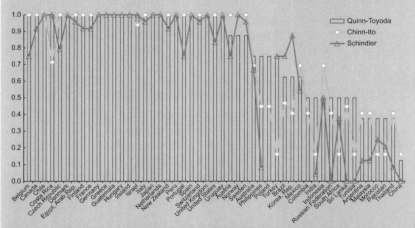

Figure 9.2.3 Capital Account Openness Indices, 2005

Source: Vargas (2014).

TABLE 9.4

Current Account Balances (*Percent of GDP*)			
	1990–97 (Average)	2000–12 (Average)	2013
Indonesia	−2.5	1.8	−3.3
Malaysia	−5.6	11.9	3.9
Philippines	−3.7	1.8	3.5
Singapore	12.3	18.9	18.3
Thailand	−6.4	2.9	−0.6
Brunei Darussalam	43.4	44.1	31.5
Cambodia	−2.8	−3.8	−8.5
Lao P.D.R.	−6.6	−16.2	−27.7
Myanmar	...	−0.4	−5.4
Vietnam	−6.8	−2.3	5.6

Source: IMF, *World Economic Outlook*, October 2014.

of GDP a year during 2000–12 (Table 9.4). Malaysia's net capital exports were even larger, averaging 12 percent of GDP a year during this period.

ASEAN countries' net exports of capital in the first decade of the 2000s reflected the accumulation of official reserves for self-insurance and precautionary purposes in the aftermath of the Asian financial crisis. As of 2015, reserves seem broadly adequate in most ASEAN countries, so there is scope for a change in the direction of intraregional and interregional net capital flows. Park and Takagi (2012) note that the tendency of most ASEAN countries to maintain relatively tighter controls on outflows has discouraged capital inflows from within ASEAN, while encouraging inflows from advanced countries outside the region.[6]

ASEAN capital account liberalization will be an ongoing process with the end goal of achieving a high degree of capital account openness while preserving adequate financial stability. Discussions among the member countries continue to be led by guidelines established in the AEC Blueprint: (1) ensuring an orderly capital account liberalization process consistent with member countries' national agendas and readiness of their economies; (2) allowing adequate safeguards against potential macroeconomic instability and systemic risk that may arise from the liberalization process, including the right to adopt necessary measures to ensure macroeconomic stability; and (3) ensuring that the benefits of liberalization will be shared by all ASEAN countries.

An important challenge for capital account liberalization is to harness benefits while minimizing risks. Ishii and others (2002) recommend a gradualist approach, emphasizing the need for careful sequencing and establishment of preconditions to be observed before a country could safely move from one step to the next. As

---

[6] As noted earlier, because of home bias, ASEAN-based investors tend to invest a relatively large share of their portfolios in their home regions. Therefore, a relaxation of ASEAN countries' controls on outflows could be expected to lead to a disproportional increase in capital outflows to other ASEAN countries.

observed by Park and Takagi (2012) and ADB (2013), ASEAN countries maintain several classes of restrictions that may currently be providing legitimate safeguards against speculation and preventing the buildup of financial sector risk. These include restrictions on the offshore use of almost all ASEAN countries' currencies and external lending in domestic currency, as well as limits on the ability of investors to hedge foreign currency risk. Some of these restrictions may need to be phased out as the region moves along the path to regional financial integration. It may be appropriate, however, to maintain these restrictions until relevant thresholds for upgrading macroeconomic and financial policy frameworks are met.[7] Empirical research suggests that financial depth and institutional quality are the two most important preconditions for foreign capital inflows to have a positive effect on economic growth.

PROMOTING SAFE FINANCIAL INTEGRATION IN ASEAN

This section reviews policies that could be adopted by ASEAN countries, individually and collectively and with regional and multilateral partners, to promote safe financial integration in ASEAN. These policies would be particularly relevant for FDI inflows and banking integration. This section also considers the present state of and future prospects for regional surveillance and financial cooperation initiatives, including the ASEAN+3 Macroeconomic Research Office (AMRO) and the Chiang Mai Initiative Multilateralization (CMIM—see also Box 9.1). The section also briefly discusses (1) the lessons for Asia from the failings of European integration efforts; and (2) risk mitigation within ASEAN, including in the context of the CMIM, and the role of the IMF.

Policies to Help Enhance Financial Integration and Mitigate Risks

In the medium and longer terms, ASEAN banking links are likely to expand further as the AEC's financial integration goals are gradually realized. As ASEAN financial systems become more open, they will become more exposed to developments abroad. The potential result of such exposure is exemplified by the difficult global economic and financial environment that developed in the aftermath of the global financial crisis. There are various aspects to this. Duval and others (2014) find that greater banking and portfolio integration between two economies reduces the economies' output comovement in general. However, during a period of crisis (such as the global financial crisis) banking integration appears to increase the synchronization of cycles across countries. In such cases, global banks pull funds away from all countries, amplifying output comovement for countries that are financially integrated and reliant on foreign capital flows (Kalemli-Ozcan,

---

[7] The ADB (2013) proposes, as a safeguard measure, retaining the restrictions on cross-border trading of forwards and derivatives as well as on offshore currency use.

Papaioannou, and Perri 2013).[8] This points to the potential merits of regional banking integration: a greater role for regional banks could reduce the impact of financial shocks originating in advanced economies.

As noted earlier, international experience suggests that rapid bank expansion in new markets can pose challenges because bank risk management and supervisory monitoring may fail to keep pace. Uneven supervisory quality in host markets can also contribute to the masking of vulnerabilities. Although an ASEAN-wide single supervisory mechanism would be the best solution, it may not be technically and politically feasible in the near term. In fact, as of early 2015, ASEAN has not indicated that it is considering a single supervisory mechanism or forming a perfectly integrated banking sector. Instead, ASEAN countries have shown a trend toward harmonizing regulations (including in securities markets). While this harmonization takes shape, one option to mitigate risks may be greater host control over foreign branches, as is being implemented in Singapore (see next paragraph). Alternatively, risks can also be mitigated by reciprocity arrangements. The principle of reciprocity has governed banks from non-EU member states that open branches in the EU. The reciprocity principle is also a cornerstone of the Basel Committee on Banking Supervision's framework for countercyclical capital buffers. A certain degree of harmonization—for example, in the definition of capital—is necessary for mutual recognition. Malaysia's Financial Sector Blueprint highlights the need to further deepen home-host cooperation in supervision and crisis prevention.

In Singapore, the important role played by foreign branches creates exposure to their parent banks. The IMF's 2013 Financial Sector Assessment Program report for Singapore (IMF 2013d) notes that Singaporean banks have large capital and other cushions and appear able to withstand major shocks. It also observes that the Monetary Authority of Singapore has adopted measures to mitigate the risks posed by the presence of the large number of foreign branches. Accordingly, the Monetary Authority of Singapore has (1) set high standards for approving foreign entrants, applying the same prudential qualifications as it applies to its own locally incorporated banks; (2) limited the number of foreign branches permitted to accept retail deposits; and (3) recently adopted a program that requires so-called qualified full banks with large retail presences to locally incorporate their retail operations. The Monetary Authority of Singapore has also established good working relationships with home supervisors of the foreign branches and proactively engages with management of the parent banks to ensure that they take responsibility for any risks or shortcomings identified in the branches' operations.

As discussed in this chapter, with greater financial integration come risks from credit booms and volatile and unpredictable capital flows. These risks underscore the importance of sound macroeconomic management in a world of high capital

---

[8]The impact of the ongoing deleveraging by European banks appears manageable. In fact, European bank retrenchment has represented an opportunity for ASEAN banks (and those from elsewhere in Asia). The pullout of U.S. banks from emerging markets following the Latin American debt crisis of the 1980s and the deleveraging by Japanese banks in Southeast Asia after Japan's financial crisis in the 1990s are cautionary tales.

mobility. If the risks originate in the banking system, it makes sense for countries to adopt macroprudential tools such as tightening conditions for housing loans or having banks hold more capital. If the risks are associated with capital flow surges, implementation of temporary capital flow management measures might prove useful. At the same time, deeper financial market development still has benefits. As Bank Negara Malaysia Governor Zeti Akthar Aziz has pointed out, mature financial systems can handle capital flows without being overwhelmed. The retrenchment of euro area banks from Asia following the global financial crisis underscores the importance of having well-developed, well-regulated, and deep financial markets in Asia as a means of absorbing external shocks.

The development of the domestic banking sector and increased banking sector integration can proceed in tandem. A key challenge for policymakers and supervisors in Asia is to design and implement policies that support an efficient and resilient integrated banking system. Harmonization of the regulatory and supervisory frameworks can accelerate the pace of financial integration. As banking sectors develop and integrate, supervisory capacity needs to keep pace with increasingly complex banking institutions and their cross-border operations. Making the most of financial integration also means establishing better global rules, such as the reforms envisaged in Basel III. Perhaps paradoxically, the various ongoing efforts aimed at enhancing regional integration could lead to greater regulatory fragmentation. Such fragmentation could happen if inadequate coordination between ASEAN and other regional integration initiatives were to result in the adoption of conflicting regulations.

Policy reform initiatives related to the creation of the AEC can have far-reaching effects on other policy fields such as domestic monetary and fiscal policy. And capital account liberalization can lead to a loss of policy independence and a resulting need to strengthen fiscal policy and structural reforms. The experience of Malaysia and Indonesia in 2013 provides strong support for the assertion made in ADB (2013, 16) that "the best strategy for living with an open capital account is to pursue sound macroeconomic policies." In the first half of 2013, when once-large surpluses on the current account of the balance of payments narrowed significantly (Malaysia), or turned into deficits (Indonesia), international investors blamed overly loose macroeconomic policies and started to sell their asset holdings in these countries. Capital outflows from both countries subsided after the adoption of strong packages of macroeconomic policies.

Europe's experience with financial and monetary integration of highly heterogeneous economies is relevant in thinking about the path to ASEAN (and greater Asian) financial integration. An important lesson that has emerged from Europe is that monetary and financial integration without fiscal or political integration is fraught with danger, especially when member countries are highly heterogeneous with regard to fiscal discipline, export competitiveness, institutional advancement, and other macrocritical dimensions. Unlike the euro area, ASEAN countries do not share a common currency and monetary and exchange rate policies. Therefore, exchange rate movements can help absorb shocks. Nevertheless, Asia will be well served in the future by adopting a measured, gradual, and evolutionary approach to financial integration.

Risk Mitigation within ASEAN and in Collaboration with the IMF

The growing interconnectedness between economies and financial systems is increasing the risk that national and international financial markets will be subjected to protracted bouts of instability. This is true globally as well as in the Asian region. Efforts are ongoing to strengthen the region's safety net to address ASEAN+3 countries' potential need for short-term liquidity if balance of payments difficulties were to arise. In this context, the ASEAN+3 Finance Ministers and Central Bank Governors, at their May 2012 meeting, adopted proposals to double the CMIM's size to $240 billion and to introduce a crisis prevention facility. The increase went into effect in July 2014, following the required ratifications.

As is the case with other regional organizations and financing arrangements (IMF 2013b, 2013c), the IMF has long been engaged in fruitful dialogue and cooperation with ASEAN and ASEAN+3 institutions. Building on this working relationship, collaboration is being strengthened in the areas of surveillance, liquidity support arrangements, and capacity development. For example, at their May 2014 meeting, the ASEAN+3 Finance Ministers and Central Bank Governors endorsed the "Guidelines for the Further Cooperation with the International Monetary Fund." Collaboration between the IMF and regional organizations focuses on the IMF's macrofinancial areas of expertise. The IMF regularly presents its research and analysis at various regional forums, including its work on capital market development and capital account liberalization. Similarly, the IMF organizes joint seminars and conferences (for example, in January 2014 in Tokyo and in March 2015 in Seoul, jointly with AMRO), in which issues such as macroprudential policies in ASEAN are discussed. In addition to research and analysis, the IMF helps with regional institution building in ASEAN by sharing with AMRO its expertise gained from cross-country analyses.

CONCLUSION

This chapter highlights that further ASEAN intraregional integration (through increased trade, FDI, portfolio investment, and cross-border banking) could be an important source of growth, employment, and more inclusive development, as well as a source of resilience to shocks for ASEAN countries.

Trade and financial integration within ASEAN have increased considerably in recent years. Nevertheless, there is significant scope for further financial sector liberalization and capital account liberalization. In particular, it is well known that financial integration in Asia, and particularly in ASEAN, lags behind such integration in the rest of the world. Although this is changing (for example, Singaporean and Malaysian banks' activities in the region are expanding), more needs to be done to address the continued fragmentation of financial systems in Asia and in ASEAN. In fact, financial integration is an important component of ongoing initiatives to create a single ASEAN market for goods and services. The Blueprint for the AEC calls for regulatory harmonization and the strengthening of policy coordination among member states. Although coordination is appropriate, the recent experience in the EU underscores that it is equally important to take a regional approach to financial stability. In particular, a supranational oversight framework may be necessary for the planned single AEC market for financial services. Europe's experience also suggests the need to reinforce regional macrofinancial surveillance mechanisms (for example, AMRO) and regional financial safety nets (for example, the CMIM). These regional efforts are ongoing and actively supported by IMF staff, where possible.

The ongoing strengthening of regional macroeconomic surveillance and financial safety nets is welcome, but it is also important to monitor financial systems to ensure early detection of the emergence of possible vulnerabilities. ASEAN countries are at different stages of economic development, and ongoing financial integration means that countries with relatively low credit-to-GDP ratios are catching up with the front-runners. Such financial deepening is valuable but, as is well known from economic history, the resulting strong growth of credit could give rise to financial sector vulnerabilities and risks. The challenges faced by some of the ASEAN countries in the context of their domestic financial sector development need to be taken into account when decisions are made about the correct pace of ASEAN financial sector liberalization. Therefore, the diligent and careful approach taken by ASEAN countries in moving forward is appropriate. However, the ASEAN/AEC framework leaves open the possibility that more advanced economies will move faster with financial integration. Once adequate safeguards are in place, it would be in the interests of these countries to remove protectionist barriers to regional banking integration.

REFERENCES

Aizenman, Joshua. 2009. "Hoarding International Reserves versus a Pigovian Tax-Cum-Subsidy Scheme: Reflections on the Deleveraging Crisis of 2008–9, and a Cost Benefit Analysis." Working Paper No. 15484, National Bureau of Economic Research, Cambridge, Massachusetts.

Almekinders, Geert, Satoshi Fukuda, Alex Mourmouras, and Jianping Zhou. 2015. "ASEAN Financial Integration." IMF Working Paper No. 15/34, International Monetary Fund, Washington.

Asian Development Bank (ADB). 2012. "Facts and Data about Southeast Asian Infrastructure." Manila: Asian Development Bank. http://www.adb.org/features/fast-facts-asean-infrastructure-fund.

———. 2013. *The Road to ASEAN Financial Integration: A Combined Study on Assessing the Financial Landscape and Formulating Milestones for Monetary and Financial Integration in ASEAN.* Manila: Asian Development Bank. http://www.adb.org/sites/default/files/pub/2013/road-to-asean-financial-integration.pdf.

Association of Southeast Asian Nations (ASEAN). 2008. "ASEAN Economic Community Blueprint." January. http://www.asean.org/news/item/declaration-on-the-asean-economic-community-blueprint.

Basu Das, Sanchita, Jayant Menon, Rodolfo Severino, and Omkar Lal Shrestha. 2013. *The ASEAN Economic Community: A Work in Progress.* Singapore: Asian Development Bank and Institute of Southeast Asian Studies. http://www.adb.org/sites/default/files/pub/2013/aec-work-progress.pdf.

Chinn, Menzie D., and Hiro Ito. 2008. "A New Measure of Financial Openness. *Journal of Comparative Policy Analysis* 10 (3): 309–22.

Claessens, Stijn, and Neeltje van Horen. 2014. "Foreign Banks: Trends and Impact." *Journal of Money, Credit and Banking* 46 (1): 295–326.

Cubero, Rodrigo, Shanaka J. Peiris, Purichai Rungcharoenkitkul, and Dulani Seneviratne. 2014. "Growing Strong Together: An Analysis of Trade Linkages in ASEAN." Unpublished, International Monetary Fund, Washington.

Duval, Romain, Kevin Cheng, Kum Hwa Oh, Richa Saraf, and Dulani Seneviratne. 2014. "Trade Integration and Business Cycle Synchronization: A Reappraisal with Focus on Asia." IMF Working Paper No. 14/52, International Monetary Fund, Washington.

Fiechter, Jonathan, Inci Otker-Robe, Anna Ilyina, Michael Hsu, Andre Santos, and Jay Surti. 2011. "Subsidiaries or Branches: Does One Size Fit All?" IMF Staff Discussion Note No. 11/04, International Monetary Fund, Washington.

International Monetary Fund (IMF). 2010. "Does Asia Need Rebalancing?" In *Regional Economic Outlook: Asia and Pacific*. Washington: International Monetary Fund, April. http://www.imf.org/external/pubs/ft/reo/2010/apd/eng/areo0410.pdf.

———. 2012. "The Liberalization and Management of Capital Flows: An Institutional View." IMF Policy Paper, November 14, International Monetary Fund, Washington. http://www.imf.org/external/np/pp/eng/2012/111412.pdf.

———. 2013a. "Guidance Note for the Liberalization and Management of Capital Flows." International Monetary Fund, Washington. http://www.imf.org/external/np/pp/eng/2013/042513.pdf.

———. 2013b. "IMF Explores Ways to Enhance Cooperation with Regional Groups." IMF Survey. July 2, International Monetary Fund, Washington. http://www.imf.org/external/pubs/ft/survey/so/2013/POL070213A.htm

———. 2013c. "Stocktaking the Fund's Engagement with Regional Financing Arrangements." IMF Policy Paper, April 2013, International Monetary Fund, Washington. http://www.imf.org/external/np/pp/eng/2013/041113b.pdf

———. 2013d. "Singapore Financial System Stability Assessment." IMF Country Report No. 13/325, Washington, October.

———. 2014. *Annual Report on Exchange Arrangements and Exchange Restrictions*. Washington: International Monetary Fund.

Ishii, Shogo, Karl Habermeier, Jorge Ivan Canales-Kriljenko, Bernard Laurens, John Leimone, and Judit Vadasz. 2002. *Capital Account Liberalization and Financial Sector Stability*. Occasional Paper No. 211. Washington: International Monetary Fund.

Jeanne, Olivier, and Anton Korinek. 2010. "Managing Credit Booms and Busts: A Pigouvian Taxation Approach." Working Paper No. 16377, National Bureau of Economic Research, Cambridge, Massachusetts.

Kalemli-Ozcan, Sebnem, Elias Papaioannou, and Fabrizio Perri. 2013. "Global Banks and Crisis Transmission." *Journal of International Economics* 89 (2): 495–510.

Mourmouras, Alexandros, and Steven Russell. 2013. "Financial Crises, Capital Liquidation, and International Reserves." Unpublished, International Monetary Fund, Washington.

Park, Yung Chul, and Shinji Takagi. 2012. "Managing Capital Flows in an Economic Community: The Case of ASEAN Capital Account Liberalization." Working Paper No. 378, Asian Development Bank Institute, Tokyo.

Pongsaparn, Runchana, and Olaf Unteroberdoerster. 2011. "Financial Integration and Rebalancing in Asia." IMF Working Paper No. 11/243, International Monetary Fund, Washington.

Purisima, Cesar V. 2014. Keynote remarks at the Center for Strategic and International Studies, forum on "The Promise of Regional Integration: Protecting and Strengthening ASEAN Centrality," Washington, April 10.

Schipke, Alfred. 2015. *Frontier Asia: The Next Generation of Emerging Markets*. Washington: International Monetary Fund.

Vargas, M. 2014. "Quinn-Toyoda and Other De Jure Indices of Capital Account Openness." Unpublished, International Monetary Fund, Washington.

World Bank. 2014. *East Asia and Pacific Economic Update April 2014: Preserving Stability and Promoting Growth*. Washington: World Bank. http://documents.worldbank.org/curated/en/2014/04/19543743/preserving-stability-promoting-growth.

CHAPTER 10

Capital Flows: A Prospective View

Edda Zoli, Sergei Dodzin, Wei Liao, and
Wojciech Maliszewski

MAIN POINTS OF THIS CHAPTER

- During the past two decades capital flows to Asia have been large and volatile, creating both opportunities and challenges for regional policymakers.

- In the period following the Asian financial crisis, net capital flows to the region were mainly driven by domestic GDP growth, which was high in comparison with U.S. growth, U.S. interest rates, and investor risk appetite.

- In both the short and long terms, additional factors will also shape the size and composition of capital flows. These factors include quantitative and qualitative monetary easing in Japan, capital account liberalization (most notably in China), increasing financial integration and development, and changes in saving patterns driven by demographics.

- All of these factors will contribute to capital flow volatility, requiring sound macroeconomic and microprudential policies as well as macroprudential policies to build resilience and mitigate risk.

INTRODUCTION

The past two decades have seen waves of large capital inflows sweeping through Asia. The first wave started in the early1990s and ended abruptly with the Asian financial crisis in 1997. The second one began in the early 2000s and came to a halt with the global financial crisis. The third wave started in mid-2009 and ended in May 2013, when the U.S. Federal Reserve signaled plans to exit from its quantitative easing (QE) program. Capital inflows delivered economic benefits, but they also posed significant challenges for policymakers because of their potential to generate overheating, loss of competitiveness, and increased vulnerability to crises.

Yitae Kim, Raphael Lam, and Jongsoon Shin also contributed to this chapter. The authors thank Jingzhou Meng and Sidra Rehman for excellent research assistance, and Joong Shik Kang, Kwok Ping Tsang, Jerry Schiff, Chikahisa Sumi, and Jianping Zhou for helpful comments.

Against this background, this chapter takes a prospective look at capital flows to and within Asia, and explores the factors that will shape their size and composition in the short, medium, and long terms. Important policy changes and structural transformations, which are under way in the region and globally, will affect capital flow movements in Asia. Such changes include, in the short to medium term, monetary policy normalization in the United States and quantitative and qualitative monetary easing (QQE) in Japan. In the medium to long term, they include capital account liberalization—most notably in China—increasing financial integration and development, and changes in saving patterns driven by demographics.

First, the chapter reviews stylized facts about past capital flow cycles, capital flow composition, and geographical origin and destination, and presents a new empirical analysis of the main drivers of capital flows to Asia after the Asian crisis. This empirical evidence is then used to discuss the outlook for capital flows in the short to medium term. Then, the chapter focuses on the possible impact of Japan's QQE, China's capital account liberalization, and other structural changes in capital flows to and within Asia.

Although the full implications of all of these factors on future capital flows cannot be predicted, it is clear that volatility of cross-border capital flows will persist, creating significant policy challenges. Therefore, Asian economies need to continue building resilience to confront these challenges. Sound macroeconomic and microprudential regulation and supervision will be essential tools. In addition, macroprudential policies—which have already been used extensively in the region—can provide supplementary instruments to mitigate systemic risks. Hence, the final section of the chapter reviews Asia's experience with macroprudential policies, and also highlights how the existing framework could be further strengthened to enhance resilience and improve the response to economic fluctuations. Because capital flows can bring important benefits to Asia, the final section also reviews policy measures that can help channel capital flows to productive uses.

CAPITAL FLOWS IN RETROSPECT

Stylized Facts on Capital Flows to Asia

Capital flows to Asia have been highly volatile since 1990. After a significant surge in the early 1990s, they saw a massive reversal with the Asian financial crisis. Since the middle of the first decade of the 2000s, capital flows have resumed, but remained volatile, recording a boom from the fourth quarter of 2006 to the third quarter of 2007, followed by a sharp decline during the global financial crisis, and another upswing from the third quarter of 2009 to the third quarter of 2011 (Figure 10.1). Although the pattern of capital flow movements was similar for both advanced Asia (comprising Australia, Japan, and New Zealand) and the rest of Asia, the latter experienced larger shifts in flows, especially in the 1990s and in 2012–13.

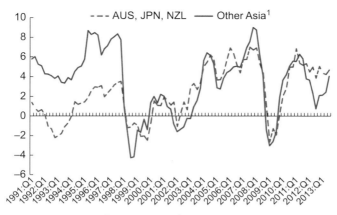

Figure 10.1 Nonresident Non-FDI Inflows to Asia (*Four-quarter moving average, percent of GDP*)

Sources: IMF, International Financial Statistics and World Economic Outlook databases; and IMF staff calculations.
Note: AUS = Australia; JPN = Japan; NZL = New Zealand. FDI = foreign direct investment.
[1]Other Asia comprises China, Hong Kong SAR, India, Indonesia, Korea, Malaysia, the Philippines, Singapore, Taiwan Province of China, Thailand, and Vietnam.

Net capital flows were also volatile, particularly in Asian economies other than China. This volatility was due to their composition. Flows to Asia, excluding China, have been dominated by portfolio and other investment, mainly bank loans (Figure 10.2). Both are volatile sources of funding: portfolio investment is considered more mobile than are other flows, and bank loans are typically short term. Both types of flows are also highly sensitive to external financial conditions, particularly in advanced economies. Similarly to the most recent surge in inflows, flows to Asia in the run-up to the Asian financial crisis were related to a declining trend in interest rates in the advanced countries and to a search for yield.

Capital flows to China have been dominated by more stable foreign direct investment (FDI), but in 2012 the "other investment" flow category started to become more volatile. A gradual liberalization of exchange rate restrictions contributed to this additional volatility. The liberalizing of surrendering requirements in 2012, together with changes to near-term perceptions about currency appreciation, produced a shift to foreign deposits. This shift caused a large negative swing in the "other investment" category, which was partly reversed in 2013.

Capital flows to low-income Asian countries have been small compared with those to the rest of the region, but they have been increasing, especially since the global financial crisis. FDI has been the major component of capital flows to this country group, also reflecting greater investment in natural resource sectors following the spike in commodity prices after 2005. FDI inflows have increased rapidly especially in low-income Asian countries with significant natural resources, such as Mongolia, and to a lesser extent, Lao P.D.R. China was the source of part of these FDI flows.

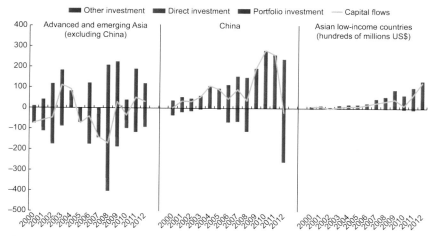

Figure 10.2 Asia: Capital Flows, Net (*Billions of U.S. dollars*)
Sources: IMF, Balance of Payments Statistics; and IMF staff calculations.

As in the early 2000s, most portfolio inflows to Asia continued to originate from the United States and advanced Europe, exposing Asia to spillovers from those regions (Figure 10.3). Intraregional portfolio investment has grown somewhat since then. The share of portfolio investment of Asian origin increased from about 15 percent to about 24 percent between 2001 and 2012, reflecting, in part, a deepening of domestic financial markets such as local currency bond markets. Portfolio outward investment within Asia also grew, from 10 percent to 18 percent, over the same period. As of 2012, about 70 percent of direct investment originated within the region, and most of Asian FDI was directed toward the region.

Asian economies also have been the recipients of bank loans from Europe and the United States (Figure 10.4). European banks have been important sources of both direct and indirect credit to the region. The banks' direct lending has been to private sector agents in the region through cross-border transactions and through lending by local subsidiaries and branches. Direct lending has included the area of trade finances. Indirectly, banks have played a role in the wholesale funding of regional banks, particularly in Australia, Hong Kong SAR, Korea, New Zealand, Singapore, and Taiwan Province of China (IMF 2012b). European banks reduced their lending to Asia in the aftermath of the global financial crisis, with credit from euro area banks not fully recovering to precrisis levels. The impact of European banks' deleveraging has been partly offset by regional banks, especially those in Japan, that have stepped in (see Box 10.1 below).

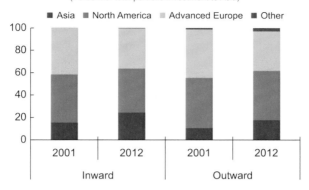

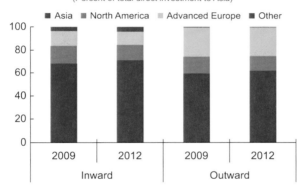

Figure 10.3 Asia: Regional Composition of Portfolio and Direct Investment

Sources: IMF staff calculations; Coordinated Portfolio Investment Survey; and Coordinated Direct Investment Survey.

Drivers of Capital Flows to Asia in the Post–Asian Crisis Period

To gain a sense of the drivers of capital flows to Asia in the post–Asian crisis period a model of net capital inflows was estimated using a panel of 14 Asian economies from 2000:Q1 though 2013:Q4.[1] (See Annex 10.1.) The results suggest that domestic GDP growth, U.S. short-term interest rates, the U.S. QE program, and investor risk appetite—proxied by the Chicago Board Options Exchange

---

[1] See Annex 10.1 for background information on the empirical analysis and regression results.

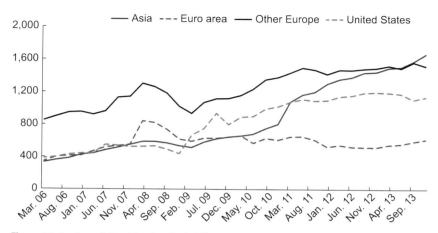

Figure 10.4 Consolidated Foreign Banks' Claims on Asian Economies (*Billions of U.S. dollars, on immediate borrower basis*)

Source: Bank for International Settlements.

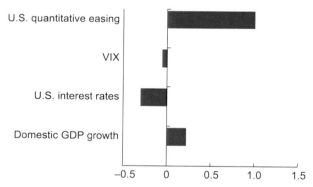

Figure 10.5 Asia: Quarterly Response of Net Capital Inflows to Domestic and External Variables (*Percent*)

Source: IMF staff estimates.
Note: VIX = Chicago Board Options Exchange Market Volatility Index.

Market Volatility Index (VIX)—have been key determinants of net inflows to the region.

The analysis found that U.S. monetary policy was a more important driver of net capital flows to Asia than was domestic monetary policy. In fact, a 1 percentage point increase in U.S. short-term interest rates was estimated to reduce the ratio of net capital inflows to GDP by 0.3 percent after one quarter (Figure 10.5). Conversely, domestic short-term rates were found not to have a significant impact on net capital inflows. The coefficient associated with the QE dummy variable was estimated to be positive and significant in some model specifications, suggesting that the Federal Reserve's QE programs may have boosted net capital flows to the region. In contrast, dummies for quantitative easing operations conducted in the United Kingdom and Japan were found not to be significant.

Domestic GDP growth has also been an important determinant of net capital inflows, with a 1 percentage point increase in growth estimated to boost the ratio of net capital inflows to GDP by 0.2 percent after a quarter. U.S. GDP growth by itself was not found to be a significant factor in explaining net capital flows to Asia, but in an alternative model specification, the growth differential between Asian economies and the United States was found to be a significant driver of capital inflows to the region. Investor risk appetite also plays a part in explaining net capital flows to Asia. A 1 percentage point rise in the VIX—indicating an increase in uncertainty and a decline in global risk appetite—is associated with a reduction in net capital inflows by close to one-tenth of a percent of GDP after a quarter. Institutional country characteristics, although not explicitly modeled, played a role in explaining cross-country differences in the net capital flow movements, as indicated by the high significance of cross-section fixed effects. Similar findings were obtained when net inflows excluding FDI were used as a dependent variable, instead of total net inflows.

A model of gross capital inflows to Asia over the same period was also estimated (Annex 10.1).[2] Results indicate that gross capital inflows are not very sensitive to U.S. short-term interest rates, and that, instead, they mostly respond to domestic growth, U.S. growth, or the differential between the two growth rates—as well as to the VIX and a dummy for U.S. QE.

PROSPECTIVE CAPITAL FLOWS: WHAT WILL SHAPE CAPITAL FLOWS TO AND WITHIN ASIA?

The empirical analysis provided some insights on what explained net capital flows to Asia in the past. Now, however, the relevant question is: What is the outlook for capital flows? Because Asia is expected to remain a global growth leader, it will very likely continue to receive large capital flows. Nevertheless, a number of global and regional factors will affect interregional and intraregional flows, and most likely will also contribute to capital flow volatility. In the short to medium term, the Federal Reserve's exit from unconventional monetary policy and the normalization of global interest rates will likely play a role. The Bank of Japan's (BoJ's) QQE program could also have an impact on capital flows to and within the region. Beyond the medium term, capital flows to and within Asia will be largely shaped by capital account liberalization, most notably in China. Other factors, such as financial integration within and outside the region, financial development, and savings patterns—in turn driven by demographics—also are expected to shape capital flow movements, including within the region. These aspects are discussed in the next section of this chapter.

---

[2] Studies on capital flow volatility emphasize the importance of analyzing gross capital flows instead of just net flows (for example, Forbes and Warnock 2012; Milesi-Ferretti and Tille 2011).

Factors Shaping Capital Flows in the Short to Medium Term

Monetary Policy Normalization in the United States

Since May 2013, expectations of a gradual unwinding of QE by the Federal Reserve have led to significant portfolio adjustments on the part of global investors. As a result, capital flows to Asia reversed sharply. The QE program ended in 2014, and U.S. policy rates are expected to start rising in 2015. Given the sensitivity of Asian capital flows to those U.S. policy rates, a rate hike in the United States could lead to a temporary reversal of capital flows in Asia. However, solid domestic GDP growth, especially compared with that of the United States and other advanced economies outside of Asia, will likely continue to attract capital flows to the region in the short to medium term.

Quantitative and Qualitative Monetary Easing in Japan

The BoJ initiated its QQE program in April 2013, as part of Prime Minister Abe's three-pronged strategy to exit deflation and lift growth. The BoJ's plan to double the monetary base by about ¥130 trillion (27 percent of GDP) in two years—coupled with concerns about increases in U.S. interest rates—could trigger capital outflows from Japan to other countries in and outside Asia in the short to medium term.

Japanese investors have often been net purchasers of foreign assets (mostly foreign bonds and notes) in the past decades, with an average of about ¥12½ trillion (less than 3 percent of GDP) in purchases per year and never exceeding ¥25 trillion (about 5 percent of GDP) per year. QQE will likely have an impact on Japanese capital outflows through the following channels (IMF 2012c, 2013b):

- *Firms expanding abroad*—Japanese firms have increasingly moved abroad, often to the Asian region, to reduce production costs and exploit local markets, with a positive impact on destination countries' growth. A rise in domestic inflation from QQE, accompanied by depreciation of the real effective exchange rate, could slow the rising trend of outward FDI flows.[3] However, outward FDI is a long-term trend, because firms aim to locate where demand is growing and take advantage of cost differentials. Therefore, a reversal of increasing overseas production or FDI abroad is unlikely, given the relatively high rates of return on these investments.

- *Rebalancing of portfolio flows*—QQE and a sustained difference in monetary policy stance between the BoJ and other major central banks are expected to trigger a shift in the portfolio composition of Japanese investors—especially financial institutions—away from domestic government bonds and into riskier financial instruments, including foreign assets.

Portfolio rebalancing of Japanese financial institutions is progressing. Domestic banks have reduced their holdings of Japanese government bonds

---

[3] Empirical evidence suggests that, for instance, a 10 percentage point depreciation in the real effective exchange rate would slow the overseas production ratio by 1.3 percentage points.

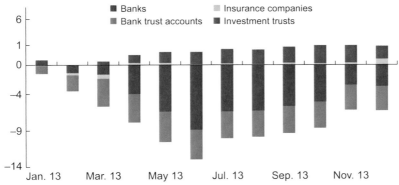

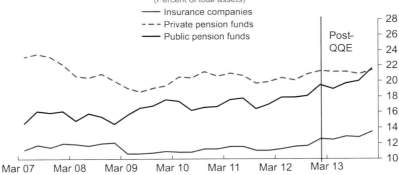

Figure 10.6 Japan: Outward Portfolio Investment and Foreign Security Holdings

Sources: Bank of Japan; and IMF staff estimates.
Note: QQE = quantitative and qualitative easing.

since April 2013 and increased outward portfolio investment. But they have also accumulated significant excess reserves at the BoJ, which could be used for further foreign portfolio investment in the future. Holdings of foreign securities have picked up somewhat for public pension funds, but only modestly for insurance companies and private pension funds (Figure 10.6). Nevertheless, the following factors suggest that more capital outflows could take place in the coming years:

- Insurance companies have announced a gradual diversification toward foreign securities in the medium term in their investment plans, although few insurers intend to substantially unwind their Japanese government bond holdings.
- Japan's Government Pension Investment Fund—with total investment assets of about 27 percent of GDP—has revealed plans to gradually diversify

toward emerging markets for higher yields in the medium term. Benchmark limits on investment in risky assets, which have constrained the acquisition of foreign bonds and equities, were eased in June 2013, resulting in an increase in foreign security holdings (Figure 10.6).[4]

- Households in search of higher yields could reallocate more of their savings toward foreign assets, which currently represent only 2½ percent of household financial assets.

Bank Lending Abroad

As QQE encourages financial institutions to shift away from government bonds, Japanese banks will likely increase domestic lending as well as foreign lending, especially to other Asian economies, to boost profits. Overseas activity of Japanese financial institutions has already risen significantly since the middle of the first decade of the 2000s (Box 10.1), and access to ample liquidity under QQE is likely to provide a further boost to cross-border expansion.

An illustrative scenario analysis assuming that Japanese investors broadly maintain the current portfolio composition in their overseas investment strategies suggests that potential capital outflows could be $80 billion to $100 billion (1.6 to 2.0 percent of GDP—IMF 2014a). This analysis takes into account the easing of benchmark limits for the Government Pension Investment Fund, rising interest rate differentials with the United States, domestic credit demand growth, and banks' large excess reserves. If Japanese investors were to change their strategies, that is, if they were to more aggressively rebalance their portfolios toward foreign securities, capital outflows could be higher, as much as $260 billion (about 5 percent of GDP). A large portion of rebalancing would likely be toward North America and Europe, which historically have been the recipients of about 70 percent of both Japanese portfolio and bank lending flows. Although Asian emerging markets would likely receive a smaller share, the estimated potential capital flows to these economies could be as much as $30 billion—more than half of their peak reserve loss during 2013.

Factors Shaping Capital Flows in the Medium to Long Term

Capital Account Liberalization

Financial accounts in Asia are less open than they are in other regions (Figure 10.7). Based on the Chinn-Ito index,[5] although the capital account openness of some Asian economies (Hong Kong SAR, Japan, New Zealand, and Singapore) is comparable to that in the euro area and North America, other countries maintain considerable capital flow restrictions. For low-income economies in particular, capital account liberalization would likely induce further FDI inflows, given their growth prospects and recent trends.

---

[4] Under the new policy mix, the Government Pension Investment Fund can invest 12 percent (±5 percent) and 11 percent (±5 percent) of assets in foreign stocks and bonds, respectively.

[5] The Chinn-Ito (2006) index is a commonly used measure of capital account openness, based on the IMF's *Annual Report on Exchange Arrangements and Exchange Restrictions*.

Box 10.1. Cross-Border Activities of Japanese Financial Institutions

Cross-border activities of Japanese financial institutions have risen since 2005, particularly to the Asian region, with a temporary decline during the global financial crisis. Cross-border consolidated claims of Japanese banks abroad reached nearly $3 trillion (about 30 percent of total banking and trust assets) in December 2013—growth of 40 percent since 2005. Claims on Asia have more than doubled since the global financial crisis and now account for about 10 percent of total foreign consolidated claims (Figure 10.1.1).

Japanese banks expanded their overseas networks through various forms of ownership. Besides setting up local branches and subsidiaries, banks have sought to expand their customer bases and business functions through business alliances and investments in overseas financial institutions. They have also sought to exploit different ownership structures tailored to local markets. As a result, major Japanese banks have attained an important global and regional presence, especially in the areas of syndicated lending and project finance, and now overseas gross profits account for about 30 percent of total gross profits. At the same time, major brokerage firms and life insurers have sought acquisitions or strategic partnerships overseas, especially in Asia.

Empirical analysis indicates that limited domestic credit demand owing to stagnant growth has created incentives for Japanese banks to seek opportunities abroad (Lam 2013). Also, abundant yen liquidity, supported by a stable deposit base, and strengthened capital ratios have allowed Japanese banks to take on more foreign exposure. Large financing needs for infrastructure in emerging Asia, increasing outward foreign direct investment and trade links of Japanese firms, robust growth in Asia, and European bank deleveraging in the region have offered new business opportunities abroad for Japanese banks. Higher interest rates in destination countries have provided an additional incentive to expand overseas.

The expansion trend overseas is likely to continue under the quantitative and qualitative monetary easing framework. Ample liquidity in the domestic market will act as a push factor for banks' lending activity both domestically and abroad. Japanese financial

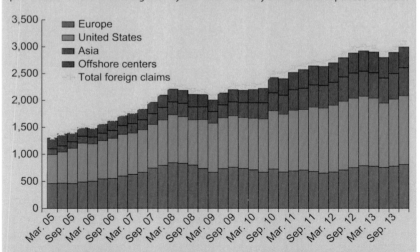

Figure 10.1.1   Consolidated Foreign Claims for Japanese Banks (*Billions of U.S. dollars*)

Source: Bank for International Settlements.

Box 10.1. (*continued*)

institutions would benefit from a more diversified income base as they expand abroad, although they may want to use a gradual and cautious approach in overseas strategies given that they will need to maintain adequate capital ratios under the global regulatory reform agenda (for example, Basel III). Furthermore, rapid expansion could lead Japanese financial institutions to buy foreign assets at high prices or enter into unfamiliar local markets. This could, in turn, lead to heavy losses as occurred in the late 1980s and 1990s. Higher overseas exposure may add to risks that would require continued close monitoring by supervisory authorities, which would be accompanied by an increase in cross-border supervision challenges.

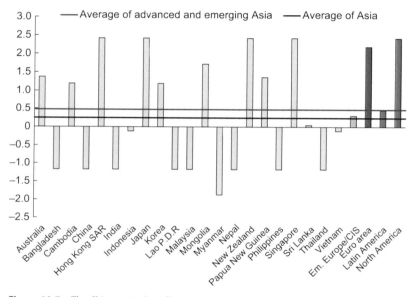

Figure 10.7   The Chinn-Ito Index of Financial Openness, 2012 (*Index number*)

Source: Chinn and Ito (2006).

Note: Em. Europe/CIS = emerging Europe and the Commonwealth of Independent States.

China and India are the largest Asian economies, and they have relatively closed financial accounts. Their liberalization could have a significant impact on capital flows to and within the region in the medium to long term. Existing evidence, however, suggests that capital account liberalization in India would not have a very large global effect, given that restrictions have already not been truly binding, and the scale of potential flows is lower (Ma and McCauley 2013;

Bayoumi and Ohnsorge 2013).[6] For this reason, this section focuses on developments and implications of capital account liberalization in China.

According to both de jure and de facto measures, China's capital account is still relatively closed. Besides scoring low for financial openness according to the Chinn-Ito de jure index, China ranks 138th in its ratio of international assets and liabilities to GDP, a widely used index of de facto financial openness. Moreover, the spreads between implied returns on currency forwards in China and the off-shore renminbi markets—another measure of de facto financial openness—have been persistently high, indicating that capital flows have remained restricted despite the increasing share of foreign assets and liabilities in GDP (Ma and McCauley 2013).

Some gradual steps toward liberalization have already been taken (Box 10.2), and capital account liberalization has been listed among the key reforms in the authorities' blueprint announced in 2013. Steps, yet to be defined, will likely include further expanding the list of qualified domestic and international investors for outward and inward foreign portfolio investment transactions, and gradually increasing quotas. The Shanghai Free Trade Zone has been launched, and a pilot program loosening certain restrictions in the zone is being rolled out. In parallel, the Chinese authorities are actively promoting the internationalization of the renminbi for transactions among nonresidents.[7]

Size of Potential Flows

How large could the potential flows from further capital account liberalization in China be? The adjustment in the gross investment position could potentially be very large. Chinese assets abroad and foreign assets in China are currently much smaller than what would be expected given the scale and characteristics of the Chinese economy, and also in light of other countries' experiences (He and others 2012; Bayoumi and Ohnsorge 2013).

Estimates point to a potentially large expansion in China's outward portfolio position, and a smaller increase in its inward portfolio position. These estimates are based on the sensitivity of capital inflows and outflows to changes in capital account restrictions in a sample of emerging markets. The adjustment of Chinese assets abroad—mostly reflecting portfolio diversification—could be on the order of 15 percent to 25 percent of GDP, while the adjustment of foreign assets in China could be on the order of 2 percent to 10 percent of GDP. This would imply a net accumulation of Chinese net international assets of 11 percent to 18 percent of GDP ($1 trillion to $1.5 trillion, or 1.3 to 1.2 percent of the world's GDP— Bayoumi and Ohnsorge 2013). Other analyses also point to a projected increase

---

[6] India's existing portfolio assets are much lower than are China's. Indeed, India's bond and stock market sizes are about one-quarter of China's (Bayoumi and Ohnsorge 2013).

[7] Trade settlement in renminbi now accounts for nearly 20 percent of China's total trade, and the renminbi is also widely used for trade financing. At the same time, offshore renminbi markets have been developed in Hong Kong SAR, Singapore, and London, and China has signed currency swap agreements with numerous countries.

in the net outward position of about 10 percent of GDP (nearly $1 trillion, or 1.3 percent of the world's GDP) by 2020 (He and others 2012). It is difficult to speculate about the destination of such outflows, given that data on the current geographical composition of China's outward portfolio investment are not available.

Similarly, China's outward FDI position will likely increase by more than inward FDI. He and others (2012) estimate that the stock of outward FDI could increase by 22 percent of GDP by 2020, while inward FDI could rise by 11 percent of GDP

Box 10.2. China: Steps toward Capital Flows Liberalization and Their Impact

China has been taking gradual steps toward liberalizing capital flows.

Inward foreign direct investment (FDI) and its liquidation remain subject to approval requirements, but since early 1990, administrative barriers have been gradually eased. As a result, inward FDI annual flows increased from less than 1 percent of GDP in 1990 to 3.1 percent of GDP in 2012, making China the destination for 18 percent of global FDI and the world's largest recipient.

Outward FDI has been largely liberalized, even though investments are still subject to administrative regulations and approvals. Although China's outward FDI stock in 2012 amounted to only 6.1 percent of GDP (compared with 31.3 percent of GDP in the United States), it increased sharply from $64 billion in 2005 to $503 billion in 2012 and it is now the world's fifth largest (Figure 10.2.1).

Portfolio investment is subject to tight, but gradually increasing, quotas:

- *Inward portfolio investment* is channeled through qualified foreign institutional investors, subject to a three-month lock-in period and an aggregate ceiling. In 2011, a Renminbi Qualified Foreign Institutional Investors scheme was established to allow qualified investors to invest offshore renminbi in domestic securities markets, with certain restrictions on asset allocation and subject to an overall ceiling. In 2013 the scheme was further expanded, and restrictions on asset allocation were loosened. In addition, eligible institutions outside of mainland China may invest in China's bond market, subject to limits but not lock-in periods.

- *Outward portfolio investment* is channeled through qualified domestic institutional investors, subject to institution-specific ceilings. Under this program, licensed domestic institutions are allowed to raise funds from domestic investors to invest in foreign capital markets. Since the program was launched in 2006, the investor base has gradually expanded to include banks, mutual funds, and retail investors. The scope of eligible investment instruments has also been broadened.

Other investment. Foreign borrowing is subject to a ceiling or approval requirements, but lending abroad is largely unrestricted. The holding of cross-border accounts also requires approval. Domestic correspondent banks may offer renminbi financing accounts to banks participating in foreign renminbi operations within certain limits and maturities. Hong Kong SAR and Macao SAR renminbi clearing banks may participate in the domestic interbank market.

Box 10.2. (*continued*)

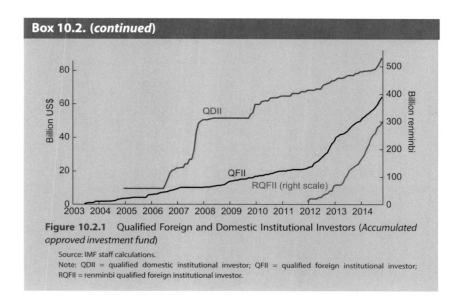

Figure 10.2.1 Qualified Foreign and Domestic Institutional Investors (*Accumulated approved investment fund*)

Source: IMF staff calculations.
Note: QDII = qualified domestic institutional investor; QFII = qualified foreign institutional investor; RQFII = renminbi qualified foreign institutional investor.

during the same period. This would imply net FDI outflows of 11 percent of GDP ($1 trillion, or 1.3 percent of world GDP). A large portion of flows could be directed to the rest of Asia, which is currently the recipient of 85 percent of China's FDI. Continuing the trend of the past few years, low-income countries in Asia, especially those with large natural resources, would likely be among the recipients of FDI.

However, even though the literature points to a substantial increase in Chinese net foreign assets in the postliberalization equilibrium, arbitrage conditions will likely continue to play a major role in driving capital flows in the short to medium term, for a number of reasons including the following:

- Non-FDI capital flows to China have been sensitive to arbitrage conditions even under restrictions. Regression analysis confirms that appreciation expectations play a major role in driving these flows, together with U.S. interest rates and growth prospects in China. Appreciation expectations are probably a better proxy for return on investment than are interest rates, which were heavily regulated in the past (Table 10.1).

- Arbitrage could continue to attract capital inflows after opening up. Projected productivity developments in tradable and nontradable sectors will likely lead to further appreciation pressures of the renminbi in the

TABLE 10.1

Determinants of Non-FDI Capital Flows to China, January 2002 to November 2013			
	(1) **OLS**	**(2)** **OLS2006**	**(3)** **ARCH**
Interest differential[1]	0.561	0.983	0.769**
Standard error	0.548	0.602	0.323
P-value	0.308	0.106	0.017
12-month NDF premium[2]	−2.173***	−2.544**	−2.161***
Standard error	0.581	1.008	0.414
P-value	0	0.013	0
Output growth in China[3]	0.875**	1.256*	0.776***
Standard error	0.423	0.672	0.273
P-value	0.04	0.065	0.005
Lagged non-FDI flow	0.427***	0.405***	0.371***
Standard error	0.069	0.078	0.041
P-value	0	0	0
R^2	0.54	0.56	0.531
Durbin-Watson statistics	1.872	1.78	1.745

Source: IMF staff estimates.
Note: Heteroscedasticity autocorrelation robust standard errors are reported. ARCH = autoregressive
    conditional heteroscedasticity; FDI = foreign direct investment; OLS= ordinary least squares.
[1] Interest differential = China one-month repo – U.S. one-month Treasury bill rate.
[2] The NDF premium is measured by the gap between the non-deliverable forward (NDF) on renminbi and the
    renminbi/U.S. dollar spot rate and defined as 100×(NDF−spot)/spot, capturing appreciation expectations.
[3] Output growth in China—capturing growth prospects—is the monthly growth rate of industrial production.
$*p < .1; **p < .05; ***p < .01.$

medium term driven by Balassa-Samuelson effects.[8] At the same time, financial market liberalization—another key reform in the Chinese authorities' blueprint announced in 2013—will likely bring interest rates closer to a "natural" level consistent with relatively high marginal product of capital.[9] The correction of exchange rate undervaluation, trend appreciation, and the high natural interest rate all constitute strong incentives for inflows.

The size and direction of flows will depend on the interplay between portfolio diversification and arbitrage flows, with risk premiums playing a major role. Given the large gap between "equilibrium" and the current foreign asset position, incentives for diversification will likely be strong. Moreover, relatively weaker institutional development in China could become an additional incentive for outflows, reducing arbitrage incentives through risk premiums. But these factors could still be outweighed by appreciation pressures and higher interest rates.

---

[8] Balassa-Samuelson effects refer to increases in productivity and wages in the tradable goods sector that lead to higher wages in the nontradable (services) sector, and appreciation of the real exchange rate.
[9] He, Wang, and Yu (2014) estimate the "natural" interest rate to be about 4½ percent.

Given the size of potential flows and the weight of the Chinese economy, potential implications of opening up for the region are significant:

- Opening up of the capital account could magnify short-term risks. Financial markets in China are still relatively shallow, and the reaction of asset prices to sudden swings in capital flows could be destabilizing. In particular, liberalization could have immediate repercussions for China's real estate market. Given that real estate has been one of the key drivers of growth, a price correction and a slowdown in the market could affect economic activity, with strong international spillovers. A sharp price correction would have a particularly large effect on Japan and Korea (Ahuja and Myrvoda 2012).

- Expanding investment opportunities for Chinese households could lead to lower incentives for precautionary savings in the longer term, and possibly result in higher global interest rates (Nabar 2011).

- Inflows could still dominate at the early stage of liberalization, generating a typical boom and bust cycle. The results of a boom-bust could create strong spillovers, both directly through economic activity and trade linkages, and indirectly through the perception of regional risks.

- Liberalization would also change the role of the renminbi in the region. Opening up of the capital account and greater exchange rate flexibility will help diversify risks and free monetary policy in China. But the implications for the region would be more mixed. Fixed exchange rates in China proved to be a stabilizing force during times of financial turbulence in the past, for example, by helping crisis-struck countries restore competitiveness faster during the Asian crisis of the late 1990s. Greater renminbi flexibility and potentially large fluctuations related to capital flows could require stronger and faster policy responses in the region. Moreover, significant advances in the internationalization of the renminbi could amplify the transmission of Chinese policy and domestic shocks.

Other Medium- and Long-Term Drivers of Capital Flows

While China's capital account liberalization process is likely to be the main factor affecting the size and direction of capital flows to and within Asia in the medium to long term, other variables will also be at play, including the following:

- *Financial development*—Differences in the speed and pattern of financial sector deepening can create changes in the demand for, and supply of, domestic and foreign financial assets. Residents in Asian economies with less-developed financial markets, and hence limited domestic access to financial instruments, may have high demand for instruments issued in countries with deeper and more diversified financial sectors. However, as local financial markets develop, the pattern of demand for domestic versus foreign assets may change.[10] Similarly, foreign investors will likely increase their demand for Asian financial instruments as local markets deepen and become more liquid. For example, foreign holdings of Asian bonds have grown since the middle of the first decade of the 2000s as local bond markets developed (see Chapter 5).

- *Financial integration*—A number of initiatives are under way to strengthen regional financial markets and promote integration in Asia. These include regional economic surveillance processes in the Association of Southeast Asian Nations (ASEAN) and ASEAN+3, the Chiang Mai Initiative, the Asian Bond Markets Initiative, and the Asian Bond Fund Initiative. The push for integration is particularly strong in ASEAN (see Chapter 9). The development of cross-border financial regulation and practices will have an impact on the capital flow pattern within the region.

- *Savings and demographics*—A high share of economically inactive dependent population is typically associated with lower national savings, with an impact on current account balances and capital flows (Higgins 1998; IMF 2008). Aging trends within Asia are expected to become more diverse, with population aging projected to intensify, especially in China, Japan, and Korea (see Chapter 8), with possible implications for capital flow movements.

POLICY IMPLICATIONS: BUILDING RESILIENCE AND REAPING THE BENEFITS OF CAPITAL FLOWS

Several important factors will shape the size and composition of capital flows to and within Asia in the short to long term. Although it is not possible to predict how all of these drivers will interact and what the final outcome will be, Asia is likely to remain the recipient of large capital flows, given the prospects of sustained strong regional growth, increasing financial openness, and deepening capital markets. It is also clear, though, that significant changes in capital flow movements may occur, and volatility is likely to persist. Although these flow movements could bring important benefits to Asia by providing new financing for productive uses, they will also create challenges.

Abundant inflows can inflate asset prices and fuel credit booms and imbalances in some sectors. These inflows can also generate strong exchange rate appreciations, eroding competitiveness and possibly creating currency risks in firm and household balance sheets. In addition, capital flow volatility can contribute to boom-bust cycles (IMF 2011). Therefore, a range of policy tools is needed to build resilience against these risks, while reaping the benefits of capital flows.

Sound macroeconomic policies will be essential to build resilience as well as to manage capital flow volatility. Strong microprudential policy, including effective supervision and enforcement, will also be crucial to contain and address

---

[10]Theoretical models on the relationship between financial development and capital flows are presented, for example, in Caballero, Farhi, and Gourinchas 2008.

vulnerabilities in individual financial institutions. However, in the past these tools have proved to be insufficient to contain systemic risk. Therefore, policymakers in Asia and other regions have increasingly used a range of policy tools that explicitly focus on system-wide vulnerabilities—macroprudential policies. Have these measures been effective in Asia? And can they help in the future?

Asia's Experience with Macroprudential Policy

Zhang and Zoli (2014) analyze a sample of 13 Asian economies and 33 economies from other regions since 2000 and find that Asia has made extensive use of housing-related macroprudential measures—especially loan-to-value caps. In fact, Asia has done so to a larger degree than has other regions. Changes in reserve requirements on local currency deposits have also been quite common, both in Asia and elsewhere, probably reflecting their use as a monetary policy tool.[11] However, other liquidity tools, such as credit limits, dynamic provisioning,[12] restrictions on consumer loans, and capital measures, have been rarely used in Asia. Measures to discourage transactions in foreign currency have been deployed less frequently in the region than they have been in Central and Eastern Europe and the Commonwealth of Independent States—where foreign-exchange-denominated or indexed loans were widespread—and Latin America. Residency-based capital flow management measures have been employed only to a small extent in Asia.

There is significant cross-country heterogeneity in the tools that have been used in Asia since 2000, because Asian economies had to confront different potential threats to financial stability. New Zealand introduced a minimum requirement on core funding and has revised its macroprudential framework to introduce countercyclical capital buffers, overlays to sectoral capital requirements, and loan-to-value restrictions. Hong Kong SAR and Singapore have predominantly relied on housing-related tools. Korea, in addition to housing measures, imposed a levy on bank non-deposit foreign currency liabilities and a ceiling on bank foreign exchange derivative positions. China and India have been heavy users of reserve requirements (as a monetary policy tool). Among ASEAN economies, domestic prudential tools and reserve requirements on foreign exchange deposits have been used. Capital flow measures have been adopted in Indonesia and Thailand, including minimum holding periods for central bank bills in the former, and withholding taxes for nonresident investors in the latter.

To get a sense of how macroprudential and capital flow management policies evolved and built up over time in Asia and other regions, two aggregate indices were constructed—one for macroprudential policies and one for capital flow

---

[11] Reserve requirements are categorized as macroprudential policies in several studies (for example, IMF 2013c).

[12] Dynamic provisioning requires building a cushion of reserves during the upswing phase of the business cycle that can be released when the cycle turns.

measures.[13] Based on these indices, there appears to have been a structural tightening of the macroprudential policy stance that is particularly pronounced in Asia (Figure 10.8). Macroprudential policies were most heavily used in the precrisis boom period during 2006–07, and then again after the crisis, as capital flowed back into the region and asset prices inflated. By contrast, Asian economies have tightened residency-based capital flow measures or instruments to discourage transactions in foreign currency less frequently than have other regions.

An empirical investigation of the effectiveness of macroprudential and capital flow management measures in Asia from 2000:Q1 through 2013:Q1 suggests that housing-related macroprudential instruments contributed to the reduction in credit growth, house price inflation, and bank leverage in the region (Zhang and Zoli 2014).[14] Housing-related instruments that have been particularly effective include loan-to-value ratio caps and housing tax measures. On average, a tightening in housing-related tools is estimated to have reduced credit growth in Asia by 0.7 percentage point after a quarter and by 1.5 percentage points after a year. The impact of these instruments on housing price inflation has been larger: a tightening in housing-related measures is estimated to have lowered house price growth by 2 percentage points after one quarter.

Other non-housing-related domestic macroprudential tools, measures to discourage transactions in foreign currency, and residency-based capital flow management measures have not had a significant impact on lending, leverage, housing price growth, or portfolio inflows in Asia. Nevertheless, these policies may have affected the distribution of risks in the financial system and the resilience of the system to systemic pressures. For example, foreign-exchange-related macroprudential policy can contain currency, maturity, and liquidity mismatches within the banking system, without having a strong impact on loan growth and asset prices. Indeed, foreign-exchange-related measures have helped mitigate vulnerabilities from short-term foreign borrowing in Korea (Box 10.3). However, it has to be recognized that macroprudential policy also entails costs, mainly arising

---

[13] To construct these indices, first, changes in macroprudential policies and capital flow measures were coded numerically using a simple binary variable, taking on value 1 for tightening actions and –1 for loosening ones. Then, these dummy variables were cumulated over time since 2000. The macroprudential policy index aggregates housing-related and non-housing-related domestic prudential measures, while the capital flow measure index summarizes policy actions aimed at discouraging transactions in foreign currency as well as residency-based capital flow management measures. This categorization between macroprudential policy and capital flow measures involves some degree of judgment, given the overlap between certain macroprudential and capital flow management measures. Nevertheless, it tries to reflect as closely as possible the broad definitions of macroprudential and capital flow measures discussed in IMF 2012a and 2013b.

[14] A number of empirical studies have tried to assess the effectiveness of macroprudential policies on a sample of countries from different regions, and typically find that some individual macroprudential instruments, such as loan-to-value caps, debt-to-income ratios, and reserve requirements, have been effective in curbing excessive credit and asset price growth (Lim and others 2011; Arregui and others 2013; Kuttner and Shim 2012). Other studies have provided illustrative evidence that macroprudential policy can contain credit booms (Dell'Ariccia and others 2012).

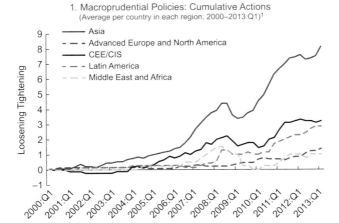

1. Macroprudential Policies: Cumulative Actions
(Average per country in each region; 2000–2013:Q1)[1]

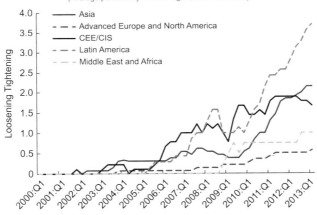

2. Capital Flow Management Measures: Cumulative Actions
(Average per country in each region; 2000–2013:Q1)[1]

Figure 10.8 Use of Macroprudential Policies and Capital Flow Management Measures by Region

Source: IMF staff calculations.
Note: CEE/CIS = central and eastern Europe and Commonwealth of Independent States.
[1]Index summing up housing-related measures, credit measures, reserve requirements, dynamic provisioning, and core funding ratio. Simple average across countries within country groups.

from higher intermediation charges and their effect on long-term output (Arregui and others 2013).

Because macroprudential policies appear to have helped mitigate the buildup of financial risks in Asia, they can play an important role in the future in managing systemic risks from capital flow volatility in the region. But how can the region's existing macroeconomic policy framework be further enhanced? One relevant

Box 10.3. Foreign-Exchange-Related Macroprudential Policy in Korea

Korea has traditionally been highly vulnerable to capital flow reversals, mainly owing to short-term borrowing in the banking sector that creates maturity mismatches and foreign exchange liquidity problems. The aggregate short-term external debt of Korean banks reached $160 billion in 2008:Q3—a sharp increase from the $60 billion level it reached in 2006:Q1. However, in the four months following the Lehman Brothers bankruptcy, nearly $70 billion left the country. The volatility of capital flows was higher in Korea than it was in other economies during the global financial crisis (Ree, Yoon, and Park 2012).

To mitigate vulnerabilities from short-term foreign borrowing, Korea adopted a series of macroprudential policies beginning in June 2010, including a ceiling on banks' foreign exchange derivatives positions and a macroprudential stability levy on noncore foreign exchange liabilities. The former measure was intended to reduce maturity and currency mismatches. The ceiling is designed to be adjusted depending on the credit cycle. The stability levy is a tax on banks' noncore foreign currency liabilities. It is also adjustable and can be used as a countercyclical tool when capital flow surges seriously threaten financial stability, with the maximum rate of 50 basis points. Its proceeds flow into the Foreign Exchange Stabilization Fund, which is separate from the government budget and can be used as a buffer in the event of a financial crisis. Other important measures include limits on foreign currency bank loans and prudential regulations to improve the foreign exchange risk management of financial institutions.

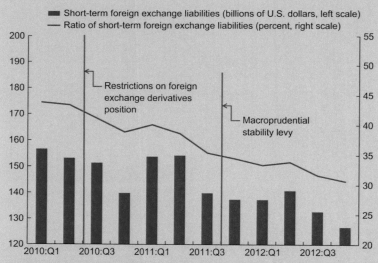

Figure 10.3.1 Korea: Macroprudential Policy and Bank Foreign Exchange Liabilities

Sources: Bank of Korea; and IMF staff calculations.

Box 10.3. (*continued*)

While Korea's experience in the use of these tools is limited, preliminary evidence suggests that the tools have been effective in containing overexposure to funding shocks and putting a brake on procyclical lending. Indeed, banks' short-term net external debt, including that of foreign bank branches, declined steadily from $153 billion in June 2010 to $126 billion in December 2012, and the short-term external debt ratio fell continuously, reaching 30.6 percent by the end of 2012, after peaking at 51.9 percent in the third quarter of 2008 (Figure 10.3.1). The sensitivity of capital inflows to global conditions fell after the imposition of the levy, relative to a comparison group of countries (Bruno and Shin 2012). Rollover risks for domestic banks also fell because their external debt maturities lengthened (IMF 2012a). The sensitivity of exchange rate volatility to changes in the Chicago Board Options Exchange Market Volatility Index (VIX) declined, too, reflecting lower foreign exchange liquidity mismatches (Ree, Yoon, and Park 2012).

issue is how macroprudential policy could be used in the event of asset price declines, slowing credit growth, or capital flow reversals. Although macroprudential policies have sometimes been loosened in a countercyclical fashion, most notably in 2008–09 as the global financial crisis unfolded, more experience needs to be gained on whether and how these instruments should be recalibrated when the financial cycle turns. Nevertheless, theory suggests that a loosening of macroprudential policies should be considered to prevent excessive deleveraging in the downward phase of the financial cycle.[15]

Against this background, consideration could be given to the adoption of countercyclical capital requirements and dynamic provisioning, which, at present, barely exist in Asia.[16] These could be helpful instruments in a context of high volatility, because they are specifically designed to build buffers during the upswing phase of the cycle that can be used during a downswing (Ghilardi and Peiris 2014; IMF 2014c). Even though there is little empirical evidence about their effectiveness, these instruments seem particularly useful in increasing resilience, as well as the predictability of regulatory changes through the cycle.[17]

---

[15] On theoretical grounds, the use of macroprudential policy as a countercyclical tool can be justified in a context in which financial frictions create procyclicality in the financial system, exacerbating business cycle fluctuations (for example, Angeloni and Faia 2013; N'Diaye 2009).

[16] China introduced countercyclical capital requirements in 2010 and New Zealand introduced its countercyclical capital requirements framework in 2013.

[17] Apart from theoretical exercises and assessments that are numerically simulated, empirical studies of how the countercyclical capital requirements mechanism actually works are absent. Jiménez and others (2012) provide some empirical evidence on the effectiveness of dynamic provisioning in Spain.

In addition to macroeconomic policy and micro- and macroprudential measures, other policy initiatives can strengthen Asia's resilience to shocks and its ability to cope with the volatility of capital flows. Continuing ongoing efforts to develop local currency bond markets would further reduce the use of short-term—and, hence, more volatile—inflows from outside Asia to finance long-term investment projects. Enhancing cooperative mechanisms, such as the Chiang Mai Initiative, making them more operational, and strengthening regional surveillance from within the region would also improve Asia's resilience and ability to respond to funding shocks.

Channeling Capital Inflows to Productive Use

In spite of the policy challenges they create, capital flows can bring important benefits to Asia. They can help finance domestic productive investment projects, contribute to the development of financial markets, enhance international risk sharing, facilitate technology transfer (for example, through foreign direct investment), promote trade, and contribute to greater consumption smoothing.

Capital flows could also provide financing to address two important issues in the region, namely financing constraints for small and medium-sized enterprises and shortfalls in infrastructure. The channeling of capital flows to productive uses could be facilitated by measures to further develop bond and equity markets. These measures would include enhancing and streamlining disclosure requirements for bond and equity issuances; improving transparency about issuers, for example, through standardized reporting and wider credit scoring; enhancing central clearing counterparties to reduce counterparty risks; and strengthening the legal and regulatory framework as well as corporate governance (Chapter 5).

CONCLUSION

Since 1990, capital flows to Asia have been large but volatile, creating opportunities as well as significant challenges for policymakers. In the period following the Asian financial crisis, net capital flows to the region were mainly driven by high domestic GDP growth (which was also high in comparison with U.S. growth), U.S. interest rates, and investor risk appetite. These factors will likely continue to play a role. U.S. monetary policy will probably have an impact in the short to medium term. In the same time frame, the BoJ's QQE program will also affect capital flows to and within the region, mainly through its impact on portfolio rebalancing and bank cross-border lending. In the medium to long term, China's capital account liberalization could have significant implications for capital flow movements, although views differ on whether net capital inflows or outflows to the country will prevail. Financial market development, financial integration, and changes in savings patterns will also likely continue to affect capital flows to and within Asia.

All of these factors will contribute to capital flow volatility, requiring policy-makers to take preemptive measures. Macroeconomic and microprudential policies will be essential tools for strengthening resilience, but macroprudential policy can also help mitigate systemic risks. Indeed, empirical evidence shows that Asia's experience with macroeconomic policy has been positive. The existing macroprudential toolkit could be further enhanced in the future with the adoption of countercyclical requirements and dynamic provisioning, which appear to be suitable instruments to strengthen resilience and respond to volatility. Policy measures to foster the development of bond and equity markets could help channel capital flows to their most productive uses.

ANNEX 10.1. EMPIRICAL ANALYSIS OF DRIVERS OF CAPITAL FLOWS TO ASIA IN THE POST–ASIAN CRISIS PERIOD

A number of empirical studies have assessed the impact of U.S. interest rates and the Federal Reserve's QE program on capital flows to advanced economies and emerging markets, but the focus was not specifically on Asia. Among the most recent studies, IMF 2011 finds a negative impact from a hike in the U.S. rate on net capital flows, which is more pronounced when the rate increase is unanticipated. Fratzscher, Lo Duca, and Straub (2013) find that U.S. unconventional monetary policy has had a sizable impact on capital flows to emerging economies, but those effects were relatively low compared with other factors. Ahmed and Zlate's (2013) empirical analysis indicates that U.S. unconventional monetary policy has not had a significant impact on net flows to emerging markets.

Unlike the existing literature, the model presented in this chapter focuses on Asian economies. The model is a cross-section and time fixed-effects panel.[18] The dependent variable is net capital flows as a percentage of GDP. The explanatory variables include the domestic short-term interest rate; domestic real GDP growth; U.S. real GDP growth (or the differential between domestic and U.S. growth); the U.S. short-term interest rate; the VIX, as a proxy for investor risk appetite; changes in the nominal effective exchange rates; and a dummy taking the value of 1 when the Federal Reserve's QE programs were introduced. Regression results are reported in Annex Table 10.1.1.

---

[18] Cross-section fixed effects were included to control for institutional country characteristics (for example, institutional quality and restrictions on capital flows). Formal tests strongly reject the null hypothesis that these fixed effects are redundant.

ANNEX TABLE 10.1.1

Regression Results: Determinants of Capital Flows to Asia

	Dependent Variable					
	Net Capital Flows as a Percentage of GDP			Gross Capital Inflows as a Percentage of GDP		
	(1)	(2)	(3)	(4)	(5)	(6)
Lagged domestic rates	0.1	0.1	0.1	0.4	0.4	0.3
P-value	0.4	0.4	0.4	0.2	0.2	0.3
Lagged U.S. short rates	−0.3	−0.3	−0.3	−0.2	−0.2	−0.2
P-value	0.0	0.0	0.0	0.5	0.5	0.6
Lagged VIX	−0.1	−0.1	−0.1	−0.4	−0.4	−0.5
P-value	0.0	0.0	0.0	0.0	0.0	0.0
QE dummy	1.0	1.0	0.9	3.0	3.0	2.3
P-value	0.1	0.1	0.1	0.1	0.1	0.2
Lagged domestic growth	0.2	0.2		1.8	1.8	
P-value	0.0	0.0		0.0	0.0	
Lagged U.S. growth	0.0	0.0		−0.9	−0.9	
P-value	1.0	0.9		0.0	0.0	
Lagged growth differential			0.2			1.7
P-value			0.0			0.0
Lagged D(NEER)		0.1			0.0	
P-value		0.2			0.9	
R^2	0.5	0.5	0.5	0.6	0.6	0.6

Source: IMF staff calculations.

Note: NEER = nominal effective exchange rate; QE = quantitative easing; VIX = Chicago Board Options Exchange Market Volatility Index.

REFERENCES

Ahmed, Shaghil, and Andrei Zlate. 2013. "Capital Flows to Emerging Market Economies: A Brave New World?" International Finance Discussion Paper No. 1081, Board of Governors of the Federal Reserve System, Washington.

Ahuja, Ashvin, and Alla Myrvoda. 2012. "The Spillover Effects of a Downturn in China's Real Estate Investment." IMF Working Paper No. 12/266, International Monetary Fund, Washington.

Angeloni, Ignazio, and Ester Faia. 2013. "Capital Regulation and Monetary Policy with Fragile Banks." *Journal of Monetary Economics* 60 (3): 311–24.

Arregui, N., J. Benes, I. Krznar, S. Mitra, and A. Oliveira Santos. 2013. "Evaluating the Net Benefits of Macroprudential Policy: A Cookbook." IMF Working Paper No. 13/167, International Monetary Fund, Washington.

Bayoumi, Tamim, and Franziska Ohnsorge. 2013. "Do Inflows or Outflows Dominate? Global Implications of Capital Account Liberalization in China." IMF Working Paper No. 13/189, International Monetary Fund, Washington.

Bruno, Valentina, and Hyun Song Shin. 2012. "Assessing Macroprudential Policy: Case of Korea." Working Paper No. 19084, National Bureau for Economic Research, Cambridge, Massachusetts.

Caballero, Ricardo, Emmanuel Farhi, and Pierre-Olivier Gourinchas. 2008. "An Equilibrium Model of 'Global Imbalances' and Low Interest Rates." *American Economic Review* 98 (1): 358–93.

Chinn, Menzie D., and Hiro Ito. 2006. "What Matters for Financial Development? Capital Controls, Institutions, and Interactions." *Journal of Development Economics* 81 (1): 163–92.

Dell'Ariccia, Giovanni, Deniz Igan, Luc Laeven, Hui Tong, Bas Bakker, and Jérôme Vandenbussche. 2012. "Policies for Macrofinancial Stability: How to Deal with Credit Booms." IMF Staff Discussion Note No. 12/06, International Monetary Fund, Washington.

Forbes, Kristin J., and Francis E. Warnock. 2012. "Debt- and Equity-Led Capital Flow Episodes." Working Paper No. 18329, National Bureau of Economic Research, Cambridge, Massachusetts.

Fratzscher, Marcel, Marco Lo Duca, and Roland Straub. 2013. "On the International Spillovers of U.S. Quantitative Easing." Working Paper No. 1557, European Central Bank, Frankfurt.

Ghilardi, Matteo, and Shanaka J. Peiris. 2014. "Capital Flows, Financial Intermediation and Macroprudential Policies." IMF Working Paper No. 14/157, International Monetary Fund, Washington.

He, Dong, Lillian Cheung, Wenlang Zhang, and Tommy Wu. 2012. "How Would Capital Account Liberalisation Affect China's Capital Flows and the Renminbi Real Exchange Rates?" Working Paper No. 09/2012, Hong Kong Institute for Monetary Research, Hong Kong SAR.

He, Dong, Honglin Wang, and Xiangrong Yu. 2014. "Interest Rate Determination in China: Past, Present, and Future." Working Paper No. 04/2014, Hong Kong Institute for Monetary Research, Hong Kong SAR.

Higgins, Matthew. 1998. "Demography, National Savings, and International Capital Flows." *International Economic Review* 39 (2): 343–69.

International Monetary Fund. 2008. *Exchange Rate Assessments: CGER Methodologies.* Occasional Paper No. 261. Washington: International Monetary Fund.

———. 2011. "International Capital Flows, Reliable or Fickle?" In *World Economic Outlook.* Washington, April.

———. 2012a. "The Liberalization and Management of Capital Flows—An Institutional View." International Monetary Fund, Washington.

———. 2012b. "The Likely Effect on Asia of a Sharp Deleveraging by European Banks." In *Regional Economic Outlook: Asia and Pacific.* Washington, April.

———. 2012c. "Spillover Report—Background Papers, IMF Policy Papers." International Monetary Fund, Washington.

———. 2013a. "The Interaction of Monetary and Macroprudential Policies – Background Paper." International Monetary Fund, Washington.

———. 2013b. "Key Aspects of Macroprudential Policy." International Monetary Fund, Washington.

———. 2013c. "Spillover Report—Background Papers, IMF Policy Papers." International Monetary Fund, Washington.

———. 2014a. "Japan: 2014 Article IV Consultation-Staff Report." Country Report No. 14/236, International Monetary Fund, Washington.

———. 2014b. "People's Republic of China: 2014 Article IV Consultation-Staff Report." Country Report No. 14/235, International Monetary Fund, Washington.

———. 2014c. *Regional Economic Outlook: Asia and Pacific*. Washington, April.

Jiménez, G., S. Ongena, J. L. Peydró, and J. Saurina. 2012. "Macroprudential Policy, Countercyclical Bank Capital Buffers and Credit Supply: Evidence from the Spanish Dynamic Provisioning Experiments." Working Paper No. 628, Graduate School of Economics, Barcelona, Spain.

Kuttner, K., and I. Shim. 2012. "Taming the Real Estate Beast: The Effects of Monetary and Macroprudential Policies on Housing Prices and Credit." In *Property Markets and Financial Stability*, edited by A. Heath, F. Packer, and C. Windsor. Sydney: Reserve Bank of Australia.

Lam, Raphael. 2013. "Cross-Border Activities of Japanese Banks." IMF Working Paper No. 13/235, International Monetary Fund, Washington.

Lim, C., F. Columba, A. Costa, P. Kongsamut, A. Otani, M. Saiyid, T. Wezel, and X. Wu. 2011. "Macroprudential Policy: What Instruments and How to Use Them? Lessons from Country Experiences." IMF Working Paper No. 11/238, International Monetary Fund, Washington.

Ma, Guonan, and Robert N. McCauley. 2013. "Is China or India More Financially Open?" *Journal of International Money and Finance* 39 (C): 6–27.

Milesi-Ferretti, Gian-Maria, and Cédric Tille. 2011. "The Great Retrenchment: International Capital Flows during the Global Financial Crisis." *Economic Policy* 269 (66): 289–346.

Nabar, Malhar. 2011. "Targets, Interest Rates, and Household Saving in Urban China." IMF Working Paper No. 11/223, International Monetary Fund, Washington.

N'Diaye, Papa. 2009. "Countercyclical Macro Prudential Policies in a Supporting Role to Monetary Policy." IMF Working Paper No. 09/257, International Monetary Fund, Washington.

Ree, Jack, Kyoungsoo Yoon, and Hail Park. 2012. "FX Funding Risks and Exchange Rate Volatility—Korea's Case." IMF Working Paper No. 12/268, International Monetary Fund, Washington.

Zhang, Longmei, and Edda Zoli. 2014. "Leaning against the Wind: Macroprudential Policy in Asia." IMF Working Paper No. 14/22, International Monetary Fund, Washington.

CHAPTER 11

Operating within the New Global Regulatory Environment

Rina Bhattacharya, James P. Walsh, and Aditya Narain

MAIN POINTS OF THIS CHAPTER

- Asian banks tend to be well capitalized and liquid, with broadly strong supervision—although there are some gaps.
- Crisis management frameworks are strong in most countries, but bank resolution remains an issue.
- Policymakers must address the issue of institutions considered "too important to fail" in Asia, particularly because the region has relatively few globally systemically important financial institutions.
- Extending the regulatory perimeter to nonbank lending, particularly in rapidly growing areas such as shadow banking, will be essential.
- Spillovers from the global regulatory reform agenda are likely to be contained.

INTRODUCTION

Asia is home to a wide and diverse range of financial sectors. The region encompasses several advanced economies (Japan, Australia, and New Zealand), international financial centers (Singapore and Hong Kong SAR), emerging market economies (China, India, Malaysia, and Thailand), and still-developing economies (Bangladesh, Cambodia, Lao P.D.R., Myanmar, and Nepal). Japan and China are home to global systemically important financial institutions (G-SIFIs)—three in Japan and two in China. Other countries have institutions that are domestically systemically important and must guard against the contagion effects of the distress of these institutions on other entities in the system. The degrees to which the preconditions for successful regulatory and supervisory frameworks are met vary widely, but some regional similarities exist.

Chief among these similarities has been the response to past financial crises. As discussed in Chapter 5, the Asian financial crisis had a profound effect on policymaking. The region's willingness to overhaul financial regulation and supervision after the crisis contributed to its resilience during the global financial crisis, and continues today as new risks are identified and as the global regulatory reform agenda gets under way.

At the top of this agenda are new requirements under Basel III, which Asian countries have already begun to adopt. On the surface, the very success of Asia's well-capitalized and highly liquid banks seems to imply a minimum of difficulty in adhering to new capital and liquidity requirements, but the need for robust risk-assessment frameworks and stepped-up demand for high-quality liquid assets do present challenges for some systems and some institutions. The implementation of these new regulatory shifts in the rest of the world will also have spillover effects in Asia.

Even at home, the very nature and success of Asia's growth models have created new challenges. Deeper and more complex financial sectors mean more potential for systemic risks, and here, Asia's experience with previous financial dislocations has led it to become a world leader in macroprudential frameworks. Rising integration, in Asia as elsewhere, has lowered costs and diversified risks. However, it has also heightened the need for cross-border cooperation in supervisory and, in times of crisis, resolution frameworks.

Larger financial sectors also lead to larger financial institutions. The emergence, both actual and hoped for, of regional financial champions will run up against global concerns about "too-important-to-fail" banks, an area in which Asian supervisors, along with their global colleagues, have found it challenging to mitigate risks. At the other extreme, a diverse and rapidly growing sector of nonbank financial institutions poses challenges for regulators as interconnectedness and complexity rise. These firms have helped broaden access to finance and have increased competition in some countries in which banking has not been especially competitive. At the same time, however, rapid growth and tighter regulation of banks means the perimeter of regulation needs to be rethought.

This chapter explores each of these themes. The section titled "Asia's Banking Sectors" assesses the framework for supervising banks in Asia, and looks at what changes will be necessary to further improve stability and bring the region in line with global reforms. The section titled "Macroprudential Policy Frameworks" looks at systemic financial risks and macroprudential policy, and the section titled "Nonbank Issues" looks at the changing role and supervisory priorities for nonbanks.

ASIA'S BANKING SECTORS

Asia's experiences during the Asian financial crisis of the late 1990s and the global financial crisis of 2008–09 spurred an effort to strengthen the regulation and supervision of the region's banks:

- The Asian financial crisis prompted many Asian economies, both emerging market and advanced, to embark on ambitious financial sector reforms. Identified gaps in regulatory and supervisory frameworks were addressed through new laws and institutions. Policy measures were taken to strengthen risk-management policies and corporate governance, and supervisory agencies were given enhanced powers to intervene and conduct regular examinations, both on site and off site.

- After the global financial crisis, many emerging market economies also took measures to upgrade their financial market infrastructures (Chapter 5). Countries in Asia that were less directly affected by the crisis (such as China and Sri Lanka) improved the quality and timeliness of supervision—often through existing prudential criteria or by restructuring supervisory processes. Several countries reformed their legal frameworks by clarifying supervisory mandates and powers. Some also sought to improve their financial infrastructures, such as by establishing deposit insurance and credit registries (Schneider and others 2015). As a consequence, banks in emerging Asian economies were in a better position to cope with the direct and indirect effects of the global financial crisis, and were, therefore, relatively unaffected by it.

- The global financial crisis affected advanced Asian economies more significantly than it affected Asian emerging market economies. The advanced economies are where G-SIFIs play a major role, and where domestic regulatory changes have mirrored developments in other advanced economies. For example, Japanese and Australian banks expanded their cross-regional lending activities in Asia as European banks deleveraged from the region.

At the same time, Asia is part of the global initiative to reform regulation and supervision. Priorities include implementing Basel III capital regulations; strengthening prudential supervision by securing resources for and independence of supervisors; restoring confidence in bank balance sheets; developing and implementing effective domestic and cross-border resolution regimes, especially for systemically important financial institutions (SIFIs); facilitating implementation of over-the-counter derivatives reforms through further cross-border coordination; and enhancing the monitoring of shadow banking (IMF 2014b; and FSB 2012b).

Capital and Liquidity

Most Asian countries have taken, or are in the process of taking, measures to fully implement Basel III capital and liquidity requirements. Basel III phase-in arrangements require Tier I capital (including a capital conservation buffer of 2.5 percent) to rise steadily to a minimum of 8.5 percent of risk-weighted assets by January 2019, and Common Equity Tier 1 capital to rise steadily to 7.0 percent of risk-weighted assets. In addition, the Basel III requirements call for an additional countercyclical buffer of up to another 2.5 percent of risk-weighted assets.

The latest progress report by the Basel Committee on Banking Supervision (BCBS) shows that the final rules for the Basel III capital requirements are already in force in many Asian economies (see Tables 11.1 and 11.2; BCBS 2014). As of September 2014, all reporting Asian countries had legally adopted the final Basel III–based capital regulations. The BCBS is also currently assessing the quality of implementation of its members through Level 2 assessments of its Regulatory Consistency Assessment Program (RCAP). Regulatory authorities in

TABLE 11.1

Implementation of Basel Frameworks

Countries

Advanced Asia

Australia	Draft rules to implement Basel III liquidity requirements issued in November 2011. Final rules to implement Basel III capital requirements issued in September 2012.
Hong Kong SAR	Draft rules to implement Basel III capital requirements and associated disclosure requirements issued in August and June 2012, respectively.
Japan	Implementation of Basel III started end-March 2013 (except for capital conservation buffer and countercyclical buffers, which are expected in 2014/15).
New Zealand	Implementation of Basel III to start January 1, 2015.
Singapore	Final rules for implementation of Basel III published on September 14, 2012.
Korea	Draft rules to implement Basel III published in September 2012.

Emerging Asia

Bangladesh	Preparing to implement Basel III from 2014.
China	New capital regulations that combine Basel II, 2.5, and III were released in June 2012 and became effective January 1, 2013.
India	Final rules for implementation of Basel III issued in May 2012 and came into force January 1, 2013.
Indonesia	Consultative paper on Basel III, which contains draft regulations for implementation of Basel III, was released in June 2012 for industry comments.
Malaysia	Intends to follow the BCBS's timetable for implementation of Basel III, with capital and liquidity requirements to be phased in over the period 2013–19.
Philippines	The Philippine Central Bank approved the implementing guidelines of the revised capital standards under the Basel III Accord in January 2013. Universal and commercial banks are required to meet the standards by January 1, 2014.
Sri Lanka	Intends to follow the BCBS's timetable for implementation of Basel III, with capital and liquidity requirements to be phased in over the period 2013–19.
Taiwan Province of China	Intends to follow the BCBS's timetable for implementation of Basel III, with capital and liquidity requirements to be phased in over the period 2013–19.
Thailand	Basel III capital adequacy requirements implemented January 1, 2013.
Vietnam	Partial adoption of Basel I, no firm plans to implement Basel III.

Source: Bank for International Settlements; and individual country central bank reports and statements.

Japan and Singapore have amended their domestic regulations, contributing to more consistent national implementation of the Basel III framework. The preliminary results for China have been encouraging—China has so far promptly rectified issues identified by the RCAP reports and is continuing with regulatory reforms.

However, some Asian countries may need to slow the moves their industries are taking to the internal-model-based approaches to computing regulatory capital given the problems in ensuring consistent implementation revealed in recent cross-country studies. The RCAP reports found considerable variations in average

TABLE 11.2

Basel Capital Progress Index, 2014

Country	Basel II Rules (1)	Basel II Implementation (2)	Basel 2.5 Rules (3)	Basel 2.5 Implementation (4)	Basel III Rules (5) 2012	Basel III Rules (5) 2014	Total (Maximum = 48) (6) = (1)×(2) + (3)×(4)	Basel Capital Progress Index (Basel II and 2.5) (7) = (6)/48 2012	Basel Capital Progress Index (Basel II and 2.5) (7) = (6)/48 2014
Australia	4	6	4	6	2	4	48	1.00	1.00
China	4	6	4	6	2	4	48	0.67	1.00
Hong Kong SAR	4	6	4	6	2	4	48	1.00	1.00
India	4	6	4	6	2	4	48	1.00	1.00
Indonesia	4	6	2	4	1	4	32	0.31	0.67
Japan	4	6	4	6	3	4	48	1.00	1.00
Korea	4	6	4	6	1	4	48	1.00	1.00
Singapore	4	6	4	6	2	4	48	1.00	1.00
Comparators									
United Kingdom	4	6	4	6	2	4	48	1.00	1.00
United States	4	6	4	6	1	4	48	0.36	1.00
European Union	4	6	4	6	2	4	48	1.00	1.00

Sources: IMF staff estimates based on Basel Committee on Banking Supervision (2012, 2014).

Note: The data for the Basel capital rules given in BCBS 2012 and BCBS 2014 are as of end-March 2012 and end-September 2014, respectively. For technical details on methodology, see Annex 3.4 of IMF 2012.

risk-weighted assets for credit risk across large banks, a significant portion of which is not explained by portfolio differences and points instead to inconsistent interpretation and implementation. The higher capital requirements arising from the reform agenda may create incentives for banks to use the advanced internal-ratings-based approach, instead of the standardized approach, to achieve lower implicit risk weights with the same balance sheets. Alternatively, banks might restructure business lines toward more nontraditional banking activities that conserve risk-weighted assets, particularly those activities that require strong supervisory capacity and experience to monitor proper implementation.

Implementation of the Basel III liquidity and leverage regulations could be more challenging. This is likely to be the case for countries with shallow financial markets and a lack of high-quality liquid assets used in the calculation of the liquidity coverage ratio and the net stable funding ratio. Also, foreign currency risk may increase if banks use foreign currency assets to meet shortfalls of liquid assets in domestic currency. The Basel Committee proposed several approaches for addressing the scarcity of high-quality liquid assets, including allowing banks to access contractual committed liquidity facilities provided by the relevant central bank for a fee. Australia, for example, in November 2011 introduced such a facility. The fee-based approach would give supervisors discretion to allow banks to hold liquid assets in a currency that does not match the currency of the associated liquidity risk,[1] or to allow banks to hold additional Level 2 assets (such as corporate debt). However, these strategies to address the scarcity of eligible high-quality liquid assets could expose banks to higher market and credit risk, as well as to foreign currency risk.

Overall, global regulatory reforms are likely to have only a small impact on Asian lending rates. Higher capital and liquidity safety margins required under the global regulatory reforms, outlined elsewhere in this chapter, will lead to an increase in lenders' operating costs. There is disagreement, however, about how much the additional safety margins will cost in terms of higher lending rates.[2] Elliot, Salloy, and Santos (2012) find a notably smaller impact than did earlier studies, in part because of the assumption that equity investors will reduce their required rates of return on bank equity as a result of the safety improvements, and that banks will take measures to reduce costs in response to the regulatory changes (Figure 11.1). On average, the

---

[1] Provided that the resulting currency mismatch positions are justifiable and controlled within limits agreed to by the supervisor.

[2] For example, the Institute of International Finance (2011) projects that the proposed Basel III reforms will increase lending rates by 243 basis points in the United States, 328 basis points in Europe, and 181 basis points in Japan during the period 2012–19. By contrast, Slovik and Cournède (2011) at the Organisation for Economic Co-operation and Development project that, during a five-year transition period, lending rates will rise by only 64 basis points in the United States, 54 basis points in Europe, and 35 basis points in Japan. These projections are very much in line with a quantitative study by the Bank for International Settlements on the impact of the Basel III capital and liquidity changes on lending rates (Basel Committee on Banking Supervision 2010). A study by the IMF finds an even smaller impact, with lending rates rising by 28 basis points in the United States, 18 basis points in Europe, and only 8 basis points in Japan in the long term (Elliot, Salloy, and Santos 2012).

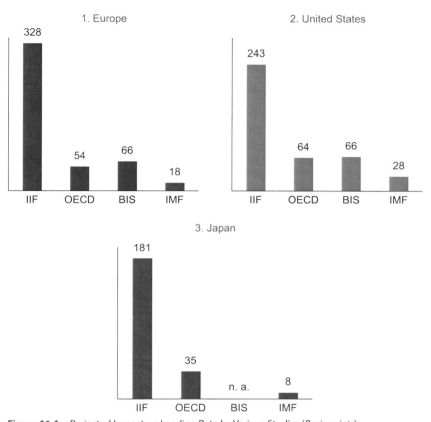

Figure 11.1 Projected Impact on Lending Rate by Various Studies (*Basis points*)

Sources: IIF (Institute for International Finance); OECD (Organisation for Economic Co-operation and Development); BIS (Bank for International Settlements); and IMF (International Monetary Fund).

estimated impact of the regulatory reforms on bank lending rates in Asia is relatively small.

There is evidence that cooperative and rural banks in Asia are less financially sound and profitable than are Asian commercial banks. This lack of soundness is reflected in the stress test results reported in recent Asian Financial Sector Assessment Program (FSAP) reports, including the Financial System Stability Assessment (FSSA) for Australia.[3] However, there are important exceptions. For example, several regional banks in Japan are affected by low core profitability, relatively thin capital positions, and large duration gaps, making them particularly vulnerable to slow growth and market yield shocks. Among emerging market

---

[3] The FSSA is a published report written by IMF staff that details the findings of the FSAP on issues relating to financial stability (as opposed to financial development) for the particular country concerned.

economies, the FSSA for India notes that, although stress tests confirm that commercial banks are well positioned to withstand a range of severe shocks, this is not the case for a significant majority of noncommercial banks (notably, regional rural banks and cooperative credit institutions that target underserviced rural and urban populations). The banking sector in the Philippines appears to be generally resilient to a broad range of macroeconomic risks, but the asset quality of thrifts, cooperatives, and rural banks is relatively weak, and provisions are low. Basic stress tests of Bangladesh's commercial banks suggest that credit risk continues to be a particular concern.

Crisis Management and Resolution

Another strength identified by some recent Asian FSAP reports is generally robust crisis management frameworks. Japan, for example, has developed a robust and time-tested crisis management framework. Malaysia, India, and Thailand have in place sound crisis management frameworks to facilitate prompt and coordinated action in the face of a crisis, and the Bank of Thailand's contingency planning and business continuity framework is also advanced. In contrast, the FSSA for Indonesia (published in September 2010) concludes that important gaps remain in crisis management and in dealing with problem banks, and that supervisory powers to intervene and resolve insolvent insurance companies are incomplete. Since then the Indonesian authorities have taken steps to improve their Prompt Corrective Action framework. In China, a more robust framework is needed to resolve weak financial institutions in a timely manner. In Thailand, too, the pace of disposal of stressed assets is slow, and there is a need to move to a more transparent and well-defined process for addressing troubled financial institutions.

Bank resolution frameworks present a more mixed picture. Singapore's solid legal framework for crisis management includes an excellent resolution regime, with tools and responsibilities clearly allocated among several public bodies, and robust arrangements for information sharing and coordination. In Thailand, however, the FSSA comments on the slow pace of disposal of distressed assets acquired by asset management companies and the need to move to a more transparent and well-defined process for addressing troubled financial institutions. China and India also need more robust frameworks to resolve weak financial institutions in a timely manner.

Too Important to Fail

Addressing the too-important-to-fail problem in Asia is urgent but efforts to do so could face legal and regulatory challenges. The *Key Attributes of Effective Resolution Regimes for Financial Institutions* (Financial Stability Board 2011) seeks to ensure that national frameworks are designed in a manner that enables and encourages authorities to cooperate with their counterparts in other jurisdictions in the resolution of a cross-border financial institution or group. Clifford Chance and ASIFMA (2013) find that most advanced Asian economies (Australia, Japan, Korea, and Singapore) as well as Indonesia, have in place "special resolution regimes" aimed at meeting these attributes, but this is not so in China, India, and Hong Kong SAR.

Several powerful forces could push already-large financial institutions in Asia to become even larger. These forces include a funding advantage for financial institutions believed to be "systemic" or too important to fail and, thus, implicitly backed by the government;[4] remuneration schemes linked to size or number of deals rather than risk-based profitability; and a belief that a "full-service" global bank is necessary to service clients requiring global reach and broad product capabilities (Kodres and Narain 2010). For example, large Korean firms are reported to prefer global banks, such as Citibank, as their financial partners for global projects because Korean banks cannot provide, on competitive terms, the comprehensive financial services they need. This situation may spur domestic institutions to become both larger and more complex, as discussed in Chapter 6. In addition, the depression of return on equity observed during the global financial crisis may influence behavior. If investors in financial institutions continue to demand precrisis rates of return on equity, there is a clear risk of further concentration of trading activities in even fewer global institutions as these investors attempt to combine their funding advantages with economies of scale.

At the same time there are forces pushing in the opposite direction. Many features of the global regulatory reform agenda are explicitly aimed at changing the existing financial landscape and making it more expensive to become systemically important. Moreover, as the *Global Financial Stability Report* October 2012 (IMF 2012) points out, banks that focus on commercial banking with a stable retail deposit base, particularly smaller banks, would be considerably less affected by the Basel III liquidity requirements than would those that focus on investment banking—with universal banks falling in between. In this context, regulatory reforms, when combined with measures taken by many emerging market Asian economies to promote financial inclusion and extend banking services to underserved regions and segments of the population, may actually promote the development of smaller, cooperative banks that can meet the credit needs of small and medium-sized enterprises and many households, while also providing profitable outlets for investing their savings.

The most likely outcome will be a more bifurcated financial system, with some financial institutions becoming larger and others opting for a more focused business model. Some banks may be willing to pay the de facto "systemic risk tax" and remain large or even grow larger, taking advantage of their too-important-to-fail status and their belief that governments will come to their rescue if they run into serious financial difficulties (Kodres and Narain 2010). Other financial institutions may prefer to avoid the additional costs associated with systemic importance

---

[4] Chapter 3 of the April 2014 *Global Financial Stability Report* (IMF 2014a) notes that systemically important banks tend to receive implicit funding subsidies that come from the expectation that the government will support large banks if they become distressed. Although financial reforms since the global financial crisis have helped reduce the size of these subsidies, estimates presented in the chapter show that they remain sizable, particularly in the euro area and, to a smaller extent, in Japan and the United Kingdom.

by retreating from some business lines, and by effectively shrinking in size to avoid paying the systemic risk tax. Regulatory efforts, such as capital charges, can help lean against the drivers behind too important to fail.

Supervision

A regional comparison of compliance with international regulatory and supervisory standards shows Asia performing as well as, or even better than, other regions. This is shown in Figure 11.2. On Basel Core Principles (BCP) standards, Asia appears to perform particularly well in corrective and remedial powers of supervisors.[5] For example, the Singapore FSSA states that the country's current regulation and supervision of its financial institutions are among the best globally. However, a more detailed regional comparison of BCP (2006) Core Principle 1 shows that Asia's compliance with standards relating to independence, accountability, and transparency of supervisory agencies is relatively low, even though supervisors do enjoy high levels of legal protection. With regard to insurance, Asia has shown strong compliance with International Association of Insurance Supervisors standards on supervision and disclosure. However, as with the BCP standards, Asia shows relatively low compliance with standards on independence (autonomy) and powers of supervisory agencies. With regard to compliance with the International Organization of Securities Commissions standards for regulation of securities markets, Asia performs particularly well on interagency cooperation and accounting and disclosure standards.

Recent FSAP reports on Asian countries have highlighted a number of pressing areas for strengthening regulation and supervision of these countries' financial sectors (Table 11.3). These reports suggest that reform priorities vary somewhat from emerging market to advanced Asian economies. At the same time, several common challenges must be addressed by almost all countries in Asia. Key reform measures proposed by the IMF include (1) reinforcing staff and technical capacity at supervisory agencies, particularly in the form of risk-based supervision and surveillance of nonbank financial institutions; (2) reducing concentration risk by tightening the definition and monitoring of "connected lending" (that is, large exposures to single borrowers, related parties, or both)—a key recommendation in almost all Asian FSAPs; and (3) promoting better risk-management practices in financial institutions through stronger regulation and enhanced disclosure requirements. India, for example, has a large exposure limit of 55 percent of a banking group's capital, which is much higher than the international practice of 10–25 percent, depending on the borrower and collateral.

Several Asian FSAP reports highlight the need for national supervisory agencies to develop and strengthen their frameworks for consolidated supervision. Conglomerates are an important feature of many Asian economies and, as mentioned earlier, their links to the state further challenge effective

---

[5]The BCP standards assessment is a standard component of an FSSA that assesses the country's compliance with international standards on banking supervision and regulation.

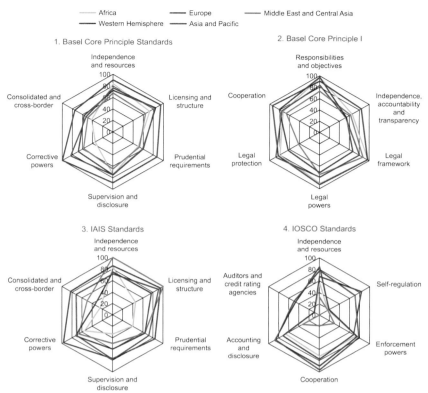

Figure 11.2 Regional Comparison of Compliance with International Standards on Regulation and Supervision

Source: Standards and Codes Database.
Note: BCP = Basel Core Principles; IAIS = International Association of Insurance Supervisors; IOSCO = International Organization of Securities Commissions.

consolidated supervision. In the Philippines, for example, about 60 percent of bank assets are controlled by banks that belong to conglomerates. Furthermore, a large proportion of listed companies (estimated to be 75 percent of effective market capitalization) also belong to conglomerates. For the moment, most Asian banks are focused on relatively straightforward traditional deposit-taking and lending activities. However, as these institutions become more complex, and move into new areas of business, the need for consolidated supervision will further increase.

Strengthening cross-border cooperation and information exchange on regulation, supervision, and resolution of financial institutions should be a high priority for many Asian countries. As Asian banks and financial institutions expand their cross-border operations, it is important that both home and host countries have (1) sufficient data and information to regulate and supervise these banks and institutions effectively, and (2) the necessary resolution tools and capacity to cooperate across borders to resolve these institutions without systemic disruption

TABLE 11.3

Priorities for Financial Sector Reform Identified by Published FSSAs

Framework for Prudential Regulation and Supervision
- Enhance independence of central bank and domestic supervisory agencies, ensure adequate legal protection for supervisors—Bangladesh, China, India, Indonesia, the Philippines, Singapore, Thailand[1]
- Enhance resources (including staffing) and technical capacity of central bank and domestic supervisory agencies (including stress-testing capabilities)—China, India, Indonesia, the Philippines, Japan
- Enhance consolidated supervision—India, Indonesia, the Philippines
- Strengthen coordination and information sharing among home supervisory agencies—China, India, Indonesia, Japan, the Philippines, Thailand[1]
- Enhance cross-border cooperation and information exchange—China, India, Indonesia, Japan, Singapore

Financial Stability
- Improve data collection and analysis, and reporting requirements—Bangladesh, China
- Enhance accounting and auditing rules and practices—Bangladesh, China, India, Thailand[1]
- Strengthen monitoring of systemic risk, develop or strengthen framework and tools for macroprudential policy—Australia, China, Indonesia, Japan
- Tighten limits on, and enhance monitoring and control of, large exposures and related party lending—India, Indonesia, the Philippines, Japan
- Strengthen regulation of securities markets, autonomy and funding for securities regulatory agency—Australia, Bangladesh, Japan
- Reform over-the-counter derivatives markets—Singapore

Crisis Management and Bank Resolution
- Enhance framework for crisis management and resolution of financial institutions—Australia, China, India, Indonesia, the Philippines
- Enhance cross-border cooperation and information exchange—China, India, Indonesia, Japan, Singapore

Role of Government
- Divest government ownership of banks, strengthen governance in state-owned banks, limit role of government in financial sector—Bangladesh, China, India, Thailand[1]

Source: IMF staff compilation.

Note: FSSA = Financial Sector Stability Assessment.

[1] The Thailand FSSA notes that, in the period between the Financial Sector Assessment Program discussions and the finalization of the report, Thailand had passed a number of critical legal financial sector reforms that addressed most of the legal and regulatory shortcomings identified in the assessments of the regulatory and supervisory standards. Nevertheless, there was too little time to assess *implementation* of the legal reforms.

and without exposing taxpayers to losses. Although Singapore is an important international financial center, the 2013 FSAP identified the further facilitation of cross-border cooperation in bank resolution as a reform priority. Moreover, in India, domestic banks have established overseas operations in more than 45 jurisdictions, but there are material gaps in information flows with overseas supervisors. However, the Reserve Bank of India has memoranda of understanding with only two overseas counterparts, and limited informal arrangements with others, and overseas inspections are also not conducted regularly. In other countries with less integrated financial sectors, progress lags even further.

Data gaps and weak legal frameworks hamper supervision across the financial sector. Some needed reforms include the following:

- Improving the availability, timeliness, and quality of financial sector data, as well as the technical capacity to analyze them and take appropriate actions if needed. For example, the FSSA for China notes the difficulty of assessing the magnitude of potential risks to the Chinese financial system, and how these risks could permeate through the economic and financial system, given the data gaps, the lack of sufficiently long and consistent time series of key financial data, and the weaknesses in the information infrastructure.

- Strengthening loan classification and provisioning practices and enforcement of prudential standards.

- Improving accounting and auditing rules and practices and bringing them up to international standards. This has been identified as an important priority for Bangladesh, China, Indonesia, and Thailand.

- Providing greater autonomy and independence to central bank and supervisory agencies, and ensuring legal protection for all supervisory staff.

The Role of the State in Asia's Financial Systems

A defining feature of the Asian financial systems continues to be the high degree of government involvement in financial intermediation. These close interactions have led to some specific outcomes across the region which, collectively, may restrain market development. Examples include the following:

- *Reliance on rules-based approaches*—Asian regulatory frameworks tend to be rules-based, with a focus on achieving compliance with these rules. Excessive reliance on rules-based supervision often detracts from supervisors' using their own judgment and employing forward-looking, risk-based supervisory techniques.

- *Limited supervisory independence*—This is reflected in insufficient or ineffective corrective action frameworks because supervisors are challenged in disciplining the state and its agents. The China FSAP shows how the operational autonomy of supervisors is often undermined by the use of the commercial banking system for development purposes. The Malaysia FSAP points to the need to address existing legal provisions that can undermine the operational independence of supervisors. The India FSAP calls for greater de jure independence of all regulatory agencies.

- *Weak implementation of rules on large exposures and related-party lending*—These rules are often not observed because the state seeks to direct bank credit to fund activities and institutions considered important in national contexts. In India, for example, state-owned banks have been major conduits for funding large public sector projects deemed to be of national importance. The FSAP points out that these large exposure limits are almost double those considered good practice internationally. The Malaysia FSAP points to the need to strengthen the definition of both connected lending and related lending.

- *Inadequate institutional frameworks for consolidated supervision*—State ownership of major players in the financial system complicates consolidated supervision of conglomerate structures spanning state-owned players in the banking and nonbank sectors.

- *Weaknesses in bank recovery and resolution frameworks*—State ownership can hamper recovery and resolution efforts by supervisors. For example, in Thailand, the FSAP finds that continuing state involvement in asset management companies has led to reduced recovery rates of nonperforming loans and recommends that the state take more effective measures to reduce its stake in intervened commercial banks and that the central bank refrain from managing and owning such stakes.

Reducing state involvement can pay significant dividends. China, India, and Vietnam should consider gradually phasing out administrative controls and promoting market-based measures for regulating the financial system, as well as divesting government ownership of banks and strengthening governance in state-controlled banks and other financial institutions. Such measures would help improve the profitability and strengthen the balance sheets of their financial sectors by increasing the commercial orientation of their financial institutions. These measures would also place the state-owned banks in a stronger position to cope with the challenges posed by the growing size, complexity, and interconnectedness of the financial sectors.

Spillovers from Global Regulatory Efforts

The emphasis in the reform agenda on raising the cost of riskier activities could affect Asia both directly and indirectly. Basel III and globally systemically important bank surcharges, aimed at addressing too-important-to-fail problems (discussed elsewhere in this chapter), will raise the cost of borrowing from such institutions. Structural measures that restrict certain risky business activities or ring-fence retail from wholesale banking will add to these effects. These regulatory initiatives could have a direct impact on Asian financial institutions, or they could indirectly affect Asian financial markets, if globally active foreign banks alter their exposures to Asia.

Global regulatory reforms may encourage internationally active banks to lower their exposure to Asia by deleveraging or shifting their activities. Higher liquidity requirements under Basel III, as well as G-SIFI surcharges, may increase the cost of operating in some jurisdictions and negatively affect cross-border lending and investment activities—or prompt changes to banking group structures. The impact is likely to be mitigated to the extent that highly liquid banks in mature Asian markets such as Japan, Hong Kong SAR, and Taiwan Province of China decide to expand their lending activities in fast-growing emerging Asian economies that offer profitable investment opportunities such as India, Indonesia, Thailand, and Vietnam (Wyman 2012).

National regulatory reforms in advanced economies designed to restrict and ring-fence the activities of domestic financial institutions could prompt international banks to retrench from their operations across Asia. Although the effects are difficult to quantify, these reforms could induce parent banks in advanced Western countries to alter their global business models and lower their exposures to Asia, either by reducing direct lending or by cutting back on their activities in derivatives and securitization markets in Asia. Foreign parent banks may reduce funding to their local

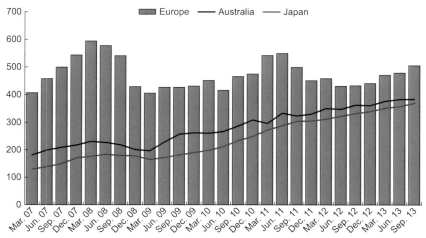

Figure 11.3 Australia, Europe, and Japan: Cross-Border Bank Exposures to Asia (*Billions of U.S. dollars*)

Source: Bank for International Settlements - Table 9D (data extracted February 4, 2014).
Note: Asia excludes Australia and Japan; Europe excludes the United Kingdom.

branches and subsidiaries in Asia, forcing them to raise funding locally or to reduce their local lending activities. Cross-border lending may be further adversely affected if Asian economies start ring-fencing their domestic financial institutions by placing limits on the size and scope of their activities (Viñals and others 2013).

However, pressures for deleveraging are likely to be mitigated by two factors:

- First, the global financial crisis suggests that retrenchment by Western banks had not posed a significant problem, at least for those countries with sound macroeconomic policies and strong growth potential. In many cases, deleveraging by Western (mainly European) banks in Asia was offset by increased lending by regional Asian banks, notably Australian and Japanese banks (Figure 11.3).

- Foreign banks, on average, have a relatively low presence in Asia, compared with their presence in other regions. This is true whether their presence is measured by their share of the total number of banks operating in the country, or by the share of total bank assets in the region. Nonetheless, there is considerable cross-country variation, with a high foreign bank presence in Australia, Hong Kong SAR, and Singapore, and a low foreign bank presence in China, Japan, and India.

MACROPRUDENTIAL POLICY FRAMEWORKS

FSAP reports recommend that many Asian countries strengthen their monitoring of systemic risks and enhance their frameworks for macroprudential supervision. The FSSA for Australia, for example, recommends that the country devote more resources to stress testing to enhance the ability of the Reserve Bank of Australia to identify and monitor emerging systemic risks. The FSSAs for China, Indonesia, and Japan make similar recommendations. Also important in this context is the need to enhance cooperation and the exchange of information among domestic supervisory agencies. The FSSA for Japan, for example, recommends bolstering oversight of systemic risk through more regular interagency information sharing and enhanced cooperation on macroprudential policy and contingency planning. Similar recommendations were made for China, India, Indonesia, the Philippines, and Thailand.

Nevertheless, some countries have put in place innovative elements in their macroprudential policy frameworks. Indeed, Asia as a region has been ahead of advanced economies in implementing macroprudential policies. India, for example, has been a pioneer in the use of macroprudential policy and has made continued efforts to strengthen systemic oversight, facilitated by a policy coordination structure that brings together major stakeholders under the leadership of the finance ministry and the central bank. Malaysia has made effective use of sectoral macroprudential instruments to limit the risks posed by strong growth in unsecured personal loans and residential mortgage loans. Several Asian countries have also been innovative with liquidity tools designed to reduce vulnerabilities from a system-wide increase in wholesale, short-term, and foreign exchange funding. These tools include the introduction of a Macroprudential Stability Levy by Korea in August 2011, and a Core Funding Ratio by New Zealand in October 2009 (IMF 2013).

NONBANK ISSUES

Securities Markets

Asian securities regulation is broadly in line with global International Organization of Securities Commissions standards. The region performs particularly well in interagency cooperation and accounting and disclosure standards, but areas for improvement remain. For example, a reform priority identified by the FSSA for Australia is to ensure adequacy and stability of core funding for the Australian Securities and Investments Commission so that it can carry out proactive supervision. The FSSA for Japan calls for strengthening oversight of securities firms through expanded and more risk-based inspection programs, extending auditing requirements, and improving the registration process. Among emerging market economies, for Bangladesh a key FSSA recommendation is to address urgently the shortage of resources of the securities regulator, and to provide the Securities and Exchange Commission with greater autonomy in budget and personnel decisions and rules enforcement.

Nonbank Finance and Shadow Banking

Nonbank financial intermediation remains relatively small in most countries. As discussed in Chapter 2, among the Asian countries for which data are available, only in Korea do the assets of nonbank financial intermediaries constitute more

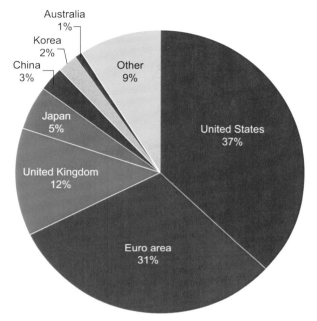

Figure 11.4 Share of Assets of Nonbank Financial Intermediaries at End-2012 (*20 jurisdictions and euro area*)

Source: Financial Stability Board (2013a).

than 50 percent of total bank assets (FSB 2013a).[6] The recorded assets of Asian nonbank financial intermediaries constitute a small share, less than 15 percent, of the global total; only two Asian countries—China and Japan—have a share of 3 percent or more of the global total (Figure 11.4). However, as it has expanded, the nonbank sector has become increasingly complex and interconnected with the rest of the financial system.

Nonetheless, the nonbank financial sector has been growing fairly rapidly in Asia and posing additional challenges for regulators and supervisors. In 2012, nonbank financial intermediation grew by more than 20 percent in China and India, and by more than 10 percent in Indonesia and Korea. Against this background, the FSSA for Japan recommends that the Bank of Japan extend its stress-testing analysis to a wider range of financial institutions, including systemically important nonbank financial institutions. In a similar vein, the FSSA for China notes that, as the range of financial services on offer widens, so should the regulatory and supervisory perimeter. The FSSA also calls for stronger supervision of financial groups and robust systemic oversight.

---

[6]The ratios are Korea: 55.4 percent: Australia; 26.4 percent; Hong Kong SAR: 23.5 percent; India:19.0 percent; Japan: 18.7 percent; Indonesia: 14.3 percent; China: 10.0 percent; and Singapore: 7.0 percent.

Tightening bank regulation may push financial intermediation outside the banking sector and toward capital markets or shadow banking. Higher capital requirements and other regulatory constraints on banks will raise the cost of bank credit and likely prompt companies to access credit through capital markets (for example, equity and corporate bond markets) or through the shadow banking system. The 2010 China FSAP lists shadow banking ("the rise of off–balance sheet exposures and of lending outside of the formal banking sector") as one of the key risks to near-term domestic financial stability.

Still, nonbank finance is not expected to challenge the primacy of bank finance in the foreseeable future. Several factors are working against a declining trend in the size of the banking sector (relative to GDP or to total financial sector assets). These factors include the funding advantage that banks have compared with nonbanks, particularly banks that are seen by investors as too important to fail, as well as their access to central bank liquidity support. And several Asian countries, including India, Indonesia, the Philippines, and Vietnam, have strong medium-term economic growth potential and rapidly growing working-age populations—some 40 percent of which have an account at a formal financial institution. The demand for banking services in these economies is likely to grow rapidly. It is also important to note that several emerging market Asian economies, such as India, are taking active measures to promote financial inclusion and extend banking services to underserved areas.[7] Moreover, quite a few countries in Asia have large state-owned banks that are unlikely to be privatized soon. These factors may well serve to offset any impact on the cost of capital resulting from regulatory changes.

The rising importance of nonbank financial institutions points to the need to extend crisis frameworks to cover them. The Financial Stability Board argues that a priority focus of policymakers should be not just reform of crisis management and resolution regimes for banking institutions, but also the strengthening of crisis management and resolution regimes for nonbank financial institutions (FSB 2013b). The FSSA for Japan, for example, states that an effective resolution regime needs to extend to systemically important nonbank financial institutions as well as banks.

Progress in this area has been slow. Several countries, including Australia, have made substantial headway in these areas and are taking steps to introduce resolution powers and tools consistent with the *Key Attributes of Effective Resolution Regimes for Financial Institutions* (FSB 2011) endorsed by the Group of 20 at Cannes in 2011.

---

[7] For example, a Reserve Bank of India committee has suggested setting up specialized banks to cater to low-income households to ensure that all citizens have bank accounts by 2016. These banks would be designed to provide payment services and deposit products to small businesses and low-income households with a maximum balance of 50,000 rupees per customer, and could be set up with a minimum capital requirement that is one-tenth of what is required to set up a full-service bank. Moreover, a key eligibility criterion to obtain one of the new banking licenses issued in 2014 was the applicant's strategy and vision for financial inclusion. The Reserve Bank of India's recent award of a banking license to only two specialized banks, one of which is a microfinance institution, from a wide field of applicants, is in line with this vision.

Even in advanced Asian economies, with fairly well-developed resolution regimes for banks, considerable progress is still needed on resolution regimes for insurers, and securities and investment firms. In countries lacking such frameworks for banks, progress is correspondingly slower. Moreover, many jurisdictions in Asia have not yet given their national resolution authorities the framework and powers needed to resolve financial groups and conglomerates.

Corporate Bond Markets

Global regulatory reforms are likely to promote the development of domestic capital markets, particularly if accompanied by supportive national policies. As discussed in Chapter 4, Asian banks currently hold significant amounts of government bonds but very limited amounts of corporate bonds. However, with the recent rapid growth in corporate bond issuance (and a corresponding decline in syndicated lending), this situation is beginning to change. As global and domestic regulatory reforms raise the cost of bank intermediation, and as oversight of non-bank financial institutions improves, corporate bond markets can be expected to continue to grow.

Developing country institutional investors can catalyze this process. The regulatory reforms currently on the global agenda may keep banks from playing a leading role in Asian domestic corporate bond markets to the extent that they require banks to hold more high-quality liquid assets to meet Basel III liquidity requirements and as collateral for derivatives trading. Conversely, aging populations in several countries, and demand by growing middle classes for insurance products and other savings vehicles, should spur the development of insurance and pension funds that can actively purchase corporate bonds.

It is also possible that national regulatory measures, such as the Volcker Rule, may reduce liquidity and depth in corporate bond markets, and raise the costs of debt issuance. The Volcker Rule largely prohibits proprietary trading activities by U.S. banks in the United States and abroad. It also prevents non-U.S. banks from executing or clearing their proprietary trading on U.S. financial infrastructures. Market making, underwriting, and risk-mitigating hedging are exempt, as are transactions in obligations of the U.S. government and agencies. However, in practice it may be difficult, costly, and onerous to prove that certain trading activities are market making and not proprietary trading.

However, the effects of these new rules are likely to be small. Affected economies and entities include the regional hubs of Hong Kong SAR and Singapore, the Chinese and Japanese G-SIFIs, as well as countries (such as Japan, Korea, and Malaysia) that are dependent on portfolio inflows from the United States. Nonetheless, any adverse impact will be mitigated by the increasingly important role of hedge funds in trading activities, and by the exemptions granted under the Volcker Rule for trading in foreign sovereign instruments. Moreover, as discussed elsewhere in this chapter, recent developments have provided no indication that global regulatory reforms will adversely affect the market for domestic corporate bonds in Asia.

Derivatives Markets

Progress in reforming over-the-counter derivatives markets has been slow. Derivatives markets in emerging Asia are relatively underdeveloped and mostly based on over-the-counter transactions (Goswami and Sharma 2011). As members of the Group of 20, six Asian countries (Australia, China, India, Indonesia, Japan, and Korea) agreed in 2009 to implement three major reforms by the end of 2012: (1) trading all standardized over-the-counter derivatives electronically or through exchanges, and clearing them through central clearing parties; (2) reporting all over-the-counter derivatives trades to trade repositories to improve transparency and price formation; and (3) subjecting non-centrally cleared over-the-counter derivatives to higher capital requirements. However, only Japan, together with the United States and the European Union, had fully implemented these reforms by the end-of-2012 deadline. Other countries appear to be waiting for the United States, the European Union, and Japan to finalize their frameworks so that they can maximize consistency and safeguard financial market infrastructure when they reform their own frameworks.

Over-the-counter derivatives reforms are expected to bring many benefits, but regulatory authorities will need to ensure that these reforms do not unduly impede the development of derivatives trading in Asia. Global regulatory reforms relating to over-the-counter derivatives trading are designed to promote better monitoring of systemic risks and to minimize the risk of disorderly liquidation of financial contracts. However, there is considerable concern that a lack of eligible instruments for collateral could make it very difficult and costly to post collateral at central clearing parties in many emerging Asian economies, thereby impeding the development of the domestic derivatives market. Moreover, changes in the market landscape resulting from the reforms in advanced economies may not only raise hedging costs for end users in Asia, it may also place smaller domestic central counterparties at a competitive disadvantage in relation to global ones, and lead to the underdevelopment of the domestic derivatives markets (FSB 2012a).

Global regulatory reforms could further slow the development of domestic derivatives markets in Asia. In many Asian countries G-SIFIs play a critical role in securities markets and derivatives, and also in trade finance. The provision of services in these areas could therefore be negatively affected by the higher capital charges and other regulatory reforms currently being contemplated for G-SIFIs. Supply of such services could also be affected by the extraterritorial aspects of regulatory reform measures adopted, or under consideration, by advanced Western countries (Viñals and others 2013). However, it is too early to have an idea of the likely magnitude of the impact of global regulatory reforms on the composition of finance in Asia.

CONCLUSION

Some of the regulatory gaps observed in the rest of the world are absent in Asia. The region is well on its way to full implementation of Basel III capital requirements, and capital positions across the region's main financial systems are strong.

However, implementation of liquidity and leverage requirements could present challenges for countries in which financial markets are shallow or poorly developed. Crisis management is broadly satisfactory in many regions, although quite a few countries lack important tools for resolution of distressed financial institutions. In general, the impact of the global regulatory reform agenda on Asia—through national implementation and spillovers from elsewhere—is expected to be relatively limited.

Institutions considered "too important to fail" are a problem in Asia. Although the region has relatively few G-SIFIs, most countries have large and domestically systemic financial institutions. The funding advantage for such institutions, as well as a preference in the region for doing business with large diversified conglomerates, could lead domestic champions to become even larger. However, financial inclusion and regulatory measures aimed at containing "too-important-to-fail" institutions will lean against these trends. The growth of many of these institutions into more diversified and globalized financial conglomerates underscores the need for enhancing consolidated and cross-border supervision across the region.

The close relationship between the banking system and the state in many countries can negatively affect both financial sector supervision and development. In many countries, the state plays both a direct and an indirect role in the allocation of credit. This complicates independent supervision and often results in concentration of exposures and an excessive reliance on rules-based approaches. Reducing the role of the state, particularly in countries in which public banks dominate the financial system, would pay dividends by strengthening bank balance sheets and facilitating the growth of more responsive and competitive financial systems.

Regulatory reform may affect the availability of some products. Liquidity restrictions could reduce the availability of long-term capital, while a tighter focus on capital and new approaches toward risk could reduce the availability of financing for small and medium-sized enterprises. At the same time, moving derivatives trading onto exchanges and the broader effort to standardize and tighten regulation of derivatives and proprietary trading could add to hedging costs. To sustain growth, Asia's economies will need to make regulatory changes that strike a balance between two objectives: (1) ensuring that the underlying risks are adequately reflected in the cost of capital and (2) ensuring that financing options are not unduly curtailed.

Nonbank finance remains small, but presents risks in many countries. Already, shadow banking is growing rapidly in some countries in the region, raising the possibility that innovation is moving ahead of supervisors' ability to identify and contain risks. Regulatory reform could push more lending activity off the balance sheets of the region's banks, adding to these problems. This calls for strengthening the framework for crisis management to cover such institutions. It also calls for supervision that is sufficiently nimble to ensure that growing interconnections in the financial system, especially between regulated and unregulated firms, do not pose significant risks.

Policymakers must distinguish between the intended and potential unintended consequences of global regulatory reforms. Many of the anticipated consequences discussed in this chapter, such as the higher cost of credit intermediation through banks and of trading in opaque derivatives instruments, are precisely what the reforms were designed to achieve. However, the reforms may also have unintended consequences. A case in point is the shift in financial intermediation toward less regulated shadow banking and a reduction in turnover and liquidity in domestic corporate and government bond markets. These trends are driven by regulatory pressures on banks to lengthen debt maturities and to hold more high-quality collateral for derivatives trading.

REFERENCES

Basel Committee on Banking Supervision (BCBS). 2010. "An Assessment of the Long-Term Economic Impact of Stronger Capital and Liquidity Requirements." Bank for International Settlements, Basel, Switzerland.

———. 2012. "Progress Report on Basel III Implementation (Update Published in October 2012)." Bank for International Settlements, Basel, Switzerland. www.bis.org/publ/bcbs232.htm.

———. 2014. "Seventh Progress Report on Adoption of the Basel Regulatory Framework." Bank for International Settlements, Basel, Switzerland.

Clifford Chance and ASIFMA (Asia Securities Industry and Financial Markets Association) 2013. *Asian Bank Resolution Regimes*. London: Clifford Chance; New York: Asia Securities Industry and Financial Markets Association.

Elliott, Douglas, Suzanne Salloy, and André Oliveira Santos. 2012. "Assessing the Cost of Financial Regulation." IMF Working Paper No. 12/233, International Monetary Fund, Washington.

Financial Stability Board. 2011. *Key Attributes of Effective Resolution Regimes for Financial Institutions*. Basel, Switzerland.

———. 2012a. "Identifying the Effects of Regulatory Reforms on Emerging Market and Developing Economies: A Review of Potential Unintended Consequences—Report to the G20 Finance Ministers and Central Bank Governors." Basel, Switzerland.

———. 2012b. "Overview of Progress in the Implementation of the G20 Recommendations for Strengthening Financial Stability—Report of the Financial Stability Board to G20 Leaders." Basel, Switzerland.

———. 2013a. "Global Shadow Banking Monitoring Report 2013." Basel, Switzerland.

———. 2013b. "Implementing the FSB Key Attributes of Effective Resolution Regimes–How Far Have We Come?—Report to the G20 Finance Ministers and Central Bank Governors." Basel, Switzerland.

Goswami, Mangal, and Sunil Sharma. 2011. "The Development of Local Debt Markets in Asia." IMF Working Paper No. 11/132, International Monetary Fund, Washington.

Institute of International Finance. 2011. "The Cumulative Impact on the Global Economy of Changes in the Financial Regulatory Framework." Washington.

International Monetary Fund (IMF). 2012. "The Reform Agenda: An Interim Report on Progress Toward a Safer Financial System." In *Global Financial Stability Report*. Washington, October.

———. 2013. "Key Aspects of Macroprudential Policy." Washington.

———. 2014a. "How Big Is the Implicit Subsidy for Banks Considered Too Important to Fail?" In *Global Financial Stability Report*. Washington, April.

———. 2014b. "Shadow Banking Around the Globe: How Large, and How Risky?" In *Global Financial Stability Report*. Washington, October.

Kodres, Laura, and Aditya Narain. 2010. "Redesigning the Contours of the Future Financial System." IMF Staff Position Note No. 10/10, International Monetary Fund, Washington.

Schneider, Todd, Faisal Ahmed, Rina Bhattacharya, and others. 2015. "Addressing Financial Sector Vulnerabilities." In *Frontier and Developing Asia: The Next Generation of Emerging Markets*, edited by Alfred Schipke. Washington: International Monetary Fund.

Slovik, P., and B. Cournède. 2011. "Macroeconomic Impact of Basel III." OECD Economics Department Working Paper No. 844, Organisation for Economic Co-operation and Development, Paris.

Viñals, José, Ceyla Pazarbasioglu, Jay Surti, Aditya Narain, Michaela Erbenova, and Julian Chow. 2013. "Creating a Safer Financial System: Will the Volcker, Vickers, and Liikanen Structural Measures Help?" IMF Staff Discussion Note No. 13/4, International Monetary Fund, Washington.

Wyman, Oliver. 2012. *The Future of Asian Banking, Volume 2: Crouching Tigers–The Rise of Asian Regional Banks*. New York: Marsh and McLennan Companies.

Index

Page numbers followed by *b, f,* or *t* refer to boxed text, figures, or tables, respectively.